Roll Over, Tchaikovsky!

NEW PERSPECTIVES ON GENDER IN MUSIC

Editorial Advisors
Susan C. Cook
Beverley Diamond

A list of books in the series appears at the end of this book.

Roll Over, Tchaikovsky!

Russian Popular Music and Post-Soviet Homosexuality

STEPHEN AMICO

UNIVERSITY OF ILLINOIS PRESS
Urbana, Chicago, and Springfield

First Illinois paperback, 2017
© 2014 by the Board of Trustees
of the University of Illinois
All rights reserved
1 2 3 4 5 C P 5 4 3 2 1

∞ This book is printed on acid-free paper.

The Library of Congress cataloged the cloth edition as follows:
Amico, Stephen.
Roll over, Tchaikovsky! : Russian popular music and post-Soviet homosexuality / Stephen Amico.
pages   cm. — (New perspectives on gender in music)
Includes bibliographical references and index.
ISBN 978-0-252-03827-3 (cloth : alk. paper)
ISBN 978-0-252-09614-3 (e-book)
1. Homosexuality and popular music—Russia. 2. Gay culture—Russia. 3. Popular music—Social aspects—Russia.
I. Title.
ML3917.R8A45   2014
781.64086'60947—dc23   2013043167

PAPERBACK ISBN 978-0-252-08308-2

For my parents

Contents

Acknowledgments ix

Notes on Transliteration, Translations, Attribution of Informants' Quotations, and Audiovisual Resources xi

1. Introduction: Homosexual Bodies/Embodied Homosexuality 1
2. Music, Form, Penetration 30
3. Phantom Faggots 63
4. Corporeal Intentions 103
5. Gay-Made Space 135
6. Conclusion: The Eloquence of Flesh 167

   Epilogue 189

   List of Interlocuters and Interviewees 205
   Notes 207
   Works Cited 271
   Index 305

Acknowledgments

It is not so much with a nostalgic nod to postmodern theory as it is from the experiential standpoint of having worked on this manuscript for several years that I must aver that no text can claim to be the creation of a single author. For while one name may appear on a cover or in a database indicating the production of a specific text by a specific person, it is only with the support—intellectual, emotional, financial, even physical—of numerous others that what often begins as nothing more than an inchoate mess of vague ideas can be transformed into a theory or an argument, into prose, into words on a page through which ideas can be shared with an audience. It is with much gratitude that I thank all of those others who assisted me in this project, from fieldwork to publication, from New York to St. Petersburg to Philadelphia to Amsterdam.

The roots of this project lay in the research conducted for my doctoral dissertation while a PhD candidate in the ethnomusicology program at the City University of New York, during which time I was fortunate enough to have received financial assistance including a Richard Gillece Fellowship, the Mario Cappeloni dissertation award, a Ford Foundation grant, a CUNY Writing Fellowship, and a David Schwartz Communications Fellowship. Additional research was conducted during a postdoctoral fellowship at the University of Pennsylvania that was funded by the Andrew W. Mellon Foundation. Without the financial support received during these years, it is unlikely this project would have come to fruition, and I am extremely grateful to both institutions and the funding bodies for their extraordinary generosity.

Much like my ill-conceived (and necessarily aborted) attempt several years ago to organize my thousands of .mp3 files according to genre and style, rather than performer—doomed to failure from its inception—I find it almost impossible to "organize" my thanks according to "genre" as well: in so many instances, I cannot draw a line between confidant or colleague, between intellectual inspiration or affective resonance, between relationships that have spanned the *longue durée*, and those that are just creeping up on the threshold. Owing to what I fear might simply become random categorization, I would simply like to offer my most sincere and heartfelt thanks to the following (in alphabetical order): Nancy Albright, Nikolai Alekseev, Karina Avakyan, Brian Baer, Chantal Bax, Dmitriy Bezdenejnikh, Barbara Bliss, Liza Binford, Carolyn Birdsall, Eliot Borenstein, Denise Budd, Jim Bumgardner, Mark Butler, Vitaly Chernetsky, Jennifer Clark, Patricia Clough, Amparo Codding, Gerald Creed, Andy Curran, Ruth DeFord, Beverly Diamond, Martin Duberman, Dawn Durante, Paul Feuerman, Jason Galie, Kate Garretson, Barbara Hampton, Robin Harris Rickard, Ellie Hisama, Henkjan Honing, Judith Keilbach, Jeroen de Kloet, Wayne Koestenbaum, Igor' Kon, Jaap Kooijman, Andy Krikun, Aleksandr Kukharskii, Julia Kursell, Anne Kustritz, Susan Lees, Christoph Lindner, Sasha Lipovtsev, Heather Love, David MacFadyen, Peter Manuel, Laurie Matheson, Fred Maus, Wim van der Meer, Mara Mills, Jussi Nissenen, Pierre Noel, Julia Peterson, Kevin Platt, Tim Rommen, Dan Sheehan, Sasha Shum, Roberta Sparenberg, Markus Stauff, Wendy Steiner, Anne Swartz, Andrew Tomasello, Leo Treitler, Ilya Vinitski, Maryn Wilkinson, and Liz Wollman. Additionally, in the aggregate, I offer the same quantity and quality of thanks to the blind reviewers and the editors at University of Illinois Press, the students in my Music and the Body seminar at the University of Pennsylvania, and especially—at the risk of exhibiting preferential gratitude—all of my informants (many of whom I considered my friends) in St. Petersburg and Moscow. Without the generosity of these people, their willingness to endure my (most assuredly sometimes seemingly ridiculous) questions, their assistance in all manner of maneuverings through the post-Soviet system, their candor and warmth, this book would be little more than a lifeless compendium of arid data.

Finally, I must thank my family (Mike, Erin, Dante, and Bridget) and above all—here I unabashedly cop to preferential treatment—my parents. Throughout my life they have unconditionally supported my academic and artistic pursuits, in every way possible, and have selflessly given of themselves so that I would have access to opportunities they did not. In those moments when I doubted my ability to bring my project to fruition, they refused to allow me to quit, offering wisdom and encouragement, often from thousands of miles away. Although words are entirely inadequate to express my love, admiration, and gratitude, it is to them that I dedicate this book.

Notes on Transliteration, Translations, Attribution of Informants' Quotations, and Audiovisual Resources

Throughout this book I adhere to the Library of Congress system of transliteration, even in such cases where words may have common anglicized spellings (i.e., Igor' instead of Igor, Sofiia instead of Sofia, Iurii instead of Yuri, *bania* instead of *banya*, and so forth). The only exception to this strict adherence is the name Tchaikovsky; in this instance, owing in part to its inclusion in the book's title, as well as the overwhelming use of and familiarity with the Francophone transliteration, I have maintained the spelling currently common in English-language publications. In cases where I have cited works in translation, or have used quotations from other authors using different transliteration conventions, I have maintained the spelling from the original source, noting this in parentheses.

Unless otherwise noted, all of the translations are mine. Although I have had the assistance of colleagues in instances where a word or expression (or even tone of voice) presented me with difficulties, I am entirely responsible for any mistakes contained herein.

I have given basic information regarding each layperson quoted/referenced in a separate table at the end of the text. This list is arranged alphabetically by each person's first name (in each case a pseudonym), followed by that person's age and city of residence at the time of our meeting or correspondence. Interviews with professionals are listed in a separate table, alphabetically by that person's last name or professional moniker. The date and place of each interview follows each person's name.

Because of strict copyright rules governing popular culture productions, I have not been able to include images, lengthy musical transcriptions, or text translations. However, the interested reader may easily find a wealth of information online, via search engines such as Google, YouTube, or any number of Russian-language websites. For readers who do not use the Cyrillic alphabet, in many instances transliterated names or titles will also be sufficient for producing results via internet searches.

Roll Over, Tchaikovsky!

1. Introduction

Homosexual Bodies/Embodied Homosexuality

> The male body, as ideal and symbol, appears as the base model of homosexual culture.
> —Igor' Kon (2003: 274)

The gay pride parade, an annual fixture of the contemporary landscape in such far-flung locales as New York, Montréal, Reykjavík, Johannesburg, and São Paolo, is a complex phenomenon. Not only sites for celebration and revelry, such parades are also inherently sociopolitical actions, visible and public manifestations of communities and identities formed, in part, in relation to the variable of sexual orientation. Indeed, the very appearance of a gay pride parade may often be seen as an indicator not only of the extent to which a country (or city) has moved toward the formation of a civil society and modern liberal policies, affording equal rights to all citizens, but of the very viability of LGBT identities and communities within a specific geopolitical location. Thus, in 2005, when word of plans for Moscow's first-ever gay pride parade in May 2006 began to appear—thirty-six years after the first such event in New York City and thirteen years after the decriminalization of male homosexuality in Russia[1]—both Russian and Western observers could wonder what this might portend for LGBT politics and persons in a country whose legal-juridical suppression of the homosexual had found its most chilling incarnation in the gulag. Would Russia's tentative and partial economic rapprochement with the West be followed by, or bound up with, an adoption of the cultural mores of Europe or the United States?[2]

Whatever the desires or intentions of the parade's organizers, it quickly became clear that for many of those in power in the country's capital, quashing the affair was paramount. Mayor Iurii Luzhkov, speaking a year before the scheduled date of the event, stated that he would refuse to allow a permit for the parade and that he was intent on "protecting the interests of Muscovites," who "would categorically not support this initiative."[3] As the planned festivities neared, a Moscow court upheld Luzhkov's decision,[4] and yet at least one of the parade's organizers, Nikolai Alekseev, promised that, the absence of permits or legal sanction notwithstanding, the march would occur.[5] Luzhkov's invective continued to rise and, positing a cultural chasm between the West and the East, he asserted "our way of life, our morals and our tradition—our morals are cleaner in all ways. The West has something to learn from us and should not race along in this mad licentiousness."[6] Such invective could not but have given approbation to those groups—largely collections of neo-Fascists, nationalists, skinheads, and Orthodox Christians—who picketed and attacked participants in social events that occurred surrounding what was to have been the "main event,"[7] such actions, often replete with violence, being termed *pogroms* on some gay Russian websites.[8] Similar violence such as beatings of participants by large groups of skinheads, as well as their pelting with eggs, rocks and other debris,[9] marked the events of the day on which the parade was to occur—but did not; instead, a small coterie of participants (most of them Westerners), denied the right to march, opted instead to lay a wreath on the Tomb of the Unknown Soldier ("a monument against fascism," according to the organizers), followed by a gathering around a nearby monument to Iurii Dolgorukii, a twelfth-century Russian ruler. But even these modest events did not come to pass, as many of the would-be marchers were either arrested or physically prevented from carrying out their planned ceremonies shortly after they appeared in the vicinity.[10]

In St. Petersburg, on the same day, a group of celebrants allied with what was then one of the city's newest gay clubs, *Tsentral'naia Stantsiia* (Central Station)[11] performed on a platform on a major thoroughfare, as part of the annual carnival celebration. Such a performance of drag queens and scantily clad dancing muscle boys, a performance of gayness, was, in contrast with the events in Moscow, remarkable for the lack of violence that accompanied it. However, rather than ascribing the absence of manifest hostilities to the city's supposed reputation for "tolerance," Severianin (2006) cast a more skeptical eye on the proceedings. Noting, for example, that although a press conference was held by Aleksandr Kukharskii (founder of one of the city's oldest gay and lesbian associations, *Kryl'ia* [Wings])[12] in order to counter some of the one-sided newspaper accounts of supposed "profanement" of a Catholic church by gays during the festivities,[13] none of the reporters present published a single word of the meeting. Silence surrounding gays and lesbians was also manifest, again according to Severianin, in the fact that any mention of "sexual minorities" or "homophobia" was absent from the city's "Tolerance Program," which was inaugurated in order to combat a growing xenophobia within its environs.¹⁴ On this elision, the city's vice governor, Sergei Tarasov was quoted as saying:

> [T]here is nothing registered [about gays and lesbians in the Tolerance Program]. This program was developed with the corresponding institutes, human rights activists [*pravozashchitniki*], and everyone who was interested. None of them raised the question of sexual minorities. Yes, and I don't think that there is a direct relationship to tolerance and xenophobia. This is a little bit of a different history. ("*Tolerantnost' v Sankt-Peterburge*")

"Tolerance," it seemed, via both word and deed, would not encompass the love that should, for its own safety, continue daring not to speak its name.

Such elisions and violent interdictions in the realm of the sociopolitical, attempting to eradicate conceptual, textual, or embodied instances of homosexuality, however, should not be taken as evidence that manifestations of same-sex love and attraction were absent in all arenas in contemporary Russia. Indeed, during the same time frame, the popular music landscape was marked by scores of performers, songs, spectacles, and audiences that in many ways served as embodied and audible instances of both homosexuality and homoeroticism: the sexualized and scantily clad bodies of such male singers as Dima Bilan or Dmitrii (Mitia) Fomin, of the group Hi-Fi, transgressing gendered boundaries as objects of sexual desire; song texts of singers Boris Moiseev and Valerii Leont'ev, suggesting love between men in sometimes rather unequivocal manners; the appearance of singer Verka Serdiuchka, one of the most popular performers in the Russian-speaking world, the drag persona of Ukrainian singer/songwriter/actor Andrei Danilko; the televised singing competition *Fabrika zvezd* (Factory of Stars), the stage and audience of which were sites for (decoded) gay male performance and spectatorship; the existence of numerous gay icons, including two of the most widely known and successful *èstrada* singers of the entire Soviet era, Alla Pugacheva and Sofiia Rotaru; the thousands of men dancing at gay-only and *miks* (mixed, meaning gay and straight) nightclubs in both St. Petersburg and Moscow, often to the songs of some of the aforementioned artists, often to Western music with connections to *netraditsionnaia orientatsiia* (nontraditional orientation, a common Russian euphemism for homosexuality) such as tracks by the Pet Shop Boys, Ricky Martin, or Boy George; and the numerous press accounts elliptically or directly alleging that one or another of Russia's biggest singing stars was homosexual; all highlight the extent to which homosexuality was, and continues to be, a constitutive part of Russia's contemporary popular musics.

Such visibility/audibility was made explicit in a list of "Famous Russian Gays" ("*Izvestnye gei Rossii*") appearing on the Russian gay website qguys.ru, an inventory that included several of the most prominent male singers in the sphere of Russian popular music.[15] Yet such cognizance of manifest homosexuality was not simply confined to spheres inhabited by gay men; for example, an article in one of Russia's most widely read newspapers, *Komsomol'skaia pravda*, asked, in its title, "why have gays and lesbians filled our stage?" ("*Pochemu gei i lesbiianki zapolonili nashu stsenu?*") (Meshkov 2005). Originally accompanied by a picture of Russian male singer Shura in a dress,[16] the text begins with the author setting out on a quest to ascertain the truth about supposed homophobic legislation in the city of Perm', where vice mayor Valerii Starikov had proposed that performers of "nontraditional sexuality" would be charged higher rates for renting the city's main performance venue, colloquially known as *Mudèka*.[17] Writing with a tone of irony, if not outright sarcasm, the reporter initially finds himself in a gay café named *Mechta* (Dream) before his meeting with Starikov, a meeting in which he is ultimately assured that it is not the *sexuality* of the performers that is the object of censure, but their "behavior" onstage—a behavior that threatens to harm "the children" (and indeed, both journalist and vice mayor agree that "no one wants their children to become homosexuals"). At the meeting's close, the journalist opines that Russia's homosexuals may "sleep peacefully" (*spat' spokoino*), secure in the fact that there is no homophobia afoot.

Meshkov's assertion that homophobia played no part in Starikov's policy can be viewed only as disingenuous, naïve, and/or characteristic of a deep denial of the generally negative attitudes toward homosexuality held by the majority of the populace not only in Russia, but in many ex-Soviet republics. Such attitudes are undoubtedly at least partially a legacy of the Communist era, a time during which male homosexuality was not only a criminal offense, but also deeply pathologized, and sexual activity (either homo- or heterosexual) that placed physical pleasure over the imperative of procreation was seen as reeking of bourgeois hedonism, entirely antithetical to the imperatives of collective nation building.[18] Statistics obtained by *VTsIOM* (*Vserossiiskii tsenter izucheniia obschestvennogo mneniia*; the All-Russian Center for the Study of Social Opinion) in January 2005 show, in response to a question, "what should be done with homosexuals," that public opinion appeared at that time to be moving toward increased tolerance:

Table 1.1

Response	1999	2005	Change
Liquidate or isolate from society	38%	31%	-7
Give help	16%	10%	-6
Leave them alone	18%	49%	+31
Difficult to say	28%	10%	-18

Source: Petrov 2005b

The results of a 2006 survey carried out by the Levada-Tsentr,[19] when taken in comparison to those of an identical 2005 survey, also showed a slight decrease in negative attitudes toward homosexuality.[20] However, statistics must be contextualized not only by comparison with those obtained from other locales, but also by attention to the possible meanings of both questions and responses. As regards the former, figures obtained from the World Values Surveys from 1996 to 2002 show, on average, that homosexuality is viewed more negatively in the ex–Soviet Union than in any other area of Western or Eastern Europe surveyed; here, the average percentage of those who found homosexuality "justifiable" was only 20 percent, lower even than the Eastern Mediterranean countries (including Albania, Bulgaria, and the successor states to the former Yugoslavia), which averaged 24 percent. By comparison, the averages were 72 percent in the Nordic countries, 70 percent in Western Central Europe, 42 percent in the Western Mediterranean, and 38 percent in Eastern Central Europe (in Haavio-Mannila and Rotkirch 2012: 484–485). Regarding the latter, it is notable that the one response showing the most "positive" change—"leave them alone"—is not necessarily indicative of a move toward greater equality for LGBT persons; rather, to "leave homosexuals alone" suggests, in the context of the reactions to *public* expressions of homosexuality, a willingness to ignore ("tolerate" seems too positive an assessment) sexual minorities only if they agree to remain hidden and invisible. Indeed, according to Karlinsky, even during the Soviet period "persecution of gay men was neither continuous nor total. In the case of well-known personalities . . . the authorities were willing to look the other way, provided the man was married and kept his homosexuality out of public view" (1989: 362).[21] And while it appears that younger people may generally have more liberal views regarding homosexuality, age is hardly a guarantee of greater "tolerance" of sexual minorities or other "others" as can be witnessed in the growing numbers of xenophobic, nationalist, and antigay youth movements, the members of which may view the incursion of "outsiders" as a threat to an imagined national unity, as well as a threat to their own (economic) existence. Pilkington and Starkova (2002), for example, have examined the different worldviews of *normal'nyi* ("normal") versus *progressivnyi* ("progressive") Russian youth (the terms themselves used by young people), contrasting the outward-reaching (international, open) views of the latter to the inward-directed (nationalistic, closed) views of the former. Some of my informants made similar distinctions; Anton, for example, contrasted himself and his friends with "those people who just hang around in the courtyards of their buildings, and have nothing more to look forward to in life than getting fucked on the stairways of their apartment complex while they're drinking vodka."

In examining the connections between popular music and male homosexuality in post-Soviet Russia, the same sort of contextualization and scrutiny must be applied in order to ascertain not only how and why such connections exist—moving beyond an overly generalized and questionable assumption that gay men have always been, in all places, drawn to "the arts"—but also to discover what exploring sexuality via the musical might reveal about subject formation and intersubjective relationships. In this regard, it is my contention that Russian homosexuality in the first decade of the twenty-first century must be understood as bound up with *embodiment*, the term indicating a mode of experience of one's self, located culturally, spatially, temporally, and in relation to others, as a sentient, material, corporeal being. While I am not attempting to eclipse the numerous additional registers through which embodiment may be understood—Mauss (1973 [1934]), for example, in a seminal article examining "techniques of the body" posits a tripartite scheme encompassing the biological, sociological, and psychological as implicated in the forms human physical actions ultimately take, and both Foucault (1990 [1978]) and Butler (1993) highlight the discursive production of sexualized bodies (and bodies of sexual knowledge)—I am also wary of theoretically erasing a material corporeality. This corporeality, an integral component in the negotiation of the cultural and temporal spaces of Russia and the West, Soviet and post-Soviet is, in part, lived and experienced through, reflected in, and performed and made manifest by means of affective and somatically resonant relationships to popular musics. Although it is perhaps the norm to use the words *identity* and *community* in connection with homosexuality in the West, these words, laden with cultural, social, and political histories are at best problematic in the post-Soviet sphere.

Indeed, in examining homosexuality outside of the Western world—to say nothing of within the Western world (as if "the West," from Milan to Boise, were a homogeneous sociocultural zone)—one must situate any group with respect to its temporal, social, and geopolitical specificities and, concomitantly, avoid the casual application of Western-born conceptions of same-sex desire, these pertaining to physical, psychological, and political variables. Conversely, and concurrently, any inquiry must guard against the creation of difference for difference's sake, in a possibly subconscious effort to create a "sexual Other" who is little more than a repository for psychosexual fears and fantasies. For example, Baer (2002), engaging Tuller's (1996) chronicle of his experiences in "gay" post-Soviet Russia, and Essig's (1999) sociological-experimental inquiry into Russian "queerness," finds that both authors have invented a landscape of the sexually polymorphous, one in which the strictures of a highly rigid and binarized (hetero/homo) sexual system have been eschewed in favor of one far more fluid. Ultimately, he critiques these authors for having elided the strictness of Russia's patriarchally inflected gender hierarchy, one intimately linked to sexuality, and one that continues to do great harm to large numbers of people—generally, those who are viewed as "feminine."[22] In his estimation, both authors have based their comparisons on rather simplistic, stereotypical notions of what homosexuality in the West "is," ignoring the diversity of models of homosexual desire coexisting in a "discontinuous, nonunitary way," in both Russia and the West (Baer 2002: 513).[23]

The problematics, in fact, of defining "a" sexual identity and, concomitantly, the meanings of same-sex sexual activity even in one geographically bounded location, may be highlighted by attention to two editorials from contemporary gay magazines in Russia, both of which were aimed at defining (or suggesting) the publications' readerships. In the now-defunct monthly magazine *XXBi*,[24] for example, the October 2004 editorial made an implicit differentiation between sex and love. Noting that a search on the internet for the word *liubov'* (love), via the Rambler search engine, brings up hundreds of thousands of documents, the author finds that "the quantity of love is overflowing all imaginable limits," but that "the quality of love has fallen dramatically" ("*Bez striptiz*" [sic]).[25] Later in the essay, in an unambiguous attempt to indicate a specific type of love, the author invokes the image of Tchaikovsky—arguably the most famous of all Russian homosexuals—and, referencing director Igor' Talankin's cinematic drama, wonders, "what kind of film about Tchaikovsky could have been made, if they risked to say the truth about whom he really loved" (adding futher, "it was certainly not the horselike ass of Baroness von Meck"). Ultimately, the editor identifies the intended reader of his publication:

> *XXBi* is addressed to those who have stopped being afraid of themselves. Who honestly and without hesitation answered the question to themselves: who do I, myself, want to love? And for what? And for those who walk through life not stumbling over their own limbs.

The editorial also offers that the magazine is about "inner freedom" (*vnutrenniaia svoboda*), a freedom encompassing the ability to "follow a beloved person, to find work that we like. Hobbies for free time. Deciding for yourself your favorite city. Your favorite county."

In the monthly magazine *Kvir* (*Queer*), however, editor Èd Mishin[26] appears less concerned with "love" than exploring desires and taxonomies:

> The thing is that pure heterosexual or homosexual inclination is seldom met. And from what moment do we start to consider that someone is gay or bisexual? From the first same-sex sex? Or maybe from the tenth. ... In general, to this seemingly simple question, my interviewers can't answer. And then they begin to understand that most important thing—the sexual minority does not exist. It is impossible to divide people into groups on the basis of sexual orientation. (Mishin 2004a: 1)

Ultimately, Mishin invokes the use of the acronym *MSM* (Men who have Sex with Men) offering it as a way of acknowledging the multifarious instances of male-to-male sexuality, without defining it. In the end, one's sexual identity is unimportant; *Kvir*, according to its editor, is "for those to whom aesthetics, drive, culture is important, over sex. And it is absolutely unimportant what your sexual preferences are."

That both magazines were/are glossy monthlies on high-quality stock with equally high-quality design, layout, and photographic standards, indicates, among other things, the confluence of a market economy and sexuality, a connection that D'Emilio (1983a) has posited as essential to the construction of a modern gay identity in the United States;[27] indeed, both editorials include a desire to delineate just who the consumers of each magazine are (and, in the case of Mishin, to make that buying public as large as possible). But although *Kvir*'s editor may profess that the magazine it not strictly for homosexual men (and *XXBi* may suggest that same thing via its very name), both the covers and the contents of both publications regularly feature(d) highly homoerotic images of scantily clad and sometimes nude men and address(ed) issues of interest to at least some homosexuals (for example, gay marriage), and on Mishin's own website, gay.ru, the publication is described as "the first monthly, glossy magazine for Russian-speaking gays" ("*pervyi ezhemesiachnyi gliantsevyi zhurnal dlia russkoiazychnykh geev*") or a "monthly Russian gay magazine" ("*ezhemesiachnyi rossiiskii gei-zhurnal*").[28] Although Essig (1999) posits the existence of a "queer subjectivity," in Russia, one that does not presume a "gay identity" among men who have sex with other men, such a conclusion is totally at odds with the views expressed by the majority of my informants; in fact, despite the name of Mishin's publication, not a single person with whom I spoke could offer an explanation of what the word meant (or where it emanated from) aside from assumptions that it was another Western euphemism for gay. Moreover, when I offered an explanation of the term's theoretical bases, many of my informants were at the very least skeptical of the concept, some dismissing it as "nonsense" ("*erunda*"), or indicative of a man's "complexes" (i.e., the inability to admit to a homosexual orientation).[29]

In his discussion of the internationalization of gay identities, Altman (1996) suggests that while specificity cannot be disregarded, "it seems clear that *some form* of gay and lesbian identity is becoming more common across the world" (85), one that may draw on both indigenous practice as well as discourses emanating from the so-called "First World." Speaking, however, in the plural, he characterizes such "modern homosexualities" as sharing several characteristics: "(1) a differentiation between sexual and gender transgression; (2) an emphasis on emotional as much as on sexual relationships[;] and (3) the developments of public homosexual worlds" (83). Although the word *identity* is troublesome, my fieldwork in Russia leads me to agree with both Baer's and Altman's assessments, as opposed to those of either Tuller or Essig. Understanding that both totalizing schemes that aspire to eradicating any form of suspected divergence from the norm, and hypermicro analyses that reify difference qua difference are equally problematic, it is clear that in contemporary Russia there are large numbers of men who consider themselves "*gei,*" "*goluboi*" (literally, light blue, a common euphemism for homosexual)[30] "*takoi*" ("like that"), "*gomo*" ("homo")—words they themselves use—as opposed to "*natural'nyi*" ("natural," meaning straight) or "*getero.*" Additionally, such men have ties not only to other men who share their sexual orientation, but also to a shared expressive culture that resonates with their sense of self, ties that resonate and are made manifest via the body.

For the majority of my informants, the attainment of physical and emotional intimacy with another man was something they considered highly important, although (as in the West) the actual weight afforded to each variable certainly differed among specific individuals; some hoped for a lasting, romantic, and monogamous relationship, while others, although acknowledging their erotic attraction to other men, found the idea of two men being faithful to each other impossible. Despite such divergences, however, not only did these men understand their homosexuality as being a constituent part of their "selves"—a part that many felt to be immutable and from birth—but several were equally aware of the fact that those close to them also knew "who" or "what" they "were." For example, Kolia lived with his family in a large apartment in St. Petersburg and on occasion spent the night there with his then-current boyfriend. When I asked him what his mother thought of this (his father was not living with the family), he said:

> I'm sure she knows what's going on, even though we simply refer to [my boyfriend] as "my friend." But he has come over in the past with flowers for me, and he spends the night with me in my room, so my mother understands perfectly what the situation is. But she has always said that the most important

thing for her is that her children are happy, and if she sees I am happy with him, then she doesn't care.

Kolia's self-definition with regards to sexuality, however, was not entirely unambiguous, insofar as he first described himself to me as "bisexual." Indeed, the term enjoys a certain popularity (even stylishness) among many younger people in Russia and warrants at least a brief discussion. In both St. Petersburg and Moscow I was acquainted with men who were married, some with children, but who carried on an active sex life with other men outside of the marriage, finding male sexual partners at *bani* (singular *bania*, communal bathhouse), on the internet, at cruising spots (*pleshki*—singular, *pleshka*) or even at clubs; in fact, several clubs in St. Petersburg were known as places for bisexuals (most notably *Monro*—named after Marilyn—*Mono*,[31] and *Metro*).[32] Although several of these men identified themselves as being "bisexual," the ways in which they viewed themselves, as well as the ways in which they were viewed by others, varied. Artur, for example, who was married and the father of a small child, was in the process of trying to emigrate to the West and had not decided whether his family would follow him. In his estimation, although he lived a "one hundred percent straight lifestyle," his sex life was "almost totally gay," and he was very conflicted regarding whether he could continue living the life of a (heterosexual) husband. Far from viewing such situations as instances of "queer liminality" or "sexual fluidity," many of my informants found the use of the word bisexual to be, again, an indication of one's "complexes" (due largely to Soviet sexo- and homophobia), and/or a necessary expedient in a strongly patriarchal society, one in which family ties are often essential for social, emotional, and financial support, and heterosexual marriage is assumed. Rather than a fluid continuum, some men, like Artur, compartmentalized their public/social lives as opposed to their erotic lives (which might also include a less visible social component) along axes of hetero and homo, respectively, and some—like Maksim, Vadim, and Ivan—although they had had long-term, live-in relationships with women, ultimately left, realizing that their erotic-emotional attractions were exclusively to other men. In some cases, the assumed imperative of living a heterosexual life had deleterious effects on both partners. Maksim, for example, recounted that his time with his "girlfriend" had been one lived with constant drama, heartache, and alcohol, and was one of the "worst periods" of his life.

Indeed, while Kolia "identified" himself as "bisexual" early on in our relationship, as weeks and months went by he told me that, "the more I have sex with men, the less I want to have sex with women. In fact, I rarely think of it any more." He had been with his current boyfriend for over a year and said that the last time he had had sex with a woman was a very brief ("about five minutes") encounter over two years ago, while driving through a small town on his way to Moscow. The incident prior to that had been likewise brief and cursory, and while he said that in the past sex with women had been "not bad" ("*neplokho*"), his sexual life with men was where he had, in his opinion, found physical and emotional satisfaction. The constant variable that connected the vast majority of my informants was their understanding that their main physical, erotic attraction was to other men, something that most of them saw as defining them as *goluboi*.

Equally important to many of my informants, in addition to sexual liaisons, was the act of socializing with other gay men,[33] either in private or public spaces (at friends' apartments, clubs, cafés, parks, *bani* or gay saunas, or even one small stretch of beach on the Gulf of Finland in St. Petersburg, the *pliazh "kurort"*),[34] as well as in the growing area of cyberspace. In the past decade, as internet use has become more common, either through home computers or internet cafés (such as the chain CafeMax),[35] there has been an efflorescence of gay (as well as straight) meeting sites (*saity znakomstv*)—gay.ru, xsgay.ru, gayly.ru, qguys.ru, gaydar.net, and bluesystem.ru, among the most popular—and these sites have become a bastion of social intercourse, allowing visitors to remain relatively free from the threat of homophobic violence. In all such instances, one of the unifying elements is a shared sense of erotic attachment to members of one's own sex—a homosexual relationship—and not the type of "queerness" that Essig posits; as such, although no one word can entirely unproblematically and with exact precision serve as a universal marker for a specific sexual orientation, I have opted to use the terms *gay* and *homosexual* (rather than *queer*) when referring to my informants. Indeed, referencing the profiles filled out by many of the visitors to the aforementioned websites, while some leave the answer to *orientatsiia* (orientation) blank on their profiles, there are scores and scores who define themselves as *gei*. None of this is to suggest that the process of one's self-definition, encompassing the variable of sexual orientation, is a casual, straightforward affair; as noted above, there are indeed men for whom an unambiguous moniker in regards to their sexual-erotic-emotional lives was problematic. Yet it is equally true that for many men, the application of the term *gei*—either in terms of their own sexual orientation, or to a segment of the population (or both)—was not so thorny. As Slava told me, "there are men who have sex with other men, they like feminine boys, they like to use them. But they don't have the inner feeling, the philosophy of gay. They are simply *pidars* [faggots]; they are not gay. I have no trouble calling myself gay, that's what I am." And as one visitor commented in a reader's forum on the website gaynews.ru, "God doesn't exist, but gays exist on our planet" ("*Bog ne sushestvuet* [sic], *no gei sushestvuiut* [sic] *na nashei planete*").³⁶

If "gays exist"—including Russian gays—what role does the body play in producing a specifically homosexual sense of self and manner of being in the world? Russian sociologist Igor' Kon, perhaps the preeminent researcher on questions of gender, sex, and sexuality in the Soviet and post-Soviet spheres, has posited the body as foundational to "homosexual (sub-) culture" (as well as the importance of the homosexual gaze to the very visibility of the male body as an erotic object),³⁷ finding gay men to have a "higher level of reflexivity . . . than men of traditional orientation." They are, moreover, "conscious of the characteristics of their own and other bodies, and give them greater meaning" (2003: 275). The male body, according to Kon, is the site in which the social, symbolic, and material coalesce for homosexual men; for example, in regards to "gay phallocentrism," the male "member" (*chlen*) is not only an abstract symbol of power (*vlast'*, *mogushchestvo*), a phallus, but also "a real instrument of pleasure (a penis)" (287), and in general gay culture gives "a great importance to the sensual side of social and private life" (275).³⁸ But while many of Kon's analyses focus on homosexual men/homosexual culture in general, there are contextual reasons for highlighting the corporeality of the homosexual self in post-Soviet, Russian space.

My foregrounding of corporeality relies, in the first place, upon the numerous instances of informants themselves referencing embodiment, either explicitly or implicitly, not only in discussions of sexual orientation, but of their daily lives and interpersonal relationships as well. Before turning to these examples, however, it will be useful to offer an overview of the ways in which the body figured within the Soviet system; indeed, the foregrounding of the human body, in both its symbolic and material aspects—the one inextricably intertwined with the other—may be seen as one of the hallmarks of the Soviet era. In this regard, it was not the individual body, per se, that was considered important, but rather the physical, material body of the citizen as synecdochal for the often anthropomorphized state; as Starks notes, Soviet ideologies "created, tamed, and tempered the individual and the corporate body in the quest to create a political organism" (2008: 7). Here, the perfection of society is seen as obtaining via the perfection—or perfect disciplining—of discrete human bodies. Workers and peasants alike were impelled (or compelled), for example, to take care of their teeth, abstain from alcohol and tobacco, change their underwear frequently, and visit the *bania*. Seeing this last as "a frontline defense to promote civilized living" (172), one informational poster produced by the *Gosmedizdat* (State Medical Publisher) in the late 1920s importuned citizens, via a rhyming couplet by none other than Maiakovskii, to "get into the cultured habit—change underwear and go to the *bania* weekly" (172, 173).[39] The cleanliness of the physical body, via the inculcation of bodily "techniques" designed as means to desired, politicized ends, was thus tied to conceptions of culturedness (rather than the assumed backwardness of the peasant)—but not only; a clean and healthy body, one that ingested the proper foods (touched and prepared only with clean, washed hands); worked, slept, and relaxed the correct number of hours each day; and engaged solely in "normal" sexual activity (that is, heterosexual, with the aim of procreation), was a site of a similarly clean mind, intellectual vigor, and the very basis of industrial efficiency and productivity, military readiness, and demographic expansion. Unhealthy choices made by individuals could have negative, material consequences (for example, one alcoholic might create a dangerous situation for an entire factory), but it was not only on the level of the literal that the body was invoked; rather, a "diseased" body, or group of bodies with "unhealthy" political or ideological agendas might function as a pathogen to the collective whole. According to Starks, "the Soviet government treated society as a body, hunting out those who might be tainted by the past or pose a threat to the future and depriving them of Soviet citizenship" (24).

While hygienists battled rhetorically for the health of the individual (as part of the collective) body, providing the blueprint for fitness (physical and/as ideological), Soviet physicians also sought to bring "sexual enlightenment" (*polovoe prosveshchenie*) to the masses. Indeed, the "sex question" (*polovoi vopros*)—comprising such matters as equality between the sexes, marriage, divorce, prostitution, venereal disease, and even, to an extent, homosexuality—was seen by many in post-Revolutionary Russia as one of the weightiest, certain types of sexual relations and behaviors being viewed in many regards as vestiges of bourgeois (for the urbanite) and/or patriarchal (for the peasant) mindset and custom. As Bernstein (2007) has shown, this attempt at creating a sexually "healthy" Soviet citizen yet again stressed the indissoluble links between individual behavior and social well-being; a renunciation of pleasure, in favor of the imperative of sexual activity as primarily geared toward procreation and the needs of "collective health," was consistently stressed by the sexual enlighteners (30; see also Chapter 6). Numerous physicians, writing in popular publications, inveighed against what they considered a "sick" or "unhealthy" interest in sexual matters and activity, suggesting that such preoccupations resulted in "a withdrawal from public life, and the desire to lock oneself away in the confines of one's petty inclinations" (33); a desire for sexual pleasure diverted energy from the paramount duties of the Soviet citizen—including work, defense, and population growth—and such a "capitalistic" mindset would cause individuals to "[shirk] their communal obligations" (35).

But if the states of the body, via the affects of sentient pleasures, seemed to be targets of eradication rather than cultivation, it must be understood that enlighteners used, as the basis for their assertions, the very materiality of the body itself, translated via the lens of putatively irrefutable "objective science." Biological bases were posited not only for "healthy" sexual comportment, but also physical—largely endocrinological—suzerainty as undeniably responsible for gender difference and sexual orientation. Although equality between the sexes may have been one of the components of the *polovoi vopros*, the declarations of the enlighteners often made it clear that, while men and women might (in theory) be treated equally as citizens, they were biologically (and thus, psychologically) different, the inference of female inferiority often being far more than simply tacit.[40] Homosexuality was likewise viewed by many scientists and physicians as the result of malfunctioning glands (although some posited an environmental etiology, especially after the rise of Stalin),[41] a malady that might be "cured" by surgical intervention.[42]

Perhaps the most enduring, ubiquitous, and visible manifestation of the Soviet obsession with corporeality was the development and institution of an officially sanctioned *fizkul'tura* (short for *fizicheskaia kul'tura*), or physical culture, a culture that whether via artistic representation or viewed spectacle (parade, sporting event), was as visual as it was corporeal (to say nothing of ideological) (see O'Mahony 2006). Enacted from the earliest days of Soviet rule, *fizkul'tura* comprised not only the playing of sports, but also a wide array of healthful activities—including, as noted in the *Great Soviet Encyclopedia* of 1936, "a strict regime of hygiene . . . strengthening the organism through natural means (sun, air, water)" (2006: 16)—all of which were to be instrumental, depending upon the specific exigencies of the time, in producing physically, and thus intellectually and morally, fit citizens, resulting in a collective social body. For example, during periods of armed hostilities, or the threat thereof, physical activity was seen as a way of readying the populace for defense, while during the first Five-Year Plan, with economic development foregrounded, the physical activities of workers (as opposed to soldiers) came increasingly under the purview of labor and trade union societies. Following the resolution of World War II, *fizkul'tura* also functioned for decades as a tool of foreign policy, presenting an embodied vision of the superiority of communism over capitalism, until the dissolution of the USSR and the "brawn drain"—that is, ex-Soviet athletes seeking more financially lucrative careers overseas—signaled its demise (2006: 17–18).[43]

Whatever the intentions of the Soviet government, it is clear that the constantly disseminated dicta or spectacular propaganda concerning citizens' bodies was not universally heeded, and the legacy of a hygienic, physical culture seems in many ways to have dissolved concomitant with the Union. For example, judging by current statistics regarding the life expectancy of Russian men—60.11 years in 2012,[44] one of the lowest in the developed world and largely due to the epidemic overuse of tobacco and alcohol—a healthy, abstemious lifestyle is apparently not one adopted by large segments of the population. Certainly one may question the extent to which anterior models and practices, some decades old, have impacted upon contemporary Russians. But while none of my informants was the living incarnation of the "perfect" Soviet citizen, as imagined by the various medical and political authorities, the parallels between Soviet models, discourses, and ideologies surrounding sexuality, science, and the body, and the statements of many of these men indicate that, at least in part, such models, discourses, and ideologies have continued to be influential past the "post-"; indeed, several authors have highlighted the necessity of viewing the complex interrelatedness of the various eras within the Soviet past—and, as I believe is clear, the past and the post—rather than their supposed dissonances and the assumed fissures obtaining between them.[45] To give only one concrete example: It may be easier to imagine how such parallels might be explained in the instances where informants were older and thus spent a large portion of their lives under Soviet rule, but it is not inconceivable that even those younger men with whom I spoke, born in the era leading up to the demise of the Soviet Union, much of their childhoods and teenage years having occurred in a "post"-*glasnost'* space, would also have been regularly exposed to Soviet-era discourses of health, the body, and hygiene if one understands that many of my informants had been *pionery* (singular, *pioner*—pioneer). In many regards similar to the Boy or Girl Scouts of the United States, the Young Pioneer Association—for children aged ten to fifteen—was the first step in becoming a member of the Communist Party, and preceded joining the *komsomol*[46] as teenagers. As Starks has shown, such groups were instrumental in the hygienists' attempts to inculcate the "proper" methods and standards of corporeal care into young Soviet citizens, even publishing a book entitled, appropriately enough, *Gigiena pionera* (*Pioneer Hygeine*) (Starks 2008: 174–175).[47] I am not suggesting that any or all of my informants unquestioningly adhered to what they had learned as *pionery*—some, in fact, had joined more out of coercion than genuine desire—or that they were not aware, perhaps in retrospect, of the regimentation (if not propagandizing) inherent in their lessons. Some, however, recalled their experiences with at least a modicum of nostalgia; indeed, nostalgia was probably instrumental, in part, for the success of the song "*Pioner*" by the group Hi-Fi, a song in which the *pioner* "credo" was exclaimed—partially chanted, partially sung—over a house beat:

Pioner vsegda gotov	A pioneer is always ready
A u pionera osnovnoe delo	For a pioneer the main thing is
Bud' gotov i smelo v trudnyi boi idi	To be ready, and go boldly to the difficult fight
A na pionera vsia strana smotrela	And the whole country watched the pioneer
Kak dusha gorela v molodoi grudi	How the soul burned in the young breast

Indeed, instances of "nostalgic" pieces of Soviet culture were somewhat common in the popular musics encountered in Russia during my fieldwork, these often enmeshed—as is the case with Hi-Fi's "*Pioner*"—with discourses of the body. Del'fin's song "*Vesna*" ("Spring") featured a video made up entirely of footage of the Moscow 1980 Summer Olympic Games, the apotheosis of Soviet *fizkul'tura*, and DJ *Gruv* ("Groove") in 2004 released a track sampling and remixing the main theme music of the spectacularly popular Soviet-era film *Sluzhebnyi roman* (*The Office Romance*) (1977), a comedy that serves as an object lesson of the requisiteness of adherence to the "correct" gender attributes of one's sex.[48]

It was not only in the arena of popular music, however, that traces of the Soviet construction of the body might be found, but also in the viewpoints, statements, and accounts of my informants themselves, as previously noted. Among my informants, although I did witness, or was told of, instances of overindulgence in alcohol, the majority expressed the maintenance of good health (sometimes in relation to the physical attractiveness of their bodies), as important to them. Moreover, many of these men offered all manner of advice to me regarding matters of health and hygiene: "home remedies" for colds, coughs, sore throats, or upset stomachs, where to buy the freshest food, the necessity of keeping apartment windows open to circulate "fresh air" (and, conversely, the detrimental effects of sleeping in an overheated room), of removing one's shoes indoors to avoid tracking in dirt from outside, of leaving the city periodically to relax and rejuvenate in more rural locales, of getting sun (no mean feat in St. Petersburg) at one of the local beaches, of going to the *bania* to partake of the beneficial attributes of the steam and heat, of getting the proper amount of sleep, of brushing one's teeth properly, of washing and preparing food properly, or of exercising (among other things).

The realm of sexuality, for a large number of these men, was also seen as reliant upon the material body; many saw their sexual orientation as being biologically based (ascribing their homosexuality to either hormonal or genetic influences), something they were "born with," and sexual attraction and behavior as likewise somatically motivated. For example, several found the idea of monogamy between two men impossible on a "biological level," and questioned the viability of long-term, committed male homosexual relationships. They also often ascribed their choice of sexual partners as dependent upon the variable of physical appearance and, often, a "genuine" masculinity. Sexual activity itself was not only something that was seen as important to their sense of fulfillment and happiness but also, in many ways, the sine qua non of being gay: that is, while having a sexual encounter with another man might not necessarily mark one as gay (as Slava suggested), one could not be homosexual if one did not have the desire for physical, erotic, sexual intimacy with another man. While many of these same assertions and viewpoints might certainly be expressed by gay men in the West, it was both the frequency of such responses, as well as the absolutely certainty with which they were often pronounced, that was remarkable; when an informant said that he was born gay, that his orientation was biologically immutable, such a statement was generally made with the conviction of fact, not as an invitation for discussion of possible alternatives.

What I am suggesting then is not (or not only) that a Soviet preoccupation with corporeality is the original point from which a post-Soviet gay man, an embodied sexual self, is "constructed." Rather, the male homosexual self as embodied self existed at the very least from the later nineteenth century, not only as the contemporaneously remarked-upon denizens of the "*gomoseksual'nyi mirok*" (the "little homosexual world") of St. Petersburg (Rotikov 1998), visible by their dress, carriage, argot, and mien, but also as the assumed audience of the homoeroticized male body as represented in and by the photographs of muscular athletes taken at the studio of Karl Bulla, the paintings of Kuz'ma Petrov-Vodkin, and the kinesthetic forms of ballet dancers Vatslav Nizhinskii and his contemporaries. This homosexual body was not entirely eradicated in post-Revolutionary Russia, but in fact left pictorial and embodied traces in the very mechanisms enlisted by the state in its attempts to perfect the individual-social body: From any number of hygiene-related posters and pamphlets depicting homosocial environments populated with nude or seminude men,[49] to the spectacles of *fizkul'tura* parades (one of which was immortalized on film in 1937),[50] to the paintings and mosaics of artists such as Aleksandr Deineka (showing nude, male Soviet citizens in "healthy" activities),[51] to the very physical space of the *bania* (a space in which, as noted, the "healthy" Soviet body might be maintained, but also where the propinquity of one male body to another might lead to actual sexual activity),[52] the male body, often inherently sexualized via the foregrounding of its aesthetic and sensual attributes, served as a repository—one often apparently, mind-bogglingly incongruous in the context of a supposedly sexo- and homophobic discursive space—for the public symbolization of a male-male sexual desire that was, for all intents and purposes, blocked in all other spheres.

The post-Soviet homosexual body or, rather, the homosexual subject who experiences his sexual self corporeally, however, is not simply a continuation of an uninterrupted, constant, and eternal body (or "body culture"); rather, homosexual men in present-day Russia have concurrently repudiated, rehabilitated, and reclaimed the physicality of what was formerly the discursively and ideologically produced trace of a body. I am in no way suggesting that Russian homosexual men have somehow "returned" to a "natural" body—a type of contemporary "noble [sexual] savage"—or somehow miraculously exist outside of the realm of ideological and discursive construction (as if the discursive and the material were autonomous, mutually exclusive domains); as noted previously, the seminal works of authors such as Foucault and Butler, both of which are exemplary in regards to analyzing the complexity of how sexed and gendered bodies and subjectivities come to be (per)formed, might well be productively applied to the post-Soviet realm. However, in their significantly apolitical stances, abjuring both the Soviet and the Western conceptions of subjectivity as insalubriously reliant upon ideological, discursive, and political systems (and systems of thought), and in their lived, somatic experiences of physical sexual acts, interpersonal interactions in shared social space, travel within and outside of the country's borders and, related to each of the foregoing, popular musics—the last of which is a site in which the body figures prominently—many homosexual men in contemporary Russia have attempted to recover a corporeal self that is not used, either materially or ideologically, as a pawn in someone else's game. While it is likely that the inculcation of an ideologically corporealized *habitus* then motivates the bodily *hexis* of homosexual men in post-Soviet Russia—the "body" internalized as sociopolitical symbol and structure impacting upon bodily actions likewise sociopolitically motivated—it is a mistake to focus exclusively on the ideological/psychological at the expense of the physiological, to foreclose upon the possibility that the *hexis* itself is able to impart a specific type of nonlinguistic, nontheoretical knowledge.[53] While there is clearly a "political" component to conceptions of corporeal agency, and the "homosexual body" is not formed in isolation, but in relation to the social group (one increasingly disseminated through media and a growing consumer culture), my goal is to take seriously my informants' emphasis on the biological and the corporeal and, while not forgetting that such emphases are, in part, the effects of ideologies, examine what the dancing, listening, kissing, fucking, sweating, singing, sucking body—never free of discourse, yet never entirely defined by it either—reveals about sexuality, the self, and intersubjectivity in post-Soviet Russia and, as a consequence of this, the insufficiency of Western ideas of gay "identity" and "community" insofar as they may assume universal relevance. The homosexual body in post-Soviet Russia is a body that has repudiated the Soviet negation of physical pleasure and Western politicization of sexuality. And it is a body that shares an intimate relationship with post-Soviet popular musics.

In order to locate the relationships between music and body in a specifically post-Soviet space, it is helpful to understand that such relationships encompass not only the body of the listener, however, but that of the performer as well—and here we may once again focus on the *bania*. For if the communal bath was a site in which both physical well-being and sexual fulfillment might be obtained, it also served as a site for social intercourse that was not necessarily sexual in nature. The *Iamskie bani* in St. Petersburg was one of several in the city, and had become by the first decade of the twenty-first century a de facto gay meeting site on certain days of the week (at certain times) largely because many of the homosexual patrons had learned and communicated, through friends and acquaintances, these unofficial schedules with one another. Here, men might not only bathe and partake of the beneficial heat and steam, but also congregate in the locker rooms (or, at the *Iamskie*, a small room off the main locker area), converse, smoke, drink a beer or a tea, and spend time in the company of others. Indeed, the *bania* was not only a site for conviviality and social interaction in the city, but outside its borders as well; several men I knew regularly went out to their families' country homes (*dacha*), some of which were equipped with *bani*, not only for what they saw as the physically restorative powers of nature (as well as its aesthetic worth), but also to spend time with family, friends, and loved ones—in the *bania*, around the dining table, in the kitchen, or working in the garden.

In fact, the majority of my informants stressed the importance of close, soulful (*dushevnye*) relationships that, while obtaining on one hand a level of deep spiritual connection, were also contingent upon corporeal proximity and shared social, physical space.[54] Most of them lived with others—either family members, friends, or lovers—and, although this might have been ascribed, in part, to financial exigencies (the cost of a market-rate apartment was far beyond the reach of most), almost all indicated that this cohabitation was at least in part by choice. Gleb, for example, lived in a small apartment with his parents on the outskirts of the city, but had frequent access to private space. He had set up an arrangement to take care of the apartment of a Western expat, who maintained an apartment in the city, when the man was not in St. Petersburg (which was often). Notably, however, Gleb often chose not to stay there, as he said he felt odd living alone. Several of my informants, in fact, did not understand why I had opted to rent an apartment and live on my own, some assuming it was because I didn't know people in St. Petersburg (or Moscow); when I informed them that I simply preferred to live by myself, they found it strange and possibly proof of their assumptions that Americans were self-absorbed, materialistic, and unable to have truly *dushevnye* relations with others. Slava, for example, the only one of my informants who had actually lived in the United States, and thus had at least some firsthand experience with "American culture," said that he would never consider living in the States for any extended period of time, because "the people are too clannish, too much concerned with themselves and their small families. It's uncommon to find people who care for or live with, or even have a relationship with their grandparents. Nobody invites other people over for *vecherinki* [parties], people all go out to restaurants or clubs—they never have you over to their home."

The importance afforded "close relationships"—from the *bania*, to the *dacha*, to the city home—are witnessed in the realm of post-Soviet popular music as well, but here I must first briefly note some of the salient attributes of popular culture in post-Soviet Russia that may be viewed as an outcome of anterior Soviet practices. Barker (1999) notes that in post-Revolutionary Russia, the bifurcations of high/low and public/private tended to blur and collapse far more than in the West. In the case of the former, rather than a tension between the cultures of the "elite" and "the masses," the Bolshevik leaders, and, following them, Stalin, attempted to forge a new proletariat culture, one intended specifically for the social class that was to have superseded those otiose, pre-Revolutionary group such as the bourgeoisie, the ruling elite, and the backward peasant. The creation of such a "meta" culture was, in fact, engendered as much by a calculated effort on the part of the political elite to disseminate ideology via agitprop, as it was by demographic shifts; as Barker points out, the first Five-Year Plan not only urbanized the countryside (bringing the State apparatuses to the hinterlands), but ruralized urban centers (men and women migrating to more populous areas for work) as workers and bureaucrats embarked upon the project of nation building. Such movements "were as responsible for the merging of elitist and popular culture under Stalin as were cultural mandates from above" (24).[55]

Stalin's goal, however, differed from that of Lenin; while the latter aspired to elevate (*podniat'*) the worker's cultural understanding, the former sought instead to make culture itself comprehensible (*poniat,*' to understand) to the worker (28). In Barker's view, "under Stalin the onus was no longer on artists, educators and ideologues to *raise* the collective level of the masses, but on the artists themselves to make their work accessible or *understandable* to those same people" (28-29). Such an imperative could often produce works that bordered on, or lay firmly in, the realm of "kitsch," such as the famous Stalinist "wedding cake" architecture, or Socialist Realism in general. But again, such an endeavor could not be viewed entirely as an imposition from the top; citing Dobrenko (1997), Barker highlights that in a very real sense, as mass culture's success could be gauged only by its comprehensibility, it could not veer into the possibly arcane concerns of a cultural elite; rather, it was required to respond to the desires of the masses. In Dobrenko's view, "the making of culture [was] much less a product of party mandate and much more a function of the *narod* [people] as the prime movers of their own culture" (Barker 1999: 29). The accuracy of such a view is given credence by examination of more contemporary Soviet popular musics as well; MacFadyen (2001), for example, examining Russian popular song of the late-Soviet period, finds that the creation not only of a star's repertoire but of his or her *lichnost'* (personality) was overwhelmingly considered to be the product of "relationships" and "conversations" between singer and audience:

> [W]e see that audience tastes and their degree of support begin increasingly to *dictate* the repertoire of an artist. A dialogue of sorts ensues.... Personality for a singer is not so much discussed in terms of something engendered between a performer and the society of his or her workplace, say, but instead a spoken, fundamentally emotional entity, one forged between singer and audience (who *like* each other) and between new and old songs, current and recognized repertoires of past *lichnosti* (who are *liked*)[56]

While "prohibited" Western musics, both recordings and styles, have consistently reached Russian audiences[57]—both through Western and Russian performers—the dissolution of the Soviet Union and the relaxation of both physical and cultural borders in Russia have made musics emanating from both the United States and Western Europe far more available to the populace. It would be a mistake, however, to imagine that such an incursion has eradicated the popularity of Russian performers, many of whom have enjoyed decades of success. Tastes in popular music among my informants were varied; but while many of them initially professed a preference for "Western" musics, it became clear over time that the vast majority of them also had deep connections to—and sincerely "*liked*"—Russian songs, genres, and performers, despite the fact that such "liking" (especially among younger people) might mark them as somehow less modern, hip, or internationally oriented. As an example: while t.A.T.u's song "*Nas ne dogoniat*" (released in English as "Not Gonna Get Us," the title an accurate translation of the Russian) enjoyed at least a modicum of success in the West, the group was not terribly popular with my informants. However, when two of the greatest singers of the Soviet era, Alla Pugacheva and Sofiia Rotaru, performed the song as part of the former's televised sixtieth birthday celebration concert in 2009 (Rotaru was then aged sixty-two), three of my former informants expressed (via email) great admiration for both the performance and the artists, one even sending me the YouTube link just in case I had missed it. (Obsessed as I was with Rotaru, I hadn't.)[58] Russian popular music is a pervasive presence not only, of course, on radio, but on television as well, music variety shows such as *Nashi pesni* (*Our Songs*), *Luchshie pesni o glavnom* (*The Best Songs about What Matters*), *Zolotoi grammofon* (*The Golden Gramophone*, a Grammy-like awards ceremony), *Novaia volna* (*The New Wave*, a song competition held in Jūrmala, Latvia) being constantly broadcast on most national channels. During my time in Russia, it was, much to my delight, difficult to turn on the television on any given night, without having at least one choice of this type of show; additionally, two music-centered stations—MTV Russia and *MuzTV* (short for *muzyka* [music] TV)—were broadcast around the clock during the time I lived in St. Petersburg and Moscow and both featured not only Western but a large percentage of Russian singers and bands as well.[59] Russian performers with whom one already has a "close" connection—often through, as Kelly (1998: 146) suggests, "extreme emotion," "a key desideratum in the popular arts"—are thus also regularly "guests" in one's house, pleasant ubiquitous presences and known *lichnosti*, "real" people who are known and with whom one spends time. Music is thus an arena in which interpersonal relationships between and among embodied subjects are vital.

The dynamic of embodiment obtains on an additional level as well, one in which the music itself, rather than the performer, is implicated. One of the most salient attributes of a vast array of Russian popular music, encompassing genres from *romansy* (romances), *rok* (rock), *popsa* (roughly analogous to Western pop), *bardovskaia pesnia* (bard song),[60] *èstrada* (a uniquely Soviet genre of "stage" songs, somewhat related to either American "show tunes" or British "variety"), and *VIA*-type songs (an acronym for *vokal'no-instrumental'nyi ansambl'*, the sanitized Soviet version of "rock" bands), is the remarkable adherence to stereotypical harmonic and melodic constructions. Although some people with whom I spoke, including my informants, negatively critiqued Russian popular music for exactly this overwhelming homogeneity, the repeated exposure to harmonic progressions and melodic lines that "move" the same way, that exhibit the same "forms"—over a course of decades, via known, affectively resonant performers—engenders an embodied relationship, a musically created body *hexis*, between sound and listener. More than simply "feeling" a song (or having feelings about a song), the recurring structures become known somatically, become part of somatic memory, and are formative of the ways in which the listener locates, orients, and situates her- or himself, in the very way s/he experiences songs and/as sites. This situated and situating relationship to music, while not uniquely Russian, is fortified by the ubiquitous homogeneity of much Russian popular music, and instrumental in subjects' experience of place—specifically, experiencing themselves as either "home" or "away," either "Russian" or "Western," respectively. This spatial dissonance in which many homosexual Russian men find themselves, brought about by their ambivalent relationships to both post-Soviet and global space, is often worked through, I will argue, via relationships to popular musics—musics that either sound and *feel* familiar, of which one has a corporeal understanding, or those of foreign (Western) origin, to which one somatically relates differently.

Methodology and Scope of Study

I approach my subject through a combination of theory and ethnography—a theoretically informed ethnography, or an ethnographically based theorization—with the conviction that, as with "mind" and "body," the separation of the two results in a skewed, partial understanding of the complex ways in which human beings order, make sense of, experience, and reconcile modes of existence that are at once both "internally" motivated and "externally" acted upon—a reconciliation that takes place at the interface of the body. Guided by the belief that corporeal existence, including a corporeal relationship to music, is not reducible to either discourse or the knowledges posited by "empirical" science (including social "science"), I draw throughout this volume not only on studies of the body by scholars who critically engage the materiality of the body productively, rather than dismissively or largely skeptically—works by Elizabeth Grosz, Chris Shilling, and Robyn Longhurst, among others—but also on phenomenological thought as expressed in the works of Maurice Merleau-Ponty and Alphonso Lingis. Merleau-Ponty's *Phenomenology of Perception* and Lingis's *Foreign Bodies*, as well as Sarah Ahmed's strikingly apropos *Queer Phenomenology*, each of which highlights in different ways the essential somatic component of perception, serve as key works in exploring the centrality of the body in social space. I do not intend to offer a historical or theoretical-critical examination of phenomenology as a whole; rather, my intent has been to engage some of the major ideas presented in these works—the concepts of orientation, intentionality, synergy, gestalt; the questioning of dualistic (mind/body) or mechanistic theories of the body; the stressing of experience as foundational to abstract, second-order conceptualization; the positing of knowledges *of* the body—and, applying them to both sexuality and music, offer a different way of approaching desiring subjects and cultural production, one that takes the body seriously. As Hass, discussing Merleau-Ponty's work, notes, "the body as we live it is no thing among things, but the pulsing, carnal condition for perceiving things; it is the stable, yet elusive being around which things and the world take shape" (2008: 84). Although phenomenology has been applied in the past to ethnomusicological inquiry in varied and productive ways, I hope to add to these studies by focusing on the ways in which "experience" is in many ways rooted in "carnal conditions" and may not always be amenable to verbal translation.[61]

The majority of my time in Russia was spent in St. Petersburg—four months in 2003 and eleven months from 2004 to 2005—with an additional five weeks in Moscow in 2004. My initial visit was undertaken not only to make preliminary contacts and gain an overview of the erstwhile capital's "gay life," but additionally (and essential to the project) to undertake intensive language courses in order to be able to communicate effectively in Russian.[62] Although English may be in the process of becoming an international lingua franca of sorts, at least among a certain cosmopolitan, urban subset of people, its use in Russia is rather limited. To offer a comparison: in Helsinki—a city that I visited numerous times while living in St. Petersburg, and located only three hundred kilometers from there—the vast majority of people spoke English, so that informal conversations or the conducting of formal interviews were unproblematic for an English-speaking foreigner. In Russia, however, the inability to speak the native tongue made even the most basic, quotidian tasks difficult, as English speakers were limited in general to those sites likely to be frequented by tourists. As such, an inability to speak Russian would have significantly decreased the number of people with whom I could have spoken about issues such as sexuality and popular culture, would have seriously skewed my informant pool, and would have rendered unavailable to me a vast number of written texts (academic, journalistic, literary).

In the course of the sixteen months I was in Russia, I conducted several formal interviews with various professionals whose views were germane to the focus of this monograph; perhaps even more important, however, were the countless conversations I had with the numerous gay men with whom I became acquainted. My initial introduction to homosexual men was through a Belgian friend, a translator for the United Nations who then maintained a residence in St. Petersburg, and these introductions led to additional connections. Initially wary of having found a nonrepresentative group of men, insofar as they had contact with the West through this translator and other Westerners, I was later to realize that such a fear was unfounded; gay Russian men in St. Petersburg and Moscow without some contact to people in the West were the minority. Additionally, I was able to make the acquaintance of numerous homosexual men both at clubs and through the internet. As I was to find out, this last modality of meeting was extremely common and popular among gay men in both cities and was the preferred method of many: online introductions offered the ability to both get information about a person with whom one might potentially meet, and thus avoid the possibility of crime (such as theft or beating), as well as to "meet" outside the scrutinizing eye of the homophobic public, thus again minimizing the possibility of crime (as in, for example, cases where men have been assaulted or robbed upon leaving a gay club).[63]

I term these interlocutions *conversations* rather than *interviews* because, although all my informants were told in advance that my speaking with them was part of my research, the subject of which they were also made aware, I did not arrive with a rigid, prescribed, or essential set of questions, nor did I record or, in general, take contemporaneous notes throughout the course of such meetings.[64] In my experience, such actions would have proved deleterious to any attempt at establishing an open and communicative link with the men I met in St. Petersburg and Moscow as, while the majority of them were interested in my research topic (and most were incredulous that such a topic would be acceptable as a legitimate area of academic inquiry) and extremely willing to discuss their views and opinions with me, an air of "formality" would have hampered our interactions. As such, these conversations were open-ended and generally unstructured, some lasting an hour or so, others lasting several. And while these men were more than willing to share their insights with me, they were equally interested in learning about "gay life" in the United States, or about the United States in general because, for the vast majority of them, I was the only American they had ever met. To have closed the bidirectionality of the circuit, to have insisted they speak only about themselves, asking nothing about me, would have left me with a depleted pool of "informants" and one certainly not indicative of the wide array of perspectives to be explored.

All of the men were also told that I would not use their given or family names in any publications but, perhaps surprisingly, most of them said they were not concerned with this. Although the chance of men being identifiable by their first names is very slim, due to the fact that in Russia the pool of male and female names is relatively small (I was acquainted, for example, with several Mikhails, Alekseis, and Dmitriis), I have still chosen to use pseudonyms for everyone either quoted or mentioned in the monograph, save for those professionals who are identified by their actual names.[65] It is with much reluctance, especially in the context of post-Soviet space (but not only), that I have chosen the word *informant* to indicate or define the men with whom I spoke. Such a term—similar to the often-encountered alternative, *consultant*—seems to sanitize and, frankly, misrepresent the relationships between researcher and those upon whose insight, knowledge, and generosity she or he relies, relationships replete with myriad dynamics based on affects, desires, and power differentials emanating from both sides of the exchange. To believe that our interlocutors want nothing of us save to aid us in the "objective" furtherance of scientific inquiry, or to believe that we as researchers truly know what we want from them (or what we are trying to accomplish with those artifacts that become our scholarship) is to live in blissful ignorance of what such relationships really encompass; indeed, as Mascia-Lees, Sharpe, and Cohen note, we should be "suspicious of relationships with 'others' that do not include a close and honest scrutiny of the motivations for research" (1989: 33) (quoted in Newton 2000 [1992]: 244). In the course of nearly a year and a half, most of it spent in St. Petersburg, my relationships with these men ran the gamut from one-time, casual meetings, to friendships that have lasted to the present. That the relationship of researcher and "informant" is indeed often one of mutual affection and respect—of friendship—has certainly been noted previously,[66] yet it seems important in the context of this work, concerned as I am with the fundamental importance of interpersonal relationships and lived experience, the two intertwined and mutually constitutive, that the implied "scientific" aspect of ethnomusicology (a "social science") be at least momentarily problematized. Merleau-Ponty (2002 [1962]), often suspicious of the extent to which "empirically based," "scientific" conclusions are taken as the basis of "true" knowledge, consistently reminds us of the primacy of experience, stressing that "natural perception is not a science, it does not posit the things with which science deals, it does not hold them at arm's length in order to observe them, but lives with them" (375). "Lives with them"—as gay men in Russia live with others like them, live with the songs and images of performers they love, and as the fieldworker lives with his or her informants.

It is probably already clear to the reader that I am focusing almost exclusively on homosexual men; I will not, in the course of this monograph, be substantively engaging either lesbian listeners or "lesbian" performers—the scare quotes here indicating both those artists who make use of a type of "faux-lesbian" identity intended either to titillate heterosexual, male viewers, or to court gay/lesbian audiences (the groups t.A.T.u., Reflex, and *Andreia i*

Galena, for example), or those who, while widely assumed to be lesbian, have or had not at the time of writing "come out" (Eva Pol'na of the group *Gosti iz budushchego* [Guests from the Future], Zemfira Ramazanova of the group *Zemfira*, Svetlana Surganova of the group *Surganova i orkestr* [Surganova and Orchestra], Diana Arbenina of the group *Nochnye snaipery* [The Night Snipers], and the singer Elena Pogrebizhskaia, formerly of the band Butch).[67] Additionally, the centrality of the popular music "diva" (a word also used in Russian to describe the phenomenon, in addition to *ikon*, "icon") in gay male culture, although extremely important, will not be explored. Although these are significant lacunae, I have chosen to leave both for future work, insofar as they are both enormously rich and complex areas of inquiry, which, while related to the foci of this current volume, lie somewhat outside of the parameters of the theoretical concerns with which I am concerned (to say nothing of the practical impediments).[68] Indeed, to have fully engaged either or both of these subjects would have been impossible in the space allotted for this monograph, and a cursory examination would, in my estimation, be inappropriate.[69]

Finally, it is important to highlight specifics regarding both temporality and geography. In terms of the latter, any effort to productively describe or examine something as unwieldy as "sexuality" in a country spanning eleven time zones and perhaps innumerable local cultures—from Siberia to Kamchatka to the Petrine "window on the West"—would seem a daunting undertaking, one possibly doomed to failure. As such, my study is not an examination of all *Russian* gay men, but focuses on those men living in Russia's two largest cities, St. Petersburg and Moscow. Through the limited contact I had with men living in smaller locales within the country (and through reminiscences of those men who had moved to these urban centers from more rural, provincial locations), it was clear that one's experiences of sexuality and (popular) culture varied greatly based on geocultural location. As such, this study makes no attempt to engage those peoples or locales outside of the two mentioned, and it makes no claims to comprehensiveness in terms of the Russian Federation as an entity. In the same way that an ethnography based on gay men in New York City might say little about gay men in Tallahassee, Florida, the experiences of the men with whom I met and spoke in St. Petersburg and Moscow should not necessarily be extrapolated to suggest anything about Perm', Sochi, or Ekaterinburg.

Regarding the former, as noted previously a significant amount of my data (and lived experiences) reflect the time period of 2003–2005. Upon return to the United States in 2005, however, I continued to carry out research, including online ethnography[70] (largely discussions and informal interviews with old and new contacts via email and chat sites, as well as regular perusing of gay-themed Russian websites and forums), discussions and informal interviews with gay Russian and Russian-speaking Ukrainian men (some of whom were met during the time I lived and worked in Sheepshead Bay and Brighton Beach, Brooklyn, neighborhoods with sizable Russian-speaking populations), and habitual reading and viewing of—and listening to—all types of Russian media, including television programs, newspapers, music, and films. As such, it is important to understand that the bulk of this study, both the data analyzed and the analyses put forward, relates to a specific temporal location—roughly early 2003 to late 2011—and is not meant to suggest an eternal ethnographic present. Although several important events impacting upon gender and sexuality in Russia occurred around the time the monograph was being readied for publication—perhaps most notably the enactment of federal legislation in Russia against "gay propaganda"—I have restricted references to and discussion of these most recent events to the Epilogue that follows the final chapter.

Overview of Chapters

The chapters comprising this monograph each take a different focus in attempting to elucidate the corporeal connections between gay men and popular musics in post-Soviet Russia. In Chapter 2, I continue my discussion regarding the homogeneity of Russian popular musics, offering a detailed analysis of specific harmonic and melodic musical attributes that contribute to a Russian "sound." These attributes are important not only in terms of positive sonic markers—that is, what the music is (Russian)—but also, by dint of the fact that they stand in contrast to Western analogs, negative markers—what the music is not. Understanding that while many of my informants had (at best) ambivalent feelings about "Western" culture and society, they also professed a desire, and often a preference, for these types of musics, I relate the relationship between sound and listener to experiences of (pleasurable) penetration. Chapter 3 explores yet another seeming contradiction in post-Soviet Russian popular musics, specifically the existence of widespread homophobia, and the relatively large number of popular music performers whose sexual orientation has been questioned, both by those in the general public and the (yellow) press. In this chapter, focusing on the work of three male performers—singers Boris Moiseev, Valerii Leont'ev, and Verka Serdiuchka/Andrei Danilko—I explore the ways in which certain texts of theirs may be read as suggesting male-male sexuality, especially when coupled, as part of an entire gestalt, with the singers' bodies and performances. Additionally, I enlist the phenomenon of the phantom limb to situate historically and corporeally, and help explain this contemporary efflorescence of relatively visible/audible homosexuality.

Chapter 4 continues the focus on male performers and male bodies, segueing from the previous chapter by way of Serdiuchka's out-of-drag work *as* Danilko, then focusing on the groups Hi-Fi and Smash!! and concluding with a close reading of the work of singer Dima Bilan, the 2008 winner of the Eurovision Song Contest. In this chapter, I examine the ways in which male homosexuality is suggested via the presentation of the sexualized male body as object of the gaze—an objectifying gaze placing the male in the position of the "feminine." I further consider the role of proximity in both the implied homoerotic connections between members of the aforementioned bands, as well as the addition of the female (band members and/or audience) as a way of short-circuiting the palpably homoerotic through the triangulation with the feminine. The chapter closes with a detailed discussion of Bilan's victory at Eurovision, focusing on both the live performance and the subsequent music video of his winning entry, and relating the apparently conflicting visual, sonic, and textual contents of each to dynamics of intentionality and orientation.

The relationships among spatiality, orientation, and corporeality are the focus of Chapter 5, which examines how a post-Soviet, gay social space is engendered, in part, via popular musics. Here, as in Chapter 2, I highlight the ways in which seeming binaries—inside/outside, here/there, now/then, us/them, East/West—are experienced via musical spaces. I show, however, that such dissonances do not preclude the formation of a situated, stable, sexual self, one affectively and physically connected to both sound and space. Moreover, the importance of virtual, mediated, musical spaces in the creation of the self is explored, especially in relation to the subject's development—via sounds, images, and experiences—of the awareness of like others. Finally, in the conclusion I suggest the insights that might be gained by understanding the sexual self via the musical (rather than the political or textual) and stress the importance of the foregrounding of the living, sexual body in gay Russian men's wresting of their same-sex desires from the socially imposed shackles of pathology.

2. Music, Form, Penetration

> The outer influence must be integrated to the national [Russian] culture, and not liquidate it, as many of the aggressive supporters of the West are trying to achieve.
> —D. G. Gorin (2003)

The relative relaxation of geopolitical borders in Russia, post-perestroika, has allowed an intercourse with the West that, although certainly not absent during the Soviet era, or without restrictions in the present, increased the visibility, number, and variety of Western cultural products on Russian soil. During my time in St. Petersburg and Moscow, Western automobiles were prized commodities among those able to afford them (Mercedes and BMW, in particular), and Western "designer" clothing, cigarettes, fast food, or even home furnishings (with entrance of multinational retailer IKEA into major Russian cities), enjoyed a certain cachet for many.[1] Anglophone words related to popular culture have become part of the Russian lexicon (e.g., *bestseller* [бестселлер], *khit* or *megakhit* [хит/мегахит, hit/megahit]), in certain cases the entrance of the word into somewhat common parlance indicative of the popularity of specific (Western) genres. For example, both the *tok shou* (ток шоу, talk show) and *realiti shou* (реалити шоу, reality show) formats continue to be well represented on Russian television, with numerous offerings directed at varied audiences and demographics.[2] Additionally, Russified versions of American television shows were also common—*Sex in the City* spawned an unofficial Russian version, *Bal'zakovskii vozrast, ili vse muzhiki svo . . .* (*Balzac Age, or All Guys Are Bastards*),[3] while *The Nanny* gave rise to a virtual clone, *Moia prekrasnaia niania* (*My Beautiful Nanny*)—and American films and television shows were extremely common and consumed by large numbers of people.[4] But while Anglo-American and Anglophone products and words were commonplace, it was notable that, in contrast to any Western European country in which I had lived, or which I had visited, the audio portions of almost all imported films and television programs were generally either obfuscated or obliterated through dubbing, subtitles being exceedingly rare. Russian culture, it appeared, was neither hermetically sealed off from the West, nor entirely engulfed by it.

The realm of popular music was also a site of border crossings, with both Western and Russian musics audible and visible on radio and television, on posters advertising upcoming performances or CD releases, and in the wares of both retailers and street vendors alike. It was not, however, simply the propinquity of the discretely Western (a Pink concert, a Björk CD) to the discretely Russian (a Liudmila Gurchenko concert, a *Mashina vremeni* CD),[5] however, but also the adoption and/or Russification of Western musical styles by Russian performers that was indicative of porous boundaries. Such mixtures, increasingly common in a world defined, in part, by the dynamics of globalization, and indicative of the intricacies and complexities of contemporary cultural production, have often led to recourse to concepts of hybridity (or syncretism) in relation to the theorization of popular musics.[6] These concepts not only admit to but foreground the various "components" that serve to contribute to formations of new cultural products and new conceptions of self, the very bases through and upon which synthetic or syncretic forms come into being.[7] What is requisite in such theorizing, however, is not only attention to the "material" "end-product"—the self, the (cultural) object—but to the processes themselves, processes that occur within defined sociocultural and historical times and places, as well as to the ontological specificity of the "hybridizing components" (here, music) acting with and upon embodied beings; music, it must be stressed, does not act upon or engage a subject in the same ways as text or ideology, although certainly both may be adjuncts of musical phenomena. In this chapter, I examine the relationship between gay Russian men and both Western and Russian popular musics, including a discussion of the formal attributes of the latter that distinguish it from the former, and highlighting the ways in which lived experience—apprehended, in part, as a porosity of borders and operating as both a material and conceptual dynamic—inflects the interaction between these men and audible culture.

The material and conceptual aspects of these musical contacts, in an explicitly gay male context, may be seen as operative in two products released in St. Petersburg in 2003 and 2005—the *Gay CD* and *Gay CD Blue Edition*, respectively, with tracks assembled into a set by Russian DJs Kosinus and Slutkey via their "good friends from the Petersburg gay groups (*tusovki*)" (Gaspacho 2006).[8] Both packages featured imagery of male-male sexuality resembling the type of images often found in Western-style gay products: the first, replete with drawings of idealized, muscled, handsome young men with pronounced buttocks, pecs, and nipples; the second with a simplified graphic of two penises inside a heart, and even the "international" gay symbol, the rainbow, printed along the inside spine of the earlier release. A "review" (cum advertisement) on the Russian gay site xsgay.ru stated that the 2003 CD was meant "for those who are tired of old, deadly boring 'gay schlager,' for those who want to listen to contemporary, young music, for those who look to the future and who are developing" ("*Vpervye v Rossii!*"); the follow up, a two-CD set, included the tracks from the original release on one disc, with a second disk of new material. Included among the twenty-two tracks of the latter release were "Thru" by Kings of Tomorrow (Puerto Rican New Yorker Sandy Rivera), "Drop the Pressure" by Mylo (Scotland), "Rocky XIII" by Aloud (France), "Deepest Blue" by Deepest Blue (U.K. duo comprising Joel Edwards and Israel-born Matt Schwartz), and "Club Tropicana" by the Vinylshakerz (Germany), among others. Not only was the majority of the text on the packaging in English (or written in Latin script, as was the case with the DJs' names), but all of the vocals for the tracks—including the samples—were also in English. Neither Russian artists nor the Russian language were in evidence.

These CDs were not only engendered, in part, by globalizing processes enabling the circulation of music via the circuits of technology and capital (the internet as a site for obtaining new musics, capital enabling the importation of Western musics to Russia, international engagements for DJs such as Slutkey and Kosinus, through which they become part of the international, global dance music community, and so forth), but moreover, an example of the use of the very concepts of globalization and internationalization as affective markers of cultural (or subcultural) capital (Thornton 1996). Rather than Russian *popsa* or "schlager," this was "modern" (*sovremennaia*), "fashionable" (*modnaia*) music, music sung in a foreign language, music from different countries, music of "others"—including others marked by a "nontraditional sexuality," if not necessarily as performers, then certainly as intended audience and consumers. Homosexuality was, in fact, something that was remarked upon by several of my informants as imparting a certain prestige (marked by modernity, style, and internationality) upon a cultural product; Slutkey himself, in response to an interviewer's question as to whether he and Kosinus would "sweat" over the fact that being connected with a gay release might lead the public to question the DJs' own sexual orientations, stated that "the fact that many consider us to be gay, only increases our popularity" (Gaspacho 2006).[9]

How well the CD sold is difficult to estimate as many Russians have relied upon illegal downloading of music, via the internet, rather than the purchasing of CDs; additionally, many CDs for sale (either in stores or in the many street markets) are counterfeit.[10] According to the DJs themselves, the first CD "spread only among [our group], and didn't reach the wide masses" (Gaspacho 2006), while according to the website gayly.ru the first circulation of the CD was difficult to find in stores, having quickly sold out ("*Gay CD v Peterburge*"). Whatever the actual numbers of sales, however, many of my informants had heard of the CD, were interested in listening to what was on it, and, perhaps most importantly, evinced an affinity for the type of music that the disc contained: that is, house, disco-house, and trance, this despite the fact that many of them were not able to attach a stylistic label to the music in order to describe it. For example, on one occasion, while having coffee with Aleksei in one of the more stylish coffeehouses in St. Petersburg,[11] at one point he remarked, in reference to the music coming over the speakers (a mixture of lounge, chill-out/downtempo, trance, and house), "*this* is the kind of music I like." When I asked him if he could put a name on "this kind of music," he was not able to, continuing, "I don't know much about music or styles, I just know what I like." Similarly, one evening while driving with Konstantin, he popped one of several CDs lying on the front seat into the car's player, producing a stream of up-tempo disco-house/trance music. The CD, like the others I could see, had been burned on a home computer and was lacking any sort of information regarding performers, titles, or the like. I asked him who was playing, and he admitted that he didn't know, that it was a *sbornik* (compilation) made by a friend for his birthday, but that it was his favorite type of music—in his words, "high-quality, Western dance music." Some of my informants were familiar with the appellations of one or more genres of contemporary dance music, most all of which were used in transliterated forms—for example, *khaus* (хаус, house), *tekhno* (техно, techno), *fank* (фанк, funk), *disko* (диско), *dzhangl* (джангл, jungle), and so forth—but even these men did not know what the labels meant in terms of stylistic attributes or historical connections and geneses; no one, for example, knew that "house" had come from Chicago's Warehouse. Although a few were quite sophisticated in terms of their knowledge, these were generally the minority, and their knowledge was often related to the fact that they were then currently working, or had worked in the past, as DJs.

It was not only dance or electronic musics that many of the gay men with whom I spoke preferred, but, according to them, Western music in general. Such artists as Madonna, Annie Lennox, Björk, Mylène Farmer, Diana Krall, and the Cranberries, among others, were noted by several as being among their favorites; conversely, many claimed that they did not like Russian popular music in general, seeing it as somehow inferior to Western. For example, Konstantin, contrasting Nikita Malinin's "*Vspyshka v nochi*" ("Flash in the Night") with Darren Hayes's "Popular," two songs that were enjoying popularity in Russia in 2004–2005, noted of the former that Malinin had "no voice, no talent," and was simply famous because of his father (Russian èstrada singer Aleksandr Malinin), while Hayes's voice, in his estimation, was far superior. According to him, "in Russia, being a pop singer has nothing to do with talent, it's only about how much money you have. If you want to be a singer, and you, or your husband or your boyfriend, have money, you just record a song, make a video, you pay people to play it, and you're a singer." The view of success in Russia being contingent upon either financial or filial considerations (or both) was something that several of my informants suggested;[12] Ivan claimed that the singer Zhasmin had been able to establish her musical career solely due to her first husband (a wealthy restaurateur and businessman, Viacheslav Semenduev, several decades her senior), and others made similar claims about singer Alsou,[13] whose father, Ralif Rafilovich Safin, was the first vice president of Russia's largest oil company, *Lukoil*. In addition to Malinin, others noted Stas P'ekha (grandson of Èdita P'ekha, one of Russia's most famous and popular singers of the second half of the twentieth century), as having benefited from the stardom of family members.

Konstantin also noted that he considered the lyrics to Russian pop songs generally "stupid" or "nonsense," something echoed by other informants. While many of these men spoke little or no English, and thus were not able to comment on the quality of the lyrics of many songs emanating from the Anglophone West, Konstantin's command of the language was excellent; he had accomplished this through study in the university, and his relationships with English-speaking friends, many of whom he had met while traveling abroad, and with whom he maintained relationships via email. As such, he was one of the few who actually understood English-language lyrics, and he did admit that many of the words to Western songs were equally—in his estimation—"bad." However, he still felt that "the lyrics just *sound* better in English." Somewhat related to this, Kristina, a DJ at the gay club *Greshniki*, and thus someone who was both influenced by and influential on gay musical sounds and discourses, underscored the fact that her professional name, DJ Christy, should be written in Latin script as opposed to Cyrillic. Understanding that she spoke no English, I asked her why she preferred this Western spelling to the Russian, to which she replied, "I don't know—I just think it looks better." Both Konstantin and Christy appeared to be reacting affectively to an "imaginary West" (Yurchak 2006)—a concept to which I turn later in this chapter—one connoting the modern, the international, the global.

The idea of the affective rather than the "logical" or aesthetic as instrumental in the formation of an affinity toward specific musics may be underscored by noting the concomitantly negative reactions many informants had for such genres as *shanson*,[14] a type of Russian popular music that not only exhibits those musical attributes most stereotypically Russian but also the texts and performers of which often evince a nationalistic and/or xenophobic worldview. In contrast to the connections made by my informants between Western music and modern internationalism, *shanson* was seen by them as music for the narrow-minded and the provincial. The genre frequently draws upon imagery of the prison and the criminal, both presented in a positive, romanticized light, and singers such as Aleksandr Novikov are also known for their homophobic and anti-Semitic views. For example, Novikov was quoted as stating that contemporary Russian show business is a business of "Russian-speaking Jews... pierced through with fags [*pederasty*]... and a few of them are one in the same person."[15] In an interview with the singer in the newspaper *Pravda*, much of the same virtriol was quoted, with Novikov characterizing Russian show business as ruled in part by the "blue" (*goluboi*—that is, gay) mafia, a place where "rich fags let loose their boys who want to sing" ("*Aleksandr Novikov: '... pederasty—trusy.'*"). Having written a letter to President Putin in 2004 inveighing against (among other things) the supposed prevalence of "bordello-type prima donnas" and "militant fags" in Russian popular music, Novinkov—who has referred to himself as a himself a "patriot" (Polupanov 2004)—has excoriated Russian *popsa* and *èstrada* performers such as the group Hi-Fi and singers Katia Lel' and Alla Pugacheva, all three of whom were and are, not coincidentally, popular with many gay men.

While Novikov has appeared as one of the most hyperbolically homo- and xenophobic performers, others who evince less virulent nationalistic (and parochial) sentiment were often equally unpopular with my informants. The group *Liube*, for example, characterized not only by the stereotypically Russian style of their music, but by their references to patriotism, the military, and the "motherland," was also prone to anti-Western sentiment.[16] Speaking about the group's singer, Nikolai Rastorguev, Anton, one of the most acerbic men I knew, characterized him as "a fat pig singing garbage." Indeed neither Anton nor any of my informants (save one)[17] evinced a liking for the band. Yet it is not possible to suggest a neat heuristic scheme whereby lists of attributes are seen as either comporting with or antagonistic to "gay sensibilities." For example, while singer Kristia Orbakaite—daughter of Alla Pugacheva, one of Russia's most successful *èstrada* singers, and arguably the country's largest gay icon—was popular with many gay men, Anton also had scathing words for her remake of the song "*Katiusha*," one of the most well-known and popular war-era Soviet songs. In her version, presented on Russian television as part of a New Year's musical celebration entitled *Noch' v stile disko* (*Disco-Style*

Night), the singer was clad in a "sexy" soldier's uniform (hot pants instead of fatigues), perambulating around the stage while singing, with high kicks and swiveling hips. Anton was aghast at this performance, calling Orbakaite a "stupid bitch who ruins everything she touches," further explaining that the Soviet *Katiusha* rockets (named after the song) were "responsible for saving the lives of millions of Russians . . . during one of the worst times in our history, and she makes it into a stupid disco song."[18]

In fact, while many of my informants professed a preference for Western popular music, many of them also admitted a connection to Russian popular musics as well, although this connection was not always immediately expressed (at least to me, a Western foreigner) and was sometimes implicit rather than manifest. For example, in Russia in 2004, two musical talent competitions were televised widely: *Narodnyi artist* (*National Artist*)[19] and *Fabrika zvezd* (*Factory of Stars*). Although both were imports—the first based on the original, British *Pop Idol* (which has spawned numerous identical progeny all over the globe),[20] the second, a Russian version of the original Spanish *Operación triunfo*[21]—among the majority of men I knew, the latter was far more popular, possibly due to the fact that it was simply more "Russian." For while both shows had the same general concept, there were also several differences contributing to the latter's being considered and accepted as more "indigenous." First, while on the former contestants were required to sing live, contestants of the latter show lip-synched their performances, as was the practice of most televised (and often "live") concerts of Russian pop performers. Second, approximately half of all performances on *Fabrika* were constructed duets between the contestants and some of Russia's most famous *popsa* and *èstrada* singers, in contrast to the solo performances of *Narodnyi artist*. In these performances, stars' current songs were rerecorded to include vocals of the contestants, alongside those of the original artists, and were performed (lip-synched), onstage, in their newly revised forms. Third, songs were often "staged" with props and/or costumes—for example, a winter scene with the singers huddled together wearing mittens, scarves, and hats, or a "jazz" number with men in fedoras—thus adding to an overall artifice or "staginess" sometimes typical of Russian *èstrada*. Fourth, the content of *Fabrika* was not limited to the contest itself; rather, the show, in keeping with the "*realiti shou*" (reality show) format so popular in Russian television during the same period, featured large amounts of footage of the contestants living together, rehearsing, meeting with the artistic directors, and sometimes engaged in amorous liaisons with one another.[22] The foregrounding of the social, rather than simply the competition on the stage, is also likely to have resonated with Russians' belief in the importance of the interpersonal. And finally, *Fabrika* became, in 2004, allied with Alla Pugacheva, who served as the show's artistic director and occasionally sang as well. As previously noted, Pugacheva was not only an icon in the generic sense, but was considered by many to be "the" gay icon among pop singers.[23]

Although the majority of songs performed on *Fabrika* were of Russian origin, there were instances of covers of Western songs as well, such as contestant Mikhail Veselov's performance of "*Moia vina*" ("My Fault"), Air Supply's "All Out of Love" with different, Russian lyrics (not a translation of the original). Additionally, on occasions when American songs were performed, they might serve as an opportunity for contrasting the Russian contestant with the American originator, casting the contestant in a more positive light; thus, contestant Viktoriia Daineko (the ultimate winner of the sixth season) was introduced on one occasion as ready to sing Jennifer Lopez's "Ain't It Funny," "better than Jennifer Lopez herself." In a similar vein, Ivan told me that Daineko was one of his favorites on the show, calling her a "Russian Mariah Carey," and adding that she was "even *better* than Mariah Carey." Admiration of Russian music was often concomitant with a sense of pride in Russia's culture and history and, conversely, a critique of the materialism and "vulgarity" characteristic, in their eyes, of the West; as Gleb told me, although the word *vulgar* had become part of the Russian lexicon ("*vul'garnyi*") it was, in his opinion, something not encountered in Russia, but rather distinctly American. However, the fact that excessive venality was often a critique they levied against Russian singers is but one of many complexities precluding any simple, binarized analysis of gay Russian men and popular music.

The porosity of borders may be seen on a lexical level as well. Numerous words associated with the music business in the West—*proiudser* (продюсер, producer), *aranzhiment* (аранжимент, arrangement), *remeik/remiks* (ремейк/ремикс, remake/remix), or *khit/superkhit* (хит/суперхит, hit/superhit)—were and are widely seen in Russia, as are abundant instances of transliterations of genres including, in addition to the dance genres mentioned previously, *rok* (рок, rock), *rèp* (рэп, rap), *dzhez* (джез, jazz), and *bliuz* (блюз, blues), among others.[24] Several performers, perhaps in a bid for international success, and with the understanding that the Cyrillic alphabet is not readily comprehensible to the majority of people outside the Slavic-speaking world,[25] use both Latin and Cyrillic versions of their names (e.g., singers Alsou/Алсу, Shura/Шура, and Jasmin/Жасмин, and groups Hi-Fi/Хай-Фай, Reflex/Рефлекс, and A'Studio/А-Студио, among others), opt solely for Western names (groups Fantasy, Sky, A-Sortie, Quest Pistols, PUNCH, Smash!!, singer Ana$tezia), or even combine the two, sometimes within the same moniker (e.g., the group Иванушки [*Ivanushki*] International). DJs, both those who are recording artists and those who play in local clubs, frequently use their names in Latin script (e.g., DJ *Gruv* [Грув,

Groove], DJ Rudenko, Moscow's DJ Manana, St. Petersburg's DJ Christy, as well as Kosinus and Slutkey), although the letters "DJ" are sometimes encountered, when used as a descriptive noun, in their transliterated, Cyrillic form (Ди-джей).

English words or short phrases are included in numerous lyrics, including MC Vspyshkin's "*Khorosho*," ("Good," which contains the slang word "motherfucker") *Diskoteka avariia*'s "*Surovyi rėp*" ("Severe Rap"), Nikita Malinin's "*Vspyshka v nochi*" ("Flash in the Night"), Zhasmin's "*Kis-kis*" ("Kiss-kiss," a transliteration of the English),[26] *BiS*'s "Mister DJ" (the title of which is generally written with a combination of Cyrillic and Latin script, i.e., "Мистер DJ"), *Vintazh*'s "*Roman*" ("Romance")[27] as are—although less frequently—both German (*Gliuk'oza*'s "*Shvaine*" ["*Schwein*," "Pig"],) and French, as in the following lyrics from *Gosti iz budushchego*'s "*On chuzhoi*" ("He's Another's"):

Proiti po shagam moi dni, oh yeah	My days go by, by steps, oh yeah
Vse bylo by tak zhe	Everything would be the same
Bol'she ne budem odni	We will no longer be alone
Vybrana s kornem, pogibaiu ot zhazhdy	Torn out with the roots, I perish from thirst
Nezhno sheptala "tu es ma vie"	I whispered gently, "you are my life"[28]

In Sky's "*Mal'chik ishchet mamu*" ("Boy Looking for [his/a] Mom"), the chorus features rapped phrases interspersed with those sung, the former provided by Mr. Slan, the latter by the group's lead singer, Irèn:

On idet k sebe domoi (He goes home alone)
Baby boy he's nothing but a bum
V luzhe raspleskalsia blesk nochnoi (In a puddle spilled a nighttime brilliance)
What you gonna do in the world full of drama?

On several Russian lyric sites, however, the first of Mr. Slan's lines was translated as "Baby boy he's not to find a mum," "Baby boy needs nothing but a mum," or "Hey be boy, he's nothing but a vamp," while the second, although more often translated correctly, also produced "What she gonna do in a bowl full of drum?"[29] As Yurchak (2006: Chapter 4) notes in his discussion of late Soviet interaction with the "imagined West," literal meanings are clearly not important to all interlocutors; while foreign words may not be understood entirely, they no doubt continue to carry the cachet of the international nonetheless.[30]

Other artists shuttle between Russian and English in the same song (e.g., *Elka*'s "Movie Star") record entire songs in foreign languages (e.g., A'Studio's

"You Appreciate," Hi-Fi's "Childhood" and "Call Me Misha," Shura's "I Know," Nikita's "Les Mirages"), record both English- and Russian-language versions of the same song (e.g., Valeriia's "*Bol'*" ["Pain"], also recorded as "Wild") and some, such as the group Smash!!, sing almost entirely in English, with a few songs in either Russian or French.[31] English words also appear as "subtitles" in the videos of some singers (Iuliia Savicheva's "*Vysoko*" ["High"], Verka Serdiuchka's "*Ia popala na liubov*'" ["I Fell/Wound Up in Love"], Valeriia's "*Po serpantinu*" ["By the Winding Road"]), although here the entire texts are not translated; rather, key words, giving the gist of the song, appear along with the images (for example, "high," "easy" in the first, "dangerous," "love" in the second, and "Woman in Love Again?" in the third).[32] Although I have categorized these examples as occurring on a lexical register, it is important to understand that they exceed this level by dint of their production via the human voice, indexing a human—a Russian—body. One may read any number of English, French, or German words (whether transliterated or not) on the streets of Moscow or St. Petersburg; reading, seeing, however, is far different from hearing such words emanating from the voices, the bodies of Russian singers, a corporeal instance of porous borders. Process, as noted earlier, must not take a back seat to artifact in the examination of globalization and ensuing hybridities, not only insofar as attention to the former may guard against the assumption of unidirectional circuits of power and influence (cf. Neederveen Pieterse 2004), but also to the extent that process almost necessarily implies interpersonal relationships (Frith 2000). What must be remembered is that the "social actors" taking part in such relationships are not simply concepts or empty conduits through which cultural information flows, but embodied, in-the-flesh beings. The emanations from the human vocal tract are not incidental to the "texts" they carry; they are the body made audible, equally as important as the Cyrillic or Latin alphabets at the (human) site of reception. *Gosti iz budushchego* was easily one of the most international-leaning groups in Russia during the last decade, much of their output comporting with Western stylistic and aesthetic norms, and several of their songs featuring English lyrics. Yet the response of one of my informants, Vadim, reminded me of my own intellectual myopia. When asking why he thought Eva Pol'na, the group's lead singer, was so popular, he replied, almost puzzled, "listen to her voice."

Russian Popular Music: Formal Attributes

Before progressing further, it will be helpful to elucidate specific formal attributes in order to ground the discussion contrasting the Russian and the Western[33] on an explicitly musical level. In the following pages I offer graphic representations (charts of harmonic structures and transcriptions of melodies) of examples of Russian songs exhibiting what I have found to be some of the most salient characteristics of "Russian-sounding" musics from the genres of *popsa*, *èstrada*, and *romansy* (romances). Although only a few are given, there are literally thousands of other examples of songs with these same attributes; they are ubiquitous and widely dispersed in terms of both genre and historical placement. For the musically literate reader who may be unfamiliar with the actual sound of Russian popular musics, such examples will serve to make known such traits in a number of different musical contexts. My main goal in offering theses musical examples, however, is to highlight the fact that music is apprehended not only via texts/lyrics, but also through sound structures and sonorities (understanding, of course, that transcription cannot fully communicate all of the salient attributes of such sonorities). Many of the examples I have given to this point have included those of a visual, discursive, and/or linguistic nature, but this is not meant to eclipse the importance of specifically sonic elements. Indeed, I view such elements as inextricably linked to one's embodied experience of and with music, perhaps especially in the case of the nonmusician or nonacademician.

As I have noted, the gay men who shared their opinions with me regarding popular musics often contextualized their preferences and dislikes within a context of a Russian/non-Russian (Western) split, and indeed this bifurcation played out in the creation of both physical and sonic space in many of the locales frequented by gay men.[34] However, Russian and Western musics of all sorts—"classical" or "art," jazz, popular, traditional or "folk"—have intermixed for centuries, across both geopolitical and generic boundaries. Both jazz and rock music, even during the height of the Cold War, reached Soviet Russians' (and Soviet Russian musicians', performers', and composers') ears, and not always via unofficial channels. As Yurchak (2006) notes, jazz—depending upon whether it was seen as "cosmopolitan" (read: bourgeois) or "internationalist"—could be either lauded or denounced, and rock could be "contained" by its being performed (under surveillance) by state-approved bands in state-sponsored clubs.[35] My intention, however, is not to suggest that borders have been eroded or erased, resulting in a genuinely hybrid Russo-Euro-American music but, rather, to highlight the complexity and, in the end, irony of this interchange. And much of this complexity hinges upon harmony.

Numerous authors, in their examinations of a putative "national style" in Russian "art" music of the nineteenth century, have suggested that identifying such a style is far more complex than simply noting a composer's embracing of or departure from Western harmonic language, or the inclusion of "authentic" or ersatz "folk" musics.[36] Indeed, Western functional harmony had a strong presence in Russian musical language for several centuries, not only in terms of Russia's "art" or concert repertoires, but in nonclassical, "traditional" musics as well—musics that, in the context of growing urbanity, straddled a line between oral and literate, "folk" and popular. For example, Taruskin (1997b) suggests that Nikolai Alexandrovich Lvov's 1790 *Collection of Russian Folk Songs with Their Tunes* (*Sobraniye narodnïkh pesen s ikh golosami*), the piano accompaniments[37] of which "transformed each *narodnaya pesnya* . . . into a diminutive art song with a well-wrought if conventional keyboard accompaniment prefiguring the idiom of the so-called domestic romance (*bïtovoy romans*) of the next generation" (17; author's transliteration) were less adulterations of a supposedly pristine, cloistered Russian "folk" tradition than examples of an extant musical language that had appeared in the urban settings, one which drew upon both the musically "oral" and the "literate." As such, "there is every reason to suppose, in particular, that Pratsch's notorious leading tones, long regarded as 'Western' disfigurements, were endemic to the melodies in question at the time and in the place of their collection" (20). In short, the positing of a pristine state of "authentic" Russian popular *or* traditional musics unsullied by the encroachment of Western musics, at least in the nineteenth century, and following, is probably untenable.

Zemtsovsky (1999) finds similar connections between both Russian popular and traditional musics, and those musics of foreign provenance making use of a Western harmonic language. He notes, for example, that some early-twentieth-century Russian lyric songs came from street barrel organs, "which played an international repertory of popular songs (including Neapolitan songs, and even Argentinian [*sic*] tangos" (766).[38] He finds a similar syncretism in the music of Russia's cities, noting of the "urban song" that its influences included "the old peasant song; new musical instruments with harmonic possibilities (the guitar and the piano); military band music and European dances, introduced during the reign of Peter I; the three-part harmony of the secular *kant* . . . the link with professional music and poetry; Gypsy singing . . . and vaudeville" (2001: 6). Finally, the complexity and circuitousness of just how the influence of "the West" in particular occurs can be clearly seen by attention to the musical. Highlighting the importance of the *Rom*, Zemtsovsky finds from at least the late eighteenth century, and on through the nineteenth, a "process of Gypsy instrumentation of Russian tunes, choral orchestration and harmonization," and that "even the traditional polyphony of the Russian peasants was adjusted . . . by Gypsies" to Western functional harmony, a "'translation' into the Western European musical language" (2001: 6).

Ironically, it is just such elements of Western functional harmony that Zemtsovsky mentions, as well as the leading tones discussed by Taruskin, that feature prominently in several genres of Russian popular music of the twentieth century and contribute to its "Russian sound": specifically, a stress *on* the leading tone, especially in the context of dominant-tonic cadences and, related to this, the use of secondary dominant chords, augmented 6th chords (as pre-dominants or dominant substitutes), and progressions based on the circle of fifths. In addition to this, melodic sequences[39] (often in combination with the aforementioned types of progressions) also occupy a prominent position in contemporary popular music in Russia. The following examination of songs from different eras shows these musical attributes over a large span of time, but it is not my intention to show either a development or evolution of these traits; rather, I simply wish to show similarities and connections.

Beginning with the prewar era, the use of secondary dominants is evident in several Russian *romansy* (singular, *romans*), many of which exhibit attributes of commercialized *Rom* musics[40] (for example, an accelerating tempo to give emotional urgency; violin, guitar, and accordion as accompanying instruments; a highly evocative, "emotional" vocal delivery; and/or chromaticism),[41] thus indicating that the genre *romans* is not, as it might seem at first blush, indicative of the "romantic" but the *Rom*. The chordal progressions of two such *romansy* follow (Examples 2.1 and 2.2); in all instances the song's title is followed by the name of the performer (where given) on the recordings from which the analyses or transcriptions were made:

Example 2.1. "*Ei, iamshchik*" ("Hey, Coachman") (Zhenia Shevchenko)

AM^7	dm	DM	em^7♭5 or gm/M^{6*}	CM	FM	EM^7	AM^7	
V	i	[I]	ii^{ø7} or iv^{6**}	VII	III	V^7 of V	V^7	
		V of iv		V of III				
AM^7	dm	DM	gm	CM	FM	EM^7	AM^7	dm
V^7	i	[I]	iv	VII	III	V^7 of V^7	V^7	i
		V of iv		V of III				

* In the second verse, this chord is changed to G minor, thus suggesting that the preceding chord—D major—may indeed be seen as V of iv.
** The "6" here indicates the addition of the sixth tone of the scale, not a chord in first inversion (as is often encountered in common practice art music).

Example 2.2. "*Starinnyi piterskii romans*" ("Old Petersburg Romance") (Alesha Dmitrievich)

dm	AM⁷	dm	CM	FM	AM⁷	B♭M	gm	dm	AM⁷	dm
i	V⁷	i	VII V of III	III	V⁷	VI	iv	i	V⁷	i

In these examples, secondary dominants play a prominent role, often as precursors of the relative major (the mediant), as in the movement from C major to F major in "*Starinnyi piterskii romans.*" Such use of secondary dominants may also be heard in one of the most popular songs of the wartime era, "*Sinii platochek*" (Example 2.3), a prime example of early *èstrada*.

Example 2.3. "*Sinii platochek*" ("Little Blue Kerchief") (Klavdiia Shul'zhenko)

FM7	b♭m	B♭M	e♭m	e♭m (b♭ bass)	b♭m	FM7	b♭m
V7	i	[I] V of iv	iv	iv	i	V7	i
FM7	b♭m	A♭M7	D♭M	e♭m	b♭m	FM7	b♭m
V⁷	i	V⁷ of III	III	iv	i	V⁷	i

The use of such secondary dominants continues through the postwar era, and here modulations to major keys, as well as even lengthier strings of secondary dominants—often related to progressions based on the circle of fifths—occur, as in Examples 2.4–2.6.

Example 2.4. "*Lavanda*" ("Lavender") (Sofiia Rotaru and Jaak Joala)

gm	cm	FM	B♭M	DM⁷
i	iv	V of III	III	V⁷

Example 2.5. "*A les stoit zagadochnyi*" ("But the Forest Stands Mysterious") (Liudmila Zykina)

am	EM⁷	am	FM	CM	GM⁷	CM⁷	FM
i	V⁷	i	am: VI FM: I	V	V⁷ of V	V⁷	I
AM⁷	dm	GM⁹	CM	AM⁷	dm	am	EM⁷	am
V⁷ of vi	vi	V⁹ of V	FM: V am: III	V of iv	iv	i	V⁷	i

Example 2.6. "*Dorozhnaia*" ("Road Song") (Aida Vedishcheva)

dm	GM	CM	FM	B♭+⁶/B♭⁷	am
iv	VII	III	VI	Gr+⁶/♭II⁷*	i
	V of III	V of VI	(V of ♭II dim⁷)		

* The chord here may be analyzed as either a German augmented sixth chord, resolving to the tonic instead of the dominant or, perhaps better (in light of the jazzy style of the piece), a ♭II⁷ or tritone substitution, a chord often encountered in jazz. Although augmented sixth chords commonly occur as predominant chords, Tchaikovsky (1900) suggests that they may indeed resolve directly to the tonic, although he notes that this is more common in the major mode (108). See also Biamonte (2008).

The verse of "*Lavanda*"—an extremely popular recording for *èstrada* superstar Sofiia Rotaru, and Estonian singer Jaak Joala—is marked by the use of a single secondary dominant, while in "*A les stoit zagadochnyi*" there are several, as well as pivot chords enabling a temporary modulation to the key of F major. In "*Dorozhnaia*," there are three consecutive secondary dominants, related to the circle of fifths from D to A, albeit with the chord built on B-flat—a German augmented sixth chord or a tritone substitute—serving as a dominant substitute, rather than as preparation for the actual dominant, E major.

The examples I have given above are from quite different repertoires: Rotaru and Joala's song is an example of *èstrada*, Zykina's song a type of highly orchestrated, concert version of *narodnaia muzyka* ("folk music"), and Vedishcheva's epitomizing a jazzy, typically 1960s–1970s style known as *retro* (marked by the use of electric organ and guitar, close background vocal harmonies, and often upbeat tempo, similar to Western "mod" music). Such harmonic structures are also found in well-known children's songs (such as "*Kreiser Avrora*" ["The Cruiser Aurora"] and "*V trave sidel kuznechik*" ["In the Grass Sat the Grasshopper"]), many of which may have been featured in cartoons and were and are also sung by *pionery*, a group, as noted earlier, to which virtually all of the men I knew had belonged in childhood. With this last in mind, it is clear that this harmonic language was and continues to be one that is encountered and inculcated from a very early age.

Vedishcheva's "*Dorozhnaia*" from the 1968 musical film *Belyi roial'* (*The White Grand Piano*) features a harmonic progression, as noted, related to the circle of fifths, and such harmonic progressions have become a staple of songs in numerous genres of Russian popular music. In the following examples (Examples 2.7–2.11), which span a period of over thirty years, all of the harmonic progressions are quite similar, and some identical.

As with the previous examples, these songs and performers represent a wide array of genres and styles of Russian popular music. VIA-Pesniary's is an example of a *vokal'no instrumental'nyi ansambl'* song, with a *narodnaia*

Example 2.7. "*Vologda*" ("Vologda") (VIA-Pesniary, 1978)

gm	CM	FM⁷	B♭M	e dim	AM
iv	VII	III⁷	VI	ii°	V
	V of III⁷	V⁷ of VI	V of ii°	[V] of V*	

FM	DM	gm	AM	dm
III	[I]	iv	V	i
	V of iv			

* In the harmonic analysis, I have used [V] to indicate that, while the chord tones are not those of the actual dominant of the following chord, the supertonic chord nonetheless serves a dominant function. The indication appears also in Examples 2.8 and 2.10, *infra*.

Example 2.8. "*Otpusti menia*" ("Let Me Go") (Valeriia, 2004)

f♯m	DM	EM	AM (c♯ bass)	DM	g♯m⁷♭5 (b bass)	C♯M	f♯m
i	VI	VII	III	VI	ii°⁷	V	i
		V of III	V of VI		V of ii°⁷	[V] of V	

Example 2.9. "*Shiroka reka*" ("The Wide River") (Nadezhda Kadysheva and *Zolotoe Kol'tso*, 2004)

c♯m	f♯m	BM	EM	AM	f♯m	G♯M⁷
i	iv	VII	III	VI	iv	V
		V of III	V of VI			

Example 2.10. *Sneg*" ("Snow") (Filipp Kirkorov, 2011)

b♭m	e♭m	A♭M	D♭M	G♭M	c dim	FM	b♭m
i	iv	VII	III	VI	ii°	V	i
		V of III	V of VI	V of ii°	[V] of V		

Example 2.11. "*Ia tak skuchaiu*" ("I Miss [You] So") (*Infiniti*, 2011)

b♭m	e♭m	A♭M	D♭M	G♭M	e♭m	FM	b♭m
i	iv	VII	III	VI	iv	V	i
		V of III	V of VI				

feeling due to the use of "traditional" instruments such as *garmon'* and *semistrunnaia gitara* (Russian button accordion and 7-stringed guitar), but also featuring Western-style drum kit and electric bass and keyboard, "gypsy" violin, and a decidedly "operatic," bel canto vocal delivery at the final cadence by lead vocalist Anatolii Kasheparov; Kadysheva's is a synthesis of *narodnaia*, *èstrada*, and *popsa*, Valeriia's a cross between *popsa* and *tantseval'naia* (dance of "club" music), and Kirkorov's and *Inifiniti*'s almost textbook examples of *èstrada* and *popsa*, respectively.

In both "*Vologda*" and "*Sneg*" an uninterrupted, literal circle of fifths progression marks the refrain, with the diminished supertonic serving a secondary dominant function as V of V. In "*Sneg*" the circle of fifths progression alone makes up the harmonic language of the refrain, and in "*Vologda*" the arrival of the tonic, expected after the A major chord, is deferred for several measures with the interpolation of the F major (III) chord, leading to yet another secondary dominant (V of iv, with the minor tonic changing to major, as seen in "*Sinii plantochek*"), and ultimately the typical subdominant-dominant-tonic cadential progression. In each of the remaining examples, although the circle of fifths is not literally stated, the gestalt is similar nonetheless. In "*Otpusti menia*" the submediant replaces the expected subdominant as the second chord of the series, and the fourth and sixth chords (the mediant, A major, and the G♯ half diminished seventh chord, built on the supertonic) are presented in inversion due to the bass following a pattern of down a third/up a second—a sort of slowly migrating undulation. And in both "*Shiroka reka*" and "*Ia tak skuchaiu*" the diminished supertonic chord, most likely due to its dissonance, is replaced with a minor subdominant, allowing for the typical cadential progression also found in "*Vologda*."

Additionally, numerous songs on the contemporary pop scene are notable for relying solely upon tonic-subdominant-dominant progressions, either as the constituents of the chorus, or of the entire song;[42] in a large number of cases, the leading tone resolving to the tonic is highlighted, either by being present in the melody line, or in a particularly audible hook. And finally, in terms of harmonic content, an attribute that is obvious from the preceding is the overwhelming use of minor keys in Russian *popsa*; as opposed to the West, where songs in major keys are extremely common, they make up a small minority of the output of Russian tracks.

Certain melodic attributes are also widely found in Russian popular music, and in this instance, as noted earlier, it is the use of sequences that contribute to a "Russian sound." Here again, as in the case of harmonic language found in numerous eras, there appear to be connections between anterior forms of popular musics and the contemporary. In earlier forms, however, instead of sequences proper, there are melodies based in part on repetitions of short tonal and rhythmic motives that may be repeated at higher or lower pitch groups, though not always necessarily immediately sequentially, or literally. There are, however, several instances of such "motives" appearing sequentially, as in Example 2.12.

Example 2.12. Vocal line, verse, "*Sinii platochek*" (Klavdiia Shul'zhenko, c. 1942).

Note that the shape of the melody, both in terms of intervallic relationships and rhythm, is very similar when comparing mm 1–3 with mm 5–7; the melodic contour is virtually identical, except at the cadences, and the rhythm has been slightly changed in the second set of measures, replacing a straightforward quarter-note–based rhythm with one making use of dotted quarter and eighth notes. Even more similar are the melodic phrases of mm 9–10 and 11–12, beginning on D and C, respectively, identical save for the initial eighth note in measure 11 (which may actually represent a variation made in performance, rather than the prescriptions of any foundational written score); mm 25–26 and 27–28 are indeed identical. While there are minor differences between the melodic materials compared above, in the postwar era forward, more literal sequences can be found either in the vocal or instrumental lines, as in the song "*Brich Mulla*" (an example of *avtorskaia pesnia*) (Example 2.13). Here, the section from the pickup to measure one, through the third beat of measure two, and the section from the fourth beat of measure two to the third beat of measure three make up a literal sequence.

Example 2.13. Vocal line, verse, "*Brich-Mulla*" (Sergei and Tat'iana Nikitin, 1997).

In this instance, the melody is supported by a harmonic progression making use of secondary dominants and a partial circle of fifths; this is also the case with the melody found in the chorus of the song "*Shiroka reka*" (Example 2.14), examined earlier in Example 2.9.

Example 2.14. Vocal line, chorus, "*Shiroka Reka*" (Nadezhda Kadysheva and Zolotoe Kol'tso, 2004).

In contemporary *popsa*, there are numerous instances of sequences, again either vocal or instrumental, as can be seen in Examples 2.15a, 2.15b, and 2.15c, all of which occur in the song "*Devushki fabrichnye*" ("Factory Girls") by the group *Fabrika*. Here the sequences are literal and longer, and three separate sequences occur in the same song:

Examples 2.15a, b, c. Accordion riff, balalaika riff, and vocal line (chorus), "*Devushki fabrichnye*" (*Fabrika*, 2003).

The various constituents of a Russian sound in popular music are not, however, limited to formal attributes. For example, arrangements often draw upon those instruments that have traditionally been used in various forms of Russian popular music over the course of at least the last two centuries (*garmon'* or *baian*, Russian versions of the accordion, as well as acoustic guitar—either the 7-stringed Russian *semistrunnaia*, or the Western version—balalaika, violin, brass ensembles, and so forth), as in the previously examined "*Vologda*" and "*Shiroka reka*," as well as Verka Serdiuchka's "*Chita drita*," Blestiashchie's "*Naleteli vdrug dozhdi*" ("Rain Suddenly Came Down"), and numerous others. Additionally, the use of certain vocal timbres—rough and raspy for men, possibly in reference to the seminal work of one of Russia's premier *bard*s, Vladimir Vysotskii, or a nasal, tight chest voice for women, similar to that used in much of Russia's traditional music—serve as sonic signs of Russian-ness.

There are also several instances in contemporary Russian popular music of actual "historical" elements, either new versions of earlier *èstrada* songs, (e.g., Zhanna Aguzarova's cover of Shul'zhenko's "*Sinii platochek*"), traditional songs reworked with more modern accompaniments and arrangements (e.g., Igor' Krutoi's "*Kontrasty*,"),[43] or the use of recordings of traditional material in popular songs (Valerii Meladze and VIA-Gra's "*Okean i tri reki*" ["An Ocean and Three Rivers"]). Bands such as *Ivan Kupala*[44] have formed the majority of their work around recordings of Russian traditional music, often that of female vocal soloists or ensembles. However, it is not only "folk" or traditional music that references the past, as the use of samples of both music and dialogue from famous Soviet-era films—as noted in the previous chapter—has become popular in recordings of dance music in recent years (e.g., DJ *Gruv*'s "*Sluzhebnyi roman*" ["Office Romance"], Vengerov and Federoff's or DJ *Krot*'s "*Zdravstvuite, ia vasha tetia*" ["Hello, I'm Your Auntie"—a loose, Russian adaptation of *Charley's Aunt*]), or Vengerov and Federoff's "*Kavkazkaia plennitsa*" ["Caucasian Captive"]).

Often, the more closely a song adheres to the most stereotyped harmonic, melodic, instrumental, and timbral attributes, the more closely it resembles and/or is considered *shanson* (rather than *popsa*), although as in the West, rubrics under which various musical forms are subsumed are never absolute or unquestioned. Furthermore, in some instances, while the majority of my informants evinced an antipathy to this genre of popular music, there were instances where such aesthetics were enjoyed by them, although such approbation often depended upon the specific performer. For example, a *shanson*-like song by drag queen Verka Serdiuchka, Alla Pugacheva, or *èstrada* singer Nika[45] were much more likely to meet with approval despite the possible connotations of their stylistic conventions.

But these stylistic conventions, embedded in and constitutive of innumerable "conceptual" discourses (regarding nation, aesthetics, the superstar, and the cultural-historical, to name but a few) are not simply idealized abstractions; rather, they are in large part productive of a specifically embodied mode of perception, one that links musical experience to corporeal existence. I am not speaking here (only) of, for example, Meyer's (1956) conception of "embodied meaning" (which is, one can argue, an "interior," "psychological" apprehension of harmonic and/or melodic movement, producing alternately tension and resolution), or Keil's (1966) conception of "participatory discrepancies" (which focuses on an interactive, "productive" state of music *making*), or Davies's (2001) finding of a congruence between sonic and corporeal morphology, or even Kaufmann's (2000) or Clarke's (2005) positing of the interrelationship between musical structure and somatic movement; rather, from a phenomenological standpoint, I am suggesting that the very perceptions of the movements of these harmonic and melodic conventions—patterns of melodies that rise, or cascade, or step upward or downward, bass lines of harmonic progressions whose patterns vacillate between an upper point and a lower point, sometimes evoking a slowly migrating circle—are dependent upon one's perceiving *via* a body, a body that is the precondition for experiencing the world from a specific vantage point, a vantage point that is a precondition for the concepts of "up" or "down" (Merleau-Ponty 2002 [1962]: 353–354). As Merleau-Ponty notes, our understanding of a cube, for example, is predicated upon our very corporeal existence:

> It is a question of tracing in thought that particular form which encloses a fragment of space between six equal faces. Now, if the words "enclose" and "between" have meaning for us, it is because they derive it from our experience as embodied subjects. In space itself independently of the presence of a psycho-physical subject, there is no direction, no inside and no outside.... In order to be able to conceive the cube, we take up a position in space, now on its surface, now in it, now outside it, and from that moment we see it in perspective. (236–237)

Yet these musical "objects" are not simply things in and of themselves; rather, they *exceed* themselves and point toward other similar objects, perceived by others in other places; they are "[objects] for everybody ... open to a plurality of thinking subjects" (71),[46] objects "spilling out" spatially and temporally, encompassing somatic and affective memories of *pioner* songs from childhood, *romansy* heard (and perhaps sung along to) at bars or parties, perhaps under the veil of alcohol (the smell of which becomes vivid), *popsa* tunes heard on the radio at work, or on television in the midst of the winter holiday season, the sounds of *Novogodnyi goluboi ogonek* (*The New Year's Little Blue Light*, an annual holiday musical variety show) infusing the familial space, or dance remixes of *popsa* tunes danced to, sweating, in a gay club in St. Petersburg. Surrounded by family, friends, lovers, or sexual liaisons, these structures as sound are not "conceptual," "abstract" "formal devices" but, rather, polyvalent, sonic, and kinetic "things" the perception of which is not only dependent upon their situation within complex *Gestalten* (the singer's voice singing *this* sequence, the *baian* playing *this* chordal progression), but upon, again, a living body.[47] It is not that Russians (let alone gay Russian men) have a monopoly on such relationships to musical sounds and structures; but the fact that the sounds of Russian popular musics, via their structures, are so overwhelmingly homogeneous in comparison to Western analogs, encompassing such a wide variety of styles, genres, and temporalities, and that such sounds and structures are constituent parts of the contexts in which so many physical interpersonal relationships occur suggests a deep and profound relationship of corporeal existence to the auditory in Russia.

Music, Politics, Penetrations, and the Homosexual Body

Discussion of the somatic apprehension of one's "own" (or perhaps better said, one's "deeply known" or "homegrown") music highlights the embodied nature of musical experience. What, then, might be the nature of such corporeal experience concerning musics of "others"? I have previously referenced Yurchak's (2006) concept of the "imaginary West," one that he enlists in an attempt to explain the supposed contradiction inherent in Soviet citizens' acceptance of Western cultural products which, at face value, appeared to be in ideological opposition to the most foundational tenets of the Soviet system. Yurchak contends, however, that such cultural products were in fact "emptied" of their constative meanings (as were, often, "official" Soviet rituals or speech), and that their use "introduced a shared imaginary world into the Soviet reality, deterritorializing it, making it neither Soviet nor Western" (204). The troubling of a binarized model of us/them (Russia/West) via the introduction of a third term is important, and certainly in line with much thinking on the dynamics of hybridity and syncretism.[48] However, the relationships between Western cultural products and Russian citizens in both late-Soviet and contemporary Russia can additionally be read on a distinctly somatic, not entirely psychological ("imaginary") level, using some of the very examples from Yurchak's text.

First, Yurchak notes the importance of Western styles for late-Soviet youth: the duplication of hairstyles, the procurement of genuine Western garments or, for those unable to accrue the considerable sums necessary to purchase the authentic, the ingenious copying and creation of articles of clothing of a Western appearance. Such an attraction was not only to the historical past, as demonstrated by the *stiliagi*,[49] but still operates today; young gay men in Benetton, Diesel, or Izod were not uncommon sights on St. Petersburg or Moscow streets (or in clubs in both cities), and even those whose budgets precluded such expenditures might often be attired in what was then currently fashionable in the West (mulletlike haircuts, deconstructed T-shirts—often with English or French words on them—combat pants, track jackets, and so forth). Such displays are just that: displays of the body that has been attired to present itself as Western. But it would be a mistake to consider such objects as objects "on" the body only; rather, as Grosz (drawing on the work of Schilder [1978]) notes, clothing can have a transformative effect on the body. Objects that come into contact with the body long enough will be "incorporated into the body image," will mark the body's "gait, posture, position"; indeed, "subjects do not walk the same way or have the same posture when they are naked as when they wear clothing" (1994: 80). Clothing on and of the living, acting body clearly operates additionally on a nonimaginary, highly material, somatic level.

Second, we can highlight the corporeal elements of late- and post-Soviet interactions with foreign music as well; while undeniably discursively, ideologically, and "imaginarily" apprehended, the body is also a locus that must be foregrounded. As both Yurchak (2006) and Pilkington (2002) have noted, Russians themselves explicitly remarked upon the physical relationship between themselves and Western music.[50] What I want to highlight here, and in what follows, however, is the ability of music, through the subject's experience, to trouble the very idea of bodily impermeability. For while the actual, physical sources of music may be outside the listener's body (the body of the musician, his or her vocal chords or instrument, the mp3 or CD player, the speakers, the stores that sell the CDs, the encoded .mp3 or .wav files on a physical hard drive, and so forth), outside the listener's place/space (emanating from a foreign locale), at the same time it is experienced inside the listener as well via the cognitive and affective circuits in the body *and* mind, and the actual organs of reception: the ears, of course, as well as the eyes which take in surrounding discourses, as well as the entire body, the gut of which may be (either or both metaphorically and/or physically) vibrated. Despite the now decades-long worry about "cultural grayout," as well as the admitted increasing presence of Western musics on Russian soil, music emanating from Europe and the United States is still very much considered, to varying degrees, foreign; it is absolutely not so entirely "normalized," via ubiquity, as to be undifferentiated from contemporaneous Russian popular musics. But any attempt to discern how such corporealized relationships obtain must certainly take into consideration the specific historical and social placement of the subject, a subject who must not be defaulted to a presumed heterosexuality.

The opening of Russia's borders, the allowing of ingress and egress of bodies and bodies of information, engendered in the first decade of the twenty-first century a sense of siege among many Russians, some of whom feared an ensuing threat of foreign (often Western) encroachment. Owing in part to the strained relationships between the Kremlin and both Ukraine and Georgia,[51] as well as the tension produced between Russia and the West in association with the Baltic States' having become members of NATO in 2004, public sentiment not only against the West, but against all "outsiders" was and is, in the first decades of this century, a palpable reality. The Russian government itself was criticized for having intensified a growing intolerance, making use of a "manageable xenophobia" (Kolesnikov 2005) in order to solidify the "us" of the *narod* (people, nation) against the "them" of the interloping other.

Although government officials may have claimed that "for Russia, multiculturalism is now reality and standard practice,"[52] a rise in xenophobic violence painted a grim corrective to this hopeful, rosy picture. Attacks on and murders of foreigners, including foreign students, gained media attention in the mid-2000s,[53] as did hate crimes against ethnic minorities from the Caucuses. In one particularly disturbing instance, a nine-year-old Tajik girl, Khursheda Sultanova, was stabbed to death in St. Petersburg by a group of skinheads, allegedly yelling "Russia for [ethnic] Russians."[54] Indeed, Russia is reported to have the largest population of skinhead groups in the world,[55] and such groups have been responsible not only for violence against "foreigners," but against anyone deemed to be anti-Russian. In two separate and brutal instances in St. Petersburg in 2005, ethnologist Nikolai Girenko[56] was shot to death in his apartment (in front of his daughter), and twenty-year-old musician and university student Timur Kacharava was repeatedly stabbed in the neck on *Nevskii prospekt* (the city's main, central street), in broad daylight, possibly in response to the outreach work for the homeless he was part of that same day. He died while waiting for an ambulance to arrive.[57]

Xenophobic sentiment is not restricted to groups of neo-Nazis, however, as political parties have also been implicated in attempting to arouse anti-"Other" sentiment as well. In 2005, ultranationalist party *Rodina* ("Motherland"), headed by Dmitrii Rogozin, aired an advertisement on Moscow television in which racist, stereotyped images of Caucasian people were featured (loafing around the street, eating watermelon, and so forth).⁵⁸ The "dark-skinned" "foreigners" are told by a party leader to "pick up their watermelon skins," after which they are addressed as children, and asked "do you understand Russian?" (Piper 2005).⁵⁹ The commercial, which was ultimately taken off the air due to mounting criticism, ended with the tag line "clean your city." The idea of "cleansing"—to a state of (anterior) purity?—may also be seen in connection with other ultranationalist, neo-Fascist groups, such as *Nash gorod* (Our City), whose internet home page featured an embellished swastika above the phrase "*ochisti svoi gorod*" ("clean your [own] city").⁶⁰ The use of Nazi symbols is something common with such groups, and the swastika also figures prominently, albeit minimally disguised, in the logo of the *Slavianskii soiuz* (Slavic Union), a "national-socialist movement" ("*natsional-sotsialisticheskoe dvizhenie*").⁶¹

The anxieties of some Russians regarding the threat of the foreign is not, however, confined to specific geographic sites and ethnic others, and cannot be seen as a response to material circumstances only; rather, as Borenstein (2008) has convincingly argued, the anxieties are often related, in part, to Russia's relationship to the voracious West, a relationship which took on, in the years following perestroika, a manifestly sexual character in Russian political discourse. Here, Russia, figured as a female body, is seen as a "weakened, passive importer of prepackaged cultural and physical commodities" (24), "misused at the hands of either the . . . leaders . . . the country's perceived internal enemies (usually Jews, Chechens, and businessmen), or the depraved West" (42): in short, Russia, to make use of the biological metaphor clearly underlying much of this discourse, was "getting fucked." Such corporeal metaphors are apparent in a video found on the website of the previously noted *Slavianskii soiuz* where Nikolai Kur'ianovich—then deputy of the State Duma from the Liberal Democratic Party of Russia (*LDPR*; *Liberal'no-demokraticheskaiia partiia Rossii*)⁶²—flanked by the group's leader Dmitrii Demushkin, states that "the Slavic union and skinheads are . . . useful organizations," "the healthy reaction of an organism" battling an implied infection—a penetration by a virus rather than a penis (or phallus).⁶³

It is not surprising that this sort of discourse, drawing upon the biological, the West, the Other, and penetration, should invoke the homosexual—a figure that has been, as Healey (2001a) shows, historically constructed as either the denizen of the "backwards East" or the "debauched West." As an example, the previously noted group *Nash gorod*, calling for support of its antigay "actions," made use of the biological-homosexual nexus. One web page in particular, seeking support against the proposed 2006 gay pride parade in Moscow, and featuring a photograph of one man licking the penis of another, through the latter's briefs (a shot apparently taken from gay erotica), is overlaid with a block of text full of fallacious "data," noting that, for example, "eighty percent of fags [*pederastov*] have a venereal disease, including AIDS," or "scientists consider homosexuality [*pederastiia*] a psychological illness, similar to schizophrenia." In larger red letters, near the center of the photograph, appears the text, "We are absolutely against faggots infecting our children with diseases of the body and soul. NO to a Western infection. NO to a parade of faggots."[64] The biological, the homosexual, and the Western are here joined together as constituent parts of a "problem" threatening the integrity of the anthropomorphized Russian (social) body,[65] one that must guard itself against such foreign bodies and must strive to return to its putative insularity, solidity, impermeability. Vladimir Zhirinovskii, on hand at the attempted "gay parade" in Moscow in May of 2006, also invoked the specter of the Western homosexual as threat, warning the assembled crowd "that Russia would become like 'putrid America and dying Europe' if it permitted the 'gay mafia' to triumph, and led the crowd in chanting 'gays and lesbians to Kolyma'—the Stalin-era prison camp" (Human Rights Watch 2006).

The anxieties surrounding the homosexual are, I believe, not simply invoked by the concatenation of gay men with Westernization and/or psychosocial disease; rather, it is the very symbolic nature of the homosexual body and, especially, the anus that engenders fear. In *Homosexual Desire*, Hocquenghem posits that "Homosexuality primarily means anal homosexuality, sodomy" (1978: 84); however, this assessment is of a conceptual nature, not meant to indicate the actual physical, sexual practices of gay men.[66] Here, Hocquenghem is suggesting that the anus is defined in opposition to the "public" phallus, the "great signifier" around which society is organized (82). Indeed, Hocquenghem asserts that "ours is a phallic society, and the quantity of possible pleasures is determined in relation to the phallus.... Our society is so phallic that the sexual act without ejaculation is felt to be a failure" (81–82). In contrast to the hypervalued phallus, its (conceptual) visibility, its centrality, is the anus—the very symbol of the private, the concealed, an organ that must, in a society in which all desire is mandated as phallocentric, be devoid of any "desiring use" (84). To attach desire to that which operates outside the public (a public space controlled by phallocentricity) is to destabilize the very foundational tenets and dynamics of society. Hocquenghem, however, asserts that it is only through the reinvestment of the anus with desire, a desire that threatens the supremacy of the phallus, that change (including the abolition of homophobia) can be effectuated; furthermore, such desires must be "grouped"—that is, a grouping of homosexual desire (rather than solipsistic desire) that refuses the supremacy of the phallus and, in relation to this, the social order.[67]

However, the conflation of the anal and homosexual may serve another symbolic function, insofar as the anus, in the context of sexual desire and activity, may be indexically or metonymically related to penetration—and a penetrable body is one that has relinquished a conceptual *masculine* impermeability.[68] Yet even if anal sex is not, in fact, practiced among gay men with the regularity that some might imagine, the fact remains that, for most gay men, some form of penetration is part of sexual activity. In the instance of anal intercourse, Russian men, like Western men, do make distinctions regarding the role played by the partners: *aktiv*, the insertive partner, *passiv*, the receptive partner, and *universal* (or *uni*), a man who performs both roles.[69] But oral sex requires, obviously, a penetration as well and, although certainly sexual proclivities cover a wide range of possibilities, it may be rarer to find that man who is either entirely "active" or "passive" in terms of fellatio;[70] the fact that such categorizations as those surrounding roles with regard to anal penetration are not encountered with the same frequency when associated with oral penetration would seem to indicate that such specificity in sexual role has not solidified to an extent requiring linguistic labels.[71] Still, the symbol of the anus, an organ around which sexual desire may indeed coalesce, and one that cannot penetrate but is penetrable, seems to me an apt focus for homosexual desire; gay men's bodies, although equipped with a penis (and thus the power to penetrate in keeping with phallic power), are also sites of possible penetration *by* phallic power, whether the anus, the mouth, or even "the fist" which can unclench and be "penetrated" by the penis/phallus as it is manually pleasured. Insofar as the anus is *the* organ signifying solely penetrability (mouths, with tongues, can penetrate, as can the fingers of an open fist—or the fist itself), then homosexual desire—a desire encompassing the acts of penetrating and/or being penetrated—may indeed be seen as one that is anal.

Penetration, I want to suggest, is thus not for homosexual Russian men seen as the "threat" it is often portrayed as, not only in such extreme instances as the ones I have discussed above, but in the general, often homophobic, press as well; rather, penetration, based upon psychic and corporeal experience, is often a correlate of pleasure. Here it is also essential to relate such dynamics of penetration to specifically musical cultural contact, insofar as music has the power to penetrate not only symbolically and discursively, but physically as well; it "does not stop at the skin," it "reach[es] inside" (Burrows 1990: 20-21; in Austern 2002: 5) or, more nefariously, "rapes" the ear

(Austern 1998:615). The sonic, as opposed to the visual, problematizes the insularity of subject and object, as sound "inhabits the subject just as the subject might be said to inhabit sound" (Bull 2000: 2). Music does literally get inside the listener, producing numerous avenues for affective response in the process; it not only gets inside the "mind," saved as memories (with attendant affects), but also acts upon and enters the body, vibrating the very internal organs of hearing, vibrating the viscera, vibrating the larynx when singing along with a performance or recording. All of these at least partially explicitly physical occurrences are, indeed, pleasurable if the subject is not predisposed to view penetration negatively. And in theorizing, it is vital to understand that that which is *conceptualized* is not first *cognized*, but *somatized*; indeed, Merleau-Ponty and others, operating from a phenomenological stance, posit experience as foundational and conceptual abstraction as a second-order process. Moreover, both Merleau-Ponty and Lingis reference the penetrative components of perception in general. Merleau-Ponty posits a symbiotic relationship between subject and perception, noting the "certain ways the outside has of invading us and certain ways we have of meeting this invasion" (2002 [1962]: 370). And in a characteristically poetic passage, Lingis also references the subject's permeability:

> The echoes and the murmurs that wander off things, the odors that emanate from them, the voluptuous contours and hollows of things and of the waves and rain that caress, the mossy forests and nocturnal fragrances that fondle one's surfaces and penetrate one's orifices, and the night they cast about their luminous outcroppings belong to the reality of things and make the things visible and real. (1994b: 42)

Conceiving of penetration as pleasure, and music and perception as penetrative, it is understandable that many gay men may feel more receptive to transgressing not only physical borders, but musical and cultural borders as well. Further to this, understanding that many of my informants had had physical, sexual interactions with Western men is not simply a prurient footnote; rather, the fact that they had experienced physical intimacy with an "embodied West" contributes to their experiential formations of relationships with somatically powerful cultural productions such as music. I do not want to suggest that Russian men are constitutionally "passive," on their backs (or bent over) ready to bottom for a powerful, tumescent West; rather, my contention is that an embodied subject understanding penetration as something potentially pleasure-inducing (rather than humiliating, an assault on physical, psychic, or symbolic/metaphoric integrity), either for the self or for the partner, is one who is open to the very idea of permeability.

Additionally, the fact that many heterosexual Russian males have strong positive connections to Western musics should not be read as some sort of indication of "latent homosexuality," suggesting that penetration is the singular theoretical optic with which to describe the phenomenon. The fact that disparate groups of people may have positive reactions to or relationships with identical cultural productions does not mean that the loci of connections are not likewise disparate. My goal is not to valorize the homosexual body as universal explanans, but to enlist it—highlighting, in the process, the dangers of the too-frequent default to an assumed heterosexuality in (ethno)musicological theorization—in order to illuminate this specific dynamic.

But "penetration" itself is more complex than a simple bifurcation of inside/outside, active/passive, top/bottom (the spatial marker perhaps indicating superiority/inferiority); even in terms of sexual activity, although the "active" partner in oral sex is often assumed to be the insertive partner and is certainly seen to be such in terms of anal intercourse, it can be argued that the active partner may actually often be the *receptive* partner, insofar as he actively brings about the partner's pleasure through his bodily motion—a "passive" partner is not necessarily an immobile partner. The examination of borders, in terms of interpersonal (embodied and psychic) human relations, here specifically in the context of Russian-Western (embodied and symbolic) interaction, must be viewed with a certain amount of nuance. Kilgour (1990), for example, noting that metaphors of incorporation (the most severe of which might be cannibalism) are often used in service of both re-creating an imagined primordial unity, as well as the palliation of the anxiety engendered by the perceived encroachment on one's space (body, nation, home, and so forth) by an Other—in the latter instance, a case of "eat or be eaten," a way of eradicating difference—offers the idea of the communion and the Host as one that roils the eater/eaten dichotomy. In communion, a "reciprocal incorporation" obtains, as "man is a host in that he literally takes God, in the form of the Host into himself," while "the Host is the kind of food that converts the feeder into himself" (15). This type of mutually constitutive relationship is also engaged in phenomenological theory, often as a way to demonstrate that subjective experience does not imply solipsism but, rather, an engagement with others, "a 'coming together' of people who are irreducibly different through inter-animate behavior and conversation," and not fusion or synthesis (see Hass 2008: 122). It is through the recognition of intentional behaviors and body positions of others that one understands her or his connection to these others, others sharing a sentience and engagement with the living world that is not the purview of the "I" alone. As I have previously noted, it is not only "objects" (formal musical conventions) that index others (they are objects *for* others), but directions, postures, and corporealized aims often in relation to such structures that allow the subject to recognize "a presence of me in the other and the other in me" (Merleau-Ponty 2002 [1962]: 149).

As with Kilgour's conception of the reciprocity inherent in the relationship between the two "hosts," music likewise admits to a give-and-take relationship with the listener; if music is incorporated into the listener, changing him/her in the process, then the music itself is also changed: That which is Western becomes part of the lived experience and position of being gay and Russian, a position that situates the self not (only) as part of the *rodina* (motherland), but (also) among a widely disseminated, international gayness.[72] To imagine and feel one's self as penetrated by music of the "other" is to, in part, define one's self as "global," as part of an international community of listeners. As with the *Gay CD*, or the inclusion of travel-related articles in the *gei i lesbi* rubric of St. Petersburg's *Kalendar'/Time Out*, the homosexual is increasingly not only self-defining, but also defined via recourse to a discourse of international connections.[73] Of course, this internationality does not eclipse the domestic; as I also discuss in Chapter 5, the musical interplay between the foreign and indigenous also contributes to the formation of a gay musical space, one concurrently "here" (inside) and "there" (outside) in both St. Petersburg and Moscow. In both cities, it was possible to see gay men dance, in gay clubs, to everything from the Black Eyed Peas to the Boogie Pimps to Russian pop-dance duo *Gosti iz budushchego* to Ukrainian drag queen Verka Serdiuchka's "*Khorosho*" ("Good") or "*Chita drita*"—two songs exhibiting the most traditional of musical attributes (instrumentation, harmony, and so forth), sung by a man (Andrei Danilko) in women's clothing, the rural and the urban together, a Ukrainian "other," singing in Russian (and marketed to a Russian-speaking audience in both Russia and Ukraine), inside a Western-style space, inside the borders of Russia.

It is not only the role of the gay man in sexual activity—one in which he possesses the possibility to both penetrate and be penetrated—but his role in society, especially one undergirded by homophobia, that confirms the complexity posited by Kilgour, Merleau-Ponty, and others. For if ultranationalists or Fascists view themselves as "true" Russians, protecting the "real" Russia, the inside shoring up the boundaries against the outside, then gay men have always *been* the "outside" on the "inside." Othered by the juridical and the cultural, yet often able to "pass" as part of the "us" (as opposed to the "them"), they are dichotomous, privileged as bearers of phallic power, vilified as sites of receptive desire, both Russian and Western (by dint of their Western "debauchery," as suggested by Zhirinovskii), at once that to be battled against and that which battles against; for while the vast majority of gay men I knew were at least marginally liberal in their views regarding immigration and emigration, there were some whose virulent (and sometimes tacit) animosity toward ethnic others (Central Asians, Africans, Caucasians, generally) was freely expressed to me.[74]

Gay Russian men are not simply "Western converts" who want only to emigrate to the West—something some American or Western European gay men might see as puzzling, due to the troubling levels of homophobia in Russia. Indeed, I asked many informants about their desires, or lack thereof, regarding emigration, often in response to their assertions that their lives in Russia as gay men were far more difficult than they imagined my life—as an American—to be. Yet despite their stated difficulties, their answers were far from uniform.[75] Neither Stanislav nor Grisha, for example, had traveled outside of the country (and had traveled very little within Russia), and due to their financial situations thought it unlikely that such travel would occur in the near future; as such, neither had given much thought to the idea of vacationing, much less emigrating.[76] For those who had traveled or lived abroad, the responses to these experiences were mixed. Several had ambivalent feelings about their time in the West, several were extremely positive, while others were exceedingly negative in their assessments. Of those occupying the middle ground, Dmitrii, for example, had lived in Germany (and, after my departure from St. Petersburg, returned again, in conjunction with his job), and while he found the quality of life superior to that he had enjoyed in Russia, felt that overall things there were "too ordered, too dull" (an assessment similar to that of several other men who had been there and comparable to opinions about Finland). Zhenia had lived in Oslo and Brussels (counting the latter as one of his favorite cities) and had traveled to France as well, and although he had great admiration for the beauty of the country, said that he was not fond of the French people; for him, the French treated life like "a game" or "theater," while he preferred "being direct and to the point." But while several of my informants found the West "dull" and "boring," Oleg felt that life in Russia was just that; for him, nothing ever changed, and people were stuck in the past. Aleks noted much the same thing, saying that, while St. Petersburg was a beautiful city, full of stunning architecture, it was, for him, like "living in a museum."

There were, additionally, numerous men who were unabashedly positive in their assessments of their time spent in the West, such as Vasilii, who had studied in Germany and was highly critical of the then-current political situation in Russia, one that he saw as inhibiting the creation of basic human rights for people. Aleksei had also traveled extensively—to Germany, Austria,

Spain, and Egypt, as well as throughout Russia, in connection with his job at a chemical company—and had a great desire to see the United States (especially New York), although he said that, in comparison with Europe, New York was so distant that it was "hard to even conceive of it being real." Petia, who had traveled to England as part of an exchange program, although he at first experienced an unpleasant culture shock, found his return home to be painful, noting that "after I had been to London, I fell in love with everything there," and had "cried and cried" when he had to return to Russia, as he "didn't want to go back." Vova said that he would prefer to live "*anywhere* abroad, anywhere outside of Russia," and Artur was in the process of preparing for his language exams, in the hopes of obtaining documents necessary to emigrate to either Australia or Canada.[77]

It is important to remember, however, that "the West" is often little more than an overly broad conception,[78] and for many of the men I knew, differences among specific countries were important. Slava, for example, had traveled in both Italy and France, and although he had positive things to say about both places, had generally only negative reactions to his time in the United States (he was, not incidentally, one of the few people I met who had ever been to the country). Ivan, likewise, was largely positive regarding his impressions of Spain and Italy, but less so about the time spent living in Switzerland, which he "absolutely hated," due in part to the fact that he found life there "incredibly boring." In our discussions, it was also notable that he often countered his negative assessments of "the foreign" with positive assessments of Russia; for example, he noted that, although Switzerland was known as having some of the best ski slopes in the world, he found the skiing much better in Russia. Also, while the Swiss were "cold" and "unfriendly," Russians, in his opinion, were "warm" and "open."[79] He further noted that he had never been to the United States or the United Kingdom, and had no desire to do so, nor did he have any desire to live outside of Russia again. Negative conceptions of both England and the United States were in fact common, and it was not unusual for my informants, including Ivan, to openly criticize the United States directly to me; I was often told, for example, that Americans were greedy, vulgar, fat, uneducated, and that the country and its people were entirely without (a) "culture," this despite the fact that I was the only American the vast majority of them had ever met and that a considerable segment of their favorite musics were from the United States.

Indeed, Ivan's contempt for Americans was in direct contrast to his attitudes toward both Western music and me. Among his favorite performers he noted Enigma, Cocteau Twins, Portishead, Madonna, Britney Spears, Christina Aguilera (whom he was "embarrassed" to admit liking), and Pink (whom he though was Australian, and admired because she was "tough"). While he also mentioned, as noted earlier in this chapter, a fondness and respect for certain Russian groups or singers, in general his discussions about popular music focused on Western artists. And although among the gay men I met in Russia, he was one of the most openly contemptuous of the United States, he was also one of the most open and generous to me (for example, seeing me off from Domodedovo airport in Moscow and presenting me with small gifts from a weekend trip to his hometown outside Moscow). While Ivan may have hated "Americans" or been negatively disposed toward a certain "ideology," his positive connections and reactions to both Western music—music that I have endeavored to show is apprehended at least partly somatically—and to an embodied (not hypothetical) actor, to me, highlight the necessity of theory focusing on lived experience, experience in and of the flesh.

3. Phantom Faggots

> Detachable, separable parts of the body . . . retain something of the cathexis and value of a body part even when they are separated from the body. There is still something of the subject bound up with them—which is why they are objects of disgust, loathing, and repulsion as well as envy and desire. They remain (peripheral, removable) parts of the body image, magically linked to the body.
> —Elizabeth A. Grosz (1994: 81)

If the Soviet era was remarkable for its sexophobia, palpable as, paradoxically, an absence of explicit speech about sex or sexual matters, then the post-Soviet era, notable for a virtual explosion of unambiguous and open speech about sex—in the yellow press, as well as in academic discourse—might be seen as its garrulous corrective.[1] A televised assertion in 1987 that "sex" did not exist in Russia ("*u nas seksa net*," "we don't have sex")[2] could find its post-Soviet counterpart in 2004 in the form of the program *Pro èto* (*About This*),[3] a U.S.-style talk show that featured topics and discussions, the frankness of which would be almost unimaginable on broadcast television in the United States; for example, one program contained an extended segment on fellatio, including extremely explicit questions to both the panelists and audience members, such as whether they swallowed or spat—a frankness rendering questions such as "boxers or briefs?" positively puritanical by comparison.

An illustration of the stark differences between the present-day liberalism in matters sexual with those of the past decades, and people's cognizance of such, is also illustrated by an event that occurred during one of my first visits to the gay club *Greshniki* in 2004. Two young men were enticed, partially by the promise of free alcohol, into taking part in an amateur striptease, a spectacle that, through the promptings of the host and audience, grew increasingly ribald over the course of several minutes. Although full nudity was prohibited at the club (even for the professional strippers), both contestants bared their buttocks, and one shed his clothes entirely, holding only his hand or a piece of removed clothing over his genitals. Both bumped and ground at the audience and against each other, made facial expressions approximating sexual ecstasy (in the manner of gay porn), and seemingly took pleasure in exposing their flesh as sexualized and sexy. As things reached a sort of climax—the nearly nude boy, his back against the wall, grinding against and being ground against by the other boy, the latter's jeans at his knees, his posterior gently and rhythmically thrusting, the drag queen hostess exclaimed over the microphone, with great sarcasm, "oh, they are so modest (*skromnye*)—just like in Soviet times."

The laughter that followed her exclamation arose from the obvious knowledge on the part of the audience that this sort of spectacle—if not entirely public, then hardly wholly clandestine—was certainly the very opposite of Soviet ideals of modesty. And it was also in many ways the absolute antithesis of the position of an embodied and visibly sexualized homosexuality in Soviet Russia for the majority of the twentieth century. Whereas before 1993 homosexuality in Russia might be, like sexuality "in general," notable for its (signifying) absence from the public sphere, male-male sexuality, as well as those who practiced it, became to some extent visible following the repeal of Article 121—as characters in *detektiv* novels (Baer 2005) or theatrical productions (Beumers 2001), and even as guests on television shows; talk shows *Pro èto* and *Pust' govoriat* (*Let Them Talk*), for example, have both devoted episodes to the topic of homosexuality. Gay men, however, were and are not simply "spectacles" for the general public, and the various forms of media offer not only a representational affirmation, but also the possibility of didactic sexual information; for example, gay men with internet access who go to Russian gay sites may find banner ads referencing *analnyi seks v pervyi raz* ("anal sex for the first time"), the link from which leads to the large, online store of the gay.ru website, where a wide array of sex toys, lubricants, and sex "manuals" (such as Terry Sanderson's *The Gay Man's Kama Sutra* [2004], translated into Russian) are available. Those without internet access could also in the first decade of this century find similar items on sale in St. Petersburg's one "sex boutique" considered "gay-friendly," Pornomania, or at the gay boutique *Indigo* (with locations in both Moscow and St. Petersburg).[4]

But while there may be wholesale similarities between the various post-Soviet audibilities/visibilities of homosexuality and sexuality "in general"—repression/efflorescence, to use a horribly simple gloss—subsuming homosexuality under such a generality (one implying a universal heterosexuality) eradicates the possibility of understanding the specific places occupied and roles played by those men with nonnormative sexual identities, the degree to which such efflorescence is curtailed, the reasons for such curtailment, and the modalities via which such embodied subjects ultimately become both audible and visible. While, for example, the word "*gei*" may be uttered on a television talk show, in 2004 President Vladimir Putin could apparently not do the same. Following his meeting with the Commissioner of Human Rights of the Council of Europe Alvaro Gil-Robles, whose report had pointed out numerous infractions against the rights of minorities (including sexual minorities) in Russia, Putin assured the Commissioner that assiduous work would be done in "some directions." The implicit elision was not lost on one commentator, who noted that Putin's "some" ("*nekorotym*") made it impossible to know whether lesbian and/or gay men would be included in any initiatives (Petrov 2005a). Moreover, although media representations of homosexuality were not entirely absent, it was unusual during my time in Russia, in the country's two largest metropolitan centers, to see gay men or lesbians (that is, those who self-presented according to any of the numerous stylistic and/or social codes one might see on display in the cities' gay clubs) on the streets with any sort of regularity, alone or as small groups or couples. It is probably the case that many such men and women, due to what the vast majority of my informants saw as a pervasive and perceptible homophobia throughout Russia, choose to "pass" in "daily life" rather than risk social disapprobation—and not only from heterosexuals; indeed, on one occasion while shopping in a large retail complex in the center of St. Petersburg, accompanied by Aleksei (a gay man), he and I wound up at the check-out counter behind two men who read to both of us—via subtle clues of style, comportment, purchases, and their personal interaction—as a couple. Aleksei turned to me and whispered "I can't stand it when they have to be so *obvious*." (Apparently he believed that he and I, two gay male friends, were not "obvious.")

While it is true that there are public spaces in which gay men may congregate in both St. Petersburg and Moscow, public visibility of homosexual men nowhere approached that of such Western sites as Montréal's Gay Village, New York City's West Village or Chelsea, Philadelphia's "Gayborhood," or London's Soho, and the homophobia to which my informants referred was something I almost immediately and viscerally felt (via social interactions and exposure to Russian media) upon my first arrival. Yet this cloud of proscription, resulting in a void in lived, quotidian life, seemed not to have settled upon the realm of popular music; for, as immediately as I had noted the lacuna of visible walking, talking, living homosexual men around me, in these cities of millions of inhabitants each, I had also been almost instantly stunned by the number of apparently "gay men"[5] who were active (and popular) *popsa* and *èstrada* singers. This was not a case of a one-off Liberace, Azis, or Zeki Muren here or there, but rather a growing roster—one that was literal and kept handy in my small, always-available notebook—including well-known artists Sergei Penkin, Shura, Filipp Kirkorov, Maksim Galkin,[6] Nikolai Baskov, Vitas, Nikita, Dima Bilan, Dmitrii (Mitia) Fomin (of the group Hi-Fi), Sergei Lazarev (of the group Smash!!), and Andrei Gubin, among others.[7] Assumptions that might have been written off as a Western gaydar in need of recalibration, however, were confirmed by both informants and press accounts alike, resulting in a baffling contradiction: if homosexuality was truly anathema to the vast majority of Russians, how could so many embodied examples of a *"netraditsionnaia seksual'naia orientatsiia"* be found in the mass media, and why, specifically this form—this musical form—of popular culture? Can the post-Revolutionary disappearance of the visible and embodied gay male—a severing from the social body—and the subsequent reappearance be understood not only on sociocultural/sociopolitical and discursive levels, but corporeal as well? How is homosexuality represented or suggested in the musical output of specific contemporary singers? And finally, how can this reappearance be contextualized historically? These questions will be approached via the examination of the musics and discourses surrounding three contemporary artists: Boris Moiseev (b. 1956, Belarus), an *èstrada/popsa* performer, best known not only for his having been a dancer and choreographer with and for Russia's most successful *èstrada* singer (and arguably most venerated gay icon), Alla Pugacheva,[8] but also for his being the only male singer in all of Russian popular music to officially have "come out"; Valerii Leont'ev (b. 1949, Russia), another *èstrada/popsa* singer whose career as a recording and performing artist has spanned five decades and who has enjoyed great success in both the Soviet and post-Soviet eras; and singer/songwriter/actor Andrei Danilko (b. 1973, Ukraine), whose drag persona Verka Serdiuchka was easily one of the most widely listened-to artists in Russian popular music for several years in the first decade of this century (and whose popularity is still widespread).[9]

Disease, Infection, and Amputation

While prohibitions against male-male sexual activity existed among the Orthodox Slavs for centuries,[10] homosexuality in nineteenth- and early-twentieth-century Russia was to some extent tolerated, especially in comparison with contemporaneous Western European neighbors. Although Peter the Great's Military Articles of 1716 made *muzhelozhstvo* (literally, "men lying with men," but taken to mean male-male anal intercourse) a punishable offense, such punishment did not extend to the civilian public; this was not, as Orthodox proscription had been, punishment for a "moral failing" but, rather, one for activity that might threaten military hierarchies (Healey 2001a: 80). Sodomy for civilians was made illegal only under the criminal codes adopted in 1835 and 1845, this legislation "designed to impose a conservative European moral norm" (98) on a society that had been, at least relatively speaking, less likely to punish sexual activity between men (or between women) than its neighbors to the West. Although homosexual sodomy was punishable by exile to Siberia under Article 995, legislation that remained in effect until 1917, Healey notes that police in the early part of the twentieth century made little effort to enforce this particular law, and that the Article was "virtually a dead letter in the largest of Russia's cities by the end of the Imperial era" (95).

With the 1917 Revolution, Russia's attention to matters encompassing both sexuality and gender (including homosexuality, divorce, gender equality, abortion, and prostitution) signaled a relative openness unparalleled in Western countries, and legislation regarding such matters was "the most liberal ... in the world at the time (Riordan 1993: 2);[11] the 1922 and 1926 criminal codes, for example, omitted *muzhelozhstvo* from the list of criminal offenses.[12] Such liberalism, however, was not necessarily an indication of acceptance of homosexuality, per se; for example, Bolshevik M. Iu. Kozlovskii, a contributor to the draft legislation of the 1921 code, sought the removal of sodomy not necessarily on the basis of sexual freedom—or even equality—but from a position of advancing secularization and modernization over a religious, "moral" basis for society (Healey 2001a: 121). Moreover, Kozlovskii's belief that homosexuality was to be understood via a biological/medical standpoint, mirrored in the work and writings of numerous Soviet physicians, psychiatrists, and legislators in the 1920s,[13] may imply that while homosexuality was not considered a *criminal* offense, it might still be seen as some sort of *dysfunction*—one that, once its etiology had been investigated and discovered, might be treated. Homosexuals, thus, should be treated "humanely," seen as men who simply act according to their "nature," but it is a nature that is "abnormal," one that might be studied, understood, and eventually cured.

Whether or not such biologizing discourses might be seen as pathologizing, homosexuality was at least not a punishable offense. Yet this immunity from prosecution based on sexual orientation was not long-lived. As Stalin began to consolidate and centralize power, pragmatism replaced utopianism, groups of "social anomalies" were constructed and labeled as antithetical to the health of the state, and biological explanations for homosexuality began to be eclipsed by those postulating a genesis via social context—"nurture" over "nature." In the republics, for example, male homosexuality was seen as the outcome of "backward" social customs, as well as economic inequalities and exploitation (e.g., the *bachi* in Uzbekistan, young boys who were kept as prostitutes), while in Russia, the urban homosexual was recast as a class enemy, a "labor deserter" who preferred "decoration and dress design" (Healey 2001a: 174) to working toward Communist ideals. But it was perhaps the concatenation of homosexuality with fascism that solidified a resolve to recriminalize male-male sexual activity in the USSR, one enacted as law with the adoption of Article 121 in late 1934. The explanation for the action, first widely disseminated in 1934 via Gor'kii's article "*Proletarskii gumanizm*" ("Proletarian Humanism") in the Soviet newspapers *Pravda* and *Izvestiia*, made clear the Soviet stance that homosexuality was not to be understood as the outcome of a biological etiology but, rather, a social etiology, one that was deleterious and diametrically opposed to the very health and strength of the state. This stance could be seen as encapsulated in Gor'kii's infamous proclamation, "destroy the homosexuals—Fascism will disappear," and the connection between nonheterosexual sexuality and antistate, anticollective mindset was reaffirmed in 1936 by Nikolai Krylenko, Peoples' Commissar for Justice, who announced that "homosexuality was a product of the decadence of the exploiting classes," and that such people had no place "in a socialist society based on healthy principles" (Kon 1993b: 92). For the next fifty-nine years, male homosexuality was a punishable offense, one that led anywhere from tens to hundreds of thousands of men to imprisonment and sometimes death.[14]

The association of homosexuality with one of Russia's most powerful political-military adversaries would seem to be, in and of itself, a linkage sufficient to mandate legal proscription. Yet while biologizing discourses had largely been replaced with those of a constructivist bent—in terms of etiology—Krylenko's allusion to social health points toward the discursive production of an anathemized homosexuality that was also based upon corporeal imagery, conferring upon male-male sexual activity the status of a disease requiring eradication. Numerous authors have shown how the body functioned as a metaphor throughout the history of Soviet Russia, disseminated in the popular press, state propaganda, and literary texts. Starks (2008), for example, examines the profusion of propaganda devoted to raising hygienic standards among the populace; here, healthy, individual bodies were seen as necessary constituent parts of the healthy social body. And Livers (2004), via an examination of literary texts of the Stalinist 1930s, finds a similar reliance upon corporeal metaphors—often explicitly gendered, with the feminine constructed as "natural," the masculine "rational"—whereby a "carefully cultivated sense of social unity [was] enacted in almost corporeal terms of physical closeness and warmth" (5).[15] In this context, the homosexual body stood in opposition, by its very nature, to the health of individual, collective, and social/state bodies. Indeed, as Healey (2001a) notes throughout his volume on homosexuality in revolutionary Russia, the "good" Soviet man was configured in state ideology as clean and innocent, yet capable of being infected by male "sodomites." Such infection could have not only moral, but sociopolitical consequences; that is, homosexual men could divert male energy from the imperatives of nation building and defense, and "threatened the purity of the healthy Soviet young man and perhaps harbored opportunities for sedition" (203). Visible homosexual subcultures would need to be eradicated, not only because they had a "demoralizing" effect, but also because they could lead to a "crisis of mental or sexual hygiene, imagined by police and Politburo . . . as the seduction of innocent young men by 'pederasts'" (187).

How then was such an infection to be eradicated? One material and particularly nefarious option was of course by interment in the gulag; while homosexual activity might continue there, it was contained within a physical location populated by those who were already considered miscreants and would not be visible or available to (via some sort of powerful seductiveness) "normal," "healthy" citizens. However, a literal, physical herding of living bodies to discrete physical sites on the fringes of the geographical landscape could probably never be fully accomplished because legal, juridical, economic, and political resources were finite and already overtaxed. As such, the "pederast" was severed from the social body not only physically, but discursively as well, largely via two different modalities. In the first instance, homosexuality was figured in spatial terms, located outside of Russia; while there may have been remnants of this "disease" within certain urban locations, homosexuality was constructed as foreign, belonging to either the "depraved," "primitive" East, on the one hand, or the "neurasthenic," overcivilized, "depleted" West, on the other. In this "geography of perversion" (Healey 2001a: 252–253), the homosexual, by his very being, was formulated as not part of Russia, alien and Other.

In the second instance, however, instead of constructing the homosexual "as" "something"—as *anything*—discussion of homosexuality largely disappeared from public discourse;[16] according to Kon, by the mid-1930s "a complete and utter silence had fallen over the entire issue. Homosexuality was simply never mentioned anywhere" (1993b: 93). Indeed, the very enacting of the legislation outlawing male sodomy was "imposed without public discussion" (Healey 2001a: 183), and little documentary evidence remains as to why the initiative was adopted so wholeheartedly; it would appear that the "speech" intended for posterity was to be as bowdlerized as contemporaneous speech.[17] Furthermore, there appeared to be little information available to either the procuracy or judiciary as to how apply the new statute; one did not even speak of the law to those in charge of implementing punishment for its transgression.[18] Such imperatives of silence apparently applied to the didactic spectacle known as the show trial (*pokazatel'nyi protsess*) as well. Drawing upon archival work, Healey (2001a) found that of a sample of eight Moscow city court trials for sodomy between 1935 and 1941, six of them (involving thirty-two of the thirty-six defendants) were held behind closed doors, and he suggests that judges saw "little educative value, and possibly greater social harm" in making such trials public (214). Contrasting these trials with those held in the previous decade, he notes, "Unlike the show trials of the 1920s against clergy and monks for sexual offenses, these were not edifying spectacles mounted to demonstrate Bolshevik values to a wide audience.... These processes functioned not on the massive scale of the show trials, but primarily for the players who took part in them" (227).

Taken in the context of a pronounced somaticism regarding matters of citizen and state—citizens' bodies are of concern to the state because their health impacts upon the health of the social whole; diseased individuals (including homosexuals) may infect "innocent," "pure," "healthy" individuals; the state itself is a body comprising tens of millions of discrete bodies—the severing of the homosexual, physically and discursively, via interment, spatialization, and elision, may also be viewed as corporeal in nature. A putatively diseased part of the social body is cut off to avoid further contamination, or even death, of the whole; the homosexual is amputated from the body politic. But are such acts—on symbolic, no less than corporeal, levels—irreversible, without resultant traces? In the post-Soviet era, we may begin to see such traces on a textual level, circulating around and emanating from certain performers. Texts referencing homosexuality begin to bleed through the obfuscatory Soviet overcoatings, begin to become visible on the palimpsest.

(Yellow) Press, "Blue" Men: Moiseev, Leont'ev, and Danilko

In the summer of 2004, posters appeared throughout the streets of St. Petersburg advertising an upcoming concert. Alongside the announcements for performances by Pink, Cher, *Nochnye snaipery* (The Night Snipers, a Russian rock group), *Fabrika zvezd*, and other local and international acts, was the visage of the bleached-blond, post–middle-aged Boris Moiseev, one of the most controversial and, judging from his ability to fill concert halls, popular performers in Russia of the time. His appearance on July 7, at St. Petersburg's *Oktiabr'skii* concert hall—a large Soviet-era structure in the center of the city, not far from the major transportation hub of the *Moskovskii vokzal* and a favored spot of popular performers from around Russia—drew a huge crowd.

Nearly every seat in the theater was filled, the majority of the patrons being well-dressed (though not particularly "stylish") middle-aged women. The night of the concert, the audience became restive when, approximately ten or fifteen minutes past the slated curtain time, Moiseev had still not come to the stage. Groups of people began to rhythmically chant, "*Bor-ia, Bor-ia*,"[19] some stamping their feet in time. Perhaps in response to this, a voice sounded over the loudspeakers: "Ladies and gentlemen—in ten minutes, the world will change" ("*cherez desiat' minut, mir izmenitsia*").

While the announcement was certainly hyperbolic, Moiseev did, in the early nineties, contribute to the changing of the codes of silence in Russia regarding matters of sexuality. Although he had been active as a performer—largely as a choreographer and dancer—in the Soviet Union (Russia, Belorussia, and the Baltics, especially Latvia), as well as abroad (in Israel, the United States, and Canada), since the 1970s, with the coming of the glastnost of the El'tsin years and a relative relaxing of freedoms in the public sphere, Moiseev publicly "came out." Although his motives for the declaration have been questioned (specifically, the contention that it was done for reasons of "PR," a way to create "scandal" and thus attract listeners), Moiseev denied these charges. He insisted that his decision to reveal his sexual orientation had been made upon return to Russia, after having toured for three years in Europe and the United States, at a point when "democracy [arrived]—or ... Mr. El'tsin was building it." According to Moiseev, "someone had to say to everyone: 'Enough of hating one another'" (Morozov 2005).

Moiseev's troupe for the evening consisted of himself, six male dancers, two female dancers, and two female "background singers" (or "background lip-synchers"); the music was prerecorded, and Moiseev apparently lip-synched the entire concert, the microphone he held seemingly nothing more than a prop.[20] As some of my informants had told me, and as I had heard for myself from the Moiseev CDs I had purchased, his vocal talents were indeed minimal,[21] and recorded versions of his songs relied heavily on numerous effects and double-tracking on the vocals, in order to give more presence to a rather thin voice with a very limited vocal range. During the performance, the only "live" sounds that he produced were either syncopated, rhythmic vocables ("uh" or "eh"), or spoken exclamations such as "*davai*" or "*derzhi menia*" ("come on," "support me") interspersed into the text of a song.

While his vocal talents are unremarkable, Moiseev's physical appearance is often arresting, both on and offstage, his bearing *mannernyi* (mannered)—a word used by many of my informants to describe him. On a talk show appearance in 2004, for example, although his clothing was not entirely over-the-top, veering more toward a young, urban style (low-slung combat pants resting precariously below a middle-aged paunch, and zip-up turtleneck sweater), Moiseev went through the gamut of gay stereotypes: cross-legged and limp-wristed, he doted on his pet (in a video segment that followed him to the dog's grooming, complete with Moiseev tying the crowning hair ribbon—on the dog, that is), showed his "artistic" mettle by "sketching" on one of his headshots, and taking the challenge of styling a woman's hair blindfolded. The evening of the performance he was relatively subdued, in comparison to some of his other sartorial statements, which often rely upon chiffon, lycra, lace, satin, and/or ruffles: first appearing in a white T-shirt and red-and-white tracksuit (again, an approximation of a youthful, urban, clubby style), he later changed to a black lace T-shirt, diaphanous white overblouse, and multipocketed "club" pants, these replete with rhinestone chains. His hair, close-cropped and bleached blond was also relatively staid—far less outrageous than the wigs and/or hair extensions he has sometimes sported—although he was in full, heavy makeup, his norm. The overall image is one of theatrical gender-bending, extremely (stereotypically) feminine, often stopping just short of full drag,[22] but even here it is difficult to draw any definitive lines; at the evening's performance, although he was attired in "male," or at least unisex, clothing, Moiseev often appears, due to his gait, his movements, and his general mien, to be a woman doing male drag, rather than the opposite. Oleg, hearing that I had gone to the concert, asked me afterward how I had enjoyed the "transvestite show."

The evening's performance, which featured numerous songs from Moiseev's then-current CD, *Liubimyi chelovek* (*Beloved Person*), drew upon several conventions common in a typical "Vegas-type" show: flashing strobes and spots placed strategically around the stage to enhance the mood of the song, dry ice wafting in to add atmosphere, the two blond, female background singers (dressed in revealing, pink, sequined gowns) placed atop a dais upstage and then parading showgirl-like down the flank of stairs to meet Moiseev. The troupe of dancers provided a whir of almost perpetual motion and energy, compensatory for the comparatively torpid fifty-plus-year-old star. The dancers and singers surrounding Moiseev that evening were all extremely attractive (at least from a distance), the female dancers often wearing little more than thongs and bras, and high stiletto heels, the men's outfits—including torn jeans and white crop tops, or tight black pants and T-shirts—seemingly designed to almost continually and optimally expose an array of flat, chiseled, virtually fat-free abdomens. Despite the frequent conflation of "male dancer" with "homosexual," all of the dancers appeared to fall on the "masculine" side of the spectrum[23]—even the women, with short haircuts, lean, muscular bodies, and outfits that sometimes appeared almost bondage/fetishlike (severe, angular, and brief tops or bottoms of black vinyl/leather), their athletic, purposive bodies in direct contrast to the supple and flowing Moiseev.

Moiseev's "softness" or "gentleness" was often expressed in his effusions of "love" to the audience; for example, after the evening's first number, the singer advanced to the proscenium to pronounce, "*spasibo za to, chto vy zhyvete so mnoi, i ia s vami*" ("thank you that you live with me, and I with you"). At the end of the concert Moiseev, holding several bouquets that had been given to him by the audience members (with several more at his feet), took in his fans' adoration, exclaiming, "*ia tebia liubliu, moi Leningrad—moi Peterburg!*" ("I love you, my Leningrad—my St. Petersburg!"). Whether this was a sincere expression of affection toward an apparently adoring public, or a calculated attempt to both play on the sentiments of an older generation, many of whom may have remembered with fondness the pre-glastnost appellation of their hometown, as well as reference his latest song ("*Peterburg-Leningrad*")[24] is almost beyond the point; it is, rather, simply a fact that Moiseev's image is one in which "love"—for his fans, for the world, for music, for Russia—is an integral component of what he offers and what people expect. He is, as proclaimed from the cover of the evening's souvenir program, "*naveki Vash*" ("forever yours").

But Moiseev's unambiguous "coming out" did not apparently render him irrevocably homosexual, neither in the hands of the press, which often suggested to readers (largely via misleading headlines) that the singer might be heterosexual, nor in terms of his own self-presentation. One article in the Russian newspaper *Dni*, for example, led with the headline "How Moiseev Lost His Bride" ("*Kak Moiseev poterial nevestu*"), yet the article recounts an event in the singer's life wherein his *brother* had lost his fiancée (owing to mice in the apartment). Two others attempted to suggest the singer's heterosexuality by linking him with female partners and led with the titles "Boris Moiseev's Beloved Women" ("*Liubimye zhenshchiny Borisa Moiseeva*") and "Boris Moiseev and His Ladies" ("*Boris Moiseev i ego ledi*");[25] his "beloved" women, however, turned out to be his mother, and *èstrada* superstars Alla Pugacheva and Liudmila Gurchenko—both of whom he has performed with, and both of whom are among the greatest gay icons in the Russian-speaking (and indeed Slavic) world. Even when his homosexuality is referenced, Moiseev may be painted as a "good gay"; for example, "he doesn't use drugs, uses condoms, and believes that one should treat one's self with care and love" ("*Boris Moiseev. Biografiia*"). One newspaper also reported on the singer's donation of his salary to aid the victims of the Beslan massacre ("*Moiseev i Baskov*").[26]

The singer himself has often taken stances that may appear to be antithetical to the aims of full equality for homosexual men and women, or at the very least to distance himself from an often despised sexual identity, aligning himself instead with the "traditional," heteronormative family. In an interview in the newspaper *Segodnia*, Moiseev came out against the marriage of Elton John to his longtime partner David Furnish, opining that "gays shouldn't irritate (*razdrazhat'*)." A public gay marriage, according to Moiseev "breaks the intimacy and intrigue around the family of same-sex love," and "in a Catholic or Orthodox church is not correct, in relation to God, in relation to public opinion, and many believers . . . this irritates people, and gays shouldn't irritate" ("*Gei ne dolzhny*"). While distancing himself from gay marriage, however, the singer for over a decade suggested (and ultimately announced) that he himself was to marry a woman. As far back as 2005, in an article on the website gay.ru, Moiseev—again coming out in opposition to Elton John's wedding—averred that he would definitely have a wedding, and that he would "go down the aisle with a lady of my heart"; conversely, he turned down the offer of his male, American "friend" (a "philologist and top model") to come live with him in Moscow, saying that he "no longer needs this." The rumors of marriage to the unnamed American "*biznes-ledi*"—unnamed even in 2007, so as to protect her from the paparazzi, according to Moiseev—continued for years, but the event never seemed to materialize.[27]

Moiseev has also consistently made references to instances of child-rearing in his interviews over the past several years. In the context of what he identified as a world marked by "cataclysms, destruction, and misery," it would be better, in his opinion, to "help people, and take abandoned children into your home, and not make showy exhibitions," which "irritate the Earth's magnetic field" (Levkovich and Grinshpun 2007). He has also regularly referenced his own biological son, Amadeus (supposedly fathered out of wedlock in Moiseev's youth), although the son was never seen in public with the singer and reportedly lived in Poland; ultimately, it was revealed that the son had never existed.[28] Consistently vaunting a type of conventional, nuclear family as his implied ideal, the singer has also in several instances distanced himself from a "gay community," and even the label "gay"; in an interview in the Russian edition of *Rolling Stone* magazine, asked if his circle of friends is "the most notorious gay group [*tusovka*]," Moiseev replied that "in general, I don't hang out with gays. I and gays are completely different histories. I myself can't determine my orientation. In the newspapers they write—gay-shmay—this is all [bullshit] [*p**dezh*; *pizdezh*]. I'm oriented to love—and that's all, okay?" (Levkovich and Grinshpun 2007). Although he often expresses a belief in tolerance ("One should be tolerant, calm, respect one's own yard, home, family, country"),[29] such tolerance—not, apparently, equality—is contextualized within a conservative, even patriotic discourse.[30]

Although Moiseev's appearance as a solo artist did not occur until after the Soviet Union's dissolution, Valerii Leont'ev had been active as a singer and performer since the 1970s, and he is considered by many to be one of the most popular artists in Russian *èstrada*. Leont'ev's discs were on display in most of the music stores I visited, and his image—long, curly hair, a wardrobe consisting often of tight, leather clothing, and a face that seems to have been stretched equally tight in recent years via plastic surgery (and one that is almost always enhanced by makeup)—was in stark contrast to those of other male *èstrada* artists who favored a more "traditional," "masculine" appearance. Not only his appearance, but his peripatetic style of performance, its very theatricality, often ran afoul of the Soviet system, leading to the reshooting or editing of his television performances in "toned-down formats" (MacFadyen 2001: 187–188). Discussing pre-perestroika *èstrada*, MacFadyen explicitly contrasts Leont'ev with Lev Leschenko, another star of the same era, the former the embodiment of the "lyric" (the personal, emotional), the latter, the "civic" (the political, the social), something that he earlier relates to the idea of gender roles—respectively, feminine and masculine. Long hair and tight clothing in and of themselves do not necessarily connote homosexuality, of course, and there are certainly heterosexually identified performers of Russian rock whose personal styles may appear, in very general terms, similar to Leont'ev's; however, it is possibly this "lyricism," in appearance no less than in musical and textual content, that differentiates him from those of a "traditional" orientation. The theme of deep love (and the resultant pain), or deep emotions in general, are regular themes in Leont'ev's music (e.g., "*Ia pozabil tvoe litso*," "I Have Forgotten Your Face," or "*Nochnoi zvonok*," "Night Phone Call"). And when delivered by a singer clad, as in one performance, in skintight white trousers (almost leggings), a gauzy white top soaked through with water, a soft-rock arrangement supporting his voice, a waterfall in the back of the stage (as opposed to, say, phallic thrusts of lasers or fireworks), the text addressing a romantic night in an old hotel with a gender-indeterminate partner—the effect is less Robert Plant, more a somewhat gay(er) Air Supply.[31] The fact that certain press accounts assert that the singer's "feminine" mode of dress and carriage were evident even in his childhood years constructs a specific optic through which contemporary sartorial and corporeal statements may be viewed.[32]

In contrast to Moiseev's openness in disclosing (and reclosing?) the details of his intimate life, Leont'ev has been characterized by journalists as being highly secretive about his life offstage, labeled by one as "one of the most closed personalities of the pop world" ("*odin iz samikh zakrytykh personazhei pop-tusovki*") (Boikov 2004); in the same article, Leont'ev himself is quoted as saying "one should never tell everything about one's self . . . without enigma, a star is not a star." While many have assumed him to have a "nontraditional" orientation—the majority, judging from both my informants and press accounts—he nonetheless is equivocal about this subject. In one interview, noting his previous denial of his supposed homosexuality, he stated "earlier, I declared: 'I'm not gay!' but now I have decided to leave that question open. Think what you want. I do not refute these rumors, I'm tired of it already, and I'm not declaring [it] like, for example, Boria Moiseev" (Polupanov 2000).

Clothing, carriage, repertoire, and equivocation, however, are not the only variables contributing to the public's apparent questioning of Leont'ev's sexual orientation, and as with Moiseev, the subject of marriage is a node around which issues of sexual orientation coalesce. Most histories of Leont'ev's personal, "romantic" life assert that he met his current wife, Liudmila Isakovich, in 1972, at which time she worked as a bass player in and director of the musical ensemble "*Èkho*" (Echo) in the town of Syktyvkar; the two lived and worked together for the next two decades and established a civil (unofficial) marriage. Isakovich "emigrated" to the United States, however, when she, Leont'ev and other members of his troupe were on tour in 1993, first living in New York City and ultimately settling in Miami, where she started a business as a dog groomer. Isakovich and Leont'ev legally married only in 1998 (or 1997, depending upon the report), yet this badge of heterosexual matrimony—one that Moiseev plays with in his various self-presentations—has apparently done more to convince than disabuse a skeptical public of the singer's homosexuality. Numerous articles[33] suggest that the "civil marriage" was nothing more than Leont'ev's attempt to present the required heterosexual identity to Soviet officials in charge of deciding which performers would be allowed to appear on state-run television, after having been denied access for several years;[34] furthermore, others propose that their official marriage in Miami was for the express purpose of allowing Leont'ev to obtain a multientry/multiexit visa—something that could be acquired only if he were married to an American citizen (which Isakovich had become) (Maistrenko 2007). Additionally, not only Leont'ev himself, but also Isakovich has been assumed—possibly due to her "butch" appearance—to be homosexual in the press. Although she, like her husband, neither confirms nor denies such speculation ("let them talk," "It's all the same to me, if they talk or don't talk, it doesn't bother me"), and suggests that the matter is humorous to both partners ("Valerii sometimes brought these newspapers [in which there was gossip]. We deliberately sat, read . . . laughed, almost fell off the bed"),[35] it has done little to convince the public that either of them is heterosexual; on one internet forum, a particularly vitriolic poster, referencing a photograph of Isakovich, stated "she's a lesbian, that's why she looks like a man. Leont'ev never slept with her . . . this is more evidence of the fact that Leont'ev is a faggot [*pidar*]—a normal guy [*muzhik*] will take a normal, beautiful woman for his wife, and not a horrible lesbian."[36]

Filial matters also occupy a place in discussions of Leont'ev and his spouse, although in an unusual manner. His long-term relationship with Aleksandr Bogdanovich (termed, explicitly, his "boyfriend" in many articles)[37] is hardly secret, and indeed it became quite visible due to the "scandal" of Bogdanovich having declared himself Leont'ev's son in order to garner media attention. If the previous press accounts are to be believed, Bogdanovich, rebuked by Leont'ev, waited for two days on the steps of the *Oktiabr'skii* hall in St. Petersburg on the nights of Leont'ev's concerts there in November of 2005, bearing a large bouquet of red roses as a sign of repentance and wish for forgiveness (to which, it is said in the above articles, Leont'ev did not respond). Additionally, Leont'ev's wife, in contrast to the stereotypical, gender-appropriate desires of a "real" woman, has said that she does not want children, and never has; in response to a reporter who suggested that Leont'ev had expressed wishes of fathering a child, Isakovich replied, "if he wants to have children, let him"—the reply, not incidentally, the title of the article—adding that, while she would relate to the child as a grandson, son, or a nephew, "children grow better on other people's balconies" ("*Zhena Valeriia Leont'eva* ").

If the blemish of reproductive insufficiency, in the context of the Russian government's obsession with procreation and declining demographics, might be seen as conferring an undesirable status on an individual, such a stigma apparently did not attach to either the childless, Ukrainian actor/singer/composer Andrei Danilko, nor to his enormously popular drag persona, the middle-aged, unmarried, childless railroad steward Verka Serdiuchka.[38] Of all the singers noted thus far, Serdiuchka was, according to informants, and judging by airplay on radio and television, as well as frequency of her songs in nightclubs, bars, and discos, far and away the most popular; as Vadim told me, "everyone loves Verka, straights and gays" ("*i natural'nye, i golubye*"). Serdiuchka, according to one source, commanded up to fifty-thousand Euros per performance,[39] was a frequent hostess of television music shows (for example, the *Zolotoi grammofon*), and was so marketable a commodity as to have been able to pitch Tide laundry detergent on national television.[40]

This popularity was underscored on New Year's Eve 2004 when, following the address of President Putin (occupying practically every station on Russian television), his speech imbued with optimism in the face of some of the most horrible tragedies in recent Russian history the preceding year,[41] at the stroke of midnight *MuzTV* played their first video of 2005: Verka Sediuchka's "*Khorosho*" ("It's Good"). The song's lyrics, reiterating over the course of three verses a rather simple "make the best of it" philosophy (if you miss your train, wait for the next one; if you have a hangover, get together with friends and drink some more; if you're unlucky in love, then also go out on the town and drink with your friends), the optimism of the text matched by the up-tempo, brass-band–laden arrangement of the song, was a hopeful tonic against the very bitter realities of 2004.

The video to the song, as is often typical of Serdiuchka's style, incorporates elements of Ukrainian (and sometimes Russian) culture[42] in a tongue-in-cheek, almost kitsch manner; indeed, may of my informants used just this word ("*kitch*") to describe Serdiuchka's overall aesthetic. Verka (a diminutive form of the name Vera) and female friend, glamorously decked out for the evening (Verka in a blood-red, sequined dress—tight over her extremely ample bosom—long fur coat, and high-heeled silver sandals, and sporting a fetching, 1920s-era pageboy) are shown being brought into jail, Serdiuchka protesting with vigor. After assaulting her captor, both women are thrown into the slammer, the cell filled with the detritus of society: elderly vagrants, pot-smoking youths, low-budget prostitutes, musicians. True to the spirit of the song, Serdiuchka makes lemonade from her situation: opening her coat to reveal a secret cache of vodka, sausages, and *solen'e* (pickled foods), she invites everyone to eat and sing until the cell erupts in raucous merriment, the decibel level of which alerts the guards outside. Seeing a poster on the wall advertising the show of Andrei Danilko as Serdiuchka, the guards open the door and become part of the festivities. Her arms wrapped around the two of them, Serdiuchka sways and sings with the men, ultimately taking up an electric guitar, yelling, "come on, Rammstein!" in reference to the German, heavy metal band, imitating a "slashing" style of playing in accordance with the electric guitar heard in the song. All are caught up in the alcohol-laden revelry of the moment, singing, laughing, dancing, as Serdiuchka boozily makes her way to the cell door and—teetering a bit—exits, ultimately leaving the jail, her attractive female friend assisting her unsteady gait, their drunken singing fading into the night. Other videos show Serdiuchka in much more familial settings, eating with her rural, Ukrainian relatives—the stock and site from which she came—often wearing a tight-fitting cloche with a large, Soviet star perched atop it, oversized gradient sunglasses (similar to those popular in Miami Beach in the 1980s), and voluminous floor-length dresses that distinguish her fashion sense as one to which the words "bad taste" could easily be applied.

Several of my informants were quick not only to point out Verka's wide-ranging popularity but also to distinguish between Danilko and Serdiuchka;

for example, both Vadim and Konstantin told me that the two were "completely different people" ("*sovsem drugie liudi*"). The cognitive separation of the transvestite from the "natural," and the creation of two separate personae from one person, is perhaps what allows Serdiuchka/Danilko to operate not only with impunity, but also with great success, within a homophobic site. Serdiuchka herself is ostensibly heterosexual, as is evidenced in both her video for "*Ia popala na liubov*'" ("I Fell in Love") and even in her advertising appearances,[43] although she does have a playful penchant for squeezing or patting the breasts and buttocks of the women in her entourage.[44] But while Danilko himself has been spared some of the harsher excoriations that have greeted Moiseev or Leont'ev, questions about his sexual orientation have still surfaced, albeit a bit more elliptically. For example, a headline in *Dni* proclaimed "*Serdiuchka poteriala orientatsiiu*" ("Serdiuchka Lost Her Orientation"), clearly suggesting sexual orientation but, in fact, telling of the singer's having gotten lost after a birthday celebration.[45] Similarly, an interviewer in *Rossiskaia gazeta* (Al'perina 2004) asked for Danilko's comments, in response to those by Moscow critics who consider Verka and her songs, "not high art, parody, but . . . a real auntie" ("*ne vysokoe iskusstvo, parodiia, vot vyshla prostaia tetka*")—the word *auntie* (*tetka*) a common, and in some contexts derisive, word for homosexual. Danilko has been (almost assuredly) falsely linked romantically to performer Aleksandr Peskov, who characterizes their relationship as simply friendship, (Artem 2004), but Danilko himself notes that he has a "warm, friendly relationship" with Filipp Kirkorov, another singer—and ex-husband of Alla Pugacheva—widely assumed to be homosexual (Granishevskaia 2005).[46] Danilko's responses to direct questions about his personal, romantic life, are also often marked by an equivocation; asked once why he didn't have a girlfriend, he responded that he had had an eight-year relationship living with a woman, one he characterized as a "heavy experience" ("*tiazhelyi opyt*"), the breakup being the catalyst for increased artistic production[47] or, in another interview, that he simply didn't have any place to meet—although he does not use the word—women ("*mne vot negde znakomitsia*") ("*Andrei Danilko: Kakaia*). Queried about his taste in women, Danilko offered that "I've never had a specific type [*obraz*; literally, form]. All the relationships which I've had, and there haven't been many, started with friendship and kind feelings [*simpatiia*]. To me it's all the same if she's in jeans or in a skirt." And asked what it is about a woman that first attracts him, the singer initially offers that "there's first a general assessment," but he progresses quickly to a discussion of why he hates weddings ("Beginning with mama, who's crying. . . . Finally, someone took your cuttlefish [*karakatitsu*]![48] Papa has to get drunk, because he gave away his daughter. Some sort of amusing theater.") ("*Andrei Danilko: Kakaia*"). Such responses, connections to other men perceived to be homosexual, a career made as a drag artist, and videos frequently featuring beautiful men in abbreviated clothing (see Chapter 4) have all contributed to a general questioning of Danilko's sexual orientation, not only by my informants (many of whom assumed he was homosexual), but in the press and on the internet as well. In one internet forum, in response to a user's question as to whether or not Serdiuchka is gay, although the majority of respondents offer their opinions that he is not, several others respond in the affirmative—one defining Danilko as "100% faggot" ("*pidar*").[49]

Music(s), Text(s), Sex(es)

It is not only the singers' personal lives, as revealed (or concealed) in the (often yellow) press, or their physical appearances that index homosexuality, but the lyrics of several of their songs as well. Here, however, the ways in which each singer's texts reference male-male sexuality are quite different, either effacing or foregrounding physicality: while Leont'ev's implicitly or explicitly highlight the corporeal, almost carnal component of sexual relations, and Danilko/Serdiuchka's point to a (physical) "polymorphous perversity," Moiseev's place sexuality in the sphere of the soul or spirit. Such a view of homosexuality is in line with that of Russian philosopher Vasilii Rozanov, who used the term *spiritual homosexual* to describe those people whose primary attractions were to those of the same sex, but for whom the carnal was sublimated.[50] Although Moiseev did not write the texts to either of the songs I discuss, his personal views about love/sex, at least as expressed in one press account, seem largely to comport with the idea(l) posited by Rozanov. Discussing his "first love," Moiseev is quoted as saying:

> I fell wildly in love with Ivars, a Latvian. A romantic with huge eyes, pure and beautiful. I remember our first sex. It was not physical, but rather spiritual. It was an undressing (*razdevanie*) and a rape of the soul, but not the body. ("*Boris Moiseev: Biografiia*")

The night of the aforementioned Moiseev concert, the symbols of "love" were foregrounded throughout, culminating in an encore during which the star and company paraded around the stage carrying white flags, each of which bore a heart, striped in the three colors—white, blue, and red—of the Russian flag. Love was aloft not only in these billowing flags, but also in the words blaring from the loudspeakers, the lyrics to "*Golubaia zvezda*" ("Blue [Gay] Star"). The song, originally released the same year of the concert, tells of a great love, one emanating from the sky, and has definite connotations of homosexuality, but this was not the first of Moiseev's songs to broach the topic; rather, it was "*Golubaia luna*" ("Blue [Gay] Moon"), released in

1994 and one of the singer's largest hits, that had earlier served as a way of introducing the subject of gay love—albeit somewhat equivocally—to millions of Russians, via sound and sight, via television and radio. The narrative is presented as a "legend" or "fairy tale" concerning two brothers, one (the younger) who fell in love with a queen, and gave his heart "in the shadows of the forest"; the elder brother, one who would "never conquer the hearts of brides," however, chose "miraculously, the loneliness of the skies." The text of the chorus, which appears three times (once in an abbreviated form), explains that the blue (gay) moon is responsible for the "strange" ("*strannyi*") love of the elder brother, one for which he would never be forgiven ("*tak emu i ne prosily*").

As noted previously, the adjective *goluboi* (literally, light blue) functions as slang for gay men in Russia, and is widely understood to have such connotations; it is not arcane, subcultural argot whose meaning is lost on the broader culture. This is not to say that the meaning is unambiguous, that it does not allow for subjective interpretation; had the intent been a foreclosure upon polysemic apprehension, certainly the text could have used the words *gei* or even the somewhat archaic *gomoseksualist*. But while Moiseev's song (with text by Nikolai Trubach, who does the majority of the singing on the recording, as well as contributing a trumpet solo)[51] abjures literalness, the ways in which homosexuality is presented and situated construct it as something at odds with the vulgarity of the quotidian, with *byt*.[52] In the first place, by relating the story as a "legend"—a narrative form that often focuses on universal, transcendental issues (good versus evil, the redemptive powers of love, and so forth)—Moiseev makes it timeless; homosexuality is presented as something that is without temporal situation, something that existed in ages past, exists in the present, will exist in the future. But while the legend-like, atemporal quality of the words on the one hand defy a literal, temporal definition, on the other they imply an ancientness through the conflation of fairy tales with the anterior ("once upon a time"); so the unnamed focus of the text (read: homosexuality) is, far from a contemporary aberration—"a vice of the ruling class," "a symptom of the ills wrought by modernization," "an imported evil from the West," what have you—something with its basis in the faraway past.[53]

The text also characterizes the love of the older, *goluboi* brother as related to the sky, to immaterial space, while the younger's is rooted on the earth (the forest); there is a suggestion here of body/materiality versus soul/intangibility, an almost Dionysian/Apollonian split between the younger brother's love of a woman and the elder's love that surpasses corporeality. However, by enlisting the image of the moon, the natural world is not entirely renounced for disembodied spirit; rather, by making the moon the object of the giver and receiver of love, Moiseev's song places homosexuality in the realm of "nature." As such, it is something beyond reproach, not "mere culture," but "physical fact."[54] It is also notable that the lyrics portray the older brother, not the younger, as *goluboi*, thus liberating the idea of homosexuality from a system in which one's age bears upon one's sexual position—that is, the idea of the acceptability of homosexuality when contained within a structure wherein the older partner retains heterosexual cachet by being the "dominant," insertive partner to the "submissive," passive, younger man. It is not the age of the one brother vis-à-vis the other that is important; rather, the fact that one person in the story is coded as "older" (dominant), and that this person is also the one who is *goluboi*, removes the strictures of age and status from the act of homosexual love, thus once again placing it beyond the reach of social structure.

The final verse, perhaps the most cryptic, references a "duel for life and honor" between the younger brother and an unnamed combatant, but the elder takes the sword, saying:

Chest' moia—moia lish' chest'	The honor is mine—only mine is the honor
Ty liubi i bud' liubimym	You, love and be loved
I bud' schastliv, brat	And be happy, brother
Ia teriaiu vse, no ty teriaesh' bol'she	I am losing everything, but you are losing more

What, specifically, the elder believes the younger to be at risk of losing is not named; however, it is apparent that the younger brother's loss is even greater than the elder's repudiation of "everything." Here, the lyrics suggest, in the context of what has come previously, that while the elder has renounced all that is socially sanctioned, all that is related to the mundane, the world of *byt*, the younger, by remaining mired in the realm of the literal, constrained by the vulgarity of the physical, the political, the social, has lost even more; in Barthesian terms, it may be akin to the abnegation of *plasir* in favor of the ineffable *joissance*.

The text of "*Golubaia zvezda*" appears, in part, as both literary and commercial successor to the tale of the two brothers; it seems in fact likely that Moiseev may have tried to re-create the formula for success that had worked so successfully in the past. The text of the second song indeed references the first from the outset ("you may remember . . . the story of two brothers"), continuing with another tale of two people—this time, "princesses." The song's lyrics makes use of many of the tropes of the first: *goluboi* love as something mysterious, but natural, something that touches one but not the other sibling, something that comes from above (perhaps indicating heaven), something that is light, thus indicating visibility as opposed to darkness, secrecy, hiddenness (in direct contrast to the status of homosexuality in the quotidian realm). One of the main differences here, however, is in the gender of the characters; it is possible to imagine that if the first song was marketed to gay men, then this was Moiseev's attempt to cash in on the other half of "the gay audience"—or, less cynically, that he wanted to give equal time, visibility, and voice to lesbian women. However, the adjective *goluboi* is not used in Russian to indicate lesbians; rather, it is the stereotypical "girl's" color of pink—*rozovyi*, in its uninflected form, but *rozovaia* when referring to a feminine noun—that, as previously noted, is slang for lesbian. It is not inconceivable that Moiseev's lyricist[55] could have chosen to title the song "*Rozovaia luna*," as even the syllable count (although not the syllable stress) would have fit with the melody used.

There are numerous possible reasons to explain why the text stands as it does. Perhaps it is, as suggested earlier, simple venality, a desire to rope in the public with the tried/tired and true, the assumption being that "*golubaia*" will ring a bell that "*rozovaia*," sonically, will not. Perhaps there is something subversive, whereby the coding of male homosexuals, *golubye*, as female characters, transgresses gender norms. Or perhaps it is the opposite, an exploitation of stereotypes, so that the "princesses" are actually gay men, this in keeping with the use (often by gay men themselves) of feminine pronouns and inflections when referencing other homosexual men. Finally, it may even be an appeal to the conservative, wherein the two protagonists of the second are somehow—by whatever stretch of the listener's imagination—seen as the dates for the brothers in the first song. Ultimately, the answer is unknowable; the stress, however, is again the centering of an "elevated," spiritual homosexuality, albeit somewhat elliptically, within the Russian popular music landscape. In this instance, owing to the currency of the word *goluboi*, Moiseev's avowed homosexuality, and his roiling of gender norms, it would seem that any preteritions surrounding the texts could only be supported by the most intricate webs of denial possible.

What should not be overlooked in this focus on the lyrics, however, is the music to which they are indissolubly connected. It is notable that, although Moiseev's music makes use of current digital recording gear and instruments such as sequencers, synthesizers, multitracking, effects (including chorusers, flangers, reverb, and so forth), often attempting to approximate a "modern sound," in many cases its sonic attributes are, conversely, stereotypically Russian (or Soviet) due to its adherence to those stylistic markers discussed in Chapter 2. For example, the choruses of both songs discussed above, as well as numerous others in Moiseev's repertoire, feature prominent sequences (Examples 3.1 and 3.2).

Example 3.1. "*Golubaia luna*"—vocal line, chorus.

Example 3.2. "*Golubaia zvezda*"—vocal line, chorus.

The harmonic language of "*Golubaia luna*" is somewhat atypical in terms of the formal attributes discussed previously; here, the verses are in B♭ major, with the choruses in the relative minor. However, the melodic sequence appears over a harmonic progression in the chorus that hints at a circle of fifths progression, but does not complete it: G minor—B♭ major—F major—the beginning of the circle—but then a quick cadence on G minor. And in "*Golubaia zvezda*," the harmonic progression over which the sequences appear is identical to the type discussed in Chapter 2 (Example 3.3):

Example 3.3. "*Golubaia zvezda*"—harmonic progression, chorus

dm	gm	CM	FM	B♭	gm	AM
i	iv	VII	III	VI	iv	I
		V of III	V of VI			

Like those of Moiseev, the lyrics of several of Leont'ev's songs allude to homosexuality in, variously, more or less oblique fashions.[56] I first encountered the following song—"*Kazhdyi khochet liubit'*" ("Each Wants to Love")—at *Kabare*, a gay disco in St. Petersburg. While the men on the crowded dance floor moved and sang along to the obviously well-known tune, Alik, who had accompanied me that evening, turned to me and advised, "this is a perfect song for your research; this is an old, gay Soviet singer." The lyrics suggest, if not love, then a sexual tension (and perhaps consummation) between two men, a Yugoslavian soldier and an English sailor. The "enemies," are waiting on a bridge for the same woman (a "sharp-eyed [*bystroglazuiu*] seamstress"), but as the clouds and darkness descend, and it becomes clear that the female object of their affection has stood both of them up, they begin to look at one another with some sort of tenderness ("as if he were a close friend," "as if they had known each other for a long time"). They ultimately wind up in a bar, loud music blaring, where

Pili ognenyi spirt i zapenenyi kvas	They were drinking fiery spirits and foamy kvas[57]
I drug drugu skvoz' dym posylali ulybki	And they were sending smiles to each other through the smoke
I krichali oni, ponimaia drug druga	And they were screaming, understanding each other
Iugoslavskii soldat i angliiskii matros	The Yugoslavian solder and the English sailor

While there is no use of romantic language or tropes, or mention of the type of physical contact one might expect to find in a "heterosexual" love song—touching hands, kissing, heads on shoulders—there is, nonetheless a suggested intimacy and carnality, which might lead to physical contact after the narrative of the text has finished; the smiling at each other, understanding, even screaming—all contribute to an illustration of gay cruising, as intelligible a portrait to its specific audience as any of the tropes used in the reproduction of heterosexual courting in popular music.

A hedonistic and carnal sort of love is central to the text of another of Leont'ev's songs with overtones of homosexuality, "*Greshniki*" ("Sinners"). Here, the focus on the joys of physical intimacy "without exception, for all," the repudiation of the church's moralistic and hypocritical teachings ("fanatic of faith ... do not rush to count the sins of others before your own"), the appellation "sons of one earth" ("*synov'ia odnoi zemlia*") and the very use of the word *greshniki* all contribute to making the text relevant to the position of homosexual men in contemporary Russian society. By constructing a bifurcation of sinner/nonsinner (the church), the narrative also alludes to and critiques the contemporary sociopolitical landscape, specifically the Russian Orthodox Church's alliance with and constant iteration of the government's desire to return the country to a more conservative, "morally" upright position, including a stance against homosexuality; indeed, in my interview with Igor' Kon, he stressed that his greatest pessimism regarding the possibility of a "gay community" being formed in Russia was due to what he saw as the stranglehold of the church on the country's "morals."[58] Furthermore, by reappropriating the language of the oppressor—celebrating one's self as a "sinner," recasting it as a positive term—and contextualizing this status as one that links to similar others ("to me, each sinner is a friend and brother, every sinner is a sister"), the text evokes or invokes the tactics and dynamics of international, or Western gays, those who have likewise often attempted to render epithets impotent through reappropriation ("queer," "faggot," "dyke"), and who define themselves as part of a community.[59] That the word "equality" is used not only in the first line of the song ("*Ia pesniu ravenstva poiu*," "I sing a song of equality"), but in each chorus ("*my greshniki, my vse ravny*," "we're sinners, we're all equal") is a further indication that the text aligns with international/Western discourses of gay identity that are defined, in part, not only via political/juridical status, but by their very visibility as embodied subjects. However, the text should not be read as a complementary, parallel expression of LGBT subjectivity, identical to Western texts, insofar as religious/spiritual imagery, rather than the state political/juridical apparatus, is invoked in the service of ultimate justification ("*Edinstvennyi khoziain tvoi—lish' Bog liubvi*," "Your one master is only the God of love"). Moreover, the repeated appellation "sons of one earth" ("*synov'ia odnoi zemlia*") to describe the "sinner" highlights the extent to which the idea of nature is instrumental in defining Russian homosexuality.

It is also possible to situate these two songs in a specifically Russian context by making the connection between their texts and what were, in the first decade of the century, the two largest gay clubs in St. Petersburg: in the first instance, the *matros* (sailor) in "*Kazhdyi khochet*" can be related to the club *Kabare*, the place where I first heard the song, owing to the fact that the establishment's alternate name is *Matrosskaia tishina* (Sailors' Silence).[60] In the second, the connection is self-evident—the name of the song, *Greshniki* (Sinners), is the same name as the club. Insofar as Leont'ev's song "*Greshniki*" was released the year before the club opened in 2000, it is nearly impossible that the singer took the title from the establishment (unless he had had foreknowledge of the club's opening). However, *Kabare/Matrosskaia tishina*, open since 1997, could surely have been known to the singer. But what is important here is not so much causality as connection; that is, it is equally important that a gay disco would have taken the name of the song from Leont'ev's song, as the reverse, or that such tropes—sailors, sinners—are common enough to be used for both appellations of gay clubs, as well as in service of suggesting homosexuality in popular music. In both instances, Leont'ev's songs are linked to physical sites of male homosexuality, sites where embodied subjects congregate, and it is very possible that such links were deduced by gay men.

A connection may be drawn between songs of both Moiseev and Leont'ev, not only insofar as they have both chosen textual material with gay subtexts,

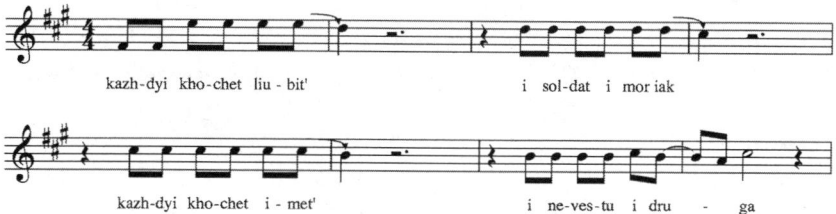

Example 3.4. "*Kazhdyi khochet liubit'*"—vocal line, chorus.

Example 3.5. "*Kazhdyi khochet liubit'*"—harmonic progression, chorus

bm	EM	AM	DM	bm	C♯M	f♯m	F♯M*
iv	VII	III	VI	iv	V	i	[I]
	V of III	V of VI					V of iv
bm	EM	AM	DM	bm	C♯M	f♯m	C♯M
iv	VII	III	VI	iv	V	i	V
	V of III	V of VI					

* The use of the major tonic (in the minor scale) as a dominant of the minor subdominant is another somewhat common harmonic characteristic in Russian pop. See, for example, Examples 2.1 and 2.3 in chapter 2 as well as Korni's "*S dnem rozhdeniia, Vika*" ("Happy Birthday, Vika").

but also owing to the use of music that uses some of the most stereotypical stylistic elements in Russian music—again, melodic sequences and chord progressions making use of secondary dominants and the circle of fifths. Leont'ev's "*Kazhdyi khochet liubit'*" is but one example of such songs in the singer's repertoire (Examples 3.4 and 3.5). Like Moiseev, he presents "nontraditional sexuality" in the context of "traditional" sound.

In terms of textual allusions to homosexuality, Andrei Danilko as Verka Serdiuchka occupies a position related to but different from those of either Moiseev or Leont'ev, insofar as his performances, texts, and music comprise two subjectivities; not a (possibly) gay man singing as a (possibly) gay man, but a (possibly) gay man singing as a heterosexual (possibly bisexual) woman. Danilko/Serdiuchka, although they are "completely different people," each bear the trace of the other; Serdiuchka comprises Danilko, and vice versa. So while Serdiuchka's references to her female beauty, or her expressed amorous longings for men[61] may be read as heterosexual in character (she has both the appropriate gender attributes and love objects), Serdiuchka cannot be present without the body of Danilko—and a man attired as a woman, singing of "his" feminine beauty and love for (other) men almost certainly troubles a simple ascription of heterosexuality to a "woman," prodigious bosom and all, who is not biologically female. Serdiuchka, in fact, troubles any number of binaries in her performances, the video for the song "*Chita-drita*" standing as an example. Here, the rural and the urban, the archaic and the modern, the Soviet and post-Soviet all commingle. Serdiuchka is shown at her *dacha*, among her friends and family: mother, the (comic) picture of the rural Ukrainian of the twentieth century, woolen headscarf, cane, and track shoes;[62] an aunt (and several young, female children) dressed in traditional Ukrainian costume; men in traditional Ukrainian shirts (*vishivanki*), some wearing suit jackets on top; three "dancing girls" dressed in stylized, Soviet-era outfits consisting of flowered dresses and matching headscarves; and three contemporary "club" types (two women, one man) with sunglasses, furs, knit cloche caps, and various hip accessories. Verka herself is resplendent in what was probably her most famous outfit of the time: a tight, blue headpiece with massive pink flower atop; her signature large, gradient sunglasses; and, first, a sequined dress with large flowers embroidered on the copious bosom, and long, brown fur coat and, later, a floor-length blue satin dress (again with the embroidery on the chest), the fur coat now white with (again) floral embroidery, floor-length like the dress. As she dances and hikes her skirts, the viewer can also see her opaque white hose and silver, high-heeled sandals. That Danilko's presentation of Verka over the years has moved from a rather low-rent version of drag (a cheap hat or hastily applied, parodic makeup) to the sort of comically glamorous visage on display in "*Chita-drita*"—one that clearly exhibits, at least in part, the desire to invoke the female/feminine with greater verisimilitude—moves him farther away *from* the comic visage of the visible male in obvious drag *lampooning* woman/femininity[63] and closer to a man who embraces this stance with both humor and affection.

It is not only this sartorial/corporeal roiling of the boundaries between masculine/feminine, male/female that suggest a nontraditional orientation, however, as references to homosexuality may be found in Serdiuchka's lyrics—references that are, in many ways, more explicit than those found in either Moiseev's or Leont'ev's texts. The song "*Devochki*" ("Girls"), for example, begins innocuously enough, chastising love for not coming when called, but appearing when least expected ("*a tut prikhodish' noch'iu bez zvonka*," "and then you come in the night without a phone call"). In the chorus, however, in the context of an imperative ("girls, love boys; boys, love girls"),[64] such unexpected ("*nezhdannaia*") love is seen as bringing happiness ("*i budet vse v vashei zhizni khorosho*," "and everything in your life will be good"). Love is not, however, restricted to those pairings via which procreation may occur, as the chorus continues

Mal'chiki, liubite mal'chikov	Boys, love boys
Devochki, liubite devochek	Girls, love girls
Ved' liubov'—ona prokaznitsa	You see, love is a mischief-maker
Vliubliaet to, chto poroi liubit' nel'zia	We sometimes fall in love with the one we shouldn't

The difference here is clear: loving the correctly gendered/sexed/genitalled object is presented as bringing abundant goodness to one's life, while loving one's own sex/gender is the result of a cupid-prankster, something that one "shouldn't" do. The latter reads as a dalliance—"it happened"—the former, a proper choice. Fine; but Serdiuchka does not leave it at that. For as the chorus reappears, four additional times in all, she reassembles the pieces so that by the second and third instances, love is still playing tricks on the same-sex couples (*"ved' liubov,' ona prokaznitsa"*), but now everything in *their* lives will be good as well (*"I budet vse v vashei zhizni khorosho"*). By the final chorus, however, love is no longer playing tricks even on them—just like their heterosexual counterparts, love will come to them unexpectedly (*"nezhdannaia"*), but they'll be entirely happy; the heterosexuals, however, although they will be happy, are now the victims of love's pranks. What begins as a seminormative, semimoralistic imperative is, by the end of the song, de- and reconstructed so that all pairings, regardless of sex or gender, may be the outcome of an impish jokester, but everyone will be happy.[65] And although the song makes much use of the stylistic attributes of 1970s disco—"scratch" rhythm guitar, four-on-the-floor beat, hooks supplied by string sections—it is also, like many of the songs of Leont'ev and Moiseev, harmonically and melodically closely aligned with the most common stylistic attributes found in Russian popular musics. The instrumental introduction of the song, for example, makes use of a modified circle of fifths progression, underlying a melodic sequence in the hornlike synthesizer melody.[66]

As I have suggested, lyrics cannot be "analyzed" without cognizance of the specifically musical forms to which they are connected. For example, Daughtry (2003), in his examination of changes in Russia's national anthem, finds attention to both music and lyrics necessary in order to ascertain the power of the piece. Noting the surrounding controversy, he explains that the original, Stalin-supported "Unbreakable Union" of 1944 (with music by Aleksandrov) was, after the leader's death in 1953, stripped of its words (which had lauded the then-denounced dictator), receiving a new text only in 1977. This new text was expurgated of references to Stalin, highlighting Lenin instead. In 1990, however, under the leadership of then-President Boris El'tsin, a new anthem was chosen, one that comprised both new lyrics and new music; while the latter was supplied by Glinka (and entitled "Patriotic Union"), it took nearly a decade for a suitable text to be found. Shortly afterward, however, in 2000, President Vladimir Putin revived the original Aleksandrov melody, but a new text was added, and Russia's national anthem became "Russia, Our Holy Power." What is key here, however, is indeed the power of melody, of music, to signify, to affect; as Daughtry notes, the resuscitation of the Stalin-era melody engendered a bitter response by segments of the Russian population (largely liberals and the intelligentsia). Quoting one columnist as remarking "no new text can erase the words that are firmly attached to Aleksandrov's music" (57), he continues that "once signification has been attached to a melody, it cannot be removed completely or with ease" (58). It should be clear that verbal expressions of homosexuality in the three aforementioned singers' repertoires cannot be cleft from the harmonic and melodic structures through and in which they are uttered.

Moreover, texts are given life and meaning not only by their connections to musical sounds and structures, but also by their having been sung, uttered, by a specific performer in a specific time and place. When Brian Molko of Placebo sings Kate Bush's "Running Up That Hill"—or Sid Vicious sings Frank Sinatra's "My Way"—the lyrics, still carrying their earlier meanings and connotations (as a result of their associations with both people and histories), are unquestionably layered with new significance, not only from their connections to new musical arrangements, but to new embodied subjects as well. The lyrics of a Boris Moiseev, or Valerii Leont'ev, or Verka Serdiuchka song, absent their connections to these specific artists, existing as "disembodied" texts only, might certainly be read as implying nothing whatsoever about homosexuality. Indeed, the composer of the music for "*Kazhdyi khochet liubit,*" Vladimir Evzerov, has denied that the lyrics reference a homosexual relationship between the two men; rather, the text—written by Russian military officer and poet Arsenii Nesmelov (1889–1945)—was based on a supposedly true story concerning a girl who had fallen in love with two men (the soldier and the sailor), "and when she reciprocated both of them, they spat at her, hugged, and went to the pub to drink and wink at each other" (Guru Ken 2005).[67] Similarly, Nikolai Trubach, author of the text for Moiseev's "*Golubaia luna,*" (somewhat incredibly) denies any imputation of homosexuality vis-à-vis either his lyrics, or the lyrics' relationship to Moiseev.[68] But an analysis only of "the object (text) itself" deals not only with an abstraction, but is an abstraction itself; it supposes an ability to comprehend, to make sense, outside of lived, contextualized experience.

Rather than abstractions, the texts of these songs must be considered not only in "dialogic" relationships with other surrounding texts[69]—those of journalists, or even unwritten, oral "social texts"—but as constituent parts of entire *Gestalten*, the lyrics linking to and indexing texts, sights, discourses, bodies, and sounds, embedded within a complex whole, the specific parts of which cannot exist as meaningful absent this situatedness. Additionally, *Gestalten* are implicated not only in terms of how "things" come to light in (viewed) perception—figures against grounds—but also in the very stance, the corporeality, of the perceiving subject. As Lingis (1998) maintains, our lives as embodied beings are guided by imperatives that emanate from those things—including other living beings—around us, so that *Gestalten* encompass not only the "postural schema," "a dynamic Gestalt that distributes the positions of our limbs, regulates the orientation of our forces . . . induced by a movement oriented toward a thing or a layout of things as toward a task," but additionally our relations to others, whereby "the sight of another person calls up within us the corresponding postural diagram that would position us in the form we see the other maintaining . . . ; each shift in posture means for us another set of faces the things turn to us" (59–60). Moreover, there is a potentiality that exceeds the literal in each response to an object; the body does not relate simply to (and is not simply) a fact in a moment, but "put[s] up a host of intentions which run from the body as the centre of potential action either towards the body itself or towards the object" in response to either movement or touch (Merleau-Ponty 2002 [1962]: 125).

Thus listening, for example, to "*Golubaia zvezda*," whether on the radio or at a Moiseev concert, what is heard, and that to which the body responds, is not simply *a* text, the "universal meaning" of which is utterable by any random agent, but *that* text sung by *that* singer in *that* social context. "*Golubiaia zvezda*" is part of an entire *Gestalt* encompassing articles in the *zheltaia pressa*, Moiseev's talk show appearances, his bleached-blond hair, his lisp, his lacy blouses and made-up face, his name as the punch line of any number of jokes, and—not at all incidentally—the stylistic conventions of the music. The listener's posture, his or her corporeal stance, when confronted with a Moiseev or Leont'ev or Serdiuchka song, is a posture in response not only to the singer him/herself but, as discussed in the previous chapter, an embodied knowledge of and relation to the very structure of the music. Moreover, the relationship to this (Russian) music, part of one's corporeal history since childhood, may be contrasted with the relationship to that (Western) music, part of one's history-in-progress; one is situated thus concurrently in relationship to home and the outside, understanding yet again that the traditional sound of the music is the very vehicle for the text in which homosexuality is at the very least adumbrated.

Such somatic stances and actions might be experienced as subtle corporeal feelings, imperceptible to others, but might also be manifest in such a way as to be gloriously visible to an entire room of people. For example, while at any number of gay clubs in St. Petersburg or Moscow, the playing of a song by Serdiuchka would very often engender a change in the movements and postures of the men on the dance floor; whereas they might have been moments ago moving to a house or disco beat, hips, shoulders, necks, legs gyrating, with the sonic appearance of "*Chita-drita*" or "*Khorosho*" (and the appearance, in consciousness, of the image of Verka herself),[70] these same men might link arms with each other, dance in a circle, and/or move their bodies up and down by alternately bending and extending their knees, all in an approximation of a type of "Slavic folk dancing." This was not, however, simply a corporeal reaction to and embodiment of "Slavic folk customs" via the stylistic conventions of the music but, rather, an embodied relationship to "the Slavic" as exemplified via Serdiuchka, part of an entire, motile *Gestalt* in which either Danilko or Serdiuchka might be foregrounded or backgrounded, in which the variable of homosexuality played a defining role. Whether for the dancer as part of the social group, the member of the audience in St. Petersburg's *Oktiabr'skii* concert hall, or the solitary listener at home in his/her kitchen, understandings of and relationships to popular songs depend not only upon texts, but upon texts embedded within complex *Gestalten*, and the somatic responses to the embodied subjects from whom such texts emanate.

Russian "Masculinity"

Despite the desire of the revolutionary reformers to liberate citizens from the shackles of an oppressive and unequal system of gender roles, one rooted in the "premodern" and "irrational" tenets of both peasant society and religion, it is in fact a rigid adherence to stereotypical gender roles that marked the majority of the Soviet period, and continues in the post-Soviet era as well. In this system, masculinity is indissolubly linked to the male and femininity to the female, and often rationalized via recourse to biological arguments of the putative inherent natures of the sexes. While notions of what constitutes masculinity or femininity have not been entirely static over the past two centuries, especially in the context of a move from an agrarian-based to an industrial society, as well as intercourse with the West,[71] contemporary Russian society—including such large, urban, "modern" sites as St. Petersburg and Moscow—is remarkable for the ways in which traditional notions of gender inform people's attitudes and behaviors. Such adherence to stereotypical gender roles does not, however, indicate only a simple continuation of anterior traditions but also a response to contemporary contexts. Relating these constructions to a nationalist agenda, Beaudoin, for example, finds that "men are expected to fulfill their masculine roles in service to the country, and women—their feminine roles, especially in the realm of reproduction" (2006: 228).[72]

There are, however, differences between the ways gender was and is lived and experienced in the Soviet and post-Soviet eras. In the former, the appellation "socialism in one gender" did not indicate an integration of the masculine and feminine (or disposal of both, in favor of an entirely new conception) but, rather, a default to the masculine. Women were "liberated" to the role of workers (resulting in what many saw as the "double burden"[73] of responsibility for both wage earning and the domestic sphere, the latter of which was still considered decidedly feminine), becoming good "comrades" working for the Soviet future; yet Lissyutkina suggests that many felt that such "emancipation" was more a compulsion, a means of enlisting the "entire population for cheap labor for the realization of the senseless utopian project of rebuilding society and conquering and exploiting nature" (1993: 275), and wrested from them their very (female) corporeality, precluding their femininity.[74] Funk (1993) highlights the post-Soviet embracing of what might be considered in the West stereotypical gender roles, noting that "in several countries [of the former Eastern bloc] . . . one response to state socialist conditions for women has been a strong essentialism: a position that women are, by nature, different from men, a difference the previous system failed to acknowledge" (6).

Men, while physically inhabiting the bodies with which masculinity might be aligned, however, also experienced gender-related difficulties in the Soviet system. While their corporeality marked them as the (potential) biological holders of masculine power, Kon, for example, suggests that "If you believe that which we write about ourselves, in Russia there are not, were not, and cannot be 'real men'" (2001b), noting:

> The economic ineffectiveness of the Soviet system, in combination with political despotism and the bureaucratization of social life left few places for individual initiative and independence. In order to gain economic and social success, it was necessary to be not daring, but sly, not proud but servile, not independent, but conforming. From early childhood to death itself, the Soviet man felt socially and sexually dependent and constrained. (2001b)

As Kon also highlights, many of the earliest authority figures encountered by children in official, social institutions, were women—for example, in schools, where teachers were overwhelmingly female, or in *komsomol* or *pioner* organizations (where three-quarters of secretaries would have been female).[75] Only informal groups offered a milieu of nearly exclusive symbols of masculinity, and such groups were often defined by an overriding sense of misogyny. Additionally, that the home remained the domain of women—women who were wage earners in the public sphere, thus further eroding patriarchal power—indicated that not only in the realm of the public, but also of the private, men's traditional roles were largely destabilized.

This erosion of male power in the Soviet Union was often compensated for in three ways, according to Kon: first, an identification with a traditional (stereotypical) form of aggressive masculinity; second, a hypercompensatory male tyranny in relation to family life, directed toward both wife and children; and third, a retreat by men from adult social and familial responsibilities (2001b).[76] The contradictions inherent in these conceptualizations—a social hypertrophy of the symbolically masculine image, in a system that eroded the ability to act accordingly, and an enervation of male responsibility within the domestic sphere, countered with both a) patriarchal tyranny on the one hand, and b) an abdication of familial responsibility on the other—made and still make for an ultimately rickety foundation for one's formation of a gendered self and often begets an overreliance on one-dimensional stereotypes. As Kay (2006) notes in her study of post-Soviet men, a corrective of the "overemancipation" of Soviet women and the "poisoning" of Soviet men is often figured in post-Soviet Russia as a need for the return to traditional gender roles—men as breadwinners, reclaiming the public sphere, and women's concomitant retreat to the home.

The enactment of a compensatory hypermasculinity, however, is not related exclusively to men's relation to women; Pilkington, for example, found that an aggressive, often violent masculinity, in relation to skinhead groups in contemporary Russia, was often articulated "through a politics of racial, ethnic, spatial and sexual superiority whose targets are depressingly familiar: 'black scum,' 'dirty hippies,' 'hen-pecked' husbands and gay men" (1996: 257). While not suggesting that large numbers of Russian men hold the execrable, xenophobic views of such neo-Fascists, it is this last group—gay men—that has, in fact, figured as target for extreme enmity in contemporary Russia, from both men and women. And the basis for this odium is exactly the same basis on which all three of the singers previously discussed have been identified as homosexual: that is, male homosexuality is viewed as a repudiation, by the male, of the masculine, and a concomitant embracing of the feminine, an alignment of biological sex with the incorrect gender attributes.[77] Moiseev's and Leont'ev's attire, their makeup and hairstyles, their focus on the "lyric" (rather than the "civic") and on love and intimacy in their musical repertoires, their physical movements (Moiseev's stereotypically "swishy," Leont'ev's overtly sinuously sexual), and Danilko's having made a career via the adoption of a female persona, appearing dressed as a woman in order to often sing about love for men, mark all three as "feminine men," the very definition, for many in contemporary Russia, of a homosexual.

It is important to highlight that this enmity is especially pronounced, and has been historically, in relation to homosexual men as opposed to women, and it appears to be a reaction not against physical acts per se but one misogynistically motivated against gender transgression in which the male abjures his privileged status, adopting the attributes of the feminine. Among the medieval Orthodox Slavs, for example, homosexual activity between women was not considered as heinous as that between men, and the greatest punishment was to be meted out for acts that placed a male in the position of a woman (namely, *muzhelozstvo*, anal penetration) (Levin 1989: Chapter 4).[78] And in Soviet Russia, while "masculine" women were often seen as carrying out gender roles comporting with acceptable notions of revolutionary quality, accepted into military service, and even (on one occasion) deemed worthy of possibly being allowed to marry (Healey 2001a: 143–144, 167–169)—their masculinity endowing them with "competence, authority, and crucially, loyalty to the modernizing (and implicitly Russian) values of the Revolution"—male femininity "could only be imagined as foreign, backward and tragic" (169). Indeed, femininity was often key to Soviet academic or legal-juridical definitions of homosexual identity; here, the passive (feminine) partner was often viewed as a true, "congenital" homosexual, while those who exhibited masculine identities and took the active role were often not regarded as "genuinely sick" (145–147).

In contemporary Russian society, the roiling of gender roles[79]—producing, in the minds of some, "weak," "impotent" men—is often figured in the context of a voracious West, the "winner" of the battle between communism and capitalism, as well as the country's perilously declining demographics.[80] In reference to the first, it is notable that all three of the singers here may be seen, despite their traditional musical forms, as in some way aligning with an anti-Soviet (linked to, but distinct from anti-*Russian*)/pro-Western worldview: Moiseev is the image of the bourgeois aesthete, Leont'ev exhibits an inordinate preoccupation with *lichnost'* (personality; that is, an obsession with the self as opposed to the social whole), and Serdiuchka appears the backward peasant who became a frivolous consumer, her body adorned by extravagant purchases, the mis-en-scène of her videos and performances often suggesting a Western disco (and her accompanying musicians resembling Western club-hoppers). They are thus dissident not only in their gender attributes, but also in their renunciation of their Socialist heritage and attendant adoption of Western mores—the West being, in the eyes of many, the very font of a visible and vocal homosexuality.[81] And in reference to demographics, the homosexual male, engaging in sexual activity not geared toward procreation, contributes to the plummeting birth rates. Meshkov (2005) commenting on what he sees as the proliferation of singers of nontraditional sexual orientation[82] in Russian popular music makes the connection between the homosexual and the Russian population explicit. Rejecting a biological, genetic basis for homosexuality, and postulating an increase in the number of gays and lesbians in Russia in the future, he states:

> In youth we also imitated idols, wore the haircuts of the Beatles, curled our hair like Hendrix. Today, the fans of Marilyn Manson play as Satanists, like he does. Naturally, this is expressed not only in the image, but also in the shocking behavior. . . . Art still forms us thus! And the powerful propaganda of homosexuality . . . without ceremony can change the direction of the obedient "chromosomes" of young boys and girls. And then, sit back, Motherland, and count the percentage![83]

Homosexuality is thus not seen as a "personal choice," or even an "alternative lifestyle," but as something with the ability to threaten the very existence of the Russian state. It is likely such a conceptualization that was at least in part responsible for recent calls to recriminalize homosexuality. For example, in 2004 Gennadii Raikov and other government deputies put forth an initiative calling for prison sentences of between two and five years. Ultranationalist Vladimir Zhirinovskii, in support of the bill, called not for prison sentences, however, but for the death penalty ("Sodomy Not a Crime").[84] Although the State Duma rejected the bill, in March of 2005 there appeared a shadow "people's government," composed of several politicians with markedly homophobic views—something that was seen as having the function of raising sagging ratings of Putin's party by pandering to antigay sentiment among the Russian populace (Petrov 2005c).[85] The vast majority of my informants agreed that, while improvements had been made, in comparison with the West (Europe, the United States, Canada, Australia), attitudes toward homosexuality in Russia were far more negative, and homophobia—including the threat of violence—far more palpable.

Incorporeal/Corporeal

In a society in which the anchors of state control and economic stability have been lost, and the very "raw material" of nation *re*-building declines precipitously each year, homosexuality, through its gendered connections to the alleged causes of the country's debility, is read as a danger. That calls for recriminalization and laws proscribing free speech have appeared in the past decade indicates that for some the question of nontraditional sexual orientation is one requiring social control. With full recriminalization unlikely in a political landscape in which Russia sees itself scrutinized by Western NGOs, juridical bodies such as the European Court of Human Rights, and the media, one might ask what form such regulation might take. But wouldn't the existence of such visible gender transgression in Russian popular culture seem to expose that very question as fallacious—that is, doesn't visibility, after decades of invisibility, of absence from the social body, suggest that homosexuality is not, in fact, viewed as a major threat? If the Russian authorities have the power to shut down television stations seen as being critical of the government (and to imprison citizens they see as political threats),[86] could they not also force control of the recording industry, making the existence of performers with "nontraditional" sexual orientations impossible?[87]

Perhaps visibility might be figured not as an effect of a social countenancing (or, at the very least, toleration) of nontraditional sexual identities but, rather, the very modality by which the threat is controlled? Could the presence of "gay" men in popular music be another instance of a disciplinary regime that requires visibility for domination—the discipline of the panopticon? Indeed, via an examination of gay characters in the contemporary Russian *detektiv* (crime novel), Baer (2009) suggests just this: anxiety about visible homosexuality in contemporary Russia has, in fact, resulted in a greater visibility, part of a "disciplinary project" to "fix homosexual desire in visibly 'homosexual' bodies" (68). But according to Baer, the project is one founded upon a contradiction: that is, if homosexuality is a threat, this suggests that there is inherent in all people the potential for homosexual desire. (Remember that in Soviet Russia, this supposed threat was seen as so powerful as to be capable of infecting otherwise "healthy" young men, and thus required a severing of the homosexual from the social body.) Yet admitting to this sort of "universalizing" model would belie the construction of homosexuality as belonging only to a specific minority of the population. According to Baer, "vigilance is now a permanent condition of the post-Soviet sexual realm" (68); and this vigilance may be carried out upon a highly visible, indeed highly stereotypical, minority, held safely out of the quotidian, *byt*, and contained by the realm of the musical—visible and audible, but not quite "among us," contained by both spectator and space, a glitzy "social ghetto of homosexuals" (Baev 2006).[88]

Certainly contemporary phenomenological analyses must take into account the power of discursive formations of and controls upon the body, and it would be fallacious to elide this dynamic in readings of cultural productions such as those under examination; a panopticon of sorts is almost certainly implicated.[89] But is surveillance the only optic through which to view visibility? While it is a given that the legal, political, and juridical apparatuses in contemporary Russia are overwhelmingly controlled by men, gender parity being nowhere near the levels in Western Europe, the United States, Canada, or Australia, to privilege a masculine disciplinary scrutiny is in some ways to default to a heteronormative patriarchy as the bedrock upon which cultural production lies, the majority audience to which it plays, and the judge and jury meting out appropriate strictures or penalties for supposed transgressions.[90] If masculine patriarchy holds sway over all forms of power, and if homosexuality is truly found to be anathema in this power structure, how can we then understand Belarusian president Aleksander Lukashenko's starstruck, almost giddy reaction to meeting Valerii Leont'ev on the stage of the musical festival *Slavianskii bazaar* in 2009, at which time he presented the performer with a special award of the president of Belarus ("*cherez iskusstvo—k miru i vzaimoponimaniiu,*" "through art—peace and mutual understanding")? Lukashenko declared that he was a "long-time fan" of Leont'ev's, and never dreamed he would be able one day to give such an award to one of his favorite artists;[91] yet he is also president of what is considered one of the most homophobic countries of the former Soviet Union and has admitted openly that he "hates fags."[92] How are we to understand that both Moiseev and Leont'ev have been socially recognized, via the conferral of state awards, as esteemed members of Russian society—Moiseev having been named *Zasluzhennyi artist rossiiskoi federatsii* (Honored Artist of the Russian Federation), in 2006, and Leont'ev having received the designation of *Narodnyi artist rossiiskoi federatsii* (People's Artist of the Russian Federation) a decade earlier?

I asked many of my informants why they thought Moiseev, in particular, was so popular, given that they also had underscored the high levels of homophobia in Russia and the former Soviet Union. Why, for example, could he be such a prominent performer not only on television, but also one who was able to sell out such large concert halls as the *Oktiabr'skii*? Some suggested that it was his association with megastar Pugacheva that had brought him fame, and had made him into a known entity; as Artur told me, "he was known, and Russians like what they know. They don't like anything new."[93] He also suggested that many of Moiseev's middle-aged, female fans, an enormous segment of his fan base, looked upon him as a "*bednyi mal'chik*" ("unfortunate boy") who needed mothering and care. Other informants suggested that it was Moiseev's constant invocations of love and beauty—often absent in the Soviet era, seen as they were reeking of a subjective narcissism, and thus considered antistate—that drew listeners and viewers, and several, including those who used the most uncomplimentary terms for the singer, underscored the fact that he was known for putting on a great show. Il'ia agreed with this last assessment ("he puts on a great show, and people like that), but also offered:

> He was a sensation, he was the first openly gay singer in Russia. He was like a freak [*urod*], a clown [*klaun*], an oddity, and people who have very dull, boring lives like to see things that are odd and strange and exciting. In my [home] town [in Siberia], for example, there are 500,000 people, one movie theatre, two restaurants and one bar. *One bar*. Of course, nothing for gay people. So when that is your life, you want to see something different, something exciting, even if it's odd or disgusting to you.

The words used by Il'ia to describe Moiseev—*urot, klaun*—were also used by other informants; in addition to these, other common descriptors included the noun *uzhas* (horror, terror), the adjective *protivno* (disgusting, revolting), and the exclamation *foo!* (ugh!). Both Moiseev and Danilko (as Serdiuchka) have been the targets of protests, and the former has had concerts canceled in both Dagestan and the city of Obninsk,[94] and was also met on one occasion with cries of "faggot" (*pidor*)[95] after exiting a performance venue in Nizhnyi Novgorod ("*Nizhnyi Novgorod: Boriu*"); on another occasion, in the same city, protestors carried signs reading "*Nizhnyi Novgorod—ne Sodom*" ("Nizhnyi Novgorod Is Not Sodom"), "*Nam ne nuzhny gei i lesbiianki*" ("We Don't Need Gays and Lesbians"), and "*Pozhelaem Bore gemorroia*" ("We Wish Hemorrhoids upon Boria") (Margolis 2006). That these same performers appear regularly to millions of fans and have established lucrative careers in the Russian-speaking world, suggests that desire and loathing are not polar opposites; as indicated by Grosz's assessment, the epigraph to this chapter, they are, rather, indissolubly linked variables, both connected to the human body.[96] Insofar as individual bodies may be considered as comprised by the social body, these discrete corporealities, severed from the whole, maintain the status of the reviled adored, those concurrently both—as Il'ia put it—exciting and freaks. Understanding this dynamic, whereby two seemingly oppositional stances turn out to be mutually constitutive parts of a complex whole, leads ultimately to an illumination of the complex interactions of the "ontological" (corporeal) statuses of the various physical bodies at play (the social whole and the individual), their relationships to sexual identity, and the entirely nonfortuitous, nonrandom appearance of the homosexual in musical space. And this illumination rests upon the phantom limb—the limb that we feel still exists after its amputation.

The phantom limb itself is a site for the amalgamation of seemingly antipodal dynamics. It is, according to Merleau-Ponty (2002 [1962]), neither a fully psychic nor organic phenomenon; rather, it comprises both, and is able to do so by existing in the space he terms *being-in-the-world*, a space itself existing at the tense intersection of an embodied experience that is neither purely reflexive nor purely intentional. The phantom limb is not a memory, but a "quasi-present," a past somatic state that becomes a present, indicating that not only bodies or spaces, but temporality itself cannot be split into binary opposites, what *was* as opposed to what *is*. The appearance of the phantom limb is a further reminder of the indispensability of the body in terms of our interaction with the world—a body that does not sully perception but is its very precondition—an interaction that is never entirely of the moment but always rife with the virtual, the possible. In his estimation:

> To have a phantom arm is to remain open to all the actions of which the arm alone is capable; it is to retain the practical field which one enjoyed before mutilation. The body is the vehicle of being in the world, and having a body is, for a living creature, to be intervolved in a definite environment, to identify oneself with certain projects and be continually committed to them. (94)

This idea of potential, of possibility is, I think, implicated in the very question of sexual orientation; sexuality, if also conceivable in terms defying binarization (for example, a "supplemental"—in the Derridean sense—relationship of the heterosexual to the homosexual, whereby each term is indispensable to the existence of the other, or as the "polymorphous perversity"—in the Freudian sense—inherent in each person prior to the alignment of the subject to a specifically genital-focused sexuality based upon heterosexual intercourse) further allows for the understanding of what may seem, at face value, a concurrent homophobia and homophilia in contemporary Russia. In this case, and in the context of a homosexuality that has been seen as a potentially and particularly virulent contagion, same-sex attraction may indeed exist, on a preconscious, corporeal level, as a "universal" potential rather than a "minority" identity (Sedgwick 1990). This is not to suggest that the popularity of Valerii Leont'ev, as a "phantom faggot," is proof of the latent homosexuality of the bulk of the Russian populace; rather, the existence of such singers, at once abject and adored, may point toward not a desire for same-sex sexual (genital) contact, or even same-sex erotic impulses, but to the desire to exist outside of a system of straitjacketing gender codes. The previously amputated homosexual, "quasi-here," is experienced in the individual corporealities comprised by the aggregate, social body.

And it is exactly due to these resistances to neat dichotomization, as well as the requisiteness of the human body in perceiving both others' and one's own sense of sexuality, that such men are found in musical space—for each dynamic that inheres in and surrounds the phantom limb, as postulated by Merleau-Ponty, finds its correlate in music. Music is, at once, the least material yet most physically effecting of all the arts; it is often experienced on a level in which the reflexive and conscious coalesce; it inherently questions the passage of linear, objective time, repeats making presents of pasts; and as voices—often met only via an electronic transmission—singers are not entirely absent (we hear them, we see them in the rarefied realm of the musical), not entirely present (but we don't see them, or those like them, in daily life), but quasipresent. That which was severed from the Soviet body remains, corporeally cathected via melody, timbre, and harmonic motion.

None of this purports to be a definitive answer, only a contribution to possibilities. There is no universal/monolithic "Russian audience" (let alone Russian populace) perceiving any or all of these three singers, and to posit one would be to once again erase the variable of sexual identity in regards to analyses of popular music and culture. One fairly common theme I did find among my gay informants, however, was that the majority loved Serdiuchka, and many respected Leont'ev, but almost all professed a loathing for Moiseev. One might assume that Moiseev's statements in the press in the past several years—including his having come out in support of Mayor Iurii Luzhkov's ban of Moscow's gay pride parade—have done little to ingratiate him to many gay men, and such statements have led one gay activist to compare him to those Jews co-opted by the Nazis in Poland to police their own "brothers" in the ghettos there (Baev 2006). Yet most of my informants also confessed that they, too, were against the idea of a gay pride parade in Russia, and would not attend if it were carried out. But politics, in the context of post-Soviet homosexuality, is for many secondary to experience, to sexual experience realized in corporeal rather than "spiritual" terms, and in this context it is more Moiseev's abnegation of lived, unapologetic sexuality than his social agenda that appear to be at least partially responsible for the negative feelings my informants had toward him. I would be remiss in failing to point out, additionally, that for many of my informants it was also Moiseev's perceived abnegation (or simply lack) of a specifically sexualized masculinity that seemed to be operative in their negative assessments of the singer; gay men, as much as heterosexual men, may be as likely to hold up the "feminine" man as an object of contempt or derision.[97] To quote one contributor to the Russian opinion website "Love/Hate" (lovehate.ru), opining over gender-bending (and "feminine") male singer Shura, "I myself am gay, but I can't stand Shura! Men love men because they are [real] guys [*muzhiki*], and not affected women [*manernye baby*]."[98]

But a final caution against universals and monolithic thinking—for although nearly every single one of my informants expressed an extreme dislike for Moiseev, and while this may be statistically representative of gay men in Russia in general, it did not mean that all gay men were likewise negatively disposed toward him. The night of Moiseev's concert, my gaydar did more than simply "ping" at the sight of three male friends, singing and skipping (indeed, skipping) down one of the hall's corridors, one of them singing a Moiseev song. The phantom was lip-synching on stage, but a speck of materiality had seeped into *byt*.

4. Corporeal Intentions

"*Muzhiki ne tantsuiut*" ("*Muzhiki* don't dance")
—DJ Gruv

Of course [Dima Bilan] is gay. You see the way he dances?
—Konstantin, 27, St. Petersburg

Lazarev, Bilan, Leont'ev, Baskov . . . gay singers are ashamed to come out [*stesniaiutsia otkryt'sia*]. They invent all sorts of stories about love affairs with women. This is because of the fear of losing the attention of most of the fans."
—Viktor Baturin, Dima Bilan's former producer

It was about 2:00 A.M. when, having earlier flagged a passing car outside of my Moscow apartment and negotiated a fare,[1] I arrived at the gay club *Dusha i telo* (Soul and Body). Located approximately twenty minutes outside of the city center, the entrance on the first floor of a large, severe, Soviet-era building complex, the establishment was packed full of hundreds of people, the spillover visible on the street as I approached. After finally making may way inside, I was glad to be out of the frigid cold, but not so glad to stand in line over half an hour to check my coat; glad to be surrounded by handsome men, but not so glad to be one of the few over forty. This being my inaugural visit, I walked around the massive space, noting that aside from the cavernous room containing the main dance floor (where hard house and other types of then-current electronic dance music styles were being played), there were several other discrete spaces—for example, one area offered pool tables for customers who might be taking a break from dancing. With hundreds of bodies coursing through the various veins of the space that morning, it was by sheer chance that I literally bumped into Kliment, an informant I had met just a few days previously. Knowing that I had not been to the club before, he showed me around the labyrinthine structure, at one point guiding me to a room marked by the sign (in English) "For Men Only."[2] Seeing and hearing light and music emanating from the room, I was fairly certain it was not a *temnaia komnata* (a "dark room," a place where men could have sexual encounters in relative darkness and anonymity), and upon entering my presuppositions were confirmed as correct; rather than a place to engage in sexual activity, it was a site for the viewing of the beautiful male body. Customers were seated on padded banquettes around the perimeter of the small room, smoking, drinking, and conversing while, to the sounds of down-tempo, chill-out, and acoustic/new-age–type music, nude men—including some of the go-go dancers from the platforms surrounding the main dance floor—entered and languorously, sinuously moved and posed to the accompaniment of the music, now standing, now draping themselves over any available open seats. More living incarnations of static painted or sculpted artistic representations of the male form than bump-and-grind strippers in G-strings, the men—entirely naked, but hiding their genitals at all times via their poses or their hands—offered themselves as visible and incarnate aesthetic and erotic objects for the male viewers assembled.

While the spectacle provided by these men was explicitly intended for the "gay gaze" ("For [Gay] Men Only"), visible male bodies that invite the eyes of the viewer exist, of course, outside of specifically demarcated spaces (a gay club) where spectators are either allowed or refused admission ("For Men Only") based on their genders and sexual identities.[3] Yet even absent the unambiguous markers of either geography or dictum, the sight of the unclothed, splendid male body often remains a site and sign for the production of assumed homoeroticism. Historically speaking, such images are visible in the paintings of one of Russia's most famous nineteenth-century artists, Alekandr Ivanov, which feature numerous instances of idealized male physicality,[4] as do thousands of photographs from the studio of Karl Bulla (active from the 1880s to the 1930s), recently unearthed by photographer Valerii Katsuba (Levy and Scott-Clark 2006).[5] Such a veneration of masculine corporeality was to reach an apotheosis of sorts in the near deification of the male form in Socialist Realist art, often with the implication that such muscular forms were synechdochal for the nation (and nation building) itself.[6] On a more contemporary front, films such as Aleksandr Sokurov's 2003 *Otets i syn* (*Father and Son*) and Hussein Erkenov's 1990 *100 dnei do prikaza* (*100 Days before the Command*), owning to their presentations of the nude or almost-nude male body, as well as the relationships between and among these bodies, have been described as "homoerotic" (although Sokurov has vehemently denied any such implications, calling the assertion a product of "sick European minds").[7]

Stratton (1996) has theorized that the emergence of the male body as a site of desire in contemporary Western culture occurred via the interplay of psychic structure, capitalist consumer culture, and the increased visibility of the previously subcultural homosexual; to the extent that Russia has in the past two decades tentatively embraced an incipient and rarefied consumer culture, Stratton's conflation of the desirability of the visible male with economic transformation may partially explain the appearance of the spectacular male body in current Russian media. Yet financial and psychological explanations, apposite as they may be in the West, do not fully explain the appearance, indeed the efflorescence, of images of male physical beauty in the musical discourses of numerous singers and bands in the first two decades of the twenty-first century in Russia and the conflation of these images with the homosexual or homoerotic. Through an examination of instances of the male body's foregrounding in the work of several Russian artists (and one Ukrainian artist)[8]—musician and composer Andrei Danilko, the groups Hi-Fi and Smash!! and singer Dima Bilan (focusing on his appearances at the Eurovision Song Contest)—I want to highlight not only the variable of the body's visibility (and, concomitantly, questions of power), but also the interrelated and phenomenologically inflected dynamics of intentionality, proximity, and orientation. A focus on such dynamics allows for an understanding of the importance of such bodies in the production of homosexual subjectivity in post-Soviet Russia, a subjectivity that is, in part, based upon one's embodied existence. Although my focus here will be largely upon filmed/video performances, the choice to focus on such visual artifacts is based upon both press and informant accounts of the bodies in question.

Frivolity/Passivity

Bodies, of course, in live performances and in videos, do not just "appear" but "do"—or fail to do—things. In the previous chapter, the work of Verka Serdiuchka was engaged in order to illustrate one of several ways that homosexuality may be alluded to in the work of a widely popular artist in contemporary Russia. But Serdiuchka's creator, Andrei Danilko, temporarily shed his drag persona in 2004, releasing a CD of instrumental songs entitled *Posle tebia* (*After You*) under his own name. In these songs and their accompanying videos, Danilko apparently attempted to move beyond the kitsch, camp, and comedy of Verka, veering toward an aesthetic of more "serious" popular music via the use of grand piano, and lush (synthesizer) "string" arrangements (as in "*Sobiraia zheltye list'ia*" ["Collecting Golden Leaves"]), at times also embracing a style more focused upon electronic timbres than traditional "folk" instrumentations. That Danilko chose to include a remake of the aria "Casta Diva"—immortalized to many by Maria Callas, one of the great gay operatic icons—indicates a connection to a specific type of homosexual culture.[9] However, it is through the use of the desirable male body as a sign that Danilko has led many, including some of my informants, to assume the artist's homosexual orientation. This particular sign is most striking in two clips, "*Posle tebia*" and "*Kukla*" ("Doll"), both of which feature the same, almost preternaturally beautiful, young man. In the first, he is shown in a stylishly dilapidated loft-type apartment, turning on the stove to boil water for tea. While a grand piano plays itself in time with the piano heard in the audio, the boy[10] waits, taking off his watch, placing it on the table. He lays on the bed, the words "What's his name is so good to me" (in English)—the title of another song on the album—emblazoned in capital letters across his T-shirt.[11] He is later seen standing, stripped to the waist, in the bathroom, posing for the gaze of the viewer, or lost in contemplation, or both. Water pours over his head; he dries it with a towel, and then returns to the table to have tea with the unseen guest. Suitcases appear and fade away; picture frames are emptied of their contents, framing only space; with the final cadence of the song, the chord of A minor the ultimate sound, he puts down his tea, and the cup splits in two.

In the second, the same boy, now in the context of a circus (replete with muscular, shirtless acrobats and jugglers) appears as a pierrot, initially putting on his sad-faced makeup, and ultimately presented in various states of undress: first, standing under a shower, the water washing away his clown's face, the camera panning down his sinuous, wet body; next running, shirtless, through the rain, his lithe frame and tight muscles on display, his jeans slung very low on his slender hips. As he runs, the seasons change, and he dons clothing, only to return to his makeup table and open a small sack holding a silver heart. The music, with its progression of i–vii (in F minor, F minor to E minor, with the latter chord serving as a substituted, "modal" dominant), and the attendant bass line jump of a major seventh (F to E), as well as the use of both calliopelike synthesizer sounds, and a sampling of a doll's speech ("mama") contribute to the video's eerie, circuslike quality; but here, the circus motif may be seen as relating the scene not only to the bizarre, but to the genre of *èstrada* as well, which has its roots in the circus (cf. MacFadyen 2001). Danilko's foray away from transvestism leads him, along with the boy in the video, into the realm of that musical genre often associated with *golubye*.

While Danilko has made use of another's male body as a sign, there are others on the Russian musical landscape who have used likewise beautiful bodies to similar effect, the difference being that—as in the case of the groups

Hi-Fi and Smash!!—the singers have used their own bodies. Both groups differ from one another in several regards, but share attributes that also differentiate them from the singers discussed in the previous chapter. First, the musical styles of the majority of their songs are not *èstrada*-related, falling more into the dance-pop category, eschewing the stereotyped harmonic and melodic devices previously discussed and making use of generally more contemporary-sounding production methods. Second, all of the participants in both groups are younger than those examined previously, ranging from their early to late twenties at the time of each group's inception.[12] Third, both groups exhibit a near-obsession with style and fashion that, although at times theatrical or outré, veers closer to European couture than Vegas-style kitsch. Fourth, both make some use of English within their works; in the case of Smash!!, approximately 95 percent of their output is sung in English. (It can be inferred, especially in the case of Smash!!, that their main audience is intended to be, if not English-speaking, then Western.) And last, both groups have a member whom many of my informants, as well as those in the general populace, assumed to be gay.

Since its inception in 1998, Hi-Fi—essentially a project of composer-producer Pavel Esenin—has most often comprised three members, two males and one female. Although the group's composition has changed more rapidly in the last few years, the two most longstanding members have been the men, Dmitrii Fomin and Timofei Pron'kin. The female member was originally Oksana Oleshko (1999–2003), and then Tat'iana Tereshina (2003–2006), Ekaterina Li (2007–2011), and finally Olesia Lipchanskaia (2011–present). Most of the members were often known by diminutive forms of their names—Mitia, Tim, and Ksiusha/Tania/Katia—but the roster might otherwise be characterized as "the blond, the brunette, and the girl," or "the gay one, the straight one, and the girl"; many of my informants assumed (or said they knew) that Fomin was gay. Some said they had heard rumors that he had previously been a dancer-stripper in gay clubs in Moscow; however, these rumors, at least in the press, are connected to Pron'kin, not Fomin. Furthermore, according to Pron'kin himself, these assertions are true.[13] But despite the fact that both Fomin and Pron'kin present their bodies, often with tight and/or revealing clothing, as sexual male bodies, and Pron'kin had put his body on display in gay clubs, it is Fomin who is most often perceived as homosexual. For example, a listener to a radio interview with the group on station *Èkho Moskvy* posed the following question in the corresponding online forum:

> I'm sorry that my question is about [your] private life, but fans want to know everything, [and] not only about your creative work [smiley emoticon]. A

question for Mitia: Is it true that you live with a man, and that you have a nontraditional sexual orientation? Simply put—are you GAY? ("*Argentum*")

The group's song "*Pro leto*" ("About Summer") is a fast-paced dance number, built partially around an incessant guitar hook that appears to be sampled from (or a copy of) Sister Sledge's "He's The Greatest Dancer"—a gay, Western classic. The lyrics of the chorus tell of summer on its way out, to the disappointment of the singer, and include the image of the rainbow—yet another possibly oblique reference to homosexuality ("*Raduzhnaia koshka, nebo za spinoi/davno ubezhala sledom za toboi*"; "A rainbow cat, the sun behind her/ Long ago ran away after you"). In the song's accompanying video, both men and Oleshko appear in gym clothes, befitting their situation in a large sports hall, full of male and female athletes and dancers. All three singers progress to the center of the hall, alternately "warming up," stretching, and then engaged in free-form dancing. They are ultimately joined by a group of male dancers, many dressed in such "urban" items as sweat pants (pushed to the knee on one leg), knit caps, and flannel shirts, who take to the mat in order to show off a gamut of "street," hip-hop dance styles. Later in the video, with Fomin atop a row of tables, and Pron'kin and Oleshko flanking him on either side, below, both men appear shirtless and soaked, as all of the dancers, instigated by Pron'kin, have begun to fling cups of water around.[14] Fomin continues his sinuous, sensual dancing, Pron'kin's veering more toward the aesthetic of the hip-hop dancers, shoulders hunched, waist bent. In the final moments, both men raise their arms and display their shaved bodies, the focus of the shot.

While both Fomin and Pron'kin exhibit their dancing bodies, only one is generally marked as gay, while the other maintains the imprimatur of heterosexuality. On the level of the visual, this may have to do with stereotypical images of what a "man" is. In this regard, Fomin, in comparison to Pron'kin, is much smaller; while both are in excellent physical shape, Pron'kin is far more muscular and larger, and he wears clothing (often cropped tees with cap sleeves, as well as extremely tight, low-cut jeans) designed to show off his huge arms, chest, and thighs. Fomin's sinewy muscles, in contrast, make him look not only diminutive, but younger. Additionally, although both appeared in some instances to shave what body hair they had, Fomin is naturally smooth; Pron'kin, in contrast, was often shown unshaved, revealing a hirsute chest.[15] Also, while both may be considered "stylish," Pron'kin's sartorial statements have been more in line with the "macho," club-hopping type of Petersburger or Muscovite, while Fomin's, often replete with large sunglasses, extravagant furs, couture-style suits, and/or numerous types of hats or headbands, are often indicative of the "dandy." (Commenting on Pron'kin's ponytail, as opposed to Fomin's ever-changing roster of hair statements, one informant offered, "no gay man is going to wear a ponytail in this era.") Fomin's dancing style also differs from Pron'kin's, the latter of whom tends to approximate (to greater or lesser success) an "urban," "hip-hop" flavor, while the former's is far more jubilant, playful—bouncy, even—but also unabashedly sexual, with sensuously gyrating hips and buttocks.

Indeed, one might even see an anal-versus-phallic split between the two, as portrayed in the video for the song "*Ne dano*" ("It's Not Given"). In the clip, each of the three is shown leaving behind his or her current life to come together in the end, perhaps as an allusion to the formation of the group. Oleshko is first shown in the midst of her wedding, from which she ultimately walks away, removing her dress in the process, continuing on in little more than a strapless top, tight micro (booty) shorts, and stiletto heels. A very young Fomin is revealed at the chalkboard of a university lecture hall, in the midst of writing a complex mathematical formula, finally putting down the chalk, and walking down the hall toward an exit.[16] Finally, Pron'kin is seen speeding along in a red sports car that he abruptly stops, exiting and walking away from it. The images of Fomin and Pron'kin are here diametrically opposed in terms of the camera's position: The former is seen from behind, the camera on the same level, his white, flowing pants accentuating his round buttocks, while Pron'kin is seen from the front, with the camera—in a "submissive" position—shooting him from below. But as with many of the visuals associated with Hi-Fi's musical output, here there is an implicit questioning of hard-and-fast gendered categories; for, while each group member is initially shown aligned with the "correctly" gendered milieu/pursuit (Oleshko/heterosexual woman/marriage; Pron'kin/heterosexual man/fast [phallic] cars; Fomin/homosexual [?] man/"thought" over "action"), the first thing each of them does is walk away from such alignments, in suspected pursuit of "reorientations." (I will return to the concept of orientation later in this chapter.)

The duo Smash!! (2001–2005), comprising Sergei Lazarev and Vladimir (Vlad) Topolov, exhibited and made use of some of the same characteristics as Hi-Fi that are contributory to one of their members' having been defined by many as gay. As with Fomin and Pron'kin, while both boys regularly displayed their bodies in videos, CD packaging, and promotional photographs, it is Lazarev who was and is "read" most often as homosexual, not Topolov.[17] On an internet forum, for example, one reader (archly adopting the screen name "Pida Rassovna"), in response to another who seemed uncertain as to whether or not Lazarev might be gay, asked whether this reader had "landed from the moon" ("*s luny upal???*"), continuing that "Lazarev has [always] been a fag [*pida*] . . . until he became a 'public face,' he really didn't hide it, just didn't advertise it." Yet another reader concurred, considering Lazarev to be "absolutely gay" (*gei stopudovo*—literally "a hundred pounds gay"), and expressing surprise that people still didn't know of Lazarev's homosexual orientation.[18]

But ideas of "passivity" are problematic in terms of stereotypes as Lazarev often appeared to be the "dominant" persona in several regards: He is arguably more handsome than Topolov (this was the general consensus of my informants, as well as the press), his physique is far more defined, his voice is superior in terms of both delivery and range, and his stage manner is more charismatic and self-assured. He is also a better, more fluid dancer, as exhibited in the numerous choreographed numbers the boys performed both in videos and on stage. In interviews, as well, Lazarev has often appeared much more confident, even more refined and charming than Topolov, although sometimes bordering on a rather manufactured sort of publicity-speak. Indeed, in response to an article about the singer on the gay, Russian site xsgay.ru,[19] one reader commented that Lazarev was "the picture of culturedness, the picture of beauty," contrasting Topolov as a "homophobic scarecrow."[20] This comports, in part, with a general characterization of gay men given to me by Stanislav. Speaking about what he saw as the connections among gay men internationally, he suggested that, in general, "gay people are those who are more educated, smarter, cleverer, more stylish, all those sorts of things."[21]

Although a large segment of their audience was teenaged girls, the gayness and homoeroticism of their act was often strong. Early publicity photos often showed both boys with open shirts, or shirtless, extremely close to one another, or even touching. And while no one with whom I spoke thought there was a sexual relationship between the two (one informant told me he even thought they were "brothers"—meaning, in this sense, not children of the same parents, but cousins)[22] their presentation as two seminaked, young, attractive boys, often in skin-to-skin contact, suggests a sensuality, if not sexuality. But sexuality is most probably part of what drew/draws their audience, and indeed a manifest sexuality imbues the lyrics of their songs. On the group's first CD *Freeway*, a sexuality in the context of love is in evidence, but on their follow-up CD *2Nite* this sexuality becomes even more carnal, more aggressive, as in the lyrics to the song "This Could Lead to Something." Here, the narrator implores the addressee to "forget those morals," confesses that he's "in it for the pleasure," and urges her (or him) to "go with a guiltless smile" and find a position of "physical, mental, spiritual, sexual" pleasure. Through the lyrics, the boys are presented as having sexual desires, desires not constrained by social mores. But to whom such sexual desires are directed is uncertain, as the gender of the object of sexual desire is left unclear, allowing for both heterosexual and homosexual readings; in fact, just such a homosexual reading was supplied by one member of YouTube who used the song as a "sound track" for a montage of scenes culled from the film *Latter Days* (2003). The film deals with the awakening of homosexual desire in a young Mormon missionary from Idaho who, upon moving to Los Angeles, falls in love with his openly gay neighbor. The member's video, drawing on the sexual content of the lyrics, features several instances of physical intimacy between the two men, including their kissing.[23]

All the performers discussed thus far are in many regards similar, both in terms of physiognomy and physique: they are boyishly handsome, glabrescent, lithely muscular, athletic, well-groomed, and stylish, presenting their bodies unabashedly and sensually. They are, in almost every regard, the opposite of one of the quintessential symbols of Russian masculinity, the *muzhik*. According to Kon, many Russian men are still influenced by this "traditional form of the strong and rough [*grubo*] *muzhik*," "a specifically Russian phenomenon," the word indicating at once "sex, age, social status, and properties of character": a mature, adult man ("a person of the sex *he* [*on*]"), a commoner, one of the lower classes (2003: 394; see also Shaburova 2002, 2005a, 2005b).[24] A *muzhik* is one who is "not a woman [*baba*],[25] not a kid [*patsan*], not a homo [*gomik*]"; he is contrasted with the "weak, alien gentleman and namby-pamby [*khliupik*] intellectual, distinguished by an increased sexuality,[26] love of liquor, strength and roughness." The *muzhik* "values his own natural characteristics, and doesn't need decoration" (394), and his behaviors and appearance—such as his beard stubble and the smell of tobacco on his body (instead of cologne)—"do not embody anything deliberate, i.e., are not the result of conscious choice and effort (Utekhin 2001: 271; quoted in Kon 2003: 394). The *muzhik* is visible not only in daily life,[27] but in politics[28] and popular music as well. In this last regard, the gruff, cigarette-smoking, gravelly voiced, obscenity-spewing Sergei Shnurov, lead singer of the group *Leningrad*, is but one of the most visible examples.[29] While Kon notes that this image of masculinity has been challenged in the early part of the twenty-first century, due in part to increased intercourse with Western ideals and commercial products, the *muzhik* is still a symbol that, for many, connotes "true" masculinity, a masculinity that is in part made visible and material via the male body.[30]

It is not only, however, the material specificity of the body that points to possible "nontraditional" sexualities of Danilko, Fomin, and Lazarev; rather, in the context of a highly rigid gender system, the use of the male body as desirable, sexual object, the object of the gaze, puts the male in the passive, stereotypically feminine, position. As Kon notes:

> [T]he gaze is power, and the only possibility of being saved from it, is to not allow other men to look at you (women don't count—they have "nothing" [i.e., a penis] to compete with a man, and they don't have the right to look at him). From this comes the typical male shyness, and related normative prohibitions.[31] (2001a: 327)

For a male to "expose" himself is, thus, feminizing, an invitation to be gazed upon (that is, judged) by other men, by power.[32] To expose the body is to expose the possibility of the myth of the phallus and, accordingly, the very power structures (phallocentricity, phallotocracy) that rest upon it. Of course, the actual penis is not exposed in any of the videos I have discussed; but by assuming the role of the object rather than subject, the male has abnegated his role as the constructor of the phallocentric gaze. Held up to the "castrating" (Kon 2001a: 326) gaze of male power, he is both transgressor, occupying the space of the feminine, and traitor: he risks admitting the male body as a site of pleasure, a body to be caressed (by, for example, the water, or the propinquity of the [singing] partner's body), rather than a body made to visit destruction and control over others. This dynamic is powerfully exhibited in the previously mentioned film, *100 dnei do prikaza*, which offers a poetically surreal and highly symbolic (as well as highly disturbing) examination of the atrocities visited upon young recruits in the Russian army. In one scene, a young enlistee, having showered, is found nude in the barracks by his commanding officer. The humiliation that ensues is largely visual in nature, related to the authority of the optic: the boy, having instinctively covered his genitals with his hands, is forcefully ordered to drop them ("*Smirno! Smirno!*," "Attention!"), exposing his full nudity to the harsh and penetrating stare of the colonel, the camera—indicating the superior's vantage point—stopping at the boy's penis. As the camera cuts away, we hear the scream of the boy, who is later found to have hung himself in a cell.[33]

There are, however, numerous instances of male bodies, in art, in advertisement, and in other cultural arenas, which are not likewise "feminized." Both Kon (2001a: 317) and Bordo (1999) note that it is not simply the sight of the male body *per se* that is feminizing, suggesting rather that dynamics of action or repose are at play—that is, the male body should be an active, not passive, body; the latter, according to Kon "makes a male vulnerable and feminine, turning him into a sexual, in this sense a homosexual, object" (2001a: 317).[34] Such gendered constructions, whereby passivity is conflated with femininity, must be understood as having a lengthy, historical basis in Soviet Russia—underpinning, for example, the presentation of women in Soviet-era art that ostensibly strove to show both women and men engaged in physical labor in support of the common good. However, as Reid (1998) suggests, even here there was a double standard at play; while men were portrayed as being engaged in an actual activity (building a ship, working in a factory), women were often depicted in sites where they *would* be working, but not actually engaged in any definable task. Using one important 1939 exhibition—*The Industry of Socialism*, "the most important art event of the decade" (134)—as archetypal, she finds that "artists perpetuated the patriarchal conception of woman as passive object of the male gaze," emphasizing "attractive physical appearance, rather than actions and abilities" (139).

The concatenation of the nonagentic/nonproductive with the feminine is likewise found in the sphere of the Soviet-era film. Dashkova (2008), for example, in an examination of eroticism of the films of the 1930s suggests that "frivolous" body movements (sometimes in conjunction with a mode of dress that called attention to one's body) may be seen as a marker of the erotic, and that such movement or comportment is often *de facto* associated with the female. In Dashkova's reading, as the "frivolous" becomes "civilized"—that is, put into service of the common good—the (female) character likewise becomes more "masculine": her appearance changes (she dons a "worker's jacket [*vatnik*], coveralls [*spetsovka*], robe [*khalat*]"), her movements are "sporty and accurate," and her bodily movements, in the company of men, mirror those *of* men—"masculine jesting codes" such as a firm handshake, a pat on the shoulder, or a punch to the chest. She has become a "*woman-comrade*, relations with whom suggest mostly working, indicating more competitiveness than intimate contact" (2008: 196).

The idea of purposelessness related to the body's form (and gender) may also be seen in Soviet-era posters calling for the populace to partake of an appropriate "Soviet physical culture" (*Sovietskaia fizkul'tura*) as opposed to a "bourgeois sport" (*burzhuaznyi sport*), the former being defined, in tacitly masculine terms, as the weapon of class struggle (Bernstein 2001: 100; 2007). In one such poster, a bodybuilder is portrayed as an example of the latter, with the words *individualism, professionalism,* and *record-breaking* ("*individualizm, professionalizm, i rekordsmenstvo*") emblazoned beneath the figure of a muscular man in a revealing wrestler-type singlet, a barbell hoisted above his head. As Bernstein further notes, the lone female figure in this visualized conceptualization of physical (and social) health is likewise found under the latter heading, here in the company of two male tennis players, all three contrasted with the image of several young men engaged in calisthenics. "Physical culture," according to the captions beneath the images is "an amusement for the bourgeoisie" ("*zabava dlia burzhuazii*"), but "a necessity for the proletariat" (*neobkhodimost' dlia proletariata*"). While in this last comparative tableau it may seem that the proletarian men are more "sexualized" by dint of their relative lack of clothing (they are clad only in abbreviated shorts, while the bourgeois tennis players are completely covered), we must focus not only on flesh, but on force, on purposiveness. In this regard, there is a stark contrast between the almost languid, casual poses of the tennis players, the foregrounded couple seated (the man with legs crossed), and the "good" Soviet sportsmen, whose kinetic bodies exude energy. Moreover, the former pictorial space is marked by strong horizontals (read perhaps as the very antithesis to progress; that is, remaining in place, on the same level), while the latter, in terms of both corporeal trajectories and the compositional strategies employed in the situating space (vertical and upward diagonal lines in abundance), the movement is resolutely and undeniably forward and upward.

Taken together, the alignment of the solopsistic (corporealized in the beautiful body) and purposeless with the feminine, the bourgeois, the antistate/anti-Soviet offers a possible explanation of how the presentation of male bodies discussed above may be read as instances of a homosexual (i.e., supposedly feminized male) body. Furthermore, that the bourgeois was often seen as the bastion of the homosexual—that is, homosexuality as the outcome of the debased upper classes—adds yet another unequivocal marker of "nontraditional sexuality." While it is true that Russian culture in the first decades of the twenty-first century is not entirely predicated upon Soviet mores, it is also clear that the simple addition of the prefix *post* does not immediately and completely obliterate constructions that existed and penetrated almost every aspect of the social, cultural, and—indeed—somatic spheres for decades. Certainly there is both room and necessity for nuance; as noted above, not all bodies (including those of Pron'kin or Topolov) are uniformly homoeroticized in the ways that Fomin's, Lazarev's, and the unnamed boy's in Danilko's videos are. As I have suggested, such an evasion of the alignment with the feminine/homosexual may be the outcome of seemingly insignificant variables as body hair (Pron'kin's), camera angle (above versus below/in front versus behind, as in Hi-Fi's "*Ne dano*"), or an overall and relative assumption of "culturedness" (Lazarev's surfeit versus Topolov's deficiency).

But the significance of the body cannot be read only through the discursive or the ideological; rather, its significance must be understood as dependent upon an embodied experience of the world, especially in the case of homosexuality, which may itself be experienced as corporeal. In this regard, it is essential to highlight the fact that objects in the world, including other bodies, are experienced as imbued with an "intentionality,"[35] and that bodies themselves, in their interactions with other object, have an intentionality as well. In the first instance, objects must be understood as projecting past the purely "visible"—they have other sides, other uses, other meanings, so that specific "qualities" are not simply abstract notions, but rather "vital value[s]," the meaning of which first arise "for that heavy mass which is our body" (Merleau-Ponty 2002 [1962]: 61); a chair (or a body), for example, is not simply *a* chair/body, but a chair/body *for* something. In the second sense, our very existence, our movements in relation to other objects and other bodies, are imbued with intentionality—that is, our physical interactions with the world, have an "intentional arc" that allows us to move past the "actual," to "reckon with the possible" (Merleau-Ponty; quoted in Hass 2008: 83). Our movements are not simply discrete points on a line (my hand is here at this moment; now, it is here), but motilities with pasts, presents, futures, directions, and possibilities—movements for and with *something*.[36] Without such an intentional arc, the unity of the senses, intelligence, sensibility, and motility "goes limp" (157).

This limpness implies, albeit in a distinctly male sense, a bond between intentionality and sexual life, one that Merleau-Ponty makes explicit. As he contends, sexuality cannot be conceived of as purely mechanistic, the reaction of an organism (or part of an organism) to some external stimulus; rather, physical states or sights may be projected into a "sexual world" or an "erotic situation," and then "maintain[ed] . . . or follow[ed] through to complete satisfaction"—a satisfaction that would be impossible for someone unable to locate sexual life within a context of intention. In Merleau-Ponty's estimation:

> A sight has sexual significance for me, not when I consider, even confusedly, its possible relationship to the sexual organs or to pleasurable states, but when it exists for my body, for that power always available for bringing together into an erotic situation the stimuli applied, and adapting sexual conduct to it. . . . [W]e are concerned, not with a peripheral involuntary action, but with an intentionality which follows the general flow of existence and yields to its movement. (181)

Sexual life cannot be collapsed into existence; rather, there is an "interfusion" between the two (196), and sexuality is at all times present like an "atmosphere" (195). Indeed, a sexed body is not simply "fortuitous"; rather, this sexed body—as a body with hands, a head, legs, upright posture, thumbs—contributes to our "distinctive way of patterning the world" (197): "The body expresses total existence, not because it is an external accompaniment to that existence, but because existence realizes itself in the body" (192).

I do not propose to eclipse the discursive or ideological with the corporeal, to posit one as origin, the other as scion, one as offering superior exegetical perspicuity than the other. Nor is it simply an attempt at theoretical thoroughness, leaving no stone unturned—just in case. I offer the reading of the corporealized apprehension of such bodies, rather, in order to underscore the danger of the often-encountered default to the heterosexual as universal subject (in ethnomusicology no less than in other disciplines) when examining a cultural phenomenon, an unreflective default that erases the homosexual. While both heterosexual and homosexual male subjects may indeed read signs of "passivity," "frivolity" (and the adjunct of "femininity") or "visibility" in bodies they define as "homosexual," gay men may also relate to such bodies via their intentionality, an intentionality that relates to actual lived experience with other male bodies. Fomin's sinewy, shirtless torso and sinuous dancing, Lazarev's navel (visible in the space between his low-slung pants and belly tee), the six-pack abs of the towel-clad model in the Danilko video—all may be "intentional" in both senses described above. I am neither suggesting that all gay Russian men would find such images so experientially rich or evocative of possibility beyond the actual (there are certainly gay Russian men for whom the *muzhik* is the sexual ideal or fantasy catalyst), nor that such "intentionality" is reducible to "fuckability." Rather, the importance is in the ability of men otherwise largely silenced in the arena of popular culture to take part in a shared expression of and reaction to images and bodies that resonate with them on the level of lived experience, and to enact these expressions materially.

If, as Shilling (2008) suggests, crises related to the body in its physical and social environment can be "a prelude to 'new beginnings' . . . encouraging people to rediscover the 'horizon of possibilities' that exists in every situation" (18), and if the attempted literal and symbolic eradication, erasure, silencing, and desexualization/castration of homosexual men in Soviet/post-Soviet Russia must be seen as such a corporeal crisis (as it must), then the appearance of previously invisible bodies, audible and indeed garrulous with intention in the realm of popular music, is far more than a callow instance of using "sex" to "sell." Indeed, the specific location of so many bodies in musical contexts seems to support Shilling's focus on the role of creativity in combating crises such as stigmatization (including the stigmatization of minority sexual identity), whereby those marginalized "discover they are more capable than society assumes, and seek to develop an alternative sense of self which can in turn have positive consequences for their health and physical capacities" (11). In his view, "robbed of their usual avenues for expression, impulses and desires push forward, and the embodied subjects seek to reestablish an effective workable relationship with the world around them" (18). Visual and audible embodiments of nontraditional sexuality are not, are never, as such, merely passive "objects" of the gaze but, rather, material instances of the creative and intentioned reclamation of the right to physical (rather than simply "spiritual") sexual existence.

Male Bodies and Triangulated Desires

The beautiful, semiclothed, male body is a site/sight with which homosexual Russian men may connect/cathect, as well as incarnate testament to the existence of such men as both consumers and producers of music: fans, singers, songwriters, musicians, producers, and video directors.[37] In the context of the palpable and widespread homophobia in contemporary Russia, however, the unambiguous flaunting of a sexualized "gay male body" would most certainly, among specific demographics, negatively impact upon the ability of an artist and his/her financial backers to sell large amounts of their product. Danilko, Hi-Fi, Smash!!, and Dima Bilan—the last of whom will be the final focus of this chapter—are or were all, in the Russia-speaking market, major artists, not indie outsiders, and music sales, touring/performing, and even product endorsement are essential to their livelihoods. As such, while a Moiseev (the spiritual "eunuch") or t.A.T.u or the group Reflex/*Refleks* (as "lesbians" for heterosexual male fantasy fodder) may be "palatable" to a wider audience, intimations of bodies aligned exclusively and unabashedly with male-to-male *physical* pleasure are often camouflaged via the proximity of the feminine, be it an actual, biological female body (or many female bodies), or even the superficial, sartorial trappings of the feminine. Here, the homosexual body is apprehended as part of a *Gestalt* in which the female is a constituent part.

Danilko's work as Verka Serdiuchka features many instances of such intersections of the visible, sexual male in close proximity to female. The male body is on display in Serdiuchka's video for the song "*Ia popala na liubov*" ("I Fell In Love"), which includes two extremely handsome, muscular, and sexual "background dancers" dressed in nothing but long, gold lamé skirts slit up the sides (slung low enough on the hips to reveal a "happy trail" of hair disappearing into the waistband), and matching neckbands, wristbands, and wings. Although the video is framed in what is a familiar, familial setting seen in some of her other productions—Verka seated at the table with her relatives, eating potatoes, peppers, scallions, and beets—the action switches to the room's television screen as one family member inserts a videocassette into the player (saying, in English, "play"). Verka looks nervously back and forth, as her performance is displayed for the assembled. In the center of a hall with chandeliers hanging from the ceiling, is Serdiuchka, dressed in gold lamé and ruffles. She is flanked on either side by her female background singers in complementary attire, including gold, ruffled headdresses, and accompanied by four dancers, two male, two female. The song, about an unrequited love follows, in parts, Verka's "stalking" of the object of her desire, a handsome male waiter, who rebukes her advances. Verka is shown as a sexual being, and the focus of her desire is a man, in a clip that continuously shows how sexually desirable men are. While in the video the erotic connections are between two biological men, the masquerade of femininity (and "camp" humor) short-circuits the implicit homosexuality for those predisposed to view such displays antipathetically.

The video also features, as noted, several attractive biological females—Verka's "background singers"—allowing for further distancing from the homosexual. Such biological females are also prevalent in the visuals associated with both Hi-Fi and Smash!!. This latter group, in certain regards, recalls the George Michael/Andrew Ridgeley team of Wham!—and not only via the use of an onomatopoeic moniker and emphatic punctuation; indeed, both bands were managed by Simon Napier-Bell, and it is clear that there was more than a subconscious attempt to draw comparisons between the two groups.[38] The boys, in fact, on *2nite* covered George Michael's "Faith," and the accompanying video was in frequent rotation in 2004 and 2005 on both *MuzTV* and MTV in St. Petersburg. Insofar as Michael publicly came out in 1998 (after his arrest for a "lewd act" in a public restroom in Beverly Hills), their covering of his song situates the boys, again, in a relation to "gayness."[39]

The connection, however, goes beyond the sexuality of the song's original performer, as homosexuality (or at least homoeroticism) is adumbrated in the narrative of several of the group's videos, "Faith" included. In it, both boys are shown surrounded by beautiful women in a setting reminiscent of Bertolucci's *The Last Emperor*,[40] although the rather explicit sexuality suggested in the lyrics seems strangely absent from what might be thought of as the site *par excellence* for the fulfillment of a boy's sexual desires: a room full of "exotic," gorgeous concubines, whose sole aim is the sexual satisfaction of the visitor. In the video, although the women are shown touching both boys in a manifestly erotic manner, the boys are passive in return, accepting the caresses, but not supplying any of their own; in fact, the only touching of the women by Lazarev appears friendly rather than erotic, a chuck on a chin, or an arm around a shoulder. A lack of "active" touching and a passive position is also evident in the video for the song "Freeway," one of their first and largest hits, in which the action encompasses both the boys' "live" performance on stage, before an exclusively young, female audience, and footage of their driving down the highway in a convertible, pursued by legions of their female fans. Although there is a palpable erotic quality to the video—the sexualness of the boys' bodies is highlighted by their tight pants, open jackets, and sheer belly tees, and two girls are shown lifting their shirts to expose their breasts—the only touching between male and female that occurs is in the final moments of the video, when Lazarev is lifted by a multitude of hands and carried out into the audience. Here, as in the previous video, his position is passive, the girls' active.

There is, however, also touching between the boys themselves. In addition to the onstage performance and outdoor shots, there are brief interspersions of Topolov and Lazarev in silhouette, shirtless, against a screen of black-and-white television or video static that open and close the video, and which occur midway through it as well. In many instances, the boys' bodies are barely touching—often back to back—until the final seconds of the video, where Lazarev puts his hand on Topolov's bare shoulder. Additionally, in one of the shots of the boys driving in the convertible, Lazarev at the wheel and Topolov directly behind him in the back seat, Lazarev takes his hands from the wheel, reaches back to Topolov's ankles (which are positioned one on each side of Lazarev's neck), and pushes his legs into the air (putting his "feet to Jesus," a common gay male idiom); Topolov's position is certainly evocative of that of the "passive," male sexual partner (the "bottom"). Thus in general, any physical contact suggests an intimacy between two males, not a male and a female.

The proximity of the feminine, with Serdiuchka, Smash!!, and Hi-Fi is a tactic used to trouble an unimpeded reading of homosexuality. In the instance of Hi-Fi, it is the female member of the group (Oleshko, Tereshina, Li, or Lipchanskaia) who performs this function, a locus for heterosexual male desire—all three of the singers comprising the group are, in fact, quite attractive—which, if it occurs on the part of the viewer, may also then be imputed to both Fomin and Pron'kin. That is, the woman's femininity, her beauty, serves as martinet of possible "nontraditional" desires, the chaperone who makes sure no inappropriate psychosexual contact occurs; should one question Fomin's sexuality, in general, or vis-à-vis Pron'kin, then the female's presence may serve as the repository for such desires, a corrective of restive gayness. Should one take uncomfortable, perhaps even noniterated interest in the shirtless, blond Fomin, then Oleshko or Tereshina or Li or Lipchanskaia may mollify any misgivings about the reasons for one's attraction to Hi-Fi. One might, at the very least, see the trio as suggesting a *ménage à trois*, wherein the specter of *exclusive* homosexuality is made more palatable by the "fashionable" suggestion of bisexuality, an option that rescues the heterosexual man from entire dissoluteness.

An implied bisexuality is, in fact, a central component of the group's video to the song "*Beda*" ("Misfortune"). The action of the video takes place in a semi-intimate, clublike setting, in several different rooms, one of which is a dressing room. In the main room, bathed in a light blue (*goluboi*) light, a shirtless Fomin, wearing a silver jacket, tight silver pants, and a light blue (*goluboi*) scarf around his neck, dances and lip-synchs in front of several scantily clad female dancers. Pron'kin, likewise surrounded by similarly dressed female dancers, and wearing an athletic warm-up jacket, "plays" the guitar, and Tereshina, situated near a vertical "stripper" pole, clad in a two-piece, abbreviated silver outfit (bra and miniskirt), dances and "sings." The narrative of the video revolves around a courtship of sorts between Fomin and Tereshina, the former vying for the latter's affections to no avail. After a brief scene in which Fomin is rebuked by Tereshina (in the presence of Moscow drag queen Zaza Napoli, who serves as a sort of "go-between"), Fomin exits to the dressing room where he removes his head, places it in a box (!), and exits in the guise of Pron'kin, dressed in foppish, eighteenth-century attire: ruffled, gold lamé shirt, long, maroon and gold brocade jacket, tight maroon knickers, knee socks, and large-buckled black shoes.[41] Accompanied on the sofa by another male similarly attired (but without pants!), the two "court" Tereshina, who is dressed almost identically to the second man (and also without pants). She rebuffs the advances of both men, including their offer of flowers, after which Pron'kin rebuffs, with a slap, the other man's offer of the flower to *him*. Although they try to physically subdue Tereshina, she runs from the room, back to the dressing room in which Fomin undertook his transformation. There, removing her wig, she spies (and is spied by) Fomin's head peeking from the box in which he had left it. As Pron'kin (Fomin?) approaches, Tereshina pulls back a rubber mask (in the style of the 1960s television show *Mission Impossible*) to reveal that *she* is actually Fomin—although Fomin's head is still peering from its box. Fomin exits again from the dressing room, and tosses his *goluboi* jacket to a puzzled Pron'kin (not Fomin?) who stares at the jacket and then, as the camera cuts back, laughs in what appears to be a moment of realization; did the *goluboi* jacket, previously on "Tania (Tereshina)" (was it Tereshina or Fomin?) serve as a clue to the hapless Pron'kin that he had, in fact, been romancing a man?. In the unsustainable narrative, Fomin appears to be all three characters simultaneously, suggesting that a connection between bodies (faces, even entire heads, are removable), and sexuality is not dependent upon gender. Fomin transforms to Pron'kin to woo Tereshina (who is dressed like a man) who, in fact, turns out to be Fomin. In the final moments of the video, Pron'kin is about to remove *his* "mask" as well, but the camera cuts away before we find out who he "is."

The video's final images are also marked by a presentation of the male gaze. Back in the main section of the club (where women and drag queens dance), the camera zooms toward the silvery, sinewy Fomin, as if someone's gaze is closing in on him. He stops dancing to meet it, and the camera quickly cuts to Pron'kin "playing" the guitar, giving the impression that he is the origin of the gaze. With the sounding of the final chord of the song—played on the acoustic guitar—Pron'kin raises and shakes his hand in a manner imitating a vibrato, also raising the neck of his guitar. Fomin is seen again, smiling, meeting the gaze head-on, but ultimately looks down and away, seemingly in deference to it. The narrative thus ends with a presentation of the male gaze directed at another male.

But male-for-male desire is not the only one represented in the video, and Tereshina's presence is interspersed throughout; indeed, the romantic relationship that seems to be the starting point of all that follows is that between Fomin and Tereshina. There is a certain type of proximity in evidence here, Tereshina functioning as part of what Sedgwick (1985) defines as a "triangulated" formation upon which "homosocial desire" rests; she is there to allay any fears of inappropriateness, to make sure the homosexual does not breach the homosocial, to focus desire on the appropriately genitalled person, while disguising the potent ties occurring between two men—the same function played by Oleshko, Li, and Lipchanskaia. This is not to say that the women's musical roles are obliterated by dint of their bodies, because, in fact, none of the women (nor Pron'kin, or perhaps even Fomin) appear to have *any* musical function in the group; rather, it is only their physical existence that matters. The majority of people with whom I spoke expressed doubt that any of the women or Pron'kin actually sang (or, in the case of the latter, played any instruments, despite his pantomime strumming of a guitar in lip-synched concert appearances) and indeed, the vast majority of tracks are built around one voice that is multitracked, supplying both lead and background/harmony vocals;[42] although there are some instances of female vocals on certain tracks,[43] the timbres of the various vocals indicate different singers, none of whom may actually be any of the women whose images and bodies are presented.[44] Likewise with Pron'kin, while there are instances of a lower male voice singing background vocals (often in unison, at the lower octave, as in "*Ia liubliu*" ["I Love"] and "*Pochtovyi poezd*" ["Mail Train"]), there is no reason to believe that he is actually supplying the voice heard.[45]

The same sort of triangulation occurs in the case of Smash!!, although here it is a motile, ductile, external femininity that takes the place of Tania (or any of the other female "singers" in Hi-Fi). In this regard, in addition to the female "characters" in the various videos—a Juliet in the Romeo-and-Juliet–themed "Talk To Me," Chinese concubines, and so forth—the omnipresent female audience may also be considered a gendered "character," a multivocal, multibodied mass of prenubile femininity. Indeed, the flocks of screaming, adoring female fans, probably planted by the band's PR directors, seem to be an immutable and indispensable part of their act not only in their "live"/

lip-synched performances, but also as featured characters (or *a* character) in videos such as that which accompanies the song "Freeway." Here the "character" works on a dual level: the female audience is both viewed and viewer, part of the triangulated configuration that it constructs in order to be able to be made comprehensible as viewed through the optics of heteronormativity.[46] In each instance, the triangulation fends off the anxiety of the homosexual, allowing for commercial success *concurrent* with gay fandom and visibility—the courting of both the homosexual and the heterosexual via a complex and multivocal *Gestalt*.

Swinging Both Ways: Dima Bilan and Eurovision

The concepts of intentionality and proximity may both be related to another central concern of phenomenology, that of orientation—how embodied subjects approach objects in the world, how perception depends upon a specific vantage point, and how such relationships thus allow the subject to *be* oriented. In her book *Queer Phenomenology*, Ahmed (2006b) links this general concept of orientation with a specifically *sexual* orientation, arguing that orientation may be conceived of as relying, in part, upon lines: lines that divide (this side from that side), that lead us places, that make certain things available and others unavailable. Such lines (which "align" us, or bring us "in line") keep bodies "directed in some way more than others," a direction that organizes movement in the aggregate—a "collective direction" (15) which, in the service of compulsory heterosexuality, acts as a "straightening device" (23; see also Chapter 2).[47] While the very existence of such lines is contingent upon their being continually followed, trodden, and thus performatively produced, certain bodies—lesbigay, queer, or trans, for example—may deviate from them, aligning with other axes that are contingent and relative, rather than essential or given, thus creating new lines, new orientations. How such linear orientations operate in the filed of post-Soviet popular music may be explored via an examination of one singer and his musical output.

Like many other Russian singers or bands, including Smash!!, Dima Bilan (the stage name of Viktor Belan), building upon a widespread popularity within the Russian-speaking sphere, embarked in the past several years upon an international career as a recording artist. Following successful, largely domestically distributed CDs such as *Nochnoi khuligan* (*Night Hooligan*) (2003) and *Na beregu neba* (*To the Shore of the Sky*) (2004), both of which featured tracks widely played on the radio, in nightclubs (in dance-version remixes), and on Russian music television, Bilan became the official entrant in the 2006

Eurovision Song Contest, placing second—Russia's highest ranking since that of Alsou in 2000.⁴⁸ In 2008, however, the singer once again won the national contest, progressed to the finals, and ultimately won the competition for Russia. Such international exposure most certainly aided him in reaching a wider audience, one that was not entirely Russian-speaking. And while Bilan's first CD had featured songs only in Russian, each subsequent release contained tracks in English, including his Eurovision numbers, both of which had been sung in English for the competitions. The 2006 entry, "Never Gonna Let You Go," appeared on the 2006 CD *Vremia-reka* (*Time [Is a] River*) in both the English and Russian versions ("*Kak ustroen ètot mir*," "How This World Is Arranged"); 2008's winning entry, "*Believe*" was likewise included as part of a CD, *Protiv pravil* (*Against the Rules*), once again in both English and Russian versions ("*Vse v tvoikh rukakh*," "Everything Is in Your Hands"). Further indicative of Bilan's increasing bid for international success, and his orientation toward both Russia and the West, both the winning song, as well as another ("*Ia tvoi nomer odin*," also released in English as "Number One Fan") were produced by American hip-hop producer and performer Timbaland, and the video for the latter was shot in London by British director Trudy Bellinger. Miazhzevich (2010), in her nuanced reading of Bilan's performance at Eurovision, highlights just this type of parallel orientation toward geographically and ideologically unique audiences, noting, for example, how his performances in the competition concurrently adopted both conventions of Soviet *èstrada* (marked by a mixing of high and low art), as well as Western performance practice (opting for "an expansiveness of gesture and boldness in the use of space") (259). Moreover, she finds that the foregrounding of sex and sexuality on the part of performers from former Soviet Union states is related to intra- and intercultural dynamics, whereby artists both adopt and critique (via the adoption) the (Western) culture of "Euro-trash."

Bilan's initial success in the Russian-speaking world was certainly due in part to what many consider to be his physical and sexual attractiveness. Although his tenor voice, honed while studying at the Gnesin State Music College in Moscow, is arguably better than those of many contemporary Russian pop singers, it is notable that on fan sites and internet forums, the singer's physiognomy and physiology are remarked upon with great frequency. His beauty has been frequently exploited in his videos, his shirtless, shaved/waxed body featured prominently in "*Ia tak liubliu tebia*" ("I So Love You"), "*Ty tol'ko ty*" ("You, Only You"), and "*Ia oshibsia, ia popal*" ("I Made a Mistake, I Was Caught"); in the clip for "*Èto bylo liubov'*" ("It Was Love"), his jeans are so low-slung as to partially and repeatedly expose his buttocks. As may be inferred from the songs' titles, much of his opus deals generally with "love"—bittersweet, unconsummated, erotic—and the "plots" of the accompanying videos often revolve around Bilan and an equally attractive female love interest.

While the addition of a female character to the video narratives, and thus unambiguous heterosexual contextualization—sometimes verging on the vulgar, with excessive grinding and thrusting[49]—is undoubtedly meant to bolster the singer's image as a heterosexual heartthrob, there are also instances of male-female pairings that, nonetheless, implicitly question normative sexuality. In "*Ia oshibsia*," for example, Bilan is the captive of a black-vinyl–clad dominatrix-cum-vampire, physically battling (and losing to) her in a cage fight, but ultimately breaking free. And in "*Nevozmozhnoe vozmozhno*" ("The Impossible Is Possible"), ostensibly a story focusing on a heterosexual pickup, the mullet-sporting Bilan appears more urban and fashionable than in early videos, the frequent shots of his crotch, as well as the narrative's inclusion of what might be read as his "cruising" of a wealthy businessman, render him more sex-for-money (gay-for-pay?) hustler than loving boyfriend.

But Bilan's attractiveness, while obviously manipulated to read partially as heterosexual, has apparently not impacted upon his concurrent popularity as a sex symbol for gay men; for example, in December of 2004 he appeared in the gay magazine *Kvir* as one of Russia's ten sexiest men, as chosen by the magazine's readers. (Sergei Lazarev, according to the editors, had just barely missed making the final cut.) And while his inclusion in a list of sex symbols *of* gay men does not necessarily connote anything about his sexual orientation, Bilan was—perhaps due to his "feminine" positioning as gazed-upon sex object, his ubiquitous, "slithery" dancing (conspicuously on display in the video for the single "Lonely"), his metrosexual attire and haircuts, and/or those "queer" video moments noted above—largely assumed to be gay by my informants. Bilan's sexual orientation was, and continues to be, questioned regularly on the internet and the press, either via direct statements or innuendo.[50] For example, one internet article leads with the headline "*Gei-skandal na press-konferentsii Dimy Bilana*" ("A Gay Scandal at Dima Bilan's Press-Conference"), reporting that the singer had been asked about his intention to marry a young Latvian man (Guru Ken 2007).[51] According to another article, designers Dolce and Gabbana purportedly approached Bilan in order to enlist his services as a model for their Eastern European campaigns; however, the designers first asked about the singer's sexual orientation, noting that all of their models were gay, because "we have that social position. We support the gay community."[52] Rather than report on the singer's answer, the article ends with the question still hanging: "Before Bilan and his team, there is now a difficult question, the answer to which will in many respects determine the future career of the singer" (Rybakova 2006).

Even Bilan's erstwhile producer, Viktor Baturin, joined the chorus of accusatory voices, intimating that his supposed love affair with (and possible impending marriage to) model and television presenter Lena Kuletskaia (featured as Bilan's exceptionally beautiful love interest in the video for his song "*Èto byla liubov'*") was entirely a sham; in a 2008 filmed interview on the website russia.ru, the businessman tells the correspondent:

> If you are principally a homosexual [*gomoseksualist*], people should also know about this. And you shouldn't dupe [*morochit' golovu*] the nymphets, [pretending] that you have a romance with Lena Kuletskaia, and you are going to marry her soon. You can't marry her, because you love the other sex.[53]

It may be assumed that the articles and interviews cited above were seen by hundreds of thousands, if not millions, of readers/viewers. More specific statistics, however, in terms of numbers of viewers can be found for each video uploaded on YouTube, where a young singer/songwriter made an "appeal" (*obrashchenie*) to Bilan, one viewed approximately 1.7 million times.[54] In the video, a young Ukrainian man, Valentin Strykalo, speaking in Russian, and appearing meek, anxious, and somewhat awkward, states that he is a fan of Bilan's. A guitar in his hands, he tells the singer that he has written a song that he believes should be performed by "none other than you" ("*imenno vy*"). As he begins to play, the plaintiveness of the minor key, slow tempo, and delicate finger picking are the perfect introduction to the first verse, the text of which reveals Strykalo's emotional turmoil ("I don't know how to overcome this pain/ how to make my heart beat again"). But what may have appeared at the outset to have been an expression/confession of somewhat hackneyed twenty-something angst begins to alter as the song progresses; the young man—now, addressing his mother in the text—links his recent sadness to the women's lingerie she has found in his closet. The stage set now with the most banal (and offensive) stereotypes, the song moves out of its minor-key verse to a major-key, aggressively strummed chorus, with the text

Vse resheno:	It's decided:
Mama, ia gei!	Mama, I'm gay
Papa, ia gei!	Papa, I'm gay
Mozhete prosto promolchat',	You can simply keep quiet
Mozhete zlit'sia ili besit'sia,	You can get angry, you can become furious
Mne na èto naplevat'!	But I don't care!

As the song continues, more "humor" is offered, his now-confessed homosexuality revealed as the cause of his unusual behavior (why he stopped smiling, why he hung a Jude Law poster on the wall), and a list of sexual liaisons (whether consummated or desired) is offered: Edik, Iarik, Marik, Nicky ("Kolen'ka"), Vasia ("Vasen'ka"),[55] Uncle Grisha, and a childhood friend of his father's. Strykalo—the stage name of singer/musician/poet/songwriter Iurii Kaplan—while making use of a far different battery of tools, and perhaps with different intentions, accomplishes the same feat as those journalists writing for the yellow press: but in this case he has literally given voice to a widespread questioning of Bilan's sexual orientation.

As might be deduced from the existing range of contemporary media accounts, neither Bilan's homosexuality nor heterosexuality are universally assumed; while some internet postings vigorously proclaim the singer's heterosexuality, others virulently characterize Bilan as the "most genuine gay, gayer simply doesn't exist" ("*samyi nastoiashchii gei, golubee prosto ne byvaet*"), "the gayest gay of all gay and non-gay gays, and moreover a bottom" ("*samyi geistyi gei iz vsekh geistykh i negeistykh geev . . . pri ètom eshcho* [sic] *i passiv*"), and one particularly malign poster opined "not only gay, but the leader of gays, he's the gay tsar, he's the gay princess of our stage, all Russian heterosexuals are sick of his faggy voice. Execute [him] immediately!" ("*ne prosto gei, on predvoditel' geev, on tsar'-gei, on golubaia korolevna nashei tseny, ego pidirastichesii* [sic] *golos proel plesh* [sic] *vsem geteroseksualam rossii. Srochno na ekzikutsiiu* [sic]*!*")[56] The point is not whether any of these "journalistic" or popular accounts in any way reports on the "truth," or which side of the hetero/homo debate is correct. Rather, what is important is the fact that the singer's sexual orientation has become an object of interest, much of this, I suggest, due to Bilan's presentation of his body as an object of indiscriminate (male/female) scopic consumption, displaying his often naked skin (including his photographs for the Russian version of *Playgirl* and the magazine *Molotok*) as sexual and sensual, rather than purposeful vis-à-vis "masculine" pursuits; that this body is often a dancing body further codes it as feminine (remembering that "*muzhiki* don't dance").[57] In the opinion of one internet forum poster, in response to the question, "why do so many people think that Dima Bilan is gay?" it is "perhaps [due to] an overt display of narcissism, and showing of his naked torso."[58]

However, as I have earlier noted, the male body cannot be simply assumed to be "gayed" through any or all self-displays (nor, conversely, can even seemingly "hypermasculinized/heteronormativized" bodies lay claim to immunity from scrutiny);[59] rather, bodies are read, consumed, and enjoyed within specific social, discursive, and historical contexts. The multivocality of the body, and the multiplicities of its reception may be seen in conjunction with Bilan's song "Believe"/"*Vse v tvoikh rukakh*," contrasting the former, sung as his winning performance at Eurovision in 2008, with the latter, the Russian version released in conjunction with a video that same year. While Bilan's physical attractiveness is visible in both, each version nonetheless foregrounds, in relation to an assumed audience, a seemingly different man (with different aims): the Eurovision performance, broadcast internationally in what is one of the most visible instances of gay fandom,[60] stands in direct contrast to the video—shot in both Russian and English versions—which played not only to an international audience, but to the mass-market Russian-speaking audience as well.

Bilan's good looks, like his self-presentation, straddle the line of the same bifurcation posited above; that is, while his dark hair and eyes, square jaw and (possibly) broken nose, occasional goatee, and musculature all point toward "manliness," his lithe frame, hairless body, wide-spaced eyes, and full, "pouty" lips read as more boyish, if not fully androgynous. Such a split of manhood versus boyhood may be seen in the overall color schemes of the singer's wardrobes in the two aforementioned performances. At Eurovision he is attired completely in white, while in the video, he is largely featured in darker clothing—the former suggesting innocence and purity (even femininity), the latter maturity, even danger (or even masculinity; consider the gendered implications of "the white prince" contrasted with "the black knight"). What the clothing makes visible or invisible is also important: While in the video Bilan's body is largely covered, the singer appearing alternately in a dark blazer and light T-shirt, black pants and vest, white shirt, and T-shirt, and finally a tan jacket over a white hoodie, for his appearance at the Eurovision final he was attired in tight white hip-huggers and a fairly sheer white shirt, partially unbuttoned and offering a glimpse of his chest. Bilan, at the emotional apex of the song—and almost concurrent with his ascent into the falsetto register—ripped his shirt open, thus exposing his bare chest at the proper climactic ("orgasmic") moment.[61]

The positioning of his body at the Eurovision finale is also telling; starting out sitting on the stage, he languorously rolls to his back (thus, a man *on* his back), and slowly moves to a kneeling position from which he delivers the first verse and chorus of the song. Although he rises to deliver the next verse and chorus, as well as the bridge section, he ends the song once again on his knees, in a position suggesting sexual supplication. In contradistinction, save for approximately two seconds in the video—the scene in which the singer is seen "performing" for an audience (and a rough analog to the Eurovision performance)—where Bilan *almost* kneels (on one knee, not both), he is filmed sitting or standing. Not only body but bodily movement and body position are indicative of subject position.

A distinction may also be made in terms of each performance's narrative (or lack thereof) and associations with either homo- or heterosexuality. In the live performance, narrative is absent, and what obtains is an air of both homosexuality (via Bilan's body) and homosociality; in the performance, Bilan is joined by Hungarian violinist and composer Edvin Martos, and Russian Olympic figure skating champion Evgenii Pliushchenko. While the reason behind Martos's appearance is clear—his violin playing is a highly audible component of the song—that of Pliushchenko is not immediately so. It is possible that the skater's celebrity (five-time European champion and 2006 Olympic gold-medalist) may have been enlisted in an attempt to garner viewer/voter interest, especially the interest of an audience assumed to be composed of figure-skating–loving gay men.[62] But the overall effect of the three men on stage, Bilan's hyperbolic vocal matched by the peripatetic, romantic violin playing of Martos, and the flowing, flashy skating of Pliushchenko, was one of male aesthetic bonding—a site not often though of as marking "masculine," heterosexual male connections.

Although the suggestion of homosexuality/-sociality may have been read in the West by Eurovision viewers, it is certainly possible that no such connotations accrued in the Russian context; as Olson (2004: 43–46) has noted, part and parcel of the Soviet project was the building of not only a new nation but a new citizenry, and the inculcation of "culture" into each person. Such "culture" was an indication of Soviet superiority (over, say, the assumed vulgarity and venality of the United States), and generally drew upon the trappings of a specifically "high," often pre-Revolutionary, culture;[63] such "culturedness" might be applied equally as well to both violin playing and figure skating, the latter of which could be related not only to Olympic sport, but also ballet dancing. But the possible implication of heterosexuality is far more apparent in the video clip for the song for both the international and domestic audiences.[64]

The lyrics of both the Russian and the English versions attempt to paint a picture of hope, courage, and perseverance, possibly in the face of adversity; and while the imagery used in each is somewhat different, both contain a similar overall message. Below are several lines from the two texts (with a translation of the Russian segments) for comparison:

ENGLISH VERSION

The courage that's inside is gonna break my fall
Nothing is gonna dim my light within . . .
. . . Nothing else can stop me if I just believe
And I believe in me

RUSSIAN VERSION

I vse v nashei vlasti
I sbudetsia odnazhdy tvoia mechta . . .
Vse eshche vozmozhno . . .
. . . Ved' vse v tvoikh rukakh

ENGLISH TRANSLATION (RUSSIAN VERSION)

And everything is in our power
And your dream will one day come true . . .
Everything is still possible . . .
. . . You see, everything is in your hands

The lyrics of both versions may seem to indicate a particularly Western, agentic self-determination, as opposed to a resignation to reliance upon an all-powerful State apparatus, and indeed some of the visuals appear to bolster the "international" flavor of the clip; for example, not only are all of the instances of printed words in English (albeit in rather clumsy translations), but the very first images are of people of color: a black man and an Asian woman in succession, both hospital workers, an immediate foregrounding that is remarkable in the Russian context.

But the visual, textual, and/or symbolic allusions to the West are largely eclipsed in the video by the contextualization of Bilan and his body within a narrative in which the dynamics and symbols of masculine patriarchy are among the most salient and pervasive. Here, the striving for something possibly impossible revolves not around the fulfillment of solipsistic, bourgeois, egocentric desire, but around Bilan and his coperformers' (Martos and Pliushchenko) organizing a "beneficent [sic] concert" in order to save a hospitalized child in need of expensive medical intervention. After an introductory section featuring Bilan singing in a sports hall (as opposed to a concert hall), the story begins with a view of the male child in a hospital bed, his mother by his side; a male doctor enters, takes the mother aside and, referencing the x-rays glowing before them, gives the mother news that causes her to collapse in tears. The sentimental pathos of the narrative is augmented by not only the interspersed shots of the angelic boy in the bed, grasping his teddy bear, but also by Martos's Romantic-style violin obligatti.

As the plot unfolds, the viewer finds Bilan in a diner, serendipitously viewing a news story of the boy's plight on the television over the counter; under the boy's image are the words "boy in need of expensive backbone surgery."[65] Immediately, he phones his (real life) producer, Iana Rudkovskaia, as well as Martos, who is in a photo session. Bilan goes to Martos, and the two, accompanied by a rather butch female photographer (in full makeup, but with close-cropped hair and sporting an olive, military-inspired jacket), progress to the sports hall to enlist the services of Pliushchenko in their attempt to save the boy. There, the four engage in another photo session, and the image of them together on the ice appears—especially when the photographer is filmed from behind—to be that of four men. The ensuing concert, at the ice rink, mirrors in some regards the performance at Eurovision, although the color story and body placement are notably different. Predictably, images of the boy being rushed to surgery are followed by those of his being wheeled from the hospital, miraculously standing, being enveloped by hugs and lifted upon the shoulders of all those in attendance—the four "men" (including the photographer) and the mother.

The hypervaluation of masculinity here is prominent; in the narrative of the video, it is a group of four biological males—Bilan, Martos, Pliushchenko, and the doctor—who are portrayed as those capable of giving life. Moreover, the Soviet dictum of art's essential power in the building of a nation is once again underscored, a concert literally saving a boy's life—a concert taking place, not incidentally, in a sports hall, a site devoted to *fizku'ltura*, yet another essential component of the maintenance of the strong, healthy individual (= state) body. That the child is male, and in need of a *backbone* no less, is also important; during the concert, with his innocent face projected behind the three performers, we are given a world in which women are absent, one in which men alone give life to (male) children. That the only other person in the video to step on the ice, and thus into the "inner sanctum," is the butch photographer (Rudkovskaia is shown at the sports hall, but only in the stands, briefly) further codes this space as masculine, as well as Soviet—rather than a genderless nation, women were de facto expected to assume the trappings of masculinity. But the references are post-Soviet as well. For although these masculine personages are contained in what might be easily read as a homosocial environment (with overtones of homosexuality), their enterprise is in service to that which is presented in the media as one of the most pressing needs in contemporary post-Soviet Russian society: a fight against decreasing demographics, and a crisis of children raised by single mothers (as the mother in the video unambiguously appears to be).[66] While at Eurovision, the boyish, sexual Bilan may be read as a sensual sybarite, reveling in the aesthetic, the bourgeois (and thus Western), the homosocial, in the video, Bilan accomplishes nothing less—with the help of his "male" companions—than providing the masculinity necessary to save male children, thus keeping Russia's population strong.[67]

Within this narrative, Bilan's body is covered, the sinuous, smooth torso so ubiquitous in his other performances conspicuously hidden. Eurovision is certainly a camp-fest; performances by such groups as Lordi (Finland, 2007) and Sylvia Night (Iceland, 2006)[68] who purposely attempt to inject over-the-top humor and theatrics into an arena often associated with "fluff," as well as offerings by performers trying, in earnest, to produce by-the-book top-40 (yet often failing miserably), all deliberately highlight what might be conceived of as the artifice, the ridiculousness, the delicious superficiality of pop. Yet Eurovision must also be understood as one of the premier sites for putting "beefcake" on display for the visual consumption by gay men; from contestants Sakis Rouvas and Kostas Martakis (Greece, 2004 and 2008) to Jonsi (Iceland, 2004) to the "boy band" Nash (Spain, 2007)—and even the "halftime" entertainment provided by the Chippendales-like group Scandinavian Hunks at Finland's final in Tampere in 2009—the competition is an internationally visible forum for gayness, in which Bilan's display of his body would serve to augment (if not eclipse) the musical components of his performance.

Conceiving of orientation as having a linear component, as Ahmed (2006b) does, may help to illuminate why such a large number of potentially homosexualized bodies appear in the context of popular music, especially if we highlight her observation that lines do not imply only spatiality, but temporality as well. The lines available to us, according to Ahmed, are not "casual," but are dependent upon lines we have already taken (21); additionally, the sedimentation of certain "straightening" linear orientations is the effect of a historical and repeated adherence *to* the line, experienced in "real" time. Music, however, while it takes place in time, and often has an inherent linearity, also implicitly questions time. The same song will occur in different locations at different times, taking the listener back or pointing toward the future. Verses and choruses unfold in time, but fold time back upon itself via the repeats; and the experience of time, when one is engaged with music, may be different than time as experienced in "daily life."[69] So, if linearity characterizes orientations—orientations that corral bodies and thrust them into specific trajectories—and such orientations are dependent upon a line that does not exist "objectively" but which must be continually and performatively reproduced (by keeping *in* line), then is it purely accidental that bodies that skew or implicitly question orientations should appear via a modality that does much the same to temporality? This is not meant to be simply a mildly clever analogy; in the same way that neither the lines available to us nor the specific physiology of the human body (upon which perception lies) may be seen as "fortuitous," cultural production, and the propinquities of the various component parts, do not fall into place by chance.

It is true, as Miazhevich suggests, that Bilan's performances attempt to engage multiple audiences, via the adoption of multiple, often apparently contradictory codes; however, it would be a mistake not only to unquestioningly accept him as (only—or even) a "Russian heterosexual performer" (2010: 260), but also to view his presentations of the codes of (global) gayness as primarily delivered ironically—as a type of *stiob*[70]—and, moreover, primarily directed to his Western audience.[71] Rather than viewing Bilan's associations to homosexuality as a type of "fakery" perpetrated on the West in order to critique Western cultural hegemony, we might also highlight them as "legitimate"—whatever the genders or genitals of his actual sexual partners—offering a model of a certain type of visible, living "nontraditional" sexual orientation, an orientation that resonates with and orients (often invisible) living, breathing homosexual Russian men. For if, as Kon (2003) asserts, it is exactly the homosexual spectator that has played such an enormous role in the history of figurative art, by "remov[ing] the spell" (*raskoldovat'*) of the "hermetically closed male body," "present[ing] it as worthy of delight and immortalization as an erotic object" (274),[72] then the removal of both this subject position and subject—the homosexual gaze(r)—from the realm of popular music is likely to recast the spell of a blind belief in a universal, "natural" heterosexuality. The abundance of visible, sexual, and intentional male bodies such as Bilan's, however, short-circuits the efficacy of any possible discursive incantation.

Visible male bodies, invoking the possibility of the homosexual, therefore, "do" many things in post-Soviet space. They provide a sight/site for gay men, around which personal desire and self-identification may coalesce, including for those men who may not wish or be able to articulate their erotic desires for other men. They serve, in a context often marked by a cultural proscription of the unambiguous presentation of the "nontraditional," the *goluboi*, as incarnate, observable, and social embodiments of the very possibility of male-to-male erotic desire, apprehended in part corporeally, related to and constitutive of lived experience. *Those* male bodies, in plain sight, relate to *my* living, male body (and not simply discursively); they both potentiate and visibly replicate (without pathologizing) my corporeal existence when other public avenues have been foreclosed. Additionally, such images engage embodied subjects other than those who self-identify as homosexual; they allow for the public foregrounding of *women's* sexual desires (e.g., female fans at concerts, in videos), the very visibility of which is a glorious affront to a patriarchy that has historically sought to circumscribe female sexuality. And they may also serve, via their function as potentiators of female sexual desire, as didactic devices, "role models" for heterosexual men who are becoming aware not only of this aforementioned female sexuality (and who may see such bodies as a way of attracting it), but of new codes of masculinity. There is also the possibility that beautiful male bodies are enjoyed by heterosexual men as well, men who may outwardly scorn such bodies as *pederasticheskie*, but may inwardly appreciate the fact that these bodies exist in the public domain, offering the ability to be gazed surreptitiously, with impunity.

I do not want to give the impression that such bodies necessarily belong to those singers most favored by gay Russian men, or that such bodies are necessary for popularity with a gay audience; most of my informants were somewhat indifferent to Bilan and Smash!! as musical performers, although they were more complimentary regarding the music of Hi-Fi (whose music was often played at gay clubs). Yet many of the same men identified one or more of these men as being *goluboi*, and admitted to finding one or more of them attractive (*krasiv* or *simpatichen*). Sergei Lazarev, who has embarked upon a successful solo singing career post-Smash!!, seemingly embraced his popularity with gay men, appearing in July of 2006 as a guest DJ (under the name Superlazer) at the gay Moscow club *Tri obez'iany* (Three Monkeys).[73] And while he continues to be presented in his videos as romantically involved with one or more women, in the press he has praised not only gay audiences ("they appreciate and love music"), but gay men themselves (finding "them" "friendlier than the majority of customers at glamorous spots," and "normal, reasonable people"), additionally characterizing Russia as a "very homophobic country" ("*ochen' gomofobnaia strana*").[74] In the same interviews Lazarev is somewhat ambiguous regarding his own sexual orientation ("I'm for people looking at their own plate, and not discussing others' preferences," "I'm generally against stamps and labels") (Ivanov 2006), but clear regarding his opinion of the public image of "the homosexual":

> The only thing that bothers me is the image of a gay man that was formed in the minds of the masses with the help of . . . show business. The majority think that a homosexual is a person who changes [into] flashy [*iarkie*], absurd outfits, who speaks with the voice of Boris Moiseev. In reality, it's totally not like this. Gay men behave and look differently, it's all individual and depends upon the character of the person."

Lazarev might be disparaged for equivocating about his own sexual orientation (especially when noting the title of his first post-Smash!! CD, *Don't Be Fake*), or for attempting to "(hetero-)normalize" gay men; however, his comments, his body, and the bodies of other such performers, offer the possibility of one type of corporeality that is somatically tangible, sexed, not "neutered" (or reoriented) via the kitsch, the camp, or the invocation of the spiritual (limp) homosexual. Here are bodies that move, the skin of which often sweats, the sweat of which has a scent; they are bodies that are potentially and *intentionally*—in all the myriad meanings of the word—sexual. The visible muscles of the male body may, at first blush, appear both analogous and homologous to those of the bodybuilder, as theorized by Lingis (1994a; see Chapter 2); otiose in terms of their functions in modern, capitalist society, removed from the sphere of purposeful work and the evolution and propagation of the species, existing only as sexual spectacle. However, far from being superfluous, their visual impact is, in fact, purposeful and necessary, reaffirming the possibility and viability of the living gay body in post-Soviet space. The fact that artists such as Lazarev, Bilan, Serdiuchka/Danilko, and Fomin are often featured in and on gay-themed magazines and websites[75] attests to their popularity as, if not (only) performers, then bodies of interest to many gay Russian men, if not (only) for their very bodies, then for the "orienting" work those bodies do.

5. Gay-Made Space

> "Space can never be that completed simultaneity in which all interconnections have been established, and in which everywhere is already linked to everywhere else. A space, then, which is neither a container for always-already constituted identities nor a completed closure of holism. This is a space of loose ends and missing links. For the future to be open, space must be open too."
> —Doreen Massey (2005: 11–12)

> In the space of musical experience, we foment transformation.
> —D. Robert DeChaine (2002: 95)

It was only in 2012 when St. Petersburg and Moscow, two of the largest cities in Eastern Europe, joined the ranks of the "virtually visible"; in February of that year, the Google Maps street view feature was finally enabled, allowing internet visitors to view some of the world's most famous sites and sights, architectural and otherwise. From the *Krasnaia ploshad'* (Red Square), to the *Èrmitazh* (State Hermitage Museum), to *Petergof* (the "Russian Versailles"), hard-core Slavophiles and the generally curious alike now had the ability to move beyond the flatness and circumscription of the still photo, to experience 360 degree views of buildings and boulevards, to "walk" (or glide, with the click of a mouse) down *Nevskii prospekt* or *Tverskaia ulitsa*, perhaps even "encountering" virtual natives along the way. Of course, even the verisimilitude offered by the latest satellite and digital technologies cannot truly replicate all that is associated with physical location within a specific space. The panoramic pictures on my laptop screen, for example, do not conjure up in me the same experiential affects as when I walked down *Moskovskii prospekt* in St. Petersburg the first time, feeling entirely dwarfed by the massive scale of the architecture, hearing the sounds of the Russian language around me, struggling to read the signs written in the Cyrillic alphabet, fearful of getting lost and being unable to ask for directions back to my apartment.

A city is not simply buildings, of course, a bounded and stable location aligning neatly with a two-dimensional depiction on a two-dimensional map (even if, with a click, it can become three-dimensional) or a linguistic signifier; rather, a city is a place comprising manifold spaces. These spaces should likewise not be considered objective, material sites into which people enter, or from which they exit; rather, space, as numerous theorists have posited, is a construction, one reliant upon relationships between and among both objects and subjects. Tuan (1977), Löw (2008), and Massey (2005) (among many others) have highlighted this constructedness to varying degrees of explicitness, rooting such constructions in the realm of lived experience.[1] Löw, for example, noting the importance of both structure and action, sees space as constituted via "performative action by synthesizing and relationally ordering objects and people," something that occurs "in day-to-day activities with recourse to institutionalized orderings and spatial structures" (43). Foregrounding the experiential, she suggests that actions are tied to perceptions that "are grounded both in the external effect of social goods and other people and in the perceptual activity of the constituting agent" (41). Moreover, Löw is highly cognizant of the affective power of space and finds that "atmospheres" of either inclusion or exclusion may be enacted via "simultaneous acts of interpretation/perception and external effects of objects in their spatial ordering" (46).

For gay men in post-Soviet Russia, the finding of spaces with amicable atmospheres is often dependent upon interpersonal relationships, word of mouth, serendipity, and even the media. In this last regard, magazines such as *Afisha* and *Kalendar'* (in both St. Petersburg and Moscow), with their listings of "cultural" happenings and sites, play a part in rendering such spaces visible, just as the publication *TimeOut* has done in such major urban centers as New York, Paris, Barcelona, and Amsterdam, among others. In fact, indicating a growing internationalism in Russia's largest cities, *TimeOut* appeared in 2004 in both cities, gradually taking over *Kalendar*.[2] The style, graphics, and layout mirrored those of all other *TimeOut*s, with listings published every two weeks, arranged under such rubrics as "film," "exhibitions," "theater," "music," "sports," "children," and "clubs." Notably missing from St. Petersburg's contents, in contrast with those of other cities, was a "gay and lesbian" section; after the first few issues, however, a very small group of such listings appeared not under its own heading, but tucked away near the back of the magazine in the section devoted to *"vzroslye igry"* ("adult games"), alongside information on casinos and strip clubs.

It was not until the summer of 2004 that St. Petersburg's *Kalendar'/TimeOut* followed the format of its sister publications, allotting a specific space within its pages for the rubric *"gei i lesbi,"* the first article in the section noting a time lag of over thirty years between *TimeOut London*'s first section for homosexuals (1968), and St. Petersburg's (Kudymov 2004a). In this short editorial, which accompanied the scant listings of gay and lesbian spaces/places in the former capital—the paucity of listings reflecting the relative paucity of actual choices—Kudymov asserts that gay men and women have been, transhistorically, occupiers of social space (noting, for example, that the number of gays and lesbians has been "surprisingly stable," having risen to its "normal" statistical level even within a few years following the mass extermination of homosexuals in Nazi Germany), and that such figures point to the fact that "love for one's own sex is a law of nature, not its mistake." The magazine's inclusion of this rubric was remarked upon by one reader in the following issue's "Letters" ("*Pis'ma*") section where, after thanking the editors, s/he remarked that the magazine had garnered another reader because the editors had proven that "the magazine works according to the principle 'everything for people.' For ALL people" ("*dlia VSEKH liudei*") ("*Pis'ma*").

But in addition to speaking *about* social space, Kudymov's article is performative of such as well; his words, in both their printed, material form and their message, actually construct a space within the magazine, as well as in social discourse. This social space was expanded via a 2006 issue of *TimeOut Moskva*, featuring a "gay map of the city" ("*golubaia karta goroda*"),³ much the same as had been accomplished via the magazine *Afisha* (literally, "Poster") two years earlier. Here, the magazine appeared on the newsstands with two different covers for the same issue: one with two handsome and stylish men, the other with two attractive women, both of whom were without makeup, natural, beautiful, and "earthy," in line with an urban/modern aesthetic.⁴ Both pairs exhibited some sort of physical contact, the women apparently purposely so, the men in close enough physical proximity to render a de facto touching. Not only the same-sex pairings but also the discreetly placed, small, rectangular rainbow in the bottom left corner that continued over the spine hinted at the contents within. But what may have been read as merely an insinuation was made explicit in one of several titles on the magazines' covers: "*putevoditel' dlia geev i lesbiianok*" ("a guidebook for gays and lesbians"). In both versions, among the regular, monthly features, departments, and listings, were several pages devoted to clubs, music, theater, and stores, among other things and spaces deemed to be of interest to or frequented by homosexuals.⁵ Likewise, the nationally distributed magazines *Kvir*, which first appeared in 2003, and *XXBi* (having appeared in 2004, only to disappear after five issues)⁶ were performative of gay spaces in both St. Petersburg and Moscow. They gave a material form to the conceptualization of "gayness" in the cities' midst; at the same time they were material objects occupying physical, visible spaces in, for example, the cities' numerous kiosks.⁷

Materiality was not, of course, limited to paper, print, or image; rather articles in magazines referenced material geographic sites, inhabited by embodied subjects. For example, Vasilii (an informant who lived, with his boyfriend, close to my apartment), noticing the newest edition of *Kalendar'/TimeOut* at my place on one occasion, told me, "my picture is in there," and proceeded to turn the pages until coming upon a short article headed by a photograph. Vasilii's back was to the camera, as were those of two other men, their arms around each other; the faces of another couple (male and female), the only two facing the camera, were blurred so as not to be recognizable. Headed by the title "*Domashnii mal'chik*" ("Domestic Boy"), the text read:

> An apartment on Fontanka. About two, three times a month there are parties here. The host of the apartment, Aleksandr, distributes invitations to his friends via SMS, and they bring their acquaintances [*znakomikh*]. By midnight, about 50 people have gathered. Practically all are homosexuals from 18 to 40 years old. The guests drink alcohol, which they've brought themselves, spreading among the company, meeting people. At the window they're discussing those who are on the sofa. On the floor they're looking at Aleksandr's photographs from his trip to Venezuela. From every side, phrases are heard, "you're Vania? They told me on the stairs," or "Hey, why are you wearing your jeans without underwear, Zhenia? You're leaving nothing to the imagination." Music plays, in the corner they're kissing. Around two, all go out to nearby clubs. ("*Domashnii mal'chik*")

The scenario presented here—private spaces of gay men, which then lead to public spaces—was one that I had experienced on other occasions. In one such instance, having been invited to a dinner party by Vadim, at the home of his friend Evgenii (an apartment he shared with his boyfriend on the outskirts of St. Petersburg), after eating our meal the suggestion was made that we flag down a car on the nearby highway, and head to one of the city's gay clubs. We, as numerous others, were oriented toward material, concrete spaces—gay clubs that had sprung up in the past decade—in which embodied subjects might link and share physical space with others so oriented. Such movement highlights the interface between corporeality and geography; while the body is oriented in certain directions, and is impacted upon by the repeated interactions with others so directed, the face of the city itself changes in response to these recurring orientations and destinations, new spaces springing up to accommodate (and reorient).[8] In this chapter, I will examine the creation of gay social space, including those spaces related specifically to music. Massey (2005) suggests a conceptualization of space as something never completed, always under construction; it is also a sphere of contemporaneous pluralities and differing trajectories, as well as a site for interrelations. Such a conceptualization comports with my observations of several "gayed" spaces in Russia, as the interactions of musics, locales, histories, and discourses—among other variables—contribute to an implicit questioning of linear time and geographic specificity. But homosexual men in post-Soviet Russia may nonetheless construct a deeply resonant and complex sense of self via their affective and physical engagements with both landscape and soundscape. Moreover, this sense of self—often in relation to "virtual," "mediated" sites, sights, and sounds—is one that is intimately, experientially related to the knowledge of like others.

Temporality and Spatiality: Soviet and Post-Soviet

Any discussion of the concept of space in relation to homosexuality must be historically and geographically situated, and in this regard it is necessary to highlight certain dynamics obtaining in contemporary Russia, many of which are related to anterior Soviet practices. Although the creation of gay space in the late nineteenth and early twentieth centuries in Russia's metropolitan centers mirrors similar geneses in such cities as London and Paris, the growth and solidification of such Western spaces in the second half of the twentieth century (San Francisco's Castro district, New York City's West Village, Paris's Marais)[9]—much of which was related to the processes of political and social movements, encompassing the quest for full citizenship—had no correlate in Soviet Russia. Insofar as the creation of "gay ghettos" has been tied to sociopolitical dynamics and discourses of constitutional rights, as well as the incursion of market forces,[10] the situation in Soviet Russia was bound to differ. Perhaps most germane to the discussion is the highly bureaucratized and stringent Soviet housing system, whereby procurement of an apartment was, if difficult for newly married couples (many of whom had to live with parents and/or in-laws for years, or had to wait until a parent's death to inherit an apartment), then virtually impossible for unmarried singles. With the dissolution of the Soviet Union, apartments that were rented from the state became the property of the inhabitants, who continued to pay only a small, monthly "maintenance" fee of anywhere from approximately ten to twenty-five dollars, a boon for those to whom the apartments officially belonged. However, such apartments were often the homes of numerous members of extended families; for those who might wish to leave the family home and find an apartment of his or her own, the rental prices—now dictated by the free market—when put in the context of the salaries of many of my informants (these averaging around four hundred dollars a month), were prohibitive. As such, a large number of single people, including many of my informants, continued to live with their parent(s) and/or other family members, some in *kommunalki* (sing. *kommunalka*), or "communal apartments" in which one or two rooms were allotted to each family, and bathroom and kitchen facilities were shared. Several of my informants who had professions that had allowed them to enter the market economy were far more mobile. Kirill and Roman (boyfriends, a translator and a teacher, who lived together in a very stylish apartment in central St. Petersburg), Boris (another translator), Konstantin (a financial analyst), Vadim (proprietor of his own landscaping business), Aleksei (a manager in a large chemical company), and even Maksim (manager of a retail store) all had the ability either to rent or even buy market-rate apartments. Others, however, were more financially constrained, and "stuck" in their living situations. Oleg, a graphic artist, lived with his mother in two rooms in a *kommunalka* in St. Petersburg; Il'ia, a dancer, shared a tiny apartment with his ex-wife in Moscow; and Gleb, who worked as a teacher, was living with his family in a small, two-room apartment on the outskirts of the city. As one of his friends told me, "he will probably live there until he eventually inherits the apartment."[11] All of these situations allowed these men little room for privacy and private space for, among other things, intimate connections with other men, but the impact was not simply upon individual people; rather, the ability to form geographically defined "communities" has been hindered both by access to capital and, concomitantly, an inability to enlist capital, often in the form of bribes, in securing rights to affordable apartments.

A view to the larger picture of gay men's access to space, beyond individual situations, reveals similar dynamics. Whereas in the West a "reverse diaspora" (Amico 2006) often occurs, whereby gay men "emigrate" from disparate, far-flung locations, converging on major urban centers,[12] such movement has also been circumscribed in Russia, once again in connection with both capital and bureaucracy. Although many people of all sexual orientations desire to move to larger cities, due to the perception of greater employment possibilities paying higher wages,[13] such movement is made infinitely more difficult, if not impossible, by statutes regarding movement within the country. One cannot, without a compelling, legitimate reason (for example, a job offer, or enrollment in a university) simply move to a different city; rather, in theory one must stay in the city in which one is a registered inhabitant.[14] However, many of my informants had indeed managed to move to St. Petersburg or Moscow (some of them legally, others not), and they often related this relocation to their wanting to escape inimical situations in their hometowns. Petia, for example, had moved from the far eastern stretches of Russia to St. Petersburg, not only to attend university, but also to flee what he saw as abuse based on his sexuality. According to him, when it became time to go to university, "I knew I had to get out of there. I just couldn't stand being talked about or yelled at every time I walked down the street. People would make fun of my clothes, or even just the way I walked. It was horrible." In comparison with the West, then, although movement has not been entirely blocked, in both the macro and the micro, economic and governmental variables have combined to inhibit the free movement of bodies and their congregating and concentrating in ways that might lead to geographically situated "communities" in contemporary Russia.

Space in post-Soviet Russia, however, cannot be examined on an exclusively material level, deeply imbricated as it is with questions of time. In his book *After the Future*, for example, Epstein (1995) suggests ways in which time may be viewed as nonlinear (and, by implication, nonteleological). For Epstein, that which was to be "the future"—the great Soviet project of building the modern, secular, and rational society, free of the corrupting ideas of superstition (read: religion) and bourgeois ideology—became, with the dissolution of the Soviet empire, the past, while that which was the pre-Revolutionary past became for many, albeit in an idealized form, the greatest hope for a future. To complicate things even further, and judging from events in Russia in the early part of the twenty-first century,[15] the "future" promised by the Communist state, although having passed *into* "the past" in the late 1980s and early 1990s, began to obtrude once again as the hope for the future, one in which the needs of the people would be provided for by the state; "the future," in this scenario, retreated momentarily—never having been "the present"[16]—but, after a brief state of morbidity, appeared again as a "present future." Perhaps in regard to a nascent visibility of gay bodies and spaces, discourses of idealized pasts could also be tied to a burgeoning homophobia. For example, noting the rise of homophobia in contemporary Russia, Kon (2006) asserts:

> Homophobia is typical of the majority of fascistic movements. Aside from many others, it is connected with militarism, which in Russia is growing stronger. Such a "consensus" is advantageous to parties and groups which don't have a positive program of action, and calls people to return to an *imaginary past*" (my emphasis). ("*I. S. Kon*")

In examining the construction of gay-centered urban spaces, we once again see the "past" returning "after the (Soviet) future." While visible gay spaces were all but obliterated during the sixty-year period marked by strict juridical proscription of *muzhelozhstvo*, Healey (1999, 2001a, 2001b, 2002a) has shown that public spaces marked by homosexuality were not only in existence, but evident and remarked upon prior to the era of criminalization. Beginning at least as early as the latter half of the nineteenth century,[17] sites of often commercialized sex between men appeared in both St. Petersburg and Moscow, centering on locations such as the *bania*.[18] In the *bania*, teams of peasant men, having emigrated to the urban centers, would work under an *artel'* system, one in which earnings were pooled and shared. Male-male sexuality in such contexts operated within defined geographical spaces, and "the *bania* supposedly kept an apparently necessary evil off the streets. 'Immoral' relations were concealed from the public" (2001b: 244). These sites also became "places of resort" for the *tetki*, sites where "the traditional masculine indulgence of same-sex eros confronted and mixed with an emerging homosexual subculture" (Healey 2001a: 33).

This homosexual subculture was connected not only to the semiprivate spaces of the *bania*, however, but to more visible sites such as public toilets or other communal spaces. Specific sites in the urban landscape, such as the stretch of *Nevskii prospekt* (one of the city's most fashionable main thoroughfares) from Znamenskaia Square to the Anchikov Bridge, extending to the Public Library and the *Passazh* (an indoor shopping center), "formed a promenade visible to initiates," and was "the city's most enduring homosexual cruising ground" (Healey 2001a: 31). This phenomenon, however, was not confined to St. Petersburg, occurring in Moscow as well and encompassing not only dynamics of geography (a spreading out) but, in conjunction with this, subcultural social formation. Relating the "significant development in the emergence of a homosexual subculture in Moscow" with "the arrival of patterns of street cruising" (1999: 46), Healey—here operating from the psychiatric records of the prostitute "Pavel"[19]—continues:

> [A] new group of "our people" [Pavel's term] also appeared in [his] account, and they had ways of recognizing each other on the boulevard (argot, gesture and dress were among the signs they used, to judge from the criminological comments about male prostitutes). Moreover, they congregated in notorious public locations to socialize and have sex. New commercialized spaces for the subculture (balls organized by "their own kind," a beer-hall with music and dancing) reflected the growing intrusion of the market even into highly specialized leisure activities." (1999: 49–50)

His assessment that the appearance of the visible homosexual and, concomitantly, visible sites of congregation, was concurrent with the appearance of "men who identified themselves as exclusively attracted to their own sex" as opposed to an earlier type of man who had sex with men, but had a "sexual identity based on a sinful but unavoidable male lust to be satisfied with either woman or man" (48) is perhaps debatable, insofar as it suggests a wholesale change in both self-definition and self-presentation.[20] But what is key here is the appearance of social spaces, in view of the public,[21] although there is the possibility that such places existed even earlier. Rotikov (1998), for example, notes that as early as 1830–1840—"Gogol''s time"—a "faggot corruption [*pederasticheskii razvrat*] reigned on *Nevskii* [prospekt]" (357). Rotikov's narrative, described in the Preface as "an aesthetic play, a literary provocation," must be approached with a certain caution;[22] still, whether or not the entirety of his assertions are based on fact, its very scope—encompassing large amounts of both geography and time, invoking names from Gogol' to Elton John—gives voice to, at the very least, the *conception* of St. Petersburg as a site in which same-sex desire was played out. Taking into account Healey's more scholarly and empirically based assertions, it seems likely that at least a portion of Rotikov's narrative reflects not only an imagined, but also a lived reality. Indeed, several of my informants had purchased, read, heard of, and/or discussed Rotikov's book; as such, its contribution to the conception of St. Petersburg as a site of male homosexuality continues.

Although homosexual activity did not completely disappear during the decades of Soviet rule,[23] its visibility was greatly diminished, homosexual men being relegated to a "culture of the toilet" (Healey 2001a: 36). Indeed, some of my informants—those who were past their late thirties, and who had lived through the Soviet era as young, sexually active adults—told me that public toilets were indeed used as sites for meeting other men during Soviet times,[24] and numerous *pleshki* (cruising spots—singular, *pleshka*) were to be found throughout the city, many of which had been dubbed with humorous monikers. Toilets used for cruising, for example, were generally referred to as *biblioteki* (libraries); in St. Petersburg, *Ploschad' muzhestva* (Muzhestva Square) and the surrounding park area were dubbed by some "*ploschad' muzhelozhstvo*," and the *Kat'kin sadik* ("Little Catherine Garden"), located in front of the *Aleksandrinskii teatr* on *Nevskii prospekt* and named for the large statue of Catherine the Great located in its center, was jokingly referred to as the "*Kat'kin zadik*"—*zadnitsa* being a word for buttocks and *zadik* its diminutive. Additionally, some said they knew of bars that were run for (and sometimes by) *tetki* during this period, although they considered these places to be for "older" ("over thirty") gay men.[25]

The perseverance of gay sites during an era of repression, however, can be contrasted with a relative efflorescence that has occurred since the dissolution of the Soviet Union, and the decriminalization of homosexuality. Not only have some of the stalwart locations remained as part of a gay landscape (the

Catherine Garden, for example,[26] as well as the *pliazh* "*kurort*" on the Gulf of Finland), but others have emerged as well, many as part of the market economy. From 2003 to 2005, for example, St. Petersburg could claim no less than three (at one point four)[27] gay male clubs, one club for lesbians (*Trièl'* [Three L's], the only one in the country), and several other establishments that either hosted gay parties or were known to be "gay/bi-friendly"[28] on certain nights. In a city of nearly 4.5 million inhabitants, this may seem a paltry number, compared not only with cities such as New York or Paris, but even much smaller cities as well; Helsinki, for example, a six-hour train ride from Petersburg, with roughly one-tenth its population, had more gay bars/clubs (six total) in the same time period. Still, taken in the context of decades of repression and a continuing palpable homophobia, both of which have inhibited the formation of infrastructure and organization of a "gay community," the appearance of such establishments—the existence of which would have been unthinkable merely twenty years prior—was something that suggested not only the possibility of a more salubrious future for homosexual men in Russia but, additionally, something that perhaps indicated a return of the pre-Revolutionary past, a time in which a burgeoning and relatively unmolested homosexual subculture appeared, as future.

Gay spaces in St. Petersburg in the early part of the twenty-first century were not, however, limited to *pleshki* and clubs situated in permanent locations. For example, certain cafés in the city center were known to be popular with gay men;[29] additionally, at least one of the city's many *bani*, the *Iamskie bani* discussed in Chapter 1, was (and continues to be) extremely popular with gay men on specific days and times during the week, at which time it was not uncommon to encounter long lines winding down the stairways. While the making of sexual contacts and engagement in sexual activity is certainly a part of the experience for many men who go there,[30] it is also a site of conviviality where they may meet with friends on a regular basis and relax, smoke, drink, and enjoy the benefits of the heat and steam. At a cost of thirty rubles per visit (approximately one U.S. dollar at the time of my last visit)—far less than the concurrent cost of approximately two hundred and fifty rubles to enter either of the gay saunas, *Nartsis* or *158B*, then in existence in St. Petersburg, or *Voda*, *Samovolka*, and *Maiakovka Sport* in Moscow[31]—it provides a site in which both the social/communal and the erotic combine, at a cost that is within reach for the vast majority of gay men in the city. Such spaces are indicative of a liminal space between gay and straight locales, having been "co-opted" by gay men without the proprietor's having envisioned or planned on attracting a specifically gay clientele. This homosexual space of the *bania*, part of the pre-Revolutionary landscape, reappeared not only in discrete locations in Russia (such as the *Iamskie bani*), but on one occasion was widely disseminated, via the mass media, as a musical spectacle: on New Year's Eve 2003, the national television station *STS* presented a roster of many of the biggest names in Russian *popsa* and *èstrada*, under the banner *Noch' v stile disko* (*Disco-Style Night*). Among the numerous acts presented was group *Ruki vverkh*'s (Hands Up) performance of the song "*Esli u vas netu teti*" ("If You Don't Have an Aunt") from the film *Ironiia sud'by, ili s legkim parom* (*The Irony of Fate, or Enjoy Your Steam*),[32] a film in which the main plot point occurs as a result of the protagonist's drinking with male friends in the *bania*. The group's two singers, Sergei Zhukov and Alekseii Potekhin, were seated downstage at a table filled with abundant amounts of food, drinking beer and lip-synching to the music (in this arrangement, appropriately, a highly electronically orchestrated version over a rapid disco beat, much different than the song's original, guitar/voice presentation). Behind them a large group of attractive, muscular men, arranged on graded benches, and clad only in white towels and felt hats,[33] carried out stylized, choreographed movements, washing themselves, washing each other, striking a neighbor (or being struck) with a *venik* (a bunch of leafy birch or oak branches),[34] leaving the benches periodically to dance behind the stars, copious amounts of artificial snow falling from the stage's rafters. While *Ruki vverkh*'s singers, as well as their target audience, appear to be heterosexual,[35] the sight of scantily clad, near-naked, handsome men (who, viewers understand, would be entirely naked in "real life"), touching each other, touching themselves, and dancing was almost certainly apprehended by homosexual men as indicative of the male-male sexuality historically and currently situated within the space of the *bania*.

Here Then There Now: Sexuality, Popular Music

The presentation on national television of homoerotic sights and sounds is only one example of popular music's relationship to homosexuality and the post-Soviet experiences of detemporalization and deterritorialization. That music might be connected to such experiences is hardly accidental, not only due to the ability of recording technology to allow sounds from "the past" to be present—without benefit of physically present performers—but also in the very act of hearing music in the here and now. Here, repetition disturbs the concept of a knowable, easily definable notion of linear time.[36] The repeating of a chorus, of a riff, of a rhythmic or harmonic pattern, may seem to simply be a matter of bringing the past into the present; however, the very act of the repeat detemporalizes and transforms the past—a past that may be recalled as having been located in a specific physical place—the listener's relation to its subsequent occurrences modulated by, among other things, having heard it before (thus, memory acting upon its present-ness).[37] Additionally, in terms of spatial location, music may contribute to both senses of fixity (via recourse to discourses of place-based authenticities) and movement (via the global circulation of sounds and musical objects) (Connell and Gibson 2003).

The elasticity or fungibility of space/time was evident in the May 2004 gay party sponsored by the group *Kul'turnyi proekt* (Cultural Project) Why Not?! The party, held at *Jakata*—one of St. Petersburg's smaller and more expensive clubs—drew a crowd of approximately two hundred and fifty people, mostly gay or bisexual men under thirty, although there were several young women there as well. Directed by two young DJs, Aleksei and Konstantin, the Project, not linked to a specific physical site but sponsoring events hosted at locations throughout the city, is spatially diffused; additionally, the announcements for events were distributed not only in various physical locations in the city, but "virtually," via email, to members of gay Russian websites as well. (I, for example, first received an invitation from VJ FaceOff while dancing at another of the city's gay clubs and several days later received one via my Russian email account.) Indeed the very party itself, the "Sunglasses Party," aimed to transport attendees both spatially and temporally. According to the invitation:

> The 21st of May is already almost summer! The organizers Why Not?! want to move it a bit closer, and have a SUMMER PARTY in the style of Disco and Garage/House. The SUNGLASSES party is *the atmosphere of the coming summer*, carefree summer days and fantastic summer music. Together with the DJs, guests will *spend the night in real travel*—from *New York* Disco from the *Studio 54 era*, to the Soulful Garage from *American black, gay clubs*. The dress code is sunglasses and *disco-style clothing*. (my emphases)

The style of both the club—featuring a lounge area in a "Moorish" style,[38] leading to a more "industrial" style room with a dance floor—and the music were very much in line with similar clubs in Western Europe operating at that time, as were the clothing styles of the guests: a Benetton-cum-Diesel aesthetic, with smatterings of "street" style. Throughout the evening, in fact, I often forgot that I was in Russia, feeling myself instead, via the music and the style, to be in "the West." Although many of the tracks played by DJ Primat were instrumental, there was a relatively steady stream of English lyrics in such songs as Karen Young's "Hot Shot" (a disco classic from 1978), and "Familiar Feelings" by Moloko (an Anglo-Irish electronic duo).[39] At the

Sunglasses Party, within the span of only a few minutes, and depending upon one's subjective position, as well as one's relationship to the various sonic, corporeal, and visual signs, one might thus experience one's self (concurrently or sequentially) in a myriad of spaces and times. As I will show in the following pages, this temporal and spatial liminality, often engendered via physical, affective, discursive, and cognitive relations to music, is a hallmark of many gay social spaces in post-Soviet Russia.

While attendees at *Jakata* that evening were met with a variety of sights, sites, and sounds through which they might place themselves, temporally or spatially, the preponderance of English-language lyrics—English being a sort of lingua franca in dance music, circulating throughout the United States and Europe—and the total absence of Russian songs with Russian lyrics, contrasted sharply with two other sites where gay men in St. Petersburg had the possibility of meeting, dancing, listening to music, and viewing a staged show on a regular basis for several years from 2003 onward. The clubs *Greshniki* (Sinners) and *Kabare* (Cabaret), owing in part to their relative permanence, their almost exclusively gay male clientele,[40] and their regular staging of drag performances, could both be contrasted with the relative cosmopolitanism at play in the clubs that hosted parties by Why Not?! (as well as a similar group, K. P. Olovo). Indeed, some of my informants, especially those who were younger and "hipper," avoided both establishments, noting what they considered bad music (Russian *popsa* and/or pop-dance), as well as the "disreputable" character of the clubs. Evgenii, for example, said that both places were "*uzhasnyi*" ("horrible"), and both he and Alik, among others, noted that they were "full of prostitutes." Andrei, in speaking about *Greshniki*, dubbed it the home of "*griaz Peterburga*" ("the dirt of Petersburg").[41] But despite such negative reactions, the vast majority of these informants had been to one or both of the clubs and, in fact, even some of the men who expressed the most negative reactions were semiregulars. Both clubs can be contrasted with the "mobile" parties discussed above, as well as with one another, on several levels.

The first concerns the general visibility of the establishments. While *Greshniki* was located in the very center of the city, with a clearly marked entrance on a main street, *Kabare* was located, although not far from the center, a bit more off the beaten track. Furthermore, the latter's location in a former "Palace of culture"[42] meant that there were several entrances to various spaces housed within the large structure; knowledge of which particular doorway led to the club was necessary for entering the establishment. While *Greshniki*'s entrance clearly showed the club's name (notably in both Russian and English), *Kabare*'s was marked only by the address and entrance number (*pod"ezd n. 3*), as well as the initials "MT," referencing the nickname of the club (*Matrosskaia tishina*, "Sailors' Silence").[43]

Greshniki's use of English was also in evidence in the club's interior, again in contrast with *Kabare*. While in the former, signs in both Russian and English noted the club's entrance and coat check fees, as well as an English-only sign offering assistance in ordering taxis home, the latter offered information solely in Russian. And while the front of the house staff (cashier and coat check) as well as some bartenders often spoke some English, inevitably using it with those customers who appeared to be "foreign" (such as myself), communication at *Kabare* was strictly in Russian. Certainly *Greshniki*'s use of English was linked, in part, to the fact that its clientele included some foreign tourists or expatriates (although in general the number of such people was rather small),[44] this probably due to the fact that the club's advertising was more visible to non-Russian speakers, a clientele they may have wished to foster due to its assumed affluence. For example, in the city's English-language newspaper, *The St. Petersburg Times*, *Greshniki* was advertised weekly, but *Kabare* was absent. However, it seems likely, in terms of the club's overarching ethos—in general, and in comparison to *Kabare*—that the club's use of the "international (Western)" language was meant to suggest a certain type of modern, stylish internationalism.[45]

The contrast of the clubs' aesthetics, and their connections to either more international or indigenous styles and discourses, was also evident on the very bodies of the customers. Similar not only to the sartorial styles described in association with *Jakata*, but to those sported by fashionable, young, European men of the time, many of the men at *Greshniki* wore hip-hugging, flared, slim-cut Diesel-style jeans, or perhaps combat-style, multipocketed pants (though tightly tailored, as opposed to the loose style of the 1990s). Both long- and short-sleeved T-shirts were worn, often with purposeful rips, tears, or other "deconstructions," or rough-edged appliqués, and many featured texts, often in English (such as "101 Percent" or "Craven,").[46] Additionally, hairstyles and accessories were often au courant, exhibiting either a retro, seventies, or mod aesthetic (longish, shag haircuts, and/or wide belts, for example) or a postpunk sensibility (leather or spiked wristbands and chains hanging from pockets or waists, along with shaved heads, or dyed or bleached, spiky/hacked hair). Notably absent were the ubiquitous pointed-toed, leather shoes then favored by many of Petersburg's heterosexual young men, various types of athletic-inspired footwear or actual trainers taking their place. Although not all of the men, the majority of whom ranged in age from approximately early twenties to early thirties, exhibited such a keen fashion sense, this aesthetic was well represented.

Conversely, although such style-consciousness was not absent on many of the men at *Kabare*, a large number of them were not quite so up-to-the-minute or on fashion's "cutting edge," and in fact, some could be seen dressed more in line with "heterosexual" styles: tight, button-front shirts, tight (often black) pants, and the aforementioned pointed, square-toed shoes. This may have reflected the fact that the clientele was marginally older than at *Greshniki*, including men who were past forty—although such men were still in the minority, and not absent from *Greshniki* either. Regarding age, it is notable that *Kabare* was viewed by most of my informants as having an older clientele;[47] whether or not statistics bore this assertion out to statistical significance, such conceptions were operative in the views of many. For example, Zhenia, although over forty, was one of the most "stylish" men I met, both in terms of his fashion sense and his taste in music. However, he preferred *Greshniki* over *Kabare*, noting that *Kabare* was a club for "older men."

The internationalism suggested in connection with the clubs' use/lack of English, and their apposite style codes, bound up with ideas of modernity, was also evident in the musics played at each, relating both establishments to temporalities and spaces on different levels: dynamics of modernity versus history, intertwined with the formation of a musical space that transcends international boundaries, while at the same time suggesting a situatedness based on both nationality and sexuality, as well as a material situatedness within the walls of a discrete site. Both clubs played musics that were at the time of my fieldwork currently popular throughout both Europe and the United States—the Black Eyed Peas's "Shut Up" and "Let's Get It Started," or Anastacia's "Left Outside Alone," which was particularly popular in both locations[48]—as well as others that were popular in smaller markets in Europe such as In-Grid's "*Tu est foutu*" ("You're Screwed/Fucked") (France), Trakan's "*Dudu*" (Turkey), and O-Zone's "*Dragostea din tei*" ("Love from the Linden Trees") (Moldova, but with Romanian lyrics),[49] thus situating themselves within the then-current contemporary, international, popular music soundscape. While many of these songs, played in remix form, were examples of the most accessible, commodified type of popular music, others such as club remixes of Bananarama's "Venus," The Royal Gigolos's "California Dreaming," and Junior Jack's "Stupid Disco" indicated a connection to a marginally more rarefied, specialist, modern musical discourse—although here again, such remixes were hardly indicative of the most cutting-edge dance music then circulating, music that was more likely to be heard at the parties sponsored by Why Not?! or *K. P. Olovo*. But even those songs and artists seen as most commodified and, as such, hardly arbiters of "modernity" in the West, must be viewed in the Russian context; although popular music "sophistication" surely exists among a certain coterie of generally younger Russians, engaging musics other than those in rotation on Russian MTV or *MuzTV*, or the radio, the very foreignness of the most popular of the pop musics suggested a connection with a post-Soviet modernity, one in which "the West" was conceptually present. Indeed, such musics must be contrasted with the large amount of Russian popular musics played at the same clubs, an amount that was often greater than that of the foreign musics; such a dynamic was different than those noted, through both personal experience, as well as assessments from various informants, at other gay clubs in such cities as Helsinki, Reykjavík, London, Paris, Montréal, Turku, or Berlin, where the vast majority of dance music would have been of Western, often nonlocal provenance. Both clubs regularly played several tracks that had been released by the then-current and previous contestants of *Fabrika zvezd*, such as Aleksa's "*Gde zhe ty?*" ("Where Are You?"), or Irakle's "*London-Parizh*" ("London-Paris"), both of which, with their four-on-the-floor beat, relatively laid-back vocal deliveries, and subtle instrumental arrangements featuring synthesizers and, in the case of the former, an acoustic guitar hook, were in line with the clubs' aesthetics veering toward popular-music–style dance songs, rather than "sophisticated," hard, dance tracks.[50] Additionally, numerous other popular Russian songs with the same types of musical attributes, performed by some of the most currently popular Russian artists were frequently heard; it was not uncommon, for example, to hear two or three songs in the same evening by Russian singer Valeriia, such as "*Otpusti menia*" ("Let Me Go"), "*Cherno-belyi tsvet*" ("Black and White") or "*Perelei voda*" ("Pouring Water").[51]

Of course, it is not a simple matter of dividing the foreign from the domestic, any more so than dividing the contemporary from the historical. For example, some of the most popular songs played, not only at clubs in St. Petersburg, but in Moscow as well, were those of Verka Serdiuchka,[52] whose music defies neat categorization in terms of either spatial or temporal variables. On the one hand, Verka is both "foreign" and "other"—she is Ukrainian,[53] she is rural, and she is also, literally, a man (Andrei Danilko) performing (as) a woman; but on the other, she is "domestic," singing in Russian (albeit with a Ukrainian accent), using musical forms and styles familiar to many Slavic people, and she is presumed by many to be the creation of a gay man. Verka is also concurrently both "historical," making use in her songs and videos of stereotypical imagery and sounds of an almost transhistorical, rurally based "Slavic-ness" (although many of her references are specifically Ukrainian), and "modern," a man whose music and performances, both as Verka and as himself, roils stereotypical gender constructions and gives voice to a relatively newly visible homosexuality (see Chapter 3).

Similarly, songs of the group *Gosti iz budushchego* (Guests from the Future), also extremely popular and frequently played at both locations,[54] exhibit some of the same complexity in terms of resisting an either/or categorization. Although the group is "domestic" and all of their songs are sung in Russian,[55] the styles they exhibit—from trance to house to chillout—are all within the realm of an international, dance music idiom; that their production values are generally extremely high also makes them appear not simply peripheral mimics, but as artists who are fluent in the musical language. They are, additionally, in the context of gay clubs, "indigenous," insofar as lead singer Eva Pol'na's lyrics (and Pol'na herself) point toward "nontraditional" sexualities.[56] And DJ Gruv, with his popular "*Sluzhebnyi roman*" ("Office Romance"), a track regularly played at many gay (and straight) clubs in both St. Petersburg and Moscow, straddles both the contemporary and the historic, by sampling both music and dialogue from the popular, Soviet-era film of the same name, and placing them within with a contemporary house arrangement. But both Gosti and Gruv, while they are operating within the modern genres of dance music, are also, by dint of language—both what the language is (Russian) and is not (Western)—related to the "past," understanding that for many of my informants, listening to *any* Russian music indicated a parochial, unsophisticated mindset, one that was backward and distinctly *not* modern.

This view was shared, to various extents, by the DJs with whom I spoke; for example, Oleg and Gavril had both worked at St. Petersburg's *Mono* Club, a tiny establishment that, while advertising itself as a club for "bisexuals," appeared, both through its advertising and clientele, to be geared almost exclusively toward homosexual men. Both professed to playing Russian *popsa* only if they received tips for doing so and said they generally preferred Western dance music such as house, techno, and jungle, both in terms of what they spun or what they listened to in their free time.[57] DJ Christy, one of the weekend DJs at *Greshniki* told me that she "couldn't stand" Russian music because of what she considered its crass commercialism; in her view, "it's all about money, not art. There's no creativity in it, no soul. It's simply all about putting out a product as fast as you can, and trying to make as much money off of it as possible.[58] Similarly, DJ Partyphone, a Moldovan in his midtwenties, spinning at one of Moscow's most popular gay parties—Sunday nights at the club *Propaganda*—expressed a similar antipathy toward Russian *popsa*, considering it to be "not of a high level" or "primitive." He stated that he would not spin it while DJ-ing "for any money," as one of his main goals as a DJ was to play the "best" music of the highest level, the most fashionable (*modnaia*), the most contemporary (*sovremennaia*).[59] While he did agree that there were certain Russian groups or projects who were putting out "high-quality" music,[60] he nonetheless preferred Western artists such as Deetron, Boogie Corporation, and Martinez, specifically noting his favorite styles as "funk" and "soul," both of which he defined as "a culture, an attitude." *Propaganda*'s Sunday night dance was indeed, according to some of my informants, one of the most "fashionable" gay sites in Moscow, where the word signifies not the conspicuous consumption of a "*novyi russkii*" ("new Russian"),[61] but a contemporary, modern, international aesthetic. Perhaps because of this, the club was popular with expatriates living in Moscow; DJ Partyphone, however, acknowledging that foreigners might indeed feel more comfortable in such a setting, insisted that the club was not "a place for foreigners," the vast majority of customers being Russian.

Although the lines between domestic and foreign, past and present (or future) are constantly, musically in flux in many gay sites, some clubs in fact effectuated a type of spatial containment of such variables. At both *Dusha i telo* in Moscow, and *Metro* in St. Petersburg,[62] different musics were segregated into specific rooms within the clubs. At the former, the cutting-edge hard house, techno and trance musics, as well as more "popular" dance tracks, such as the Benassi Brothers' "Hit My Heart," were played in the large, main room of the club, while Russian *popsa* was played in a smaller and usually packed room, upstairs; at the latter, the same dynamic obtained, although here, in contrast, the "international" room was upstairs, more sparsely populated, almost exclusively by (ostensibly heterosexual) males, while the "Russian" room was downstairs and full to overflowing with both men and women. It should be noted, however, that the borders marking this separation were far from impermeable. For example, on one night I visited *Dusha i telo* the main room was also the site of a performance by the drag troupe *Fabrika grez* (Factory of Dreams),[63] the players imitating such stars as Madonna, Beyoncé, Mireille Mathieu, Tina Turner, and Boney M. And while the "Western" component of the show was certainly pronounced, there were also several instances of distinctly Russian materials being used for comic effect; for example, as an introduction to the entrance of three performers dressed as babies—lip-synching to a comically sped-up version of In-Grid's "In-Tango"—the loudspeakers played the theme song to *Spokoinoi nochi, mal'ishi* (*Good Night, Children*), a children's television show presented nightly on Russian television for decades and watched by millions. Although not on the program the night I saw their performance, the troupe also pays homage, through drag personification, of *èstrada* and *popsa* singers such as the Ukrainian/Moldovan Sofiia Rotaru and Latvian Laima Vaikule.

Both *Greshniki* and *Kabare* had a "specialization" of spaces as well, although not along the aforementioned lines. In the case of *Kabare*, for example, the club's main room, used for dancing and the presentation of the drag shows, was contrasted with a smaller room behind the bar, where Karaoke was the feature. At *Greshniki*, the club's main space—although far smaller than *Kabare*'s, again the site for dancing and drag shows (as well as male strippers on platforms throughout the night)—was distinct from its smaller, quieter, lounge-like room upstairs.[64] But overall, the general perception was that *Greshniki* was more cutting-edge, stylish, and "gritty" or "dirty" (in both a positive and negative sense), appealing to a younger clientele, while *Kabare* was more traditional, more Soviet-era, attracting somewhat older men. The differences were not only a matter of clientele and style, however, but were additionally embodied in and engendered by the music played at each club. While, as I have noted previously, both clubs played similar musics, from international dance tracks to Russian *popsa*, the most notable difference was the total absence of more rarefied, less commercial dance tracks at *Kabare* and their inclusion in the musical discourse at *Greshniki*. In this regard, such tracks as Tweet's "Boogie2Night," Freestyler's "Push Up," and Sash's "Run" (featuring Boy George) were instrumental in defining the club's aesthetic and discourse, and contrasting it with *Kabare*.

It is essential to note, however, that discussions of "style" relate not only to what was placed on the body, or the sounds encountered by embodied subjects, as the very bodies themselves indicated connections to geographically and temporally specific standards of male beauty. In this regard, the type of masculinity on display at both clubs was far different from that one might find in many gay clubs in the United States (as well as certain European capitals). With few exceptions, the stereotypical "Circuit Party clone"—hyperbolically muscled and hyper-"masculine," often steroid-enhanced, pierced, and tattooed—was visibly absent from the clientele of both clubs. At *Greshniki*, one man did in fact exhibit the "pumped up" body of the stereotypical "Chelsea queen,"[65] and at *Kabare* another man (Tolia, whom I had met through Gleb) had a similar physique, often dancing in torn jeans, shirtless, in true Circuit Party style; they were, however, the minority. Part of this related to the greater influence of Europe as opposed to America in terms of style codes, and the general preference for leanness as opposed to muscularity, something that several of my informants noted; for them, a lean body was considered the most beautiful. Thus I was not surprised, when speaking with Tolia, to learn that he had lived in New York for several years, loved the club scene there, and had thus learned the codes of a certain subset of American "gay style." Additionally, economic factors are certainly at play; although most of my informants were concerned with their physical appearance, the vast majority lacked the resources to join health clubs, or to pay not only for "bulk-up" protein powders but for black-market steroids as well. And while many of the strippers at *Greshniki* were muscular, or at least more muscular than the majority of the club's visitors, they were still not only smaller than strippers (or gay porn stars) in America, but also far more "boyish." Some, in fact, were almost androgynous, and all were either by nature or purposefully smooth-bodied.

Embodiment, Affect, Situatedness

Understanding the lack of both temporal and spatial fixity, the fluidity of borders and bodies, it may be difficult to thus comprehend the post-Soviet gay dance club as a site for the formation of any sort of integrated or stable sense of self. Yet the foregrounding of motility should not eclipse those nodes around which such a formation—a particularly embodied formation—may occur. In this regard, the comments of one of my informants, Zhenia, regarding his reasons for preferring *Greshniki* over *Kabare*, allude to several key areas. Although Zhenia was an "older" man (he originally told me he was in his late thirties, but later admitted he was in his early forties) (thus the "typical" *Kabare* customer), he was also one of the most fashionable (thus a "typical" *Greshniki* customer). I saw him numerous times at the latter, however, but never at the former. He explained his preference with reference to the music:

> At *Kabare*, all the music is *popsa*, which I hate—I can't dance to it, I don't feel it. It's because the place is full of middle-aged men, and they all pay the DJ to play the songs they want. I prefer *Greshniki*, because at least there I can dance, and that's why I go to clubs.[66]

His attendance at *Greshniki*, however, was not based solely on the music; in fact, he noted that there were numerous other clubs in St. Petersburg—*Par'* (Steam), *Onegin*, and Red Club, for example—where the music spun by the DJs was far more to his liking. But despite his attraction to the music (and the style) of the clubs, Zhenia rarely frequented them because, not only did he find the pretensions of the *novye Russkie* clientele off-putting ("I don't feel any need to go out and show myself, and pay a hundred rubles for a glass of juice"), but he also preferred dancing with men; in his estimation, "at the straight[67] clubs, the dance floor is full of girls looking for sponsors,[68] and I'm not interested in dancing with a bunch of girls."

From Zhenia's responses emerge three main themes—feeling, music, and men—which, when taken together and examined in relation to an embodied experience of the gay post-Soviet club, offer a way of illuminating the special salience of the club for the formation of a specific subject position. "Feeling," here, is that which is affective both somatic and emotional, the two working in consort with one another through music. In terms of the former, the high volume of the four-on-the-floor beat, omnipresent throughout much of the evening, literally vibrates the body, the viscera, and is experienced as material and tactile; it is not external to the body, but produces effects which resonate in the body's very interior. This experience of internal sensation may be further effectuated by the subject's own voice. For example, in clubs in both St. Petersburg and Moscow, I often saw men who were singing along with the tracks being played throughout the evening, an occurrence at clubs throughout those cities in the United States and Europe with which I am familiar, as well. But in the case of Russian gay men, in Russia, the songs with which they were physically engaging were often in a foreign language, one that many of them did not speak. Indeed, when close enough to these men to hear the sounds they were actually producing, it was clear that many of them were not singing actual words (at least not all of the words) but, rather, producing sounds based on phonetic approximations of what they had heard. While such "singing" along may, in fact, indicate the desire to become connected to the singer, or to exhibit "cultural capital" (Bourdieu 1973) (by knowing a song, by "knowing" a foreign language), there is yet another aspect that relates to a specifically corporeal affect: that is, the pleasure in making sound.

The sounds produced in sexual excitement, or those in conjunction with physical suffering, are both obviously on one level communicative, delivering "information" about one's state. Such information is meant to be received and acted upon by another, present interlocutor. On another level, however, and especially when they are created in solitude, such creations of sounds are physical acts that by their sensual affect either augment pleasure or alleviate pain, respectively. The creation of sound by the human body in a club, often at high volume (sometimes approaching a yell or a scream), from the opening of the mouth and the stretching of the lips, to the intake and expulsion of air (the chest inflating and deflating), also encompasses the sensations of the vibrations necessary to produce sound, felt internally, from the chest to the throat to the nasal passages. Such "deep," corporeal excitation, experienced as internal sensation, contributes to the intensity of the experience for the individual, and contributes to a formation of a sense of space, place, and self that is both abstractly and somatically constructed and remembered. The somatic creation of space and place, via music, is also related to the fact that, in a very real sense, it is our ears, serving not only as sound receptors, but as organs of balance, that contribute to our sense of situatedness in our environments. Again, although the "text" is implicated in "singing along," what is most important is not the conveying of lexically based information;

words as indicators of prepositional thought are less important than as vehicles for creating pleasurable sound that resonates (in) the body, a body that "feels." Highlighting the importance of the human body, Hirschkind, in his examination of the ubiquitous and highly musical taped sermons that play an integral part in the creation of Cairo's soundscape, finds a similar dynamic in the ability of this media to form a moral and political space of belonging due not simply to its ability to disseminate ideas or ideology, but "in its effect on the human sensorium, on the affects, sensibilities, and perceptual habits of its vast audience" (2006: 2).

"Feeling," however, is not simply a case of sensation; rather, somatic experience is symbiotically intertwined with affect and emotion as well. The states of the body—moving, sweating, dancing, seeing, vibrating, singing—in the context of an hours-long auditory stream of melodies, rhythms, chordal progressions, and timbres, of songs to which one has specific relationships (as either domestic or foreign, native or exotic), in the presence of others, produces—in fact, must produce, absent psychopathology—any number of rich affective emotional responses. The affected body becomes the site for the production of emotion, and the resultant emotion is experienced and expressed in part, in and through the body. Such deeply felt states situate the embodied subject within the flux of then/now, here/there, bringing together what might have been experienced as potential destabilizations and rendering them constituent parts of a vital whole, a feeling subject with a past, present, and future. As DeChaine (2002) notes, "affect is . . . the circuit through which the past and the present, as well as imaginings of the future, become confluent. It enables the process of becoming, entangling our bodies, minds, memories, histories, thoughts, and feelings to the point where they can't be imagined apart from each other" (86).

This complexity is understood through embodiment; the dancing subject, engaging with the surrounding world, as both Brandstetter (2007) and Blacking (1983) maintain, acquires a knowledge outside of language or propositional thought, knowledge of who, where, when, and in relation to what he is. There are, of course, no "pure" affects, or "unadulterated" responses by the "natural" body to somatic sensation, culture always implicit in the way subjects choose (or are compelled) to express, make sense of, or repress emotional-physical states or order knowledges. Yet the body is not simply passive, acted upon either by stimuli or cultural scripts; as Lyon and Barbalet suggest, "the body cannot be seen merely as subject to external forces; the emotions which move the person through bodily processes must be understood as a source of agency: social actors are embodied" (1994: 50). While I would suggest that it is not affects that serve as catalysts for corporeal action but, rather, the two intertwined as a source of agency, the point is that the affected body is a body that understands not only via that which is experienced as a self, but with great dynamism perceives, and orients itself, toward the environment in order to understand. Both the dancing body (on the floor), and the comparatively stationary body (seated along the walls of the club, or standing at the perimeter of the floor, and often moving with the beat) adopt postures and assume positions and stances, so as to take in, to perceive—visually, kinesthetically, emotionally—the various postures, positions, and stances of the *male* bodies around him. For as much as the club may be about dancing and socializing with friends and acquaintances, it is also, for many, a sexually charged site, one in which apotheoses of male beauty perform (as strippers/dancers), in which one may actually have sexual encounters (in the *temnye komnaty*), in which one may initiate sexual encounters to be consummated at a later time, in another place. Men, sexual beings with sexual attractions to other men, orient themselves and are the objects of others' orientations, and physical actions are rife with sexual intentionality and possibility.

The often sexually significant interactions of these men—orienting, intentional, one appearing simultaneously as both subject and object—produce a specifically corporeal type of communication, one made necessary not only by the volume of the music (which often precludes verbal interchanges), but by the recognition of the requisiteness of communication *about* the body taking place *through* the body; the body itself has "learned to speak," the entire musculature, in its various poses, stances, and positions, "organs-to-be-seen" (Lingis 1994a: 40). In his examination of the work of Mishima, Lingis (1994a: Chapter 5) finds that the author, through his own rituals of corporeal perfection,[69] arrives at what might be seen as an inversion of certain foundational tenets of Western thought; that the body, the "surface," rather than the mind, the "interior," may be the site of profundity, and this surface acquires such a profundity and eloquence through "a community of flesh open to death," a community of "shared suffering" (1994a: 92). Such a community of corporeal eloquence and mutual intelligibility obtains, I believe, at many of these clubs for gay men, but it is not a community of shared suffering; rather, in the context of post-Soviet space, where both figurative/symbolic and literal death were more than simply vague possibilities for homosexual men, it is the relatively recent appearance of *life*—on the very flesh of dancing, collected, sexualized bodies, in spaces that only two decades ago would have been inconceivable—that emerges as the figure on the ground. As noted in the previous chapter, Shilling (2008) suggests that crisis often engenders the response of creativity, and the crisis of annihilation, pathologization, criminalization, and indeed extermination (via the gulag) faced by homosexual men for over half a century in Soviet Russia, is combated via spaces *of* creativity. Here, creativity is manifest in the very constituent and indispensable elements of the spaces themselves—the music, the DJ-ing, the design and lighting of the clubs, the drag shows and dance performances, the dancing of the individuals—as well as in the palpable sexuality of such spaces, not only insofar as sexual activity creates connections between men, but also via the very dynamic of a libidinous energy that, irrespective of any connection to procreation, may be experienced as life-affirming. None of this is to suggest, via a naïve utopianism, that such spaces do not hold the potential for significant negativity as well; from the hierarchies of corporeal beauty that relegate the "have-nots" to lower status, the sometimes excessive consumption of alcohol which may become habitual,[70] the possibility of contracting STDs through anonymous sexual encounters (sometimes because of impaired judgment brought about by the overuse of either drugs or alcohol), the inculcation of the homosexual into the gyre of capital-driven consumer culture, or even the visibility of such clubs rendering them sites for potential heterosexual colonization,[71] gay clubs may be sites of both affirmation and possible degradation. Yet the very existence of such clubs, one of the few places in which male homosexual desires might be expressed in post-Soviet Russia,[72] linked to expressive culture, played out to the sound track that highlights one's simultaneous positions in both Russian and international (gay) space, gives rise to a corporeal communication that is not simply from one to another, but all to each other—a communication that emphatically states not only that "I am," but also that "we are." The understanding that I am (a homosexual man) and we are (homosexual men), grasped through the adopted stances and positions of an embodied homosexuality, affectively motivated, are remembered corporeally and live with the subject not only in the club, but beyond its situation as well.

Virtual/Mediated Spaces

In November of 2004, a massive gay dance party, DecaDANCE, was held at the *Moskovskii dvorets molodezhi* (The Moscow Palace of Youth). Despite the brutally cold weather and heavy snowfall, it appeared as if well over one thousand men attended; neither the numerous stairs leading to the entrance, covered with ice and resembling a graded skating rink (causing more than one person, myself included, to fall more than once), nor the half-hour wait in the subzero temperatures in order to even get inside, deterred those who had traveled to the *dvorets* for the event. Inside, the huge dance floor was packed with mostly young, lean, and fashionable men (some fashionable via an antifashion stance), a steady stream of music and a viscerally stimulating four-on-the-floor beat emanating from the enormous speakers located at numerous points around the floor. Not a single note of Russian popular or dance music was heard throughout the evening, the DJs opting instead for classic and up-to-the-minute house tracks such as Bombdogs's "I Can't Explain," Gadjo's "So Many Times," Blaze's "Do You Remember House?" and David Guetta's "Stay," as well as house remixes of songs by British artists Duran Duran ("[Reach Up for the] Sunrise") and Blur ("Song 2"). The invitation to the party had promised:

> No, there won't be theatre—we won't interrupt the energy of the dance floor, moving under the best dance music from all of the best DJs of the capital.[73] However, our unusual show, continuing the length of the entire night, will be provocative, intoxicating, sobering and really—unforgettable. To say more will be simply indecent—it must be seen.

The "show" was not the type of staged spectacle presented at *Kabare*, *Greshniki*, or *Dusha i telo*, no "thing" unto itself, no sort of compilation of dramaturgical, comic, musical, or choreographic "acts" requiring the audience to stop, watch, listen, and respond; rather, a series of "vignettes" appeared on and around the dance floor throughout the evening. At one point, shirtless boys in black tights and shoes, and short skirts woven from fabric and other materials, danced and posed at various sites among the dancers; later, several boys dressed in foppish eighteenth-century attire—powdered wigs, jackets with short tails, knee breeches, hose, and so forth—appeared at various locations, adopting stylized poses in approximation of an aristocratic stance. Other "actors" included Santa Claus, a bumblebee, a few silver robots, and elves with Silly String.

Although the party was in Moscow, I ran into several of my informants from St. Petersburg, including Zhenia and Konstantin, the latter of whom had taken the train the previous day with friends of his, specifically in order to attend the event. I also saw several men with whom I had chatted on the internet, from both St. Petersburg and Moscow, as well as others whose faces I recognized from one or another Russian gay meeting site, especially qguys.ru[74]—unsurprising, as it was this site that had hosted the party[75] and distributed email invitations to each member's mailbox. Gay-themed internet meeting sites geared toward the Russian-speaking market (*saity znakomstv*, used to denote either gay or straight websites)—both those exclusively devoted to meeting/messaging and those that contained meeting/messaging sections within the site as a whole—became relatively common in the early part of this century, with sites such as qguys.ru, xsgay.ru, gay.ru, gayly.ru, and bluesystem.ru being among the most popular.[76] Such virtual destinations can be instrumental as the first step to establishing physical contact between homosexual men, especially outside of the relative cosmopolitanism of St. Petersburg and Moscow, in provincial centers where no gay clubs exist.

These gay-oriented sites, however, do not necessarily need to engender physical, face-to-face interactions in order to serve as loci for the creation of often affective and, indeed, embodied connections. In this regard, articles on "gay" fashion, literature, movies, and music, likely via a combination of influence and reflection, play a role in establishing "aesthetic" cultural bonds among men sharing the same sexual orientation. Numerous sites, including several of those mentioned, have either links or sections devoted to various sorts of musical materials (articles, streaming audio, and so forth). For example, gay.ru, the largest portal in the Russian-speaking world devoted to homosexual men,[77] has numerous pages devoted to "gay music," while both qguys.ru and gayly.ru feature streaming audio of music assumed to be of interest to gay men—either by dint of the performer's sexuality, the style of music, or historical popularity of a performer and/or style with gay audiences. The former allows the visitor to listen to tracks on the site's playlist while logged in, while the later, via a link on its home page to the site radio-indigo.ru, offers both live and prerecorded programs twenty-four hours a day, seven days a week, to anyone with an internet connection.[78] That there exist numerous Russian websites where possibly illegal and free, or extremely inexpensive downloading of music is available—a means of procuring music enlisted not only by many of my informants but by several DJs with whom I spoke, as well—ensures that the music one has listened to on any of the aforementioned gay sites is readily available and may be listened to on one's own personal audio device whenever it is desired.[79]

While in the foregoing examples music was but one component of a website catering to homosexual men, I also became aware of at least two websites devoted entirely to these two variables. The first, a bilingual Russian/English site, gaysongz.narod.ru—"*Golubye pesni*," in Russian, "Gay Songs" in English—included lists of gay-themed popular songs from Russia, Australia, Canada, Great Britain, the United States, Israel, Italy, Scandinavia, and France, each with a link to the text, a midi file, and an audio file of the song. As with those featured on both Qguys and *Radio Indigo*, the songs here might be those with an explicitly gay text (e.g., Tom Robinson's "Glad to Be Gay," or t.A.T.u's "*Mal'chik gei*," "Gay Boy"), with strong allusions to homosexuality (Boris Moiseev's "*Golubaia luna*," Valerii Leont'ev's "*Kazhdyi khochet liubit*,'" The Village People's "In the Navy"), by performers whose orientation was presumed to be "nontraditional" (Dana International, Soft Cell, Boris Moiseev, Eva Pol'na of *Gosti iz budushchego*) or by performers with large followings of gay fans (Judy Garland, Gloria Gaynor, ABBA). I had come across this website during preliminary research for my first trip to Russia and, approximately one year later, almost impossibly wound up having coffee with the site's author. Appropriately enough, I had met Anton via Qguys where I had discussed my research topic with him, but it was not until we had actually met, and I had specifically mentioned Gaysongz, that he informed me that the site belonged to him. He had started it, he said, because he was "bored," and "wasn't working enough, and had nothing to do, so I decided to try to build a couple of web pages." Additionally, because he had links to other merchants' sites on Gaysongz—for example, providers of gay videos—he saw it as a way to make money, receiving a percentage of any merchandise sold by merchants to whom customers had linked through his site. The other site, miditext.ru, which contained lyrics (for a fee) to a wide catalog of Russian and foreign popular songs as well as music-related news and event listings, used the same "business model," one that earned him a small amount of cash each month.[80]

Not surprisingly, among my informants, Anton was one of the most musically sophisticated and one who considered music to be an important part of his life. But while much of the music on Gaysongz, as well as that in his CD collection, comported with the preferences of many of my informants and was also often in line with the musical choices made by DJs at gay clubs in St. Petersburg (choices that were often based—especially in the case of smaller, less "modern" clubs—on customers' tips), he was one of my few informants who in fact never went to clubs and who expressed no interest in doing so. Yet while he may not have interacted on a face-to-face level with other homosexual men, in spaces defined in large part by their musical components, he was nonetheless linked to affect-laden sites and sounds shared by many gay men in Russia, links of which he was clearly aware. Such links—between music and sexuality, and the links engendered between and among people via their linkings to both—were also implicitly and explicitly highlighted on another website, home to the *Erektrofon*, an "encyclopedia" of "gay music."[81] Once again, the criteria for inclusion of music under this rubric largely match those discussed above, and the author(s) of the site give four reasons for his/her/their having undertaken this "extremely complex... project" ("*ves'ma slozhnyi... proekt*"): first, to illuminate the "gay" influence on music that straight people, often unreflectively listen (and dance) to, the encyclopedia serving as a "fragile little bridge between the representatives of different sexual denominations" ("*khrupkim mostikom mezhdu predstaviteliami razlichnykh seksual'nykh konfessii*"), which might later become a "huge, solid Manhattan bridge [*mostishche*]"; second, to aver that gay subculture still exists; and fourth, to possibly entreat the relatively closeted world of Russian popular music performers to follow in the footsteps of their Western counterparts. The third motive, however, is the one most germane to the current discussion:

Third: They live and get along, lonely in their blind, wild, and boring provinces, forced to hide their truth [*istinnoe*]—guys [*rebiata*], men [*muzhchiny*], and even—imagine that!—women. And often it seems to them, that they are alone in the whole wide world. And often because of this they do not want to live. Yes, as in the provinces, also in the large cities, where many of a delicate nature [*iz utonchennykh natur*] experience the same problems. And then suddenly it turns out that Elton John, and Freddy Mercury, and—unbelievably—Mick Jagger.... Well, you understand.... And to live becomes easier, and to live becomes more joyful. ("*Zachem nuzhna*")

Music here serves as a site for the formation of connections between similarly oriented subjectivities, offering a site whereby solipsism may be salubriously transcended.

But it is not only via the "new" media of the internet that such dynamics obtain, print media being another locus. In an editorial in the "gay" magazine *Kvir*, editor Ed Mishin (2004b), noting that correspondents to the publication live all over the country ("Uvat, Tavda, Asbest, Seversk, Dudinka, Tynda, Beringovskii, Chukotskaia Oblast' [Region]") offers the following:

> In such cities, villages, and corners of the taiga there are not, and are not likely to appear, gay clubs. So much happier for them, that *Kvir* has reached them. Having known about the magazine, such correspondents usually buy the entire year's publication. I hope that *Kvir* becomes that part of gay life,[82] of which many don't have enough.

Kvir's contents, like many of the gay sites noted above, has also included a variety of features and departments devoted to music. For example, a regular column, "*Terra muzcognita*" (written in a combination of Latin and Cyrillic characters, "*TERRA MУ3COGNITO*"), featured readers' responses to such questions as, "In which performers, albums today do you have the greatest interest?" "Was there a situation in your life that changed your musical preferences?" or "Which music will you listen to for driving, relaxation, or sex?" ("*Terra muzcognito*"), while images, articles, and blurbs about and from such performers as gay icons Alla Pugacheva, Sofiia Rotaru, and Madonna, the young and handsome Aleksandr Astashenok (singer from the group *Korni*), the possibly gay Valerii Leont'ev, and the faux-lesbian duo Reflex were found within the pages of the now-defunct *XX-Bi*.

To view those areas devoted to music, whether on the internet, or in print media, as simply one of many possible expressions of "gay culture" is mistaken, however. As I have shown, the sounds, structures, images, texts, and bodies associated with music hold a particular salience for homosexual men and allow for and engender a rich, embodied understanding of sexual subjectivity. Embodied subjectivity, however, is not the terminus; rather, what the musical offers is, additionally, a site for an embodied *intersubjectivity*, a site where the one, he who might imagine himself as entirely singular, understands his vital connections to others like him—not only via matters of "taste" or "aesthetics," but via an affectively motivated embodiment that might occupy and relate to space with the same postures, stances, and orientations as others like him. Although the gay dance club serves as one type of geographically defined site where such corporeal relationships to space and to others may be experienced, a literal copresence is not mandated; rather, both sounds and images of or by others, in other places, may likewise effectuate connection.

For example, videos and "live" television performances also bring images, via the media, into millions of homes throughout the country, images not only of performers, but of audiences as well. Such was the case with several musical variety/competition programs including *Fabrika zvezd* or *Narodnyi artist*, the Eurovision Song Contest,[83] or even *Starye pesni o glavnom* (Old Songs about the Most Important Things) or *Novogodnyi goluboi ogonek*,[84] the audiences of which comprised not only large numbers of girls and women, but also—here and there—young men, sometimes together in pairs. Although attendance at such musical events does not in and of itself necessarily indicate anything about a person's sexual orientation, there was, according to my informants, a stereotypical relationship between homosexual men and some of the specific programs noted above, as well as an assumed, general relationship of homosexual men to the very genres of music these programs featured—largely *popsa* and *èstrada*. In the case of *Fabrika zvezd*, one episode of the fifth season serves as an illustration of the ways in which sexual orientations of both viewers and performers contribute to the making of a site in which homosexual men may figure himself as both "I" and "we." In this episode, *popsa* star and actress Kristina Orbakaite and contestant Mikhail Veselov performed a duet version of the former's "*A ty budi menia*" ("But You Wake Me Up"), a song at that time in radio and video/television rotation. While onstage, the performers, in keeping with the sentiment of the lyrics, touched and caressed each other in the approximation of heterosexual foreplay and sensuality, the codes of homosexuality were not entirely stifled. Not only was the show itself "gayed" via the assumption of the role of the show's artistic director by the country's preeminent gay icon, Alla Pugacheva ("*Fabrika zvezd-5' ne budet*"),[85] but both singers were also connected to homosexuality: Orbakaite was linked via her mother, Pugacheva, as well as the fact that the very song she was performing that evening was concurrently being played in gay clubs in St. Petersburg, and Veselov's association to homosexuality was manifest in press accounts that had reported him as a regular visitor to one of Moscow's most popular gay clubs, *Tri obez'iany* (Three Monkeys), where he was seen "in a group of cute boys" ("*Mikhail Veselov: iz gei-kluba*"), as well as "gossip" on internet chat sites.[86] Perhaps not incidentally, the singer was also, like Mitia Fomin, Sergei Lazarev, and Dima Bilan, attractive and physically fit.

"Homosexuality" was not limited to the stage, however, appearing in the audience as well. Interspersed with the images of the singers were wide, panning shots of the assembled, as well as close-up shots of the spectators, including that of a young man singing along to the duet on stage, the chorus of which follows:

A ty budi menia potseluiami nezhnymi, nezhnymi	But you wake me with tender, tender kisses,
Usypliai menia slovami laskovymi	Lull me to sleep with gentle words,
Budu ia tebe navek i zhenoi, i nevestuiu	Forever I will be, to you, wife and bride
Budu pet' tebe pesni samye sladkie	I will sing to you the sweetest songs

In the act of changing the song from solo to duet, Orbakaite sang the first appearance of the verse and chorus alone. Veselov entered on the second verse, taking it as a solo, and the two shared the ensuing two repeats of the chorus: for what were clearly gendered reasons, on the first repeat Veselov took lines one, two, and four, while Orbakaite retained the third line, and on the second repeat the two harmonized on line one, Veselov took line two, and Orbakaite sang lines three and four alone. During these repeats of the chorus, the camera oscillated between performers and spectators, at one point focusing on the aforementioned young man singing along with the performers onstage. However, rather than suspend his singing at the moment where his gender would have precluded his assuming the role of the singer—specifically, on line three (where Veselov ceded to Orbakaite)—the young man, with camera directly on him, continued singing. As he sung himself both "wife and bride," a smile crossed his face, and his eyes briefly rolled up in a signal of irony. Rather than being simply a chance or accidental occurrence, however, such a presentation, with the camera fixed purposely on a young man assuming the role of the feminine, served a function of showing the male in the musical role of the female, in a site in many ways coded as gay.[87] I am not suggesting that to be a gay man is to be, as nonreflective and homophobic commentators might posit, a "woman in a man's body," an "urning";[88] rather, it is probably more likely for a young, homosexual man, as opposed to a young, heterosexual man, to be *unafraid* of an insouciant transgression of gender positions (to say nothing of knowing all the words to a Kristina Orbakaite song).[89]

In many ways the dynamic I am noting here has resonances with Coyne's (2010) idea of media-abetted "tuning," albeit in a possibly more "lo-tech" fashion. Drawing in part on Heidegger's concept of attunement, or *Stimmung*, and enlisting an explicitly musical metaphor, Coyne suggests that pervasive digital media enable disparate subjectivities to become "tuned" to one another. This type of tuning must be differentiated from synchronization, as the latter implies a falling in line with some final, external arbiter, while the former demands back-and-forth, intersubjective negotiations and the possibility of agency on all sides. It is this type of tuning that I find to be operative in the instances of gay men's interactions via music and musical discourses I have been discussing, whether engendered via face-to-face contact, or primarily virtually via various forms of media, or a combination of both. And such tuning, returning again to Löw, may be implicit in the formation of salubrious atmospheres that mark those spaces frequented by gay men, spaces in which intersubjectivity figures prominently.

On a corporeal level, both Merleau-Ponty and Lingis highlight the fact that connections with others, a transcendence of solipsism, occurs in part through an ability to understand our movements and positions in the physical world as—and in—the movements and positions of others. According to Lingis:

> The one who speaks of his own body taking into account what the others can observe of it and who speaks of the bodies of others as lived in the first person invokes a power to displace himself into the perceived environments of others and into the sentient and intentional postures of others. This power is in the body lived in the first person; my body displaces itself not only into the positions extended by the material layout of nature, but into the positions perceived and explored by others; it exchanges places with others in all its moves. To be sure, it makes the place that another vacated its own; it perceives what the other perceived with its own competence. (1994a: 48)

While the ability to imagine one's self in any number of others' spaces is obviously not something unique to homosexual men, or something dependent upon a shared sexual, racial, national, or other identity, in the largely homophobic space of post-Soviet Russia where homosexual men are often proscribed from manifest, highly visible forms of social intercourse with one another, to say nothing of proscriptions on their inclusion in socially sanctioned forms of symbolic discourse surrounding physical and emotional intimacy, the act of seeing one's self as a potentially simpatico other, and vice versa—the realization that one shares social and physical spaces, that one is not irrevocably, horribly singular—takes on a special profundity. One's body is thus not only a locus for possible sexual pleasure, but also for the pleasure of affiliation, pleasures that are intimately linked, on somatic levels, to music. And such pleasures and knowledges may be experienced and engendered (or "tuned") not only in "real time" in "real" spaces, but in the "virtual" as well.

In post-Soviet space, in fact, it is difficult to align conceptions of "material" or "virtual" with supposed correlates such as permanence or evanescence, respectively. For example, in the span of the first decade of the century, numerous clubs have opened, only to be closed within a matter of months. Physical sites, then, may be as ephemeral as those on the internet are *assumed* to be—but many of these "virtual" sites have, in fact, been in existence far longer than their "material" correlates. Many of the gay-themed websites or gay *saity znakomstv* discussed previously, as well as numerous others, have established a relatively permanent presence in cyberspace. In an interview in *Kalendar'/TimeOut Peterburg*, Igor' Pravdin (a pseudonym),[90] creator of the site xsgay.ru, was asked whether he thought the internet should be a site of "shared" space, where (sexual) minorities might "get used to" society (by interacting with the same sites as the majority), rather than separating themselves from it. Pravdin replied:

> I don't think so. On the internet there is a mass of specialized resources. It's senseless to mix one with the other. Every community (*soobshchestvo*) has its own clubs, interests, possibilities of meeting. . . . Moreover, very often the "implantation" ("*vzhivlenie*") of one community into another carries a negative character. Society is not ready and doesn't want to accept people who are different from the majority. (Kudymov 2004b)

Geographic spaces, cyberspaces, and media spaces, the material and the virtual, both conform to and act upon the embodiments of homosexuality; spaces are both constitutive and constituted. On the one hand, the creation of spaces in urban locales and on the internet may be seen as primary—without the space, the creation of the self, and the coalescing of the many, would not exist. Yet mindful of the rapidity with which both internet sites and discos appear and disappear in post-Soviet Russia, it is equally plausible to assume that embodied subjects whose desires—desires of both self and group—are not met, impact upon the very viability and longevity of locales, via their choices not to populate them. Regardless of such spaces' ontologies, however, filial or paternal, if homosexual men are able to continually create and re-create salubrious spaces and places, in part via their experience as embodied subjects whose corporeal existence links them to others in shared spaces and places, we might hope that the post-Soviet landscape will not be one marked by a succession of gay ghost towns.

6. Conclusion

The Eloquence of Flesh

> In novels, plays, films and other representations in dominant culture, the homosexual always dies.
> —Philip Brett and Elizabeth Wood (2002: 31)

It was 25 December 2004, and I was waiting in the frigid weather in front of the building at 28 Kanal Griboedova in the center of St. Petersburg, the typically overcast sky compounding the cold from the gray pavement that seemed to seep up through the soles of my wholly inadequate boots. Over the course of the next several minutes, five other men approached the space outside of *Greshniki* where I stood, all six of us with fists thrust deep in pockets, hats pulled tight over ears, and shoulders hunched, our jittery, bobbing, back-and-forth movements futile attempts to fend off the chill. Perhaps because I was a stranger to them, and so obviously a foreigner—marked visibly by my features (and invisibly by the fact that I was the only one for whom the day was Christmas, the Russian holiday still thirteen days ahead)—the men, some of whom knew each other, regarded me with what appeared to be a bit of suspicion, and stayed a slight distance away from my place by the door. On the other side of the canal, three more men were waiting, clearly for the opening of the club's doors and also clearly not wanting to be seen in too close proximity to an establishment for *golubye*, one whose very name—"Sinners"—unabashedly announced the dissolute, immoral nature of its guests. Indeed, if their fear had been risking the opprobrium or mockery of passersby, they had acted shrewdly, because the six of us on the "wrong" side of the water were repeatedly glared at by those on the street, one group of three giggling, whispering (with their hands over their mouths), and pointing, ultimately surreptitiously (they thought) taking out their camera and crossing the footbridge to get a wider shot of the *pedovki* in front of their natural habitat.

Shortly thereafter Aleksandr Kukharskii arrived, and after some time the manager of the club (forty-five minutes late) took out his keys, brusquely opened the doors, and allowed the ten of us inside—not for any sort of "tea dance," but for the monthly meeting of *Kryl'ia*. One of the oldest gay social/political group active in St. Petersburg,[1] *Kryl'ia* was founded in 1990 after much maneuvering through the Russian political system, and is run by one of its original founders, Kukharskii. Advertised on its website[2] as a *pravozashchitnyi LGBT tsentr* (the first word literally meaning "rights-protecting," but translated on the website—and in general—as "human rights"), *Kryl'ia* has in the past been involved in political actions;[3] however, its main function is, according to Kukharskii, "the help and support to LGTB people in crucial moment[s] of their lives." This could include anything from answering letters from gay men in the provinces seeking information, to helping track down (through a community "grapevine") an assailant who had beaten and robbed a gay man, to the running of monthly social-informational meetings such as the one we were attending.

The first subject on the agenda that day was a discussion of an exhibit then currently at St. Petersburg's *Èrmitazh* museum, *Robert Mapplethorpe and the Classical Tradition: Photographs and Mannerist Prints*, in which the artist's nude photographs were juxtaposed against classical works that also took the nude body as their subject matter. Kukharskii extemporaneously translated a review of the show, a joint effort between the State Hermitage Museum and the U.S. Solomon Guggenheim Foundation, from the English-language newspaper *The St. Petersburg Times*, offering his somewhat negative critique of modern art in general. The second agenda item was a report from a member of *Kril'ia* who had recently traveled to the ILGA (International Lesbian and Gay Association) conference in Budapest. When it came time to ask questions about this subject, it was clear that most of the men did not know what ILGA was, and the vast majority of questions posed by the attendees had nothing to do with politics; rather, most of the men's questions focused on such things as "how much does a cup of coffee cost in Budapest?" "What happened at the party [after the conference]?" "Is Budapest beautiful?" and "Are Hungarian men beautiful?" The meeting concluded with food and drink supplied by one of the members and a toast to Kukharskii from one member, who said, "to Aleksandr Aleksandrovich, without whom we would not have access to this information—I am very, *very* grateful to him for all he has done for us, he is a wonderful person who has helped us all so much."

The lack of interest in or attention to "politics" was extremely common among my informants, and the majority of them had either never heard of *Kryl'ia*, or had only negative things to say about it (or about Kukharskii himself).[4] Most had no trust in the political system, citing what they saw as widespread corruption at all levels; for example, some, echoing a view that was held by many citizens and journalists alike, cited corruption as a major factor in the terrorist siege in Beslan in 2004, which left more than three hundred people, more than half of them children, dead. Even in their daily lives, they noted that corruption and bribes were necessary to accomplish anything from registering for an apartment to getting a visa.[5] Konstantin, for example, noting that "the main difference between the United States and Russia is that we are a country without laws (*"strana bez zakonov"*), gave the following example:

> If I'm driving to work in the morning, and I'm late, and I see that the street I need to go down is closed for some reason, I'll just drive through it and have money ready to give the policeman. He'll stop me, I'll give him the money, and then I'll be on time for work. That's how things work here.

It might be argued, however, that the opening of visible gay spaces, spaces of which sexuality, music, and pleasure are constituent parts, while not overtly "political" acts (they don't strive primarily to influence legislative action or juridical processes), do, in fact, change the social landscape, and thus influence political thinking. In St. Petersburg, such dynamics could be seen in the actions of the *Kul'turnyi proekt Olovo* (Olovo Cultural Project, also known as K. P. Olovo), a group that sponsored several parties, held in different clubs, for gay men and gay-friendly club-goers. Allied with the apparently now-defunct *Molodezhnaia assotsiatsiia HS* (Youth Association HS),[6] some of the group's themed *vecherinki* (parties; singular, *vecherinka*) included "Independence Gay," "Chocolate Gay," "Red October Gay" and "Christmas Gay." However, one of the founders of the group, Ignat Fialkovskii,[7] in an interview with the website xsgay.ru, appeared to abjure "politics" as a mode of achieving freedom, in favor of experience:

> As many probably know, for a long time I was involved with "gay activism" in its classical variant—seminars, appearances in the press, international conferences—each, in a word, a noisy struggle [at] barricades. And suddenly the feeling came, that people are tired of fighting, that it's time not to struggle for the right to be "equal, free from discrimination," and so on, but simply to be exactly that—to live freely, to have fun openly, to love truly. (Pravdin 2003)

In Fialkovskii's account, the routes to "freedom" are explicitly questioned. Rather than accepting the fact that one must fight, via political channels ("gay activism") to become free, he suggests the opposite—first, "to live freely," to *embody* the actions, orientations, and possibilities of one who is free, rather than approach freedom legally, juridically, theoretically, or conceptually. Living freely is, as such, the foundation upon which legislatively engendered freedoms might obtain, and not vice versa; experience is primary to abstraction. As Merleau-Ponty notes, reacting to the Cartesian view of perception, "it is not *because* I think I am that I am certain of my existence: on the contrary, the certainty I enjoy concerning my thoughts stems from their genuine existence" (2002 [1962]: 445).⁸

But the body, and the actions of the embodied subject, however primary they might be postulated, never exist outside of the constraining structures and strictures of culture—and Merleau-Ponty's work, for example, has been critiqued for omitting these crucial variables.⁹ Some of my informants expressed concerns for their physical safety were they to appear too "out," and a few suggested that, for example, it was better to leave gay clubs only in the morning, after the sun had risen, in order to avoid the possibility of becoming a crime victim. Going to, as well as leaving, gay clubs might also be potentially dangerous, according to some; on one occasion, I was chastised by Rem, one of several gay men with whom I was sharing a car, for having told the driver we had flagged down to drop us off directly in front of *Kabare* ("we have to think of our safety. We never want people knowing where we are going, or what kind of club this is"). Another of my informants, Vadim, was a victim of an antigay attack in St. Petersburg while I was living there. When meeting one day for tea, he emerged from the metro with a swollen and cut lip. When I asked what had happened, he replied that he had been standing in the train, when suddenly a young man, about nineteen or twenty years old, came up to him, demanding, "What are you looking at, *pedovka* [faggot]?" Before he could reply, the man punched him in the face, getting off at the next stop. My apparently stupid questions as to whether anyone on the train intervened on his behalf, or if he would be reporting the matter to the police, elicited only a laugh from him.

A sense of fear also seemed to be operative in the reaction I first received when I telephoned the gay.ru online bookstore directly, asking whether or not it would be possible for me to come and personally pick up the books I had ordered, before my upcoming departure from Moscow, rather than having them sent to me in St. Petersburg (to which I would be returning in a few days)—a process that, owing to the unreliability of the Russian postal system, might take weeks (at best) or result in lost packages (at worst). At first, I was told by the person on the phone that I could come to pick up the books, but that I could not come directly to the office; rather, he would be willing to meet me at a subway stop and personally hand them to me. A second phone call, however, put me in touch with a different man who, apparently believing I was not someone who was going to cause harm to the center or any of its staff, gave me the address and a time I could come by to pick up the materials I had ordered.

In light of contemporary "pogroms" against gay men, in connection with the carrying out of both Moscow's first planned gay pride parade, as well as the associated festival (*Raduga bez granits*, Rainbow without Borders),[10] it may be argued that to "live freely" is something that is de facto proscribed due, in part, to the very real threat of physical danger; without a legally protected position, gay men's ability to enjoy the basic freedoms afforded to other citizens are severely compromised. Cognizance of the situation faced by millions of LGBT persons in Russia and ex-Soviet republics has undoubtedly been a factor leading to the nascent rights discourses among a relatively small group of politically motivated Russian lesbians and gay men, the constant and visible discrimination they face even drawing the attention of Alvaro Gil-Robles, Commissioner for Human Rights of the Council of Europe from 1999 to 2006. In his 2005 report, he noted:

> [H]omophobia has been growing alarmingly in the Russian Federation over the last few years. The statements made by representatives of the Orthodox Church and other denominations, and the actions of the Cossacks in Southern Russia and other extremist groups target homosexuals in a particularly hostile way. ... I was particularly shocked to learn from both NGOs and the press, that a group of Russian members of Parliament, comprising eminent members of the State Duma, including the heads of certain political groups, had recently tabled a bill to have homosexuality once again classified as a criminal offence. (65)[11]

Not only legal and juridical but also economic factors are essential in contextualizing post-Soviet homosexuality. Analyzing data from three waves of World Values Surveys, Inglehart and Baker (2000) have found that the move from agrarian to market-based economies can be correlated with the move from materialist to postmaterialist concerns, values shifting "from an overwhelming emphasis on economic and physical security toward an increasing emphasis on subjective well-being and quality-of-life" as well as "self-expression" (22). The former types of societies overwhelmingly maintain "traditional" values, marked not only by a reluctance to question authority, and disinterest in politics, but also by a negative reaction to "others." In their view, "people in societies shaped by insecurity and low levels of well-being ... feel threatened by foreigners, by ethnic diversity and by cultural change. This leads to an intolerance of gays and other outgroups, an insistence on traditional gender roles, and an authoritarian political outlook" (26).[12]

Traditional values are also, not surprisingly, shown to have a strong correlation to a high level of antisecularism; furthermore, in societies where the economic situation has moved in a retrograde direction (as is the case with Russia in the 1990s), such antisecularism has risen (Inglehart and Baker 2000: 41). Indeed, the economic and the religious, and their relationships to the social disapprobation regarding homosexuality in Russia, were factors noted by both Igor' Kon and Aleksandr Kukharskii in my interviews with them. Of the economic situation in Russia, Kukharskii was of the opinion that as people's financial situations began to improve, there would be a marked increase in acceptance of homosexuality; in his opinion, "when people have something of their own, when they have their own happiness, they are less concerned with ruining the happiness of others."[13] On a more pessimistic note, however, Kon stressed that as the Orthodox Christian church increases in power (perhaps filling a void left by communism), hostility toward all "others," including homosexuals, was inevitable; in his view, so long as the church held sway over the discourse of "morality" in Russia, a "gay community" would never come into being.[14] Such antipathy toward homosexuality on the part of the church was clearly evident in a letter from Aleksei II, Patriarch of Moscow, to Mayor Iurii Luzhkov, regarding the proposed gay parade in the country's capital in 2006. Referring to a "propaganda of immorality" on the part of homosexuals, and praising Luzhkov for having refused to grant the organizers a permit for the parade, the Patriarch concluded:

> I ask you, respected Iurii Mikhailovich, to accept the appreciation for your decision to guard Moscow and the Muscovites from the attempt to carry out in the capital of Russia a public parade of the propaganda of sin. I am certain that the overwhelming majority of the citizens of our country are grateful to you and the government of Moscow for the apparent concern for the retention of public morals. (Aleksei II 2006)

Additionally, Metropolitan Kirill (Gundiaev) of Smolensk and Kaliningrad—later to become, in 2009, the Patriarch of Moscow and all Russia, and a key Putin ally—at a 2005 St. Petersburg conference entitled "Religion in the contemporary system of international relations," clearly stated his aversion to the granting of rights to homosexuals, noting that Western ideas of human rights were incompatible with the moral values of Christianity. In his view, "the philosophy of human rights is used quite often in order to justify deviations from moral norms such as the cult of violence, profits and consumption, abortions, homosexuality, euthanasia, and others" ("*Metropolit Kirill*"). It is unsurprising that such views have contributed to an obvious enmity toward the Church among some gay men and lesbians in Russia; in the estimation of one internet forum poster, "Orthodoxy = Russian Nazism."[15]

Certainly the interconnections of the economic, religious, political, and juridical in relation to homosexuality are not unique to Russia. In the United States, for example, the construction of a "gay identity" has been theorized as having been concomitant with both historical events and economic variables. In what has perhaps become *the* history of the rise of a gay (sub)culture, both World War II and the growth of capitalism engendered the movements of large numbers of men from rural settings to urban centers; such migrations not only brought about liaisons between like-minded individuals (who for the first time might see others who were like themselves), but also, through new economic opportunities, such individuals became less dependent on familial ties for economic survival. According to D'Emilio (1983a):

> [T]he expansion of capital and the spread of wage labor have effected a profound transformation in the structure and functions of the nuclear family, the ideology of family life, and the meaning of heterosexual relations. It is these changes in the family that are the most directly linked to the appearance of a collective gay life. (102)

Capitalism, in his estimation, thus not only made possible the material conditions necessary for economic independence but also, in doing so, called into question the very idea of the heterosexually defined family unit.

But if capitalism may be viewed as one of the foundations of modern gay identities and communities in the West, legal-juridical encroachments upon the freedom to engage in homosexual acts, present in the West for centuries, and the attempts in the twentieth century to abolish such proscriptions were no less so. Beginning, in the United States, with the nascent homophile movements, the fight for equal rights received its most visible and galvanizing thrust from the Stonewall riots, events that have become mythologized not only in America, but abroad as well. Indeed, the concatenation in the West of the sexual with the political, legal, and juridical has been amply demonstrated by Foucault (1990 [1978]) and has either manifestly or tacitly undergirded numerous investigations of homosexuality by Western scholars,[16] so much so that to speak of a gay "identity" or "community" is to, at the very least, tacitly invoke the realm of the political, to be reminded of the indissoluble links between such terms, the people and groups to which they are applied, and the legal-juridical-political matrix. "Identity" and "community" in the West, when used in conjunction with descriptors pertaining to sexuality, are not simply indicative of either individual psychology or social group formation; rather, often conjuring images and discourses connected to Stonewall, gay marriage legislation (and the "Defense of Marriage" Act and Proposition 8), workplace parity, adoption rights, Jesse Helms, the Tea Party, the Republican Party, ACT-UP, Queer Nation, GLAAD—the list might continue almost endlessly—they are inherently politicized.

This is not to suggest that homosexuality has not likewise been politicized in Russia, Soviet or post-Soviet. As previously discussed, in Russia a de facto politicization occurred not simply via the criminalization of *muzhelozhstvo*, but by its having been linked, in the imagination of the governmental leaders, to antistate sentiment and activity; in fact, accusations of homosexuality were often conveniently invoked, absent even a shred of evidence, to dispose of political dissidents who were not found to be guilty of any other "crime."[17] Additionally, such politicization is hardly solely historical; Igor' Kon notes that in contemporary Russia political variables are implicated in the formation of heterocentrism and concomitant homophobia (2001a: 309), and the homophobic may even be considered a form of xenophobia (2006). Kon, in fact, may be considered a de facto activist of sorts, one who has bridged the assumed gap between theory and practice; he is one of the few Russian academics to have worked tirelessly for decades with and for LGBT persons in Russia, in a quest for full and equal citizenship not only for them, but for all "minorities."

To the extent the universal attainment of basic human rights for all people is a goal to which we must aspire, it is unquestionable that the fight for legal protection in such a climate is essential. Such calls for equality have been taken up not only by the more historically established groups such as *Kryl'ia*, but by newer groups as well, some of which make use of the internet for promulgation of their ideals and actions.[18] For example, on the site of the *Rossiiskaia LGBT-set'* (Russian LGBT Network) (www.lgbtnet.ru; last accessed on 7 August 2013), there appeared, in June of 2006, a "Declaration of the Rights of the Sexual Minority in Russia." In part, the document read:

> The use of the rights and freedom of a person and citizen can be limited only in the case of a threat of infringement of the rights and freedom of other persons. No person has proven that the vital choices of gays, lesbians, and transsexuals restrains the opportunities of the heterosexual majority, or threatens public safety. *On this basis, we demand the respect of human dignity and an attitude of equal rights, irrespective of the prejudices which have taken root in society, and superstitions.* ("*Deklaratsiia prav*")

The group's Declaration further notes, in reference to the ill-fated Moscow Gay Pride Parade that was to have been the country's first, that "sexual orientation, we are told, is an especially intimate business, and nothing to parade about. It will be possible to agree with this only when society and the state will respect the rights of a person for a private life." The parade organizers themselves used Mayor Luzhkov's refusal of a permit as an occasion to seek juridical protection of the sexual, with Nikolai Alekseev, one of the event's main organizers, stating that the matter would be turned over to the European Court of Human Rights ("Russian Gays Take Homophobic Moscow Mayor").[19]

But the parade, as politicized spectacle, was hardly a rallying call around which Russian homosexuals might coalesce in unanimous support. Èd

Mishin, editor of the magazine *Kvir* and founder of the website gay.ru, was also the organizing force behind the "center" *Ia+Ia* (I+I) in Moscow, which runs various groups devoted to the support of problems encountered by gays and lesbians.[20] As noted previously, while living in Moscow, I had the opportunity to drop by the physical establishment in order to pick up several books I had purchased via the gay.ru website; the "center" turned out to be an apartment in a building in central Moscow in which were housed many of the workings of Mishin's various projects, including support groups for LGBT persons. It was also the warehouse and call center for all of the merchandise sold on the gay.ru website, so that literally hundreds of boxes were stacked in any available spaces.[21] Mishin was also one of the driving forces behind the planned gay "cultural center" in Moscow, a site he envisioned as catering to "those who have no place to go alone in the evenings, and don't want the three 'b's': the *bania*, the bar, and fucks"[22] (Terskii 2004: 93). Slated to open in 2005, it never materialized, with the gay boutique *Indigo* appearing instead (first in Moscow and then in St. Petersburg, both of which were Mishin's projects).

But although Mishin's actions suggest a support for "the gay community," he clashed in print with Nikolai Alekseev, suggesting that Russia's culture was inimical to such actions as a gay parade and coming down firmly against it—in part, he claimed, because of the threat of violence to the marchers. In response, Aleekseev fired back that Mishin was, in effect, taking the position of the Kuban Cossacks, one of whose groups—the *Evraziiskogo soiuza molodezhi* (Eurasian Youth Union), an ultraconservative movement—had promised to travel to Moscow in order to prevent the parade from taking place ("*V svoem osuzhdenii gei-parada v Moskve*"). It is notable that Alekseev has often been criticized—often by gay men—for his connections to "the West," and "the West's" role in the continuing debate about gay parades in Moscow. In one article appearing in *Komsomol'skaia pravda*, *Kvir*'s chief editor Vladimir Voloshin is quoted as saying:

> In Moscow there are more than a million gays.... But parades don't interest anyone. Why fight for gay rights, if we are not harassed? And how many of our people are on television and in show business? As concerns parades—On Tverskii [Boulevard] every evening there is a parade of gays. Hundreds and thousands of homosexuals walking back and forth, making new acquaintances. And no one disperses them, no one spits in their faces. This commotion is only raised by this unknown [*nikomu ne izvestnyi*] Alekseev, and exclusively in order to see his own photograph in the Western Press. (Suprycheva 2010)

Judging from the responses of my informants, Voloshin's contention that parades "don't interest anyone" appears to have some basis in fact. When queried about their reaction to the first planned Gay Pride Parade in Moscow, my informants could largely be placed in one of two general categories: those who did not know about, and/or had no interest in knowing about the parade, and those who thought that the parade was a terrible idea. Volodia, for example, termed it a "huge stupidity," continuing that "Russia still remains a half-colonial country, like those about which Naipaul wrote in *Middle Passage*. Society is *absolutely* not ready to accept here that type of occurrence, such as a *gay's life*."[23] Volodia's comments mirror the sentiments of many informants, and the apathy and antipathy with which the very idea of this particular type of spectacle was greeted is indicative of their cognizance of the ontological and ideological status of the "Gay Parade" in both political and cultural terms and in the context of post-Soviet space. Adam, Duyvendak, and Krouwel (1999) point out in their cross-cultural discussion of gay and lesbian political movements, that there is still a difference between the West and the East, suggesting that "non-politicized identities and nonpolitical social interaction dominate in the Eastern European context . . . where desire is not framed by political interests" (348).[24] But homosexual men in Russia are "apolitical" not, I suggest, due to a hypertrophy of hedonism brought about by a newfound modicum of freedom, and the concomitant lures of consumer culture but, rather, painfully aware of the disastrous effects of the intrusion of totalizing ideological and political discourses related to sexuality into the lives of gay men, they are exceedingly wary of any conception of "identity" in which the erotic and the political are bedfellows.

Moreover, my informants' experiences and outlooks were the products not only of the social and political history of Russia and the Soviet Union, but of Russia's location within the international arena. According to Jussi Nissinen, former Secretary General of SETA (an abbreviation of *Seksuaalinen Tasavertaisuus*, Sexual Equality), Finland's national LGBT organization,[25] Stonewall became a symbol around which Finnish homosexuals could coalesce in their attempts to gain social acceptance and legal parity; in his estimation, news of the events occurring in New York (as well as in Sweden, Denmark, and The Netherlands) were like a "fresh wind," and a "beam of sun."[26] However, for gay Russian men to eagerly adopt an event of cultural and political history from the United States as an organizing trope around which their sexual identities might be formed is clearly far more problematic. For if homosexual Russian men are leery of having their sense of self allied in any way with a political apparatus that has historically been inimical to their very existence, they are no more keen on constructing themselves in the model of the "global gay," a model that is perceived by many as pointing directly to Great Britain or the United States. It would be difficult to overstate the ambivalence—if not downright hostility—that many of my informants felt for the United States in particular, a country they saw as morally and culturally bankrupt; soulless, rapacious, and arrogant in its dealings with other nations; driven by avarice in the extreme; and superciliously gloating over its "victory" in the Cold War. Gay Russian men do not want, or want to be perceived as desiring, a "liberation" via the very power that demands a complete acquiescence to its hegemonic cultural and political scripts, one that has seemingly taken great pleasure in asserting its supposed cultural and political superiority (insofar as capitalism "triumphed" over "evil" communism).

This is not to suggest that my informants saw themselves as entirely isolated from or in opposition to an "international" homosexuality. For example, when asked if they thought there was a "gay community" in Russia, many said, "no," but when asked if gay Russian men were part of an international or global "gay community," many of the same men responded, "yes." Moreover, the majority of my informants felt that, although there were certainly differences among gay men in different cultural and geographic locations, such differences were outweighed by the similarities. In both instances, these opinions held sway not only for those men who had actually traveled abroad and experienced other gay "cultures," but for those who had never been outside the borders of the Russian Federation as well. Altman expresses a skepticism regarding "sharp divides between Western and non-Western experiences of sexuality," and an increasing certainty that "we cannot discuss sex/gender structures independent of larger sociopolitical ones" (1996: 91).[27] While not wanting to eradicate difference, to posit homosexual men in Russia as being somehow entirely unlike their counterparts in the West (or other locales) may say more about Westerners' desires to "exoticize" them, to create sexual "others." Homosexual men in Russia do share experiences of sexuality with gay men in the West—including the United States—but their cognizance of connections does not imply the desire for a wholesale acceptance of a Western-style "gay identity"; as Altman suggests, their experiences are shaped not only by their sexual desires, but by their unique cultural and political heritage as well. They may consider themselves as members of a "global community," but such membership must be on their own terms.

Music, Sexuality, Culture

Discussions of self and group formation, whether global or local, must take into account not only sexual acts and desires, as well as political statuses, but cultural productions and connections. Walker (1996), in his discussion of postwar "culturalist" theories and their connection to and support of the assignation of "nation" status of various groups, argues that a "gay culture" does indeed exist, marked by institutions, didactic and support networks, ceremonies and holidays, and a "distinctively gay literature" (528), among other things. The refusal to see gays and lesbians as anything more than an interest group, he suggests, "underestimates the complexity and multifunctionality of lesbian and gay culture, while at the same time overestimating the 'thickness' or density of the culture which other national cultures provide" (521). Focusing specifically on homosexuality in Russia, Schluter (2002),[28] while positing the existence of a gay identity in Russia, finds that, instead of community, what exists is the dynamic of "fraternity." In his view, the former is based upon social *institutions* (e.g., roles, groups, activities), the latter defined as "a category of people who share some common interest or condition, and do identify themselves as members of that category, but do not interact as a group often or consistently enough to develop . . . group-level social institutions" (28).[29] Schluter does, however, also list "affective behaviors" as counting among "social institutions," and it is here that a link exists to expressive (popular) culture—the site in which male homosexuality is most audible and visible in contemporary Russia. As I have shown, male homosexuality in contemporary Russia comes about, in part, not only through pleasures of sexual activity, but pleasures of the musical—an arena which has deep roots in the Russian and Soviet cultural past. As such, a formation of the self is better understood as a combination of the modalities of corporeal experience and (with) expressive culture, such as the musical, in conjunction with (not eclipsed by, or appendages to) the political and/or juridical.

Popular music is essential to an investigation of homosexuality in post-Soviet space not simply by dint of its serving as a repository of sorts for that which is effectively blocked in other public spaces, a site "where the boys are." Rather, what I am concerned with here is not so much what has been amply stated in the musicological and ethnomusicological literature—that is, how the musical impacts upon identity[30]—but how our understanding of an embodied sexual identity can be greatly aided by its conceptualization *via* those dynamics operating in music. Here I want to stress, as I have throughout, lived, corporeal experience as primary to symbolization, abstraction, or conceptualization by examining not only the role of language in the ascription of identity but, related to this, the dynamics of musical transcription. Although perhaps seemingly unremarkable (via its naturalization), those domains in which homosexual men have gained visibility in the West and may be gaining public visibility in Russia—the legal-juridical—are often specifically those in which the written and spoken word are of paramount importance. Absent printed statutes, testimonies in courts (transcribed and later published), volumes of case law, constitutions, and the like, the modern nation state and its discourses on subjecthood are scarcely imaginable. The creation of the modern subject seems, in many respects, to be contingent upon just such linguistic primacy, in specific domains. However, it often seems as if some Western theorists have assumed an almost tautological stance with regard to sexual identity, viewing a path of causation that is both bidirectional and concurrent: that is, not only are political movements, allied with the legal-juridical, assumed to be an outcome of identity, but identity is seen as an outcome of political-legal-juridical movements.[31] Such a prejudice has also informed our historicization of homosexualities, basing assumptions of an absence of "gay identities" on either juridical proscriptions of church dogma—that is, court or church documents preserved for posterity. It is, no doubt, a dearth of existing evidence that leads researchers to rely heavily on such written testimonials, and to perform their hermeneutics thereon. However, the conclusions that have been based on such support seem at times to conflict with a cross-cultural examination of same-sex erotic interaction. As Drucker (2000b) reminds us:

> [T]he extreme reading of social constructionism asserting that before the nineteenth century there were only same-sex acts, but no same-sex identities, cannot survive even a superficial examination of pre-colonial Asian or African cultures. Many non-European languages have centuries-old words for people who habitually engage in same-sex sex, not just for particular sex acts. (13)

Moreover, we should understand that lack of access to existing discourses that may have circulated orally does not foreclose on the possibility that such "naming" existed; religious, legal or juridical documents may not have contained specific "identity words," but that does not foreclose upon the possibility of their existence. But the very idea of assuming that absent a (Western) "name" no men or women understood their same-sex attractions to be a defining part of their emotional, physical, and/or affective lives is to privilege "law" and language, abstraction over embodiment, as the arbiter of ontological status, an arbiter that is in conflict with the inarticulable. In Russia, although the word (literature, language) is afforded a high value, words alone do not fully articulate meaning; as Boym notes, "there used to be a saying among Soviet intelligentsia—'to understand each other with half-words.' What is shared is silence, tone of voice, nuance of intonation. To say a full word is to say too much" (1994: 1).

Relating this to music, we may focus, as only one particularly apt example, on the blue note—apt not only insofar as it crystallizes the dynamic I am attempting to highlight, but also by dint of its very hue, *goluboi*. Here, focusing on those attributes of music least amenable to either linguistic or graphic abstraction, it is useful to examine the enterprise of musical transcription. Middleton (1990: 103–126), for example, notes the notation-centricity that has dominated musical analysis in the West, something that leads to a reification of text, and a concomitant devaluation of process and performance. In his estimation, it is specifically those attributes most amenable to written expression (generally as prescriptive "directions") that are taken as conferring worth upon a musical "text," while those most intractable (vocal quality, phrasing, pitch inflection and so forth) are dismissed as "peripheral" phenomena.[32] But Middleton points out how both composers working "on paper," as well as singers and instrumentalists—through performance-based uses of "dirty" notes, slides, and other vocal/instrumental techniques—add to a specific musical language. In such a reading, the jazz singer's blue notes, so requisite to an affectively satisfying performance, yet transcribable in only the crudest of forms, are on a par with those symbolic representations sedimented in the written artifact. The blue note defies description in the terms specified by (patriarchal) control, changes the language that cannot name it. As the field of the legal-juridical cannot lay claim to totalizing affective, lived experience or fully articulating identity, as the Voice stands in high relief to the Word (Dolar 1996), transcription, and those enterprises invested in vaunting it as arbiter of worth, is ultimately revealed as unable to rule that which exceeds its limits.[33] Although music may be conceived of as having a relation to the linguistic,[34] the latter may not claim suzerainty over the former. As Blacking (1992) eloquently argues,[35] musical and word-based languages are distinct from one another, and it is a mistake to believe that only one holds sway in the realm of social and/or self-formation; to privilege a single domain is to impoverish the very complexity of identity. The pleasures and affects of music are often as inarticulable as those of sex and emotional intimacy, and all three—in addition to ideology and the symbolic register of language—may be used in an attempt to "translate" discourses on identity into terms more indicative of its true dynamics. As Longhurst (2001) has highlighted, although we live life in a symbolic economy, we are also embodied; but while this body has become the site of academic inquiry in recent scholarship, it is an almost idealized, transcendental body, one that does not trouble (masculinist fantasies of) rationality by remaining conceptually neat, bounded, and impermeable rather than fluid (and productive of fluids, these often relegated to the domain of the abject). Yet it is exactly this leaky skin, these messy fluids, disconcerting as they are to tidy schematization, that underline the insufficiency of the linguistic or the transcribable in regards to either music or identity. The smells, scents, and tastes of skin, sweat, semen, for example, those things so material, so viscous or salty or warm or pungent, are as eloquent as any written/transcribed theory in the domain of identity formation. In much the same way that the full affect and power of a musical performance resists reduction to written or spoken linguistic description, so does one's sense of self; it relies, to the contrary, at least in part, to the fantastic messiness of corporeal existence.

The nonlinguistically based ways in which music is related to the creation of the self are numerous. For example, musics make available, via symbolic and sensuous form, critiques of gender and power differentials inarticulable in other arenas,[36] or serve as sonic critiques of teleological historical narratives.[37] Indeed an inherent problematization of temporality may be an integral part of embodied experiences of music, often due to repetition on both the micro and macro levels;[38] but repetition also offers the possibility of situating the subject as well, and attention to musical repetition may help illuminate not only the disconnect between abstraction and experience but the obvious necessity of understanding post-Soviet homosexuality as embedded within a specific sociohistorical location. Certainly repetition is a constituent part of most musics (save perhaps for aleatory), and post-Soviet popular music is no exception: From the repetitions of songs on state-sponsored television and in (gay) discos, to the sampling of Soviet-era film songs and dialogue in dance club remixes, to the perennial returns of Soviet *èstrada* artists in contemporary guises (reinventions of the same), to the propensity of artists to "repeat" their past successes through the release of songs resembling their previous hits,[39] to—perhaps most importantly—the very attributes of much of the music itself, melodies and harmonic structures taking on extremely stereotypical forms. Voices and structures repeat, structuring repeated actions (watching a favorite music variety program, dancing at the same club, with the same people, listening to the same music while driving or working or fucking). Indeed, it is this very concatenation of sound impacting upon and reflecting action that has led certain commentators to equate musical repetition with vacuity and, worse, hegemonic control. We need not rehearse Adorno's (1990 [1941]) polemics against popular music, his charges of "structural standardization," "pseudo-individualization," and "rhythmic obedience," but neither should we assume that such critiques are limited to this era. Attali's (1985 [1977]) influential monograph is still cited with regularity, and has, despite its positing of the era of "repeating" as the nadir in the entire history of music, avoided the excoriations that have often greeted Adorno's text in recent decades. And Hainge (2004), operating from a Deleuzian standpoint, finds that "pop" is not music, insofar as it is beholden to the market-driven refrain; the refrain has no power to de- or reterritorialize, is trapped in the arboreal and conjugating, cannot bring forth the freedom of the rhizomatic and connective. In the case of post-Soviet Russia, Shiraev and Danilov (1999) attribute this type of repetition to a desire on the part of the audience to be reminded of "old and presumably better times" (223),[40] and it is probable that in new, market-driven economy, within a society not historically "raised" on the valuation of innovation, the need to cater (or pander) to an audience's tastes—part of which may, indeed, be the product of "nostalgia"—may mandate giving the public "what it wants."

The devaluation and suspicion of repetition, its equation with loss of agency, and its definition in largely negative terms is in many ways manifest in Butler's (1993) theorization of the construction—performatively enacted—of gender. Invoking Derrida's linguistically based theories, she finds:

> [P]erformativity cannot be understood outside of a process of iterability, a regularized and constrained repetition of norms. And this repetition is not performed *by* a subject; this repetition is what enables a subject and constitutes the temporal condition for the subject. This iterability implies that "performance" is not a singular "act" or event, but a ritualized production, a ritual reiterated under and through constraint, under and through the force of prohibition and taboo, with the threat of ostracism and even death controlling and compelling the shape of the production, but not, I will insist, determining it fully in advance. (95)

Repetition here is nonagentic, an external imposition, the net from which we cannot escape—although owing to the impossibility of exact repetition in each instance, the possibility of subversion exists. Such subversion—defined, in contradistinction to repetition, in overwhelmingly positive terms—features prominently in Halberstam and Livingston's (1995a) examination of the "posthuman" body, and in queer theory in general. I am not suggesting a wholesale conceptual inversion of these implied dynamics, whereby all repetition becomes positive and all subversion negative (a horrifying conceptualization to say the least); rather, I would like to highlight the fact that the *modality* of the repetition is not inconsequential, and that the (affective) import of repetition must be examined in context. In regards to the first, socially compelled repetitions of, for example, gender attributes, or even the quotidian repetitions associated with one's job or home life, are not experienced in the same manner as musical repetitions: the repetition of a bass riff on a dance floor, the repetition of a song in the same club over a period of weeks or months, the repetition of a singer's voice from decades past, now in the present, the repetition of a known melody, or known harmonic structures all bring about pleasures on numerous levels that, although hardly apprehended by an unmediated biology, nonetheless may literally touch and stimulate the listener's body, inside and out, and produce positive affective states.[41] Here, pleasure may be the product of a relationship to a specific object, but it may also be conceptualized as accruing from the engagement in the process of repetition itself—a type of musical "process pleasure" (Garcia 2005). Not that "pleasure," musical or otherwise, is free from the constraints of ideology; as Middleton notes in his discussion of musical repetitions, pleasures are not like "bran-tub goodies, freely or randomly available," but rather, already "ideologically sorted, shaped and wrapped" (1983: 268). Yet to eradicate, totally and fully, the variable of musical pleasure, often engendered by repetition, is not only to posit an almost unimaginable bleakness, but to diminish the ability to fully comprehend the importance of expressive culture.

Moreover, in regards to the necessity of contextualized applications of theoretical posits, it is essential to stress that "pleasure" must not be conceived of solely as a correlate of mindless hedonism or superficial sensation. "Pleasure" may also accrue from the succor afforded by one's sense of deep connection and belonging, of stability and purpose (often engendered via repetitions of various types of rituals), all of which were severely compromised for millions of people living in the wake of the dissolution of the USSR. Kon (1993a) finds that the destruction of the guideposts of identity in post-Soviet society—guideposts constructed, by and large, by the government—left an immense void in citizens' lives, leading to a world that was "meaningless," one in which social roles, identities, and statuses, were obliterated or made illegitimate.[42] This opinion was echoed on one occasion, on a palpably emotional level, by Pasha, as we viewed a video of Alla Pugacheva's performance of the song "*Osennii potselui*" ("Autumn Kiss," released in 1993)[43] at my apartment. Watching and listening to Pugacheva, I commented on what I perceived to be the "strangeness" of both the song and her appearance. It was odd to me, for example, that on the level of genre, this particular piece did not seem to fit into any stylistic categories under which the bulk of her material might be subsumed; it did not particularly resemble her manifestly pop/rock-influenced songs, nor was it entirely similar to the more "classic" *èstrada* pieces in her repertoire, especially insofar as the rather dark verse led to a somewhat bouncy, almost *popsa*-like chorus.[44] Moreover, the extremely low register in which the verses were written made Pugacheva's delivery seem almost awkward, striving for deep emotional expression, but not quite achieving it. The oddness of the song was matched, in my estimation, by the visage of Pugacheva herself, the singer appearing with overteased, strawlike hair and clad in a rather bizarre-looking fuchsia satin dress (a tight, strapless, bustier-type top contrasting with the full, flared miniskirt) that she had paired with a black bolero jacket, jet black hose, and black, flat ankle boots. When I expressed this to Pasha, he appeared to be not angry, but visibly moved, and told me, "of course she looks lost—you have to understand that at this time we were *all totally lost*. We didn't have any idea who we were, or what to do, or where to go, or even where to get food. Everything that we knew was gone. Everything had fallen apart." The obliteration of guideposts of identity constructed by the state was experienced as deeply disorienting, and in Kon's (1993a) estimation "individuals urgently need[ed] new self-definitions framed in more personal, non-bureaucratic, individual terms."[45]

For gay men and women in Russia, defining a new sense of self is infinitely more difficult, insofar as such constructions need not only be productive, but destructive as well; specifically, they must eschew the pathologization and criminalization of homosexuality put in place by the previous system, abjuring the patently political as a whole, yet they are ambivalent about submitting to a hegemonic Western gay (political) identity. They are aware of the extent to which the social and political climates continue to be repressive, yet owing to the importance of close family relationships for many (often not only with the nuclear family, but with one greatly extended), are not desirous of a wholesale subversion or eradication of all social structures.[46] In this regard, it appears that the "formulaic refrain," and other such musical repetitions, are salubrious sites in relation to and through which a complex, post-Soviet, homosexual self may be experienced, lived, and constructed. The musical sites, sights, sounds, and contexts that I have examined are essential to the production of a situated self, serving as situating points—the complete absence of which would result in a type of schizophrenia[47]—corporeally and pleasurably experienced, irreducible to the political, linguistic, ideological, or discursive. This is not to suggest a thanatotic stasis, however, as the dynamic interaction of the known, the repeated, with the "new," the "other" (often, the Western) frequently marks the sites in which music and homosexuality converge in post-Soviet Russia.

The Lively Tchaikovsky

At the close of my interview with Igor' Kon, as he accompanied me to the door of his apartment, I realized I had neglected to ask a question that was related to one of the most puzzling aspects of his work—puzzling for me, a Westerner, an American. Donning my coat, I asked him if he had any idea why, in a climate marked by an aversion to sexuality in general, to say nothing of homosexuality, he had been allowed to research so widely into this area of academic inquiry. Kon replied that he had no way of knowing with any certainty, but he suggested that it may have had to do with the fact that, as chief researcher at the Institute of Ethnology and Anthropology in Moscow, he enjoyed a solid reputation as an academic who had produced legitimate, respected work of high standards and thus was not someone who was merely interested in the more prurient aspects of human sexuality. However, as a researcher who had spent time in the United States,[48] he also cautioned me against simplistically seeing Western scholarship as "free" and Soviet scholarship as "constrained." As an example of this he expressed his belief that for a scholar in the West to maintain that the body held any sort of causal role in social or subject formation could often be considered tantamount to naïveté, a lack of theoretical sophistication, or a reactionary conservatism.

Indeed, much writing about the body in Western theory appears to be, in part, geared toward the emancipation of subjectivity from a supposed and poorly theorized belief in the body's causality. Such theorization has been taken up by those interested in specifically queer bodies. Halberstam and Livingston (1995a), for example, in their discussion of posthuman bodies, note the ways in which the body must be viewed as having lost its linkages to supposed biological imperatives—which, as it turns out, are more social constructions than corporeal facts—and the attendant subversive potential of the queer body to wrest the self from the somatic (the heterosexual reproductive couple, the family unit). What may be questioned here, however, is not the worth of interventions into and interrogations of the ontological status of corporeal existence, but the possibly insidious implications of a transcultural and transhistorical theory that is often not recognized as having been born in a specific place and time; that is, while the subversive potential of the suggested posthuman (and queer) body may indeed have a profound resonance in late-twentieth/early-twenty-first-century Western culture (particularly in the United States, where discourses of self-sovereignty and "freedom" appear dissonant with any sort of top-down imperatives or constraints, be they biological or cultural), and while work foregrounding this subversive potential is of inestimable value in terms of both its theoretical importance and its potential for engendering liberatory politics and practices, such theorization must not be taken as having the ability to either explicate or dictate politics, practices, or ontologies in other places and times. In the early part of the twenty-first century, although the inhabitants of St. Petersburg were, chronologically, a decade past the fall of the Soviet Union, the psychological and affective resonances of having been thrust into a gyre of absolute uncertainty—an instability that many still experienced on a daily basis—probably rendered discourses of subversion and purposeful fragmentation or deconstruction of what might be experienced as the last bastions of constancy (e.g., the family) far less resonant than in the West. Additionally, as Warner (2002), notes, the very notion of "queer" is indissolubly linked to the political bodies, mechanisms, and practices of the modern Western nation state; as such, "we should be more than usually cautious about global utopianisms that require American slang" (209).

If Russian homosexuality is to be understood, then, as more somatic in nature than its Western counterpart, a somaticity with symbolic, visual, and sensuous links to popular musics, this must certainly not be taken to suggest a naïve and unreflective belief—by social actors or academic theorists—in corporeality, a state of affairs that will inevitably "catch up" with the West in due time; on the contrary, a body-based understanding and experience of one's sexuality indicates the ways in which situated sexual bodies are intimately wedded to the contexts in which they are experienced and lived. This does not mean that one's fleshly existence in post-Soviet Russia is in perfect harmony with its environment, does not battle against boundaries, does not link to a desire for subversion of constraints. Indeed, as I have previously discussed, the homosexual body in contemporary Russia, embedded and symbolized within, and constitutive of, musical production—discursive, material, sensuous, experiential—must often seek to overthrow the constraints of a long history of pathologization (via the Soviet apparatus), as well as the suffocating hegemony of Western "gay culture." But while both of these constraints may be viewed as impositions from without, there is yet another constraint, one arguably deeply indigenous to Russian (as opposed to Soviet) culture: the castrating straitjacket of the "spiritual homosexual," a construct I have previously noted (see Chapter 3). Baer, in part via reference to Russian writer and philosopher Vasilii Rozanov's 1911 treatise *Liudi lunnogo sveta* (*People of the Moonlight*), a work in which the male homosexual is portrayed as exhibiting the intertwined attributes of aversion to the sexual and carnal and, through this "sublimation," a fecundity regarding artistic and cultural production, highlights how this "soulful" (*dushevnyi*) categorization of homosexuality is deeply ingrained in Russian culture—indeed, not only from decades past, but in the contemporary sphere, where the supposed concerns of the homosexual (soul and art) are lauded as positive attributes in contradistinction to the venality of the West (2009: 93).[49] This enduring trope is perhaps nowhere more evident than in the representations of that most famous example of Russia, music, and homosexuality intertwined, the figure of Tchaikovsky. The failed marriage to Antonina Miliukova, the "virtual" relationship to Nadezhda von Meck and, ultimately, the mythologized apocryphal "suicide" necessitated by a physical relationship with another man, on the one hand, and the postulated "artistic sensitivity" on the other keep alive to the present day the construction of the spiritual homosexual, one whose transgressions regarding male-to-male physical sexuality may only result in death. Yet as Brett and Wood (2002) suggest, a lesbian or gay approach to the composer's life "would most likely focus on his *lively* aspects" (emphasis added), a focus on breath, flesh, and sexual vitality rather than on tortured asceticism or morbid pathology. If Tchaikovsky stands as the very (tragic, pathetic, onanistic) embodiment of the musical homosexual to both Russians and Westerners,[50] then it is only by moving beyond this castrated, frustrated, caricatured, and negated Tchaikovsky, the object-lesson in the dangers of *muzhelozhstvo*, that an understanding of the pleasures and fecundities of music and sexuality might be understood. The old, sterile, homophobically created "Tchaikovsky" must be rolled over (to become "physically" accessible to sexual excitement, and/or to be rolled out the cultural door) so that the lively, sexual Tchaikovsky may take his place.

It would be a mistake, as I have suggested earlier, to view the relative liberation and concomitant foregrounding of the body among homosexual men as simply an act of hedonism. Vanina (2004) implicitly highlights such a dynamic in her assessment of the post-Soviet homosexuality, noting:

> When they abolished [Article 121] gays were able to do everything, and from the previous restraints they quickly said goodbye . . . they danced, they drank themselves to death, changed boys one for the other. More than anything the mood of that time resembles an exhausted wail—"finally!" (36)

But while pleasure should need no apologists, there is much more than self-indulgence at play in the body's centrality in the lives and musics of homosexual men in post-Soviet space. As Shilling (2008) suggests, when the subject is both physically and psychologically besieged with profound cruelty, "ritually" tending to the needs of the assaulted body is instrumental not only in transcending the tortures visited upon it, but also in bringing about social, collective bonding on levels both emotional and somatic.[51] The body is not naïve; rather, it is often tantamount to life. Beyond procreation, a body that is sexual, that is musical, that creates spaces and places, that dances, that interacts with other bodies, is one that fairly throbs with life. The homosexual is not dead, not by political apparatus, homophobia, Western cultural imperialism, or spiritual transcendence.

Epilogue

"*Pravo na Schast'e*"

Khoroshie pesni, veselye tantsy	Good songs, happy dances
Tak khochetsia zhit' i vliubliatsia	[We] so want to live, and fall in love
Byt' vmeste i nikogda ne proshchat'sia	To be together and never say good-bye
Vezde uspet' i vmeste spet'	To arrive everywhere on time, and sing together

—Mitia Fomin, "*Khoroshaia pesnia*" ("Good Song")

I my budem vmeste	And we'll be together
Kak tselogo chasti	As parts of a whole
Khoroshie pesni	Good songs
I pravo na schast'e	And the right to happiness
I vse interesnei	And everything is more and more interesting
I vse budet luchshe	And everything will be better
Khoroshie pesni	Good songs
Ty tol'ko poslushai	Just listen

—Hi-Fi, "*Khoroshie pesni*" ("Good Songs")

With the collapsing of both time and space brought about by an increasingly (if not yet fully) digitalized media society, work on studies dealing with popular music and popular culture—to say nothing of those dealing with post-Soviet space—takes on a growing sense of immediacy and urgency. Temporal and spatial bracketing become highly problematic, and the velocity with which changes in musical sounds and images, allegiances, and scenes take place suggest to those of us chronicling, researching, and interpreting popular music that fantasies of a neatly defined and quiescent contemporary "object of study"—if it ever existed—must be once and for all jettisoned. Indeed, even attempting to find a semistable node on the rushing continuum of musical trends and practices may leave one with figurative rope burns on one's palms, as that which we attempt to grab simply speeds into the distance, a mocking "catch me if you can" whistling in its wake. It appears that only by moving with infinite expeditiousness will we have even the remotest chance of catching a "thing's" essence—a time, a place, a genre, a scene—of doing explanatory or interpretive justice to it.

Such motility and velocity seem the antitheses of the very academic and institutional apparatuses in which such popular musics are often studied; if mediated sound is ever more quicksilver evanescence, then the dictates, strictures, and structures of scholarly analyses and publications, encompassing years of library research, fieldwork, funding proposals, manuscript submissions, drafts, revisions, and galley prints seem marked by a type of charmingly archaic plodding lassitude that is destined to produce work that is ever only historical in nature. But although many transformations have occurred in the cultural, political, and musical land- and soundscapes from the time of my initial visit to Russia and the final draft of this manuscript, there have been continuities as well. With a desire again to eradicate any hint of a suggestion of an ethnographic present, and with cognizance of time's forward progression and repeating refrains, it is to both that which has changed and that which has remained the same that I wish to briefly turn my attention in this epilogue.

One of the most profound changes to the shifting LGBT landscape in post-Soviet Russia was the death of Igor' Kon in April of 2012. I was greatly saddened to read of Kon's passing, not only because he had been so generous and helpful to me while I was in Moscow conducting fieldwork as a PhD candidate, but also because his death is certain to leave an audible, visible, and textual void in the chorus of oppositional voices seeking to combat homophobia. As an academic, public intellectual, and theoretically engaged activist, Kon's written works, teaching, and lectures contributed greatly not only to a more nuanced, less puritanical understanding of sex and sexuality in general, but also to efforts to depathologize homosexuality and eradicate discrimination against all "others" in post-Soviet space. As I have noted earlier, Kon was somewhat pessimistic about the possibility of equal rights—or even increased social approbation—for LGBT persons in Russia in the near future, owing to what he saw as the growing alliance between the Orthodox Church and the entrenched political apparatus and the discourse of "morality" that barely masked the undertones of xenophobia and homophobia inherent in their rhetorics. Kon was skeptical that either group would decrease in power or influence in the coming years.

Has there been political change in Russia since the turn of the century? When I left the country, Putin was firmly in charge and, if one was to believe the polls, supported by the majority of the populace; certainly most of my informants were more pro- than anti-Putin, and the majority saved their most scathing vituperation for Putin's predecessor, El'tsin. And despite a titular swap between the president and Dmitrii Medvedev—Putin moving from president to prime minister, Medvedev from deputy prime minister to "president"—at the time of the writing of this epilogue Putin has returned to (or remained in) the role of the country's top leader. According to a recent poll by the *Levada-Tsentr*, one-third of all Russians believe that Putin will remain president until 2024.[1] Clearly, however, not all Russians are convinced that political stasis is inevitable. From late 2011 into early 2012, massive protests in Moscow, in response to what many of those involved considered a flawed and corrupt electoral process and a declining standard of living, were incarnations of a fomenting desire for change (if only among a segment of the population). Anatolii Chubais, former El'tsin-era reformer, and current head of Russian Nanotechnologies Corporation (Rosnano) related this unrest to the bourgeoning Russian middle class; in his view, "the era of stability in Russia has finished," and Russia is, due to the demands and desires of this middle class, "on the brink of democratic reforms." Sergei Mironov, leader of the opposition party *Spravedlivaia Rossiia* (A Just Russia), also voiced his belief that change was inevitable, expressing confidence that it was possible to wrest control from Putin's monopolistic *Edinaia Rossiia* (United Russia) party.[2] But while Aleksei Naval'nyi, a key figure in the Moscow protests, was lauded by *Time* magazine as one of the 100 most influential people of 2012, the accolades of a Western press apparently did little to hamper a possibly politically motivated retribution; bearing disconcerting similarities to the Mikhail Khodorkovskii affair, in July of 2012 Naval'nyi was charged with embezzlement and one year later was convicted.[3]

Although it is difficult to judge from a distance of thousands of miles, it appears that many gay men in Russia, despite the recently politicized climate of the capital, as well as the recent passage of national legislation outlawing dissemination of "gay propaganda"—an event to which I will return later—have remained apolitical in their stances. A recent profile (Schwirtz 2011) of Nikolai Alekseev in the *New York Times* notes that most Russian gays appear to be uninterested in gay activism, and it has continued to be rare that my communications with Russian contacts—now online as opposed to in person—focus or even touch on politics. On the other hand, Alekseev's activism has been partially responsible for an increased awareness among Westerners of LGBT issues in Russia (more on this later), and his website—now changed from gayrussia.ru to gayrussia.eu (last accessed on 7 August 2013), and available in both Russian and English—remains a visible presence on the internet. Alekseev's site, with its attention to LGBT news, politics, society, and culture, is hardly a one-off; several others, including the *Sankt-Peterburgskaia LGBT-organizatsiia Vykhod* (St. Petersburg LGBT Organization Coming Out;[4] www.comingoutspb.ru; last accessed on 7 August 2013), and the aforementioned *Rossiiskaia LGBT-set'* have likewise established a relatively stable existence on the Web and, in the case of the latter, this has translated into the establishment (according to the site's authors) of LGBT organizations and groups in twenty regions of Russia. Like Alekseev's, the former site comprises sections accessible to English speakers, and both groups have not only taken up, at least in part, the discourse of LGBT movements in the West (with a focus on the attainment of equal human rights), but they have also established working contacts with Western political and juridical organizations in their attempts to better the position of LGBT citizens in Russia.[5] And while they are not themselves gay men, the members of the band Pussy Riot not only openly and harshly critiqued the "unholy alliance" between the Russian Orthodox church and Putin in their "punk prayer" "*Bogoroditsa, Putina progoni*" ("Blessed Mother, Drive Away Putin")—the alliance that so troubled Igor' Kon—but also brought the issue of LGBT rights to the foreground with the lyrics "the ghost of freedom is in the heavens/gay pride [*gei-praid*, гей-прайд] is sent to Siberia in chains."[6]

Perhaps the growing visibility of words themselves of Western provenance ("*gei-praid*," "*kamin[g]-aut*"), allied with a gay "identity" and "community" (these, as I have suggested, inherently linked to LGBT politics), indicate a de facto politicization on the part of gay and lesbian Russians. Both "coming out" and "queer" are now more widely encountered than in the past, the latter appearing as part of the monikers of St. Petersburg's *Kvir-fest* (Queer Fest, www.queerfest.ru; last accessed 24 June 2013), a cultural festival organized by *Vykhod*, the main goal of which is to "support the rights of each person to be himself, regardless of sexual orientation and gender identity"[7] and "to make queer-community [*sic*] visible"[8] and the relatively new website *Kvirkul'tura v Rossii* (Queer Culture in Russia, www.queerculture.ru; last accessed 24 June 2013). In the case of both, as evidenced by the contents of the websites, it is notable that the word *queer* is being used not simply as a euphemism for *gay*, but in its Western (cultural/political) sense; as defined by the authors of the

Kvir Kul'tura site, for example, the term indicates "that part of culture which surmounts the limits of traditional patriarchal culture, gender stereotypes, presents queer optics, alternative models of sociocultural gender, cultivates marginal modes of being."[9]

While websites addressed to gay and lesbian audiences have been in existence in Russia for well over a decade, the increase in number of such sites is noteworthy, and almost certainly related to the phenomenal increase in internet accessibility among the Russian populace; in the five-year period from 2005 to 2010, internet usage increased nearly three hundred percent, from 15.3 to 43.31 percent of the population.[10] Such accessibility has surely positively impacted upon homosexual men in their abilities not only to meet other gay men via the numerous gay *saity znakomstv*, but also to obtain information (often through social media) about everything from gay travel, to HIV/AIDS transmission, prevention, and treatment, to cultural events (such as *Kvir-fest*) and/or cultural-political actions, to gay sporting groups.[11] But perhaps most importantly, in the context of this study, is the proliferation of sounds and images of, as well as information about, Russia's substantial roster of popular music performers of (assumed) *netraditsionnaia orientatsiia*. In order to contextualize this proliferation it is important to understand that up until approximately 2007, it was quite difficult to find materials such as music videos, recorded interviews, or commercials once they had run their course on television; my only option was to slavishly and obsessively record, via VCR, hundreds of hours of Russian television while I was in St. Petersburg and Moscow and have the tapes converted from SECAM to NTSC format upon return to the United States. From 2007 onward, however, surely as a result of the aforementioned increasing access to the internet in Russia, there appeared an exponential growth of such materials on the internet, most notably on YouTube and similar sites. Here, for example, with extremely rare exceptions, every video or commercial or interview I had seen on television, or every song I had heard in a club, was readily available.[12] The importance lies not in the fact that such abundance is a boon to a researcher of Russian *popsa*, but rather what such abundance (and ease of access) indicates for LGBT audiences and the formation of homosexual spaces, places, and subjectivities and intersubjectivities—including the ability of people to *dis*-identify, and what such "dis-identification" suggests about homosexuality and subjecthood in post-Soviet Russia.

It was on YouTube, for example, that Boris Moiseev opened his own channel, replete with clips not only of his musical performances, but his social performances as well—specifically, the introduction of his "fiancée" Adel' Todd (an American "businesswoman"), via a segment broadcast on *MuzTV*.

In the clip, Moiseev described marriage as "the closest of all friendships," and the couple exhibited a type of physical "intimacy" that appeared so strained and cringe-worthy that it immediately brought to mind a line from *Will and Grace* ("I haven't seen a kiss that uncomfortable since Richard Gere and Jodie Foster in *Sommersby*").[13] Far from an authentic engagement announcement, the media spectacle was most certainly another instance of Moiseev's manipulation of his sexual identity for his various (heterosexual/homosexual) audiences. Although as noted in Chapter 3, the marriage had been "rumored" for years (rumors no doubt spread by Moiseev and his publicists), and was promised to have taken place in September of 2010, the nuptials never materialized at that time. Shortly thereafter, in December of the same year, Moiseev suffered a serious stroke.[14] In an interview a year after this personal tragedy Moiseev, making direct reference to the marriage, stated:

> The time for a wedding for me is over.... There's no need to confuse that which was with that which is today. It's simply a waste of time.... I always understood that I made one conscious choice in my life. I chose the stage. And no matter how lonely and sad it was in the evenings in my luxurious apartment in the center of Moscow, I decided to be an artist.... [But] I have reexamined my life. For me material wealth has receded into the background. I no longer want to take part in any kind of intrigues, and play different roles. I want to be myself. Without provocation and scandals.[15]

Once again assuming the role of the "spiritual homosexual" (suffering and alone in his fabulous Moscow apartment, castrated by an art that allows no time for physical, sexual intimacy or relationship), Moiseev's actions and disseminated images following the interview seem to gainsay his avowal to avoid "provocation" in the future: in 2012, pictures of the singer and a young woman in wedding attire, in a Moscow park, circulated on the internet and in the *zheltaia pressa* after having appeared on Moiseev's blog.[16] In addition to the images, the blog featured an entry about the event,[17] with Moiseev himself characterized as "shocking and unpredictable" ("*èpatazhnyi i nepredskazuemyi*") and the identities of the participants purposely undisclosed in order to preserve the "intrigue" ("*sokhraniv mesto dlia intrigi*"). A segment of the "wedding" itself was featured on Russia's Channel 8, subsequently appearing on YouTube, and seemed rather pathetic; despite the singer's intention to create a media event, the performance was sparsely populated, with obviously sham paparazzi on the edges of the assemblage.[18] In the end, the performance was revealed to have been a (not terribly successful) publicity stunt and film shoot for the release of Moiseev's 2012 CD *Pastor* (*The Pastor*), the role he played at the "wedding." The stunt was also meant to serve as promotion for the CD's single "*Luchshii iz muzhchin*" ("Best Man")—the very words Moiseev had written at the bottom of the "wedding photo" that had circulated via his blog, and a video for which was apparently to have been produced from the day's footage.

Judging only from statistics on YouTube, however, neither the album nor the single (or, in fact, any of the "performances" or [non-]"events" posted there) have been terribly popular or provocative; of the numerous uploads of the song "*Luchshii iz muzhchin*," for example—the "single" from his new CD—as of August 2013 not a single one had reached even twenty-five thousand hits.[19] It is probable that the demographics of Moiseev's audience do not dovetail with the demographics of the most likely internet users in Russia and that the very old-fashioned form and style of the song (virtually indistinguishable, save for higher production values, from those he had released years earlier) simply failed to resonate with younger, computer-literate listeners. Additionally, it is possible that this presumably younger, technologically savvy, more modern—even Westernized?—audience, an audience encompassing gay men and women, were simply unable to connect not only to Moiseev's dated sound but also to the archaic, obsolete model of "spiritual, semi-closeted homosexuality" he presented. The only Moiseev clip from the new CD to receive a relatively large number of hits (233,320 as of August 2013) was the one accompanying his song "*Ia ne mogu tebia teriat'*" ("I Can't Lose You")—a clip that featured an array of arrestingly beautiful men stripping down to their undershorts.[20] If the audience for this clip (and others to be discussed shortly) can be assumed to comprise viewers and listeners of myriad sexual orientations, it is possible that the "phantom" in the form of the spiritual homosexual has been replaced by a more corporeal form, albeit via digital images.

Indeed the presentation of (homo)eroticized male bodies by both male and female performers, has become a regular part of the media landscape in Russian-language pop. In June of 2012 Sergei Lazarev appeared shirtless and pumped up on *MuzTV* to perform the song "*Ia ne zdamsia bez boiu*" ("I Won't Give Up without a Fight"), a duet with Ukrainian singer and actress Ani Lorak (in Ukrainian). Yet the performance of heterosexual passion between the singers—a type of passion on display in some of Lazarev's more recent videos[21]—as well as his highly publicized, soon-to-be ex-"romance" with one of the evening's hosts, the forty-one-year-old Lera Kudriavtseva, has apparently done little to dissuade the press and public from assuming or making insinuations regarding his nontraditional sexual orientation, sometimes in rather arch manners.[22] A columnist for *TimeOut Moskva*, for example, noting that the singer had Tweeted a "recipe" for sperm on his Twitter account ("fructose, water, vitamin C, zinc, enzymes, proteins, phosphate, and bicarbonate. Add flour and a cake can be baked") wished the singer "bon appetit" ("*Chto zh Sergei, priiatnogo appetita!*").[23] In his videos and performances Dima Bilan's body has continued to be exposed and homoeroticized, but also rather aggressively heterosexualized (via propinquity to female "love objects," or being cast in "roles" with suggestions of stereotypical masculinity);[24] yet despite intentions of normative construction, Bilan's body also continues to be "gayed" not only via its very visibility, but by more subtle means. In "*Liubov'—suka*" ("Love Is a Bitch"), for example, the singer's female love object is none other than Iulia Volkova, vocalist of the "lesbian" duo t.A.T.u, and the somewhat cryptic narrative of the video suggests that both Bilan and Volkova are brainwashed into loving the same woman (the "bitch"), a scientist/therapist of sorts. And in the video for "*Slepaia liubov'*" ("Blind Love") Bilan is a constituent part of a homoerotically charged triangulation of desire, the latent homoeroticism bolstered by the fact that his nemesis/beloved is played by Ian Somerhalder, an American actor known, in part, for his portrayal of characters of nontraditional sexual orientation.

Perhaps, however, this triangulation is meant not to hinder but to foster homosexual desire. As DeAngelis (2001) suggests, ambiguity regarding sexual orientation, in the context of gay fandom, may increase desire; a desire entirely sated, after all, is no longer a desire. Mitia Fomin, having split with the group Hi-Fi, and embarked upon a solo career in early 2009, continued his performances of "triangulation" in "live" (lip-synched) appearances (appearing, à la Hi-Fi, with one male and one female dancer) and, like both Lazarev and Bilan, also featured scenes of heterosexual eroticism in his videos (as well as the [homo] eroticized display of his body).[25] Yet again, as with the other two singers, Fomin's clips referenced homosexuality in sometimes barely coded ways: "*Vse budet khorosho (la-la-la)*" ("Everything Will Be Good") was shot in Greece—referencing perhaps both "Greek love" and Mykonos's staus as a gay playground—and the music for "*Ogni bol'shogo goroda (Paninaro)*" ("The Lights of the Big City") was culled largely from the song "*Paninaro*" by gay icons/performers the Pet Shop Boys. As with Bilan and Lazarev, Fomin's digital forays into heterosexuality did little to quell suggestions in the press that he was gay. In one instance that may have been particularly embarrassing for the singer, fully nude photos of him and another man—referenced frequently as his "boyfriend"—surfaced on the internet, the photos apparently leaked by the (apparently) disgruntled (now ex-) boyfriend himself. And Fomin himself seems to have courted continued speculation by having appeared on the cover of the March 2009 issue of *Kvir*. But perhaps the most interesting aspect of Fomin's solo career is what his departure from Hi-Fi revealed: the voice on Fomin's tracks was clearly not the voice of Hi-Fi. Indeed, as many had surmised, the vocal tracks of Hi-Fi's songs had been supplied by the group's composer and producer, Pavel Esenin, and Fomin (and all of the other Hi-Fi members) functioned *as* bodies to be viewed.

Both Verka Serdiuchka and Valeriia, two of the most famous Russian-language pop singers for the past two decades, have produced recent videos featuring male bodies ("Kiss, Please" and "The Party's Over," respectively), but a slew of newer artists have also made use of such imagery in their work. Perhaps the most striking images may be found in the unabashedly homoerotic video for the song "*Podruga*" ("Girlfriend") by the (appropriately named) group *Dik*. The video, featuring Moscow drag queen legend Zaza Napoli, includes numerous shots of bared male buttocks grasped by male hands and the following lyrics which create a pun using the song's title, and slang for the posterior:

Vse prokhodit tol'ko my drug druga	Everything passes, we only have each other
Ponimaem i nikto ne znaet	We understand and no one knows
*Chto moia **podruga**—po-padruga* [=***popa druga***]*	That my girlfriend is a gi-girlfriend [=**butt friend**; *popa*=butt]
Chto moia podruga ne skuchaet	That my girlfriend isn't bored

Another song by the group uses the same sort of manipulation of words to suggest gay sexual desire; in "*Dikii mir*" ("Wild World"), the sole line of the chorus—"*Dai mne svoi dik-, mne svoi dik-, mne svoi dikii mir*"—can be literally translated as "Give me your wi-, your wi-, your wild world," but it is clearly meant to be heard as "give me your dick." The reading is supported by the video, the final images of which include the camera panning down to what turns out to be the fully naked body of one of the men, revealing an erection in time with the chorus's text.[26] That the pun encompasses Western slang for the male genitalia—"dick" is not widely used in Russian—is in itself telling.

The group Vintazh has also produced two videos in which eroticized male bodies feature prominently: "*Roman*" (with a double meaning of "Romance" and "Novel") and "Na Na Na" (with Russian DJ and producer Bobina [Dmitrii Almazov]), the latter of which displays numerous well-muscled and attractive men in stylized Ukrainian Cossack dress. In fact, many of the most explicitly homoerotic post-Soviet popular music videos have come from Ukrainian artists themselves (such as Kamon!!!'s "*Metroseksual*"), and one Ukrainian director in particular—Alan Badoev—has become a veritable fountainhead

---

* Although the spelling is different—"po-po..." as opposed to "popa"—the pronunciation, owing to the syllable stress, is the same (i.e., "popa").

of videos featuring sexualized male bodies in recent years, the vast majority of the clips belonging to Russian or Ukrainian artists, the latter of whom often sing in Russian. A partial list includes *VIA-Gra*'s "*Anti-Geisha*," BiS's "*Korabliki*" ("Little Boats"), Maks Barskikh's "*Student*," "*Teriaiu tebia*" ("I'm Losing You"), and "*Serdtse b'etsia*" ("The Heart Beats," a duet with Svetlana Loboda), Kristina Mezhinskaia's "*Do rassveta*" ("Before Dawn"), Masha Sobko's "*Nenavizhu*" ("I Hate [You]"), David Milk's "Free Love," *Mobil'nye blondinki*'s "Birthday (*Ia segodnia k tebe ne pridu*)" ("I Won't Come to You Today"), Filipp Kirkorov's "*My tak nelepo razoshlis'*" ("We Broke Up So Absurdly"), Dmitrii Khvorostovskii and Igor' Krutoi's "*Toi et Moi*," Aleksandr Lominskii's "*Vechnost'*" ("Eternity"), Alibi's "*Melodiia dozhdia*" ("Melody of Rain"), Vasilii Bondarchuk's "*Èto byvaet s kazhdym*" ("It Happens with Everyone"), *Nereal'nye*'s "*Novyi pik*" ("New Year"—in Ukrainian), *Lama*'s "*Trimai*" ("Hold"—also in Ukrainian), and Kazaky's "Dance and Change." This last group features four handsome men dancing in scant, couturelike clothing and stiletto heels, displaying startlingly perfect examples of the male physique.[27] As opposed to the videos of Boris Moiseev, Kazaky's videos (and indeed many of the others mentioned in the preceding paragraphs) have each garnered hundreds of thousands, if not millions of views on YouTube.

Dancing male bodies continue to be part of the club scenes in both St. Petersburg and Moscow, bodies of both both patrons and performers. In September of 2012, the aforementioned group *Dik*—their logo designed to have the initial letter resemble the body part suggested by their appellation—appeared at one of St. Petersburg's newer clubs, *Malevich*, which is advertised as "a place for creative people of the LGBT community" ("*mesto dlia tvorcheskikh predstavitelei LGBT soobshchestva*"),[28] catering to both gay men and women, and gay-friendly straights. The appearance of new establishments in Piter should not, however, be taken to indicate that the number of social spaces for gay men in Russia's two largest cities is increasing; rather, as noted in Chapter 5, it seems that while the number of such establishments remains low, the number of openings and subsequent closings continues to be, conversely, high. In Moscow, many of the gay sites I had visited in 2004 are still in operation (including *12-Volt*, *Stereo*, *Voda*, *Maiakovka Sport*, *Tri obez'iany*, *911*, and *Propaganda*); several newer clubs appear to have opened (according to *TimeOut Moskva*), and some have closed—perhaps most notably one of the most popular clubs in the city, *Dusha i telo*.[29] In St. Petersburg, however, the only commercial, explicitly gay site that remains in operation from the time of my fieldwork is *Kabare*, which has moved three times in the past seven years and has changed its name to *Art-Tsentr Kabare*; *Greshniki*, *Mono*, *158B*, and *Nartsis* all closed in the period between 2005 and 2012, and while both *Monro* and *Metro* are still in existence, neither is any longer a *miks* club.³⁰ In this same period, approximately twelve gay or gay-friendly sites have opened, seven of which have subsequently closed. As such, as of September 2012, St. Petersburg's tally of establishments for gay men stands at six: the aforementioned *Malevich* and *Kabare*; the club *Tsentral'naia Stantsiia*; the bars *Bunker* and *Golubaia ustritsa* (Blue [gay] Oyster), advertised as a *kruzing* (cruising) bar and a *trèsh* (trash) bar, respectively; and the gay bathhouse *Fitnes-Sauna*.³¹ As with argot related to sexual identity and politics, it will be interesting to note what the appearance of words of Western provenance related to sociosexual space—cruising, trash, fitness—performatively enacted, might mean for post-Soviet homosexuality in the coming decades.

The complexity of the intersections of the Russian and the Western in relation to homosexuality and popular culture (including popular music)—a complexity I have attempted to portray throughout this book—is once again foregrounded vividly in the enactment of and responses to the aforementioned 2013 national legislation banning "gay propaganda." Similar laws had been passed at a regional level since 2006,³² and in 2012 the city of St. Petersburg—considered by many the cultural capital of the Russian Federation, relatively liberal (in the context of Russia's overwhelming conservatism), and home to many famous (and nonfamous) homosexual men and women throughout its history—followed suit. The Petersburg legislation, which prohibits "the purposeful and unchecked spread, in a public manner, of information which could harm the health and moral and spiritual development of minors, including the formation in them of the distorted notions of the social equivalence of traditional and nontraditional marital relations [*brachnykh otnoshenii*]" was signed into law on 7 March by Governor Georgii Poltavchenko,³³ an action that provoked a corresponding *re*action by some of the country's most famous celebrities. An open letter, signed by singers Filipp Kirkorov, Nikolai Baskov, Dima Bilan, Valerii Siutkin (formerly of the band Bravo), and Valeriia, as well as Olympic gold medalist Evgenii Pliushchenko, football player Viacheslav Malafeev (goalkeeper of the St. Petersburg–based team *Zenit*) and others, was addressed to President Putin and Prime Minister Medvedev. In the letter, these members of the "elite" (as they were termed on one Russian internet news site)³⁴ voiced their concern about the "growing campaign to consolidate the image of St. Petersburg as a capital of homophobia and bigotry" and urged the president and prime minister to consider the early termination of Deputy Vitalii Milonov, one of the main sponsors of the legislation. But while it is possible that the letter may have had some symbolic impact (albeit slight), it was clearly unable to influence any sort of political or legislative change, either at the local or, ultimately, national level, as a federal version of the statute was passed on 26 June 2013 and signed into law by Putin three days later. Article 6.21, entitled

"Propaganda of Nontraditional Sexual Relationships (*otnoshenii*) among Minors," prohibits exactly this, "expressed in the dissemination of information aimed at building among minors nontraditional sexual facilities (*ustanovok*), the attractiveness of nontraditional sexual relationships, a distorted idea of the equivalence of traditional and nontraditional sexual relationships, or the imposition of information about nontraditional sexual relationships, causing interest in such relationships."[35] Notably, the penalties for infractions—fines and/or imprisonment—are substantially higher for non-Russian citizens, who might also face deportation.

But while voices in the West—activists, journalists, politicians (including U.S. President Barack Obama and German Foreign Minister Guido Westerwelle)—have weighed in heavily against the legislation,[36] reactions by some Russian gays (including gay activists) may have appeared puzzling to their North American, European, or Australian counterparts. In a somewhat confusing (if not confused) "op-edge" piece featured on the *Russia Today* website, Nikolai Alekseev concurrently underscored the need for repealing the antigay legislation, outlining his and his groups' past and planned future initiatives to this end, but also contended that the "horrific laws" (his scare quotes used to suggest sarcasm) were "rarely applied" and that their consequences would be "mostly social, not legal" (Alekseev 2013). Yet while he suggests that the implementation of the laws is actually a boon to the fight for equal rights in Russia, having had the effect of foregrounding the discussion of LGBT rights in the media to an extent unthinkable only a decade ago, he later references the disturbing present-day practices of groups who post their physical and emotional harassment of young gay men and women on the internet, "[seeing] the gay propaganda law as carte blanche for their crimes."[37] Indeed, in reference to the brutal murder of twenty-three-year-old Vladislav Tornovo in Volgograd—beaten severely, raped with beer bottles, his genitals mutilated, his skull crushed after allegedly having told two friends he was gay—Alekseev went so far as to say "political figures have provoked antigay sentiment by portraying the gay community as a bunch of freaks. . . . They are accomplices in the killing" (Winning 2013; see also Gover 2013).

Alekseev's minimizing of the legislation's effects appears to be engendered, at least in part, by his desire to inveigh against the West, Western activists, and Russian nationals living in the West. He is not only highly critical of those Russians (some of whom may not be gay and/or oppressed) who exploit the passage of the "horrific laws" in order to emigrate to the West, but also the "bandwagoning" of Western and Russian expatriate activists around the recent legislation—despite the fact that they have been virtually silent and invisible while local versions of the law (to which they were apparently oblivious, or about which they were simply unconcerned) have been implemented throughout the country for the past seven years. Moreover, he excoriates those activists behind the attempts to organize a Western boycott of the 2014 Sochi Olympics, as well as Stolichnaya vodka, seeing these merely as opportunities for staging media spectacles and evidence of how little understanding such activists have about Russian society and the ramifications of such proposed boycotts on the lives of Russians—gay and straight.

But it was not only activists such as Alekseev whose views regarding the antigay legislation might seem perplexing to westerners. When I broached the topic with a few of my online connections, they all expressed, to some degree, the opinion that such laws were not so "horrifying" or draconian as those in the West believed. Alesha thought that they were "pure politics" ("*chistoi vody politika*"), enacted in order to divert the attention of the Russian people, via the creation of an "imaginary enemy," away from a declining standard of living and the previous years' incipient "revolutions." He suggested that the Russian people themselves were to blame for having allowed themselves to be manipulated, a view shared by Danil, who repeated the oft-heard criticism that Russians are "too passive." Danil also offered, however, that the entire Russian political system, while de jure democratic, was in reality completely under Putin's control and full of "lying politicians." However, it was Ruslan's response to my query as to how things were going for him after that passage of the law that most clearly evinced the ambivalence with which the West, and Western-style identity politics, are often received by some gay Russian men. In line with the sentiments of my other informants, he also characterized Russians as apolitical and contended that, while Russians did indeed desire Western-style freedoms, they also wanted to maintain their Russian individualism. But noting that he and his partner had lived together for many years without any type of social animus or disapprobation, or physical harm, he said that he also didn't know any gay men for whom life had become any more difficult since the statute had become national legislation. In his estimation, the furor surrounding the laws was both Western-backed and anti-Russian:

> And that which is invented by the LGBT [activists], it is all attempts to misinform the global community, and undermine normal life in Russia. The LGBT [activists] simply work off the money of the enemies of Russia, on which this organization exists. And so now they call for a boycott of the 2014 Olympics, and invent all sorts of non-existent stories.

He later suggested that the LGBT activists indeed lived off Western funds, and that if "propaganda" was outlawed, they would lose their source of income. In his estimation "they are paid for their screaming, which is erected around this law which does not impact upon our lives."

It is clearly too soon to know how such legislation will (or will not) impact upon the lives of homosexual men and women in Russia in the future, nor can we predict with any certainty its effects on the types of embodied representations, interactions, and performances I have discussed in these pages. In Chapter 3, I suggested that the very existence and successes of such singers as Moiseev, Leont'ev, and Serdiuchka seemed to indicate that the Russian authorities, who had the power to shut down media outlets and imprison political opponents, apparently did *not* wish to entirely obliterate homosexuality or homoeroticism from the sociocultural sphere. And yet the passage of this legislation, once again indicating a long-running (and inconceivable) belief in the ability to be "propagandized" into—or infected by—homosexuality (as Meshkov suggested in his 2005 newspaper article on gays and lesbians on the Russian stage; as the group *Nash gorod* suggested in their calls for the disruption of a planned gay pride parade; as the Soviet authorities suggested through their belief that "innocent" young, "heterosexual" men could be "seduced" by "pederasts") would seem to call my contention into question. But while such legal interdiction may suggest that a certain type of homophobia (which I still believe to be deeply imbricated with an equally powerful homophilia) has become a legislated mandate, at this point in time the ban on "gay propaganda" has not resulted in the disappearance of videos of "nontraditional" performers from YouTube (or similar Russian sites), the closure of such artists' websites, the removal of their products from online or brick-and-mortar retailers, or their erasure from the media in general. Moiseev, for example, retains his title of *Zasluzhennyi artist rossiiskoi federatsii* and was featured on a recent episode of the *NTV* television program *Chistoserdechnoe priznanie (Frank Confession)* (aired 22 August 2013), and he is still performing in concert in both Russia and Ukraine.

Understanding, again, the complexities inherent in the interactions of the cultural, political, national, and global around the variable of homosexuality in post-Soviet Russia, it is thus not surprising that although the gay (pride) parade is perhaps one of the most performatively efficacious rituals—efficacious in its ability to materialize homosexuality as a living, breathing, perambulating presence, one that is incarnate and a constituent part of the social structure—it is exactly this performative and spectacular ritual that Russian homosexuals have been both prevented from embracing and have chosen not to embrace. On the one hand, Moscow's politicians, courts, and citizens (from skinheads to Orthodox Christians) have rallied to thwart every attempt at materializing any such public spectacle for the past eight years, the most forceful blow coming in the form of a ruling by the Moscow city government (upheld by the city's highest court) banning all gay pride events in the city for the next hundred years, until 2112[38]—this after a 2010 ruling by the European Court of Human Rights in which Russia was found guilty of having unjustifiably banned gay marches from 2006 to 2008 and ordered to pay plaintiff Alekseev a total of €29,510.00.[39] And on the other hand, it would be far too simplistic to assert that the sparse attendance at each of the attempted marches over the past several years was due only to coercion and fear of social censure and/or physical harm; many of my informants believed, as I have noted, that such parades in Russia were a "huge stupidity," a mindset that may have had as much to do with their cognizance of the political and social situation in Russia, as it did with their cognizance of such parades' Western provenance, a provenance clearly problematized by (and problematic to) informants such as Ruslan.

But if one of the purposes of Russian activists working for the materialization of any gay parade in Russia was to gain visibility not only in Russia, but in the West as well (and thus ally *with* liberal factions in the West who might aid in the battle against post-Soviet homophobia), May of 2009 might have seemed the ideal time in which to attempt to launch yet another pride march. With Dima Bilan's win at the Eurovision Song Contest the previous year, the competition was set to take place in the winner's home country; with the eyes of the (Western) world on Moscow, activists may have assumed that Russian authorities would not risk sullying their reputation as a "modern" state (worthy of inclusion in the G8, for example) by repressing the free speech and civil rights of a "minority group." And yet the authorities, initially somewhat outwitted by the activists, ultimately had no qualms about denying the would-be marchers the right to assemble, making numerous arrests, often with excessive force. According to Alekseev, however, the response of the Russian authorities was a victory for LGBT groups:

> By stopping the gay parade, [Mayor Luzhkov] has provided massive media coverage of our fight against homophobia. . . . This has hugely increased public awareness and understanding of gay people. . . . His violation of our right to protest has given us a remarkable platform, with day-after-day of publicity about lesbian and gay human rights. (Tatchell 2009)

A Western activist present at the parade concurred with Alekeev's assessment, finding that the repressive actions had engendered a "PR disaster for the Russian and Moscow authorities, ensuring that Eurovision 2009 will be forever associated with police brutality, government homophobia, and the suppression of a peaceful protest" (Tatchell 2009).[40]

At the winner's press conference in the Olympic Indoor Arena on the final day of Eurovision, however, Alexander Rybak—a Belarusian-born

Norwegian citizen, representing his adopted country—had a different take on the protesters' decision to align their action with the final day of the competition. Asked by a Swedish journalist in the audience what he thought of the police's having prevented a "manifestation for gay rights" at the time of the contest, Rybak, initially stumbling somewhat, ultimately responded:

> Like I always said actually this whole week, in that question, um, is that, I, I think it's a little bit sad that they chose to have this parade today, because, uh . . . they were spending all their energy on that parade, while the biggest gay parade in the world was tonight.[41]

If Eurovision may be considered the gay parade of pop music, then Russia's popular music may still be the gay parade of the entire country, if "parade" may be conceptualized—in contrast to Western manifestations—as not necessarily patently political, but rather as a procession or succession of personifications of gay sexuality and "gay culture" (enacted corporeally, textually, semiotically) in the public sphere, for both heterosexual and homosexual spectators and the participants themselves. But while such a conceptualization of "parade" seems to lack the power necessary to effect political and juridical change, consigned to the realm of the digital image and/or the stage, what should not be forgotten is the unabashed corporeal nature of the images at the centers of such spectacles. Their very fleshliness may indeed portend an incarnation as living, breathing, visible, audible, and tactile presences—with or without the aid of the "Western-style" parade-cum-political mechanism—of men deemed deserving of equal human rights, of *pravo na schast'e*.

List of Interlocutors and Interviewees

(*All names are pseudonyms; each name is followed by the person's age and place of residence at the time of initial meeting*)

Interlocutors

Aleks, 22, St. Petersburg
Aleksei, 28, St. Petersburg
Alesha, 31, St. Petersburg
Alik, 29, St. Petersburg
Andrei, 24, St. Petersburg
Anton, 23, St. Petersburg
Artur, 32, St. Petersburg
Boris, 40, St. Petersburg
Danil, 40, St. Petersburg
Dmitrii, 43, St. Petersburg
Evgenii, 38, St. Petersburg
Gavril, 23, St. Petersburg
Georgii, 29, St. Petersburg
Gleb, 42, St. Petersburg
Grisha, 37, St. Petersburg
Il'ia, 40, Moscow
Ivan, 31, Moscow
Kirill, 42, St. Petersburg
Kliment, 37, Moscow
Kolia, 27, St. Petersburg
Konstantin, 27, St. Petersburg
Maksim, 31, St. Petersburg

Nikita, 25, Moscow
Nikolai, 30, St. Petersburg
Oleg, 24, St. Petersburg
Pasha, 32, New York
Petia, 21, St. Petersburg
Petr, 42, St. Petersburg
Rem, 33, St. Petersburg
Roman 43, St. Petersburg
Ruslan, 44, Moscow
Senia, 26, Moscow
Slava, 37, Moscow
Stanislav, 28, Moscow
Tolia, 41, St. Petersburg
Vadim, 34, St. Petersburg
Valera, 27, St. Petersburg
Vasilii, 29, St. Petersburg
Volodia, 22, St. Petersburg
Vova, 22, Moscow
Zhenia, 44, St. Petersburg

Interviewees

DJ Christy, 13 December 2004, St. Petersburg
DJ Partyphone, 6 December 2004, Moscow
Kon, Igor,' former Chief Researcher, Institute of Ethnology and Anthropology, Russian Academy of Sciences, 3 December 2004, Moscow
Kukharskii, Aleksandr, Director, *Kryl'ia*, 21 December 2004, St. Petersburg
Nissinen, Jussi, former Secretary General, SETA (*Seksuaalinen tasavertasisus*), 27 May 2004, Helsinki

Notes

Chapter 1. Introduction

1. Although female homosexuality was never criminalized, it was nonetheless pathologized; as such, while lesbian women were not imprisoned, they were in many cases subject to forced psychiatric and medical treatment and institutionalization (cf. Healey 2001a: Chapters 2 and 9; see also Nartova 2007).

2. Healey (2012), echoing a sentiment held by many, suggests that Russia's decriminalization of homosexuality was simply a move made in order to allow the country to eventually join the Council of Europe, not one based on moral or ethical principles regarding full and equal rights for all citizens.

3. See "*Luzhkov zapretit gei-parad*."

4. See Myers (2006).

5. I contacted Alekseev via email approximately three weeks before the date of the parade, at which time he stated that it would be held as planned.

6. See "Moscow Says Banned Gays because 'Cleaner' than West."

7. For example, protesters picketed (and attacked participants at) the presentation of a speech by Merlin Holland, Oscar Wilde's grandson, at the Renaissance Event Club, having earlier in the month prevented a party at the same venue that was to be held in conjunction with the month's festivities ("Protesters Disrupt Lecture"; "*Nochnaia vylazka mrakobesov*"). Customers of one of the city's most popular gay clubs, Three Monkeys (*Tri obez'iany*), were similarly attacked by the same sorts of groups within the same time frame ("*Napadenie fashistov*"). Although a large cultural festival entitled *Raduga bez granits* (Rainbow without Borders) was to have surrounded the parade, the group's organizers, initially intent on holding the planned festivities despite threats of violence, later posted a notice on their website, http://fest.gayclub.ru/ (inactive as of 1 December 2012) that all of the events would be postponed; indeed, the *Russkii obshchenatsional'nyi soiuz* (Russian Social-National Union), a Fascist/nationalist group, had posted the times and locations of several of the planned events

on their website, found at http://www.rons.ru/net_pidoram.htm (inactive as of 24 June 2013), calling for supporters to picket all such events; note the use of the word "*pidoram*" [uninflected form, *pidory*] in the web address, which translates as "fags" or "faggots"). As such, some events to which the protesters were called were marked by a complete absence of participants ("*Fashisty po-prezhnemu*").

8. See, for example, "*Gei-pogromy v Moskve*"; Silant'ev (2006).

9. A detailed account of the events, in English, may be found in the report prepared by ILGA Europe (Anmeghichean 2006).

10. Moscow was not the only city in which physical violence and juridical interdiction occurred hand in hand with gay parades. In Riga, Latvia, for example, permission to hold the country's first gay pride parade in 2005 was initially denied by the capital's city council. Although the ban was ultimately reversed, the small group of marchers (approximately 150 to 200) was set upon by large groups of protesters who, as in Moscow, assaulted the marches with both fists and hurled objects (including human excrement). Threats of similar violence accompanied the announcement of a similar march in 2006, although this time President Vaira Vike-Freiberga unequivocally voiced her belief that the Riga City Council's refusal—again—to authorize the parade, was "unacceptable in a democratic country because Latvia's priorities are those articles of the Constitution, which enable people to express their opinion and the state should make it possible for them" ("Vike-Freiberga Lashes Out"). Similar violence greeted marchers in Warsaw, Poland.

11. It is notable that the name of the establishment points toward a "gay history" of sorts, as a gay club by the same name was in existence in Moscow in the early 1990s.

12. The name of the group is a reference to Mikhail Kuzmin's 1923 novella of the same name. Kuzmin's work, one of several of the Silver Age that engages homosexuality in a positive light, is often considered the first Russian "gay novel." I discuss the group, and Kukharskii, further in Chapter 6.

13. The charges involved accusations that one of the celebrants urinated on or near the church, and another accosted a nun. Both Severianin (2006) and Silant'ev (2006) note that most all public celebrations in St. Petersburg can count numerous intoxicated people among the participants, many of whom—regardless of sexuality—will often relieve themselves on the street. Silant'ev also suggests that the placement of the gay group in front of the Catholic church—a church, he points out, devoted to the religion of another minority in a precarious position in present-day Russia—was a calculated measure meant to pit different "others" against one another in order to "divide and dominate" ("*razdeliai i vlastvui*").

14. For a discussion of xenophobia in Russia, including violence against gays and lesbians, see Chapter 2.

15. The list can be found at http://www.qguys.ru/do/diaries/read?id=82244 (last accessed 17 August 2013).

16. The version currently on the kp.ru website does not include the image of Shura (last accessed 17 August 2013).

17. The appellation is an abbreviation, or condensation, of the theater's full name—*munitsipal'nyi dvorets kul'turi* (Municipal Palace of Culture).

18. However, Naiman (1997) notes this mistrust of nonprocreative sexual contact in the works of both pre-Revolutionary philosopher Vasilii Rozanov (1856–1919) and literary critic (and member of the Communist Party) Vladimir Friche (1870–1929), long before the Stalinist period—arguably the period in which so-called "sexophobia" reached its apex in Russia. According to Naiman, "both Rozanov and Friche lumped together the use of birth control . . . homosexuality, onanism, *and* asceticism as characteristics of the bourgeois age. . . . 'Hatred of the [hetero-] sexual act,' 'physiological weakness,' 'psychic impotence,' and birth control, Friche said, were merely separate voices composing a single 'melody' that would lead to the destruction of civilization. Rozanov . . . shared [Friche's] aversion to trends in contemporary sexuality and gave the name 'sodomites' to *all* who were disgusted by procreation . . . [including] his philosopher colleagues, the Russian Orthodox Church, and members of the Russian intelligentsia uncomfortable with or repelled by sexual intercourse" (32–33).

19. The *Levada-Tsentr* is a nongovernmental polling and research organization, named for Russian sociologist Iiurii Levada.

20. For example, to the question as to whether consensual homosexual contact between adults should or should not be prosecuted, the 2005 percentages were 45.3 and 37.4, respectively. The corresponding percentages from the 2006 survey were 37.9 and 45.3 ("*Oprosy 'Levada-tsentra'*").

21. Karlinsky notes such figures as having included "[Sergei] Eisenstein, the popular operatic tenor Sergei Lemeshev, the pianist Sviatoslav Richter, and numerous male ballet dancers" (1989: 362). I should also note that some of my informants expressed the belief that homosexuality was never vigorously prosecuted or severely punished; rather, in their opinions, homosexuality was used as an excuse to arrest someone who was in some ways dissident, and whom the authorities wished to lock up but lacked sufficient cause to do so. Obviously, men were sent to the gulag on convictions of homosexuality, but it seems impossible to substantiate whether it was nonheterosexual activity that caused arrest and prosecution, or political expediency.

22. See also Altman (1996), who correctly notes that, "Western romanticism about the apparent tolerance of homoeroticism in many non-Western cultures disguises the reality of persecution, discrimination, and violence, which sometimes occurs in unfamiliar forms" (80).

23. See also Miller (1989) who, in his journalistic exploration of gay life throughout the United States, found many men and women whose cultural, political, and social worlds were quite different from those of the stereotypical urban "guppie."

24. The demise of the magazine was, according to published accounts, due to infighting among the editorial staff, lack of capital, and—in the view of one commentator—because it was simply "uninteresting" (Bystrov 2005).

25. The title, "*Bez striptiz*," appears to be grammatically incorrect; it should read "*Bez striptiza*."

26. The name is a pseudonym used by Mikhail Edemskii. I discuss Mishin/Edemskii's other involvements with Russia's gay "community"—both business and non–business-related—in Chapter 6.

27. On the connections between gays and lesbians and consumerism, see also Chasin, who posits that such connections promote sameness and produce the chimera that consumer action can take the place of "collective progressive political action" (2000: 166). See also Peñazola (1996) and Woods (1995).

28. The first quote was found at http://gay.ru/art/literature/kvir/ (link currently dead; last accessed 10 July 2012), and the second at http://shop.gay.ru/books/kvir/ (last accessed 17 August 2013).

29. I encountered this term—*complexes*—frequently, both when speaking to informants and when perusing Russian-language gay websites, including gay meeting sites (*saity znakomstv*). Some men, for example, explicitly noted in their profiles that they were searching for partners "*bez kompleksov*" ("without complexes").

30. The hued euphemism for lesbian women is *rozovaia* (pink).

31. Although *Mono* was nominally a club for "bisexuals," many people, including my informants, considered it a place primarily for homosexual men and prostitution. A more detailed discussion of gay social space in Russia, including gay clubs, is the focus of Chapter 5.

32. According to information on the xsgay.ru website, at the time of the writing of this monograph, both *Metro* and *Monro* were no longer *miks* (mixed) clubs. *Mono* closed in 2006.

33. The majority of my informants considered their closest friends to be either gay men or heterosexual women.

34. The name is literally translated as "spa beach."

35. The vast number of gay-themed websites was noted in the press as far back as December of 2004, at which time *TimeOut Moscva* reviewed many of the most popular sites under its *gei i lesbi* (gay and lesbian) rubric. Additionally, the gay website xsgay.ru included for several years CafeMax under its rubric "*mesta vstrech*" ("meeting places")—a place for gay men to meet and to "cruise" one another (either online or in "real time"), http://www.xs.gay.ru/places/ (last accessed 14 June 2012).

36. The comment was originally left in response to an article on gayclub.ru concerning homophobia and the Russian Orthodox Church (Petrov 2006). The address at which the article and readers' forum were originally found (http://gayclub.ru/society/2225.html) is currently inactive. The article is presently available on the site gaynews.ru (apparently the successor to the previous site) (http://piter.lgbtnet.ru/society/article.php?ID=2225; last accessed 24 June 2013), but the earliest readers' comments—of which this was one—have been removed. Typing any three of the domains into one's web browser—gayclub.ru, gaynews.ru, and piter.lgbtnet.ru—currently takes the visitor to the gaynews.ru website (as of 17 August 2013).

37. Kon, focusing on figurative art, suggests that insofar as women were historically barred from discussing (or viewing) male nudity, and heterosexual men were embarrassed by it, the "homoerotic gaze" (*vzgliad*) was instrumental in the construction of a sexualized male body (2003: 274).

38. Kon also asserts that the homosexual body is not experienced as something "given" but, rather, "as something made, mutable and plural . . . a performance" (2003: 275). To the extent that this may be true, it is also important to underscore the fact

that heterosexual male bodies are likewise constructed, in order to highlight the fact that such bodies are no more "natural" than those of homosexual men.

39. The original Russian reads "*kul'turnaia privychka, priobreti ee/khodi ezhenedel'no v baniu, i meniai bel'e*."

40. Dr. I. M. Tkachenko, for example, discussing the change in gender attributes in both "castrated" men and women, notes that the castrated male becomes "womanly" and develops feminine behaviors such as "a love for finery . . . the inclination to gossip, garrulity, intrigues, a cunning, crafty mind, etc." In contrast to the overwhelmingly negative characteristics Tkachenko attributes to women, castrated females exhibit the (positive) masculine attributes of "bravery, courage, and resourcefulness" (quoted in Bernstein 2007: 53). Noting the work of Andrei Platonov, and his envisioning of communism "exclusively as a society of men," as well as the plots of NEP stories and films that "repeatedly—often ritualistically—depicted the elimination of woman as a necessary step in the long or short march to communism," Naiman highlights the inherent misogyny of post-Revolutionary Russia (1997: 274). On the masculine bias in the conception of a "socialism in one gender," see Schrand (2002).

41. On the change of views regarding homosexuality's etiology—from biological to environmental—see Healey (2001a: esp. Chapters 7 and 8).

42. Many Soviet physicians and researchers were aware of the endocrinological experiments by Austrian Eugen Steinach (1861–1944), who claimed to have "cured" homosexual men by implanting testicular tissue of "healthy" (heterosexual) men in them. Soviet (and other) scientists who attempted to replicate the supposed successes of Steinach were not able to do so, and his theories eventually ceased to be influential (Healey 2001a: Chapter 5).

43. On the relationships among sports, cultural policy, and communism, see also Riordan (1977 and 1999).

44. The figure is from the CIA World Fact Book, http://www.cia.gov/library/publications/the-world-factbook/geos/rs.html (link currently dead; last accessed 20 January 2012). The figure is even more alarming when compared to the average life expectancy of women which, at 73.18, is over thirteen years higher. The current figures for men and women, respectively, are 64.02 and 76.02; the current web address is https://www.cia.gov/library/publications/the-world-factbook/geos/rs.html (last accessed 17 August 2013).

45. Bernstein (2007), for example, suggests that rather than viewing the repression of the Stalinist era as a break with the post-Revolutionary period, the seeds for the former were in many ways present in the latter. Similarly, Costlow, Sandler, and Vowles (1993) suggest that it is "risky . . . to agree too quickly that one historical period was a time of liberation, another a time of sexual repression, or to see the two as mutually exclusive" (15).

46. The term is an abbreviation/condensation of *kommunisticheskii soiuz molodezhi*, Communist Youth Union.

47. The state, through its various hygienic apparatuses, sought to be intimately connected to subjects' minds and bodies. For example, the author of the book, former state physician and "sanitary-enlightenment activist" L. M. Vasilevskii, "advised

Pioneers to use [their] developed strength of will to regulate their bodies, suggesting they train themselves to defecate at the same time every day" (Starks 2008: 196–198).

48. DJ Gruv (Evgenii Rudin) also makes use of the Anglicized version of his name (DJ Groove), as well as the Cyrillic (as opposed to transliterated) (DJ Грув). He released several tracks that sampled the sound tracks to popular Soviet films around this time, many of which were later collected and released on a single CD as *Poslednye kinoremiksy* (*The Last Film Remixes*) (2007).

49. As an archetypal example, see the poster produced by the Moscow Ministry of Health (MOZ) entitled "Sun, Air, and Water Are the Best Holiday from Labor" ("*Solntse, vozdukh, i voda—luchshii otdykh ot truda*"), which features nude and seminude men sunbathing, swimming, and simply relaxing in the countryside (in Starks 2008: Plate 7; see also Plates 4 and 5, the first of which includes illustrations of showering men with buttocks exposed). Other examples include a well-known poster with the slogan "If You Want to Be like This—Work Out!" ("*Khochesh' byt' takim—treniruisia!*"), featuring a flexing, muscular man whose bicep is gleefully touched by the young male *pioner* seated in his lap, or another in which the suntanned, muscular body of a male swimmer—clad in tight, black swim briefs—is presented under an excerpt from Maiakovskii's "*Marusia otravilas'*" ("Marusia Poisoned Herself") that reads "There is not, on earth, more beautiful clothing than bronzed muscles and the freshness of skin" ("*Net na svete prekrasnei odezhi, chem bronza muskulov i svezhest' kozhi*").

50. The film, *Stalinskoe plemia* (*The Stalin Tribe*), subtitled "a film about the physical culture parade in the twentieth year of the October Revolution," memorialized the 1937 parade in Red Square and featured numerous muscular, athletic men, often attired in nothing but tight white shorts. On the correspondences between Soviet and fascistic (Italian and German) representations of the male body, see Kon (2003: 348; see also 2003: 265–273).

51. See, for example, his works *V obedennyi pereryv v Donbasse* (*At the Lunchtime Break in the Donets Basin*, 1935) and *Khoroshee ytro* (*Good Morning*, 1959–1960), both of which feature groups of completely nude young men (albeit with genitals either hidden, via poses, or obscured, via the artist's "impressionistic" brushwork).

52. The *bania* as social and sexual space is examined in Chapter 5.

53. I take these terms from Bourdieu, where *habitus* may be defined as an internalization by the subject of the organizing structures that are part of his or her specific social context, structures that then influence the subject's organizing and (re)production of this context. Bodily *hexis* refers to a set of specifically physical dispositions and stances that, according to Bourdieu, are able to "pass from practice to practice without going through discourse or consciousness" (1972: 87). Bourdieu is not, however, suggesting an entirely unmediated or meaningless physical response or relation to environment, as he asserts that the child (his example, here) "has no difficulty grasping the *rationale* of what are clearly series [of verbal products, practices, or objects] and in making it his own in the form of a principle generating conduct organized in accordance with the same rationale" (88).

54. On the concept of Russian *dusha*, see Pesman (2000).

55. The dissolution of borders between "high" and "low," however, may have sometimes been more matters of theory than practice. Kelly, for example, finds that "not only in the 1930s, but also in the 1960s and indeed the 1990s, [working-class Russians remained] a good deal more likely to visit the beer-bar than the ballet, or the stadium than the concert hall. Their tastes in music, art, and literature, whilst marked to some extent by schoolroom exposure to the Russian classics, still remained fundamentally different from those of the metropolitan intelligentsia" (1998: 142). Current commentators have also remarked about the "vulgarity" of much of Russia's contemporary popular music, contrasting it negatively with that of previous eras and thus highlighting the extent to which questions of quality and "taste" are still invoked in the assessment of popular culture. One journalist, for example, suggested that "about the vulgarity of the texts of contemporary supposed *èstrada*, one could write an entire dissertation" (Il'chenko 2004).

56. See also Kelly (1998) who finds that the popularity not only of such singers as Liubov' Orlova, Vladimir Vysotskii, Alla Pugacheva, and Boris Grebenshchikov, but also of portraiture in the visual arts, "suggest[s] how important is the concentration on remarkable individuals" (146).

57. See, for example, Beumers (2005); Kelly and Shepherd (1998); May (2000); Starr (1983); Steinholt (2003); Stites (1992); Troitsky (1987); Urban and Evdokimov (2004); and Yurchak (2006).

58. The performance may be found at http://www.youtube.com/watch?v=nk6AoIanWGo (last accessed 10 May 2012).

59. Both of these music-centered stations generally played popular music for a largely younger (under 30) audience, ranging from dance tracks to rap to ballads. *MuzTV*'s lineup featured (at least marginally) more Russian music than MTV, although the latter presented a large amount of Russian music as well. Both stations still broadcast in Russia as of 2013.

60. *Bardovskaia pesnia* may also be referred to as *avtorskaia pesnia* (literally, "author song"). The genre may be considered similar, to some extent, to the singer-songwriter tradition in the West.

61. See, for example, the contributions of Berger, Rice, and Titon (all 2008) to *Shadows in the Field*, a volume devoted to an examination and critique of ethnomusicological fieldwork. Berger also notes several ethnomusicological works employing phenomenological theory including Ruth Stone's *Let the Inside Be Sweet* (1982), the first to make use of such a theoretical grounding (68).

62. My language studies continued at Columbia University upon return to the United States and with private teachers during my second trip to Russia.

63. Of course such online introductions did not guarantee safety, and some informants warned me to be careful of people posing as men interested in meeting for social or sexual reasons, but who were in reality looking for (gay) victims to rob and/or assault. Highly disturbing instances of gay teens apparently entrapped and ultimately abused via just such means have recently been documented (with photographs and videos) and disseminated via social media (see McCann 2013).

64. Notes were written up immediately upon the conclusion of the meeting, however. Additionally, on several occasions, I wrote down short segments of a conversation with an informant, generally noting to him that I did not want to forget what he had said.

65. When quoted or referenced in the text, only the men's names will appear; information regarding ages and places of residence at the times of our meetings is found in a separate appendix at the end of this monograph. Within the text, in cases where specific information regarding age, occupation, or location of residence may have exposed the informant's identity—however slight the possibility—I have chosen to change these details. Aleksandr Kukharskii (cofounder and current head of Kryl'ia, a gay and lesbian organization in St. Petersburg); Igor' Kon (sociologist and chief researcher at the Institute of Ethnology and Anthropology, Russian Academy of Sciences, widely know as an expert on "sexology"); and Jussi Nissinen (founding member and former secretary general of SETA, Finland's Organization for Sexual Equality [*Seksuaalinen tasavertaisuus*]), all of whom were interviewed, will be identified by name. Additionally, two DJs—DJ Partyphone, from Moscow's *Propaganda* and DJ Christy, from St. Petersburg's *Greshniki* (Sinners)—will be identified by these professional monikers, and two other DJs who operated under their real names will be identified with pseudonyms.

66. See, for example, Grindal and Salamone (1995); Kumar (1992); Rabinow (2012); and Sluka (2012). Additionally, Burkhart, Lapovsky Kennedy and Davis, and Williams (all 1996) have engaged, in the context of gay men and lesbians in the field, the dynamics of self-exposure, openness to informant's views, and emotional neutrality, respectively. See also Berger (2008), who highlights, from a phenomenological standpoint, the importance of engaging informants' experiences (as opposed to a narrow focus only on cultural artifacts).

67. Like several of the male singers who are discussed in Chapters 3 and 4, Pogrebizhskaia's discussion of her sexual orientation is somewhat elliptical; in an article on the website newsmusic.ru, for example, the singer asserts that the "stories" of "same-sex love" surrounding her are the result of a willful manipulation of "*piar*" ("PR") ("*Butch: 'Moi rasskazy'*"). t.A.T.u's on-screen/stage actions, as well as their name—a condensation of the phrase "*ta liubit tu*" ("that one loves that one"), where both pronouns ("ta" and the inflected "tu") are feminine—are clearly designed to reference female-female love or eroticism. Their sexuality, however, is questioned not only by listeners but in the Russian popular press; both singers from the group, Lena Katina and Iulia Volkova, are often romantically linked with other pop stars, including the singers from boy band *Korni* (Roots). Both singers also appeared on the cover of the Russian version of *Elle Girl* magazine in 2004, where a visibly pregnant Volkova openly discussed her "boyfriend" (Zaretskaia 2004). That Arbenina was widely perceived as being lesbian was underscored by the inclusion of a review of the group's CD *SMS* (an acronym widely used in Russia to indicate a mobile text message) in the gay and lesbian section of the St. Petersburg edition of *Kalendar'/TimeOut* (Filippova 2004).

68. Internet sites and clubs for gay men, as well as social networks, were instrumental in my having found homosexual male informants, yet none of these three areas promised to be productive in my attempts to make contact with lesbian women. A foreign male attempting to chat online with lesbian women would undoubtedly have been met with, at the very least, hesitation; indeed, I was only able to enter the one lesbian club in the entire country, St. Petersburg's *Trièl'* (Three L's) on one occasion, this being a night specifically set aside for a *miks vercherinka* (mixed party). Additionally, in my experience over sixteen months of fieldwork, I found that gay men and lesbians did not generally socialize together, either in private or public space (save for one club, 911, in Moscow). As such, my access to lesbian women informants was extremely limited in comparison to gay men.

69. Readers interested in lesbian sexuality in post-Soviet Russia may wish to consult Baer (2011); Chantsev (2009); Healey (2001a: Chapter 2); Nartova (2007); Stella (2008); and Zhuk (1998). For those interested in the phenomenon of the (gay) "diva," my article on this theme—part of a planned monograph devoted to female superstars in Russian popular music—may serve as an introduction (Amico 2009).

70. On online ethnography or "netnography," see (inter alia) Kozinets (2010) and Kuntsman (2004).

Chapter 2. Music, Form, Penetration

1. In both St. Petersburg and Moscow, high-end stores such as Hugo Boss and Valentino were represented, as were relatively more accessible fashions from such stores as Benetton and Diesel. Marlboro, Gauloises, and Dunhill cigarettes were all widely available (and advertisements for each were common), and St. Petersburg had, in 2005, a Pizza Hut, McDonalds, and Kentucky Fried Chicken, all three of which were on the main thoroughfare, *Nevskii prospekt*. The Swedish retailer, however, encountered numerous problems with endemic corruption, leading them to suspend further investment in 2009 (Kramer 2009, 2010).

2. Of the numerous talk shows on television during that period *Printisp domino* (*The Domino Principle*) aired in the afternoon, generally aimed toward homemakers, while *Okna* (*Windows*), in the worst tradition of Jerry Springer or Maury Povich, featured the more prurient and fantastic, and *Zhdi menia* (*Wait for Me*) served as a rather lugubrious exercise in finding lost family members. Reality shows were likewise well represented with Russian versions of Western shows (e.g., *Bol'shoi brat* [*Big Brother*], *Faktor strakha* [*Fear Factor*], and *Poslednyi geroi* [*The Last Hero*, the Russian version of *Survivor*]), as well as domestic productions such as *Dom 2* (*House 2*), in which contestants competed for a house (which they were building) and "love." Additionally, the infatuation among many Westerners with design-related television shows—specifically, home design—was also evident in Russia, with its own domestic production, *Shkola remonta* (*Renovation School*).

3. Although the show is often described as "a Russian version of 'Sex in the City,'" the television station *NTV*, which produces the show, claimed "it [had] no licensing agreement with HBO, producer of the original" (Kishkovsky 2005). The term *Balzac*

age, in Russian, is a somewhat polite way of referring to a woman who is advancing in years and who may not marry; a more colloquial, less literal translation might be "women of a certain age."

4. In St. Petersburg in 2004, for example, posters for films such as *Spiderman III*, *Catwoman*, *Open Water*, and *Collateral*, among many others, were regularly seen on the streets. American shows broadcast on Russian television during the period I lived there included *Alias* ("*Shpionka*," literally "female spy"), and *The Jerry Springer Show* ("*Shou Dzheri Springera*").

5. Gurchenko, a Ukrainian actress and singer, was one of the leading figures in Russian-language popular music for decades and performed in concert during my time in St. Petersburg. *Mashina vremini* (Time Machine) is one of the most seminal bands in Russian rock.

6. See, for example, Aparicio and Jásquez (2003); Kuortti and Nyman (2007); Moskowitz (2010: Chapter 3); Pacini Hernandez (2009).

7. Researchers such as Lipsitz (1994) and Manuel (1995) have suggested that the listening subject, although (dis)located in a field marked by a multiplicity of codes and symbols (or simulacra), may assemble certain of the variables in order to form both satisfying and salubrious conceptions of self and culture. Hutnyk (2000), however, cautions that even such terms as hybridity are fraught with difficulties because they often assume an anterior purity or stability for the various components themselves, something that, at best, misrepresents an historical unity obtaining before the encroachment of globalization and, at worst, paints a romanticized picture of a state of blissful accord irreparably disfigured by a venal modernity.

8. The original Russian—"*gei-tusovki*"—is difficult to translate into an exact English analog. The noun, *tusovka* can mean a group of people related by style or interest (for example, skateboarders, rock music aficionados), as well as the meetings of such people. Often occurring in larger cities, the names of such groups could also be taken from the site where they generally congregated (for example, around certain Metro stations). The verb, *tusovat'sia*, can be translated as "meeting," "hanging out," or even "partying," and is reliant upon the context.

9. Within the text of the article, the DJs are both evasive about their orientation; Slutkey notes, for example, that "it's all the same [if] everyone thinks that we're homosexuals and live together," and "let each think what he wants." Of those men I knew who were familiar with the DJs, some thought that Slutkey was gay, but Kosinus straight.

10. Numerous articles attest to the growing problem of music piracy in Russia; see, for example, "Russia Buries 3 Million Pirated CDs in Moscow Pit" (2005); "Counterfeit Goods Overwhelm Russia's Entertainment Market" (2005); "Moscow Prosecutors Will Not Charge MP3 Web Site" (2005); "U.S. Companies Lose Billions of Dollars Annually to Russian Piracy" (2004), all from the now-defunct mosnews.com website; see also Chernov (2001) and Crampton (2006a, 2006b).

11. The establishment was part of a chain appropriately named *Kofe Khauz*. Several of the men I knew were fond of the chain, while a few reacted against its generic, commercial quality.

Notes to Chapter 2

12. The choice of Belarusian singer Natal'ia Podol'skaia as Russia's representative for the 2004 Eurovision Song Contest (edging out such artists as Anastasiia Stotskaia, Dima Bilan, and Verka Serdiuchka) caused some in the press to question whether Podol'skaia's managers had "bought" the singer's victory in the preliminary, Russian contests, a charge that Podol'skaia denied (Philips 2005). She ultimately placed low in the *Eurovision* competition, finishing fifteenth overall.

13. Zhasmin's current full name is Sara L'vovna Shor, previously Semendueva (née Manakhimova; the singer was married twice); Alsou's full name is Alsu Ralifovna Abramova (née Safina).

14. See Kiskhovsky (2006).

15. See "*Rossiiu gubiat evrei i pederasty*" ("Russia Is Being Ruined by Jews and Fags"). Novikov may be referring specifically to singer Boris Moiseev, a Jew born in Belarus, and Russia's first "out" musical performer. I discuss Moiseev's work at greater length in Chapter 3.

16. Their song "*Ne valiai duraka Amerika*" ("Don't Play the Fool, America"), for example, suggests that the United States return Alaska to its rightful place within the Russian geopolitical sphere. Kelly (1998: 152) also highlights examples of an often xenophobic nationalism in contemporary Russian popular culture, including songs of the heavy metal group *Korroziia metalla* (Corrosion of Metal), one of which was "dedicated to the opponents of 'Zionists and *natsemy*' (a derogatory term for non-Russian racial minorities), with a chorus (sung—with an irony of which the performers were apparently unconscious—in English), running 'Kill, kill, kill, kill the bloody foreigners'" (152).

17. Perhaps not surprisingly, the city in which this informant lived, while densely populated, was considered rather provincial in comparison to either St. Petersburg or Moscow.

18. The Katiusha (a common diminutive of Ekaterina) of the song's title is a peasant girl located, according to the song's lyrics, in a beautiful and pastoral Russian countryside, sending out her song to her soldier beloved. Due to the popularity of the song, as well as its sentiment, *Katiusha* became the nickname for the Soviet Army's 82 mm BM-8 and 132 mm BM-13 multiple rocket launchers, used to great advantage against the German army. The initials *BM* stand for *voinevaia mashina*—combat vehicle—although this is a mixture of both the Latin and Cyrillic characters. Strictly speaking, the initials should be *VM*, in keeping with the anglicization of the appellation; however, the *B*—the Cyrillic character resembling the Latin letter *B* but pronounced *V*—was probably seen by anglophones and, mistakenly taken for the Latin *B*, left "untranslated."

19. In Russian, *artist* may be translated as either "artist" or "expert," although it is often used to mean either actor or singer as well.

20. These progeny include *American Idol* in the United States, *Idols* in Finland, *Philippine Idol*, and Germany's *Deutschland sucht den Superstar* (*Germany Searches for the Superstar*). In Russia and Finland—the two versions I saw—the sets, lights, music, graphics, and format were practically identical to the American version.

21. Progeny of this original include two Francophone versions: *Star Academy* (France) and *Star Académie* (Québec).

22. The presentation of such amorous spectacles was criticized by at least one Russian columnist who, commenting on the general vulgarity (*poshlost'*) of Russian *popsa*, opined that "even in such free countries as the Netherlands, establishments for public demonstration of intimate relations of people are located in a concrete 'red light' district" (Il'chenko 2004). The fact that a Western format (the reality show) became a Russian favorite—and thus a marker of Russianness—indicates the need to undertake examinations of cultural productions with attention to both content and context.

23. While almost all of my informants expressed a current or one-time liking for the show (as well as specific performers and songs), several commented negatively upon what they assumed to be venality or corruption in conjunction with choosing the season's winner. Many assumed that, although the winner was ostensibly chosen by viewers' votes, it was capital and/or connections that ultimately decided the victor.

24. Omel'chenko (2000: 100–103) offers a compendium of transliterated Western popular music forms, although the majority of them are not widely encountered in contemporary Russia.

25. The vast majority of my informants—and indeed most younger Russians whom I met—were relatively comfortable reading Latin script, despite the fact that the majority of them did not speak any foreign (Western) languages with any great proficiency. One informant, Oleg, related the ability to read the letters, phonetically, to the use of mobile phones and computers, the first of which were not available with Cyrillic fonts when they initially became available on the Russian market. As a result, many young people, who often preferred sending text messages to calling (due, in part, to the lower cost), found it necessary to learn the basics of transliteration.

26. The Russian word would be *potselui*.

27. The word may also be translated as "novel," or as a man's name.

28. Several of Gosti iz budushchego's songs featured English words—for example, "*Mama, gudbai*" (a transliteration of *good-bye*) and the house-inspired "*Ia tvoia kiska*" ("I'm Your Kitty"), which makes use of an English language text for one of the track's hooks ("I wanna see you, I wanna kiss you baby") and switches back and forth between English and Russian during the bridge ("*Ot naslezhdenia plachu* baby/ *Ia ne mogu inache* maybe") ("*I cry from pleasure* baby/*I can't help it* maybe"). Lead singer Eva Pol'na—currently a solo artist—has also used the French language in one of her most recent songs, "*Ia tebia tozhe net*" ("I Also Don't [Love] You") which is subtitled "*Je T'aime*" ("I Love You").

29. See, for example, the translations at http://pesenki.ru/authors/sky/mal_4ik-i6et-mamu-lyrics.shtml (last accessed 21 August 2013).

30. During my time in St. Petersburg, Russian popular music was also remarkable for the number of Latin (or Spanish)-influenced songs achieving much popularity—drawing upon such styles as salsa, rumba, tango, and flamenco—including Zveri's "*Iuzhnaia noch'*" ("Southern Night"), Nochnye snaipery's "*Kuba*" ("Cuba"), and

Tutsi's "*Ia liubliu ego*" ("I Love Him," featuring lyrics referencing vacations in Miami), among many others. Also, songs of foreign provenance, either Latin or Latin-styled (e.g., Aventura's *bachata* hit "Obsession" or Toni Braxton's "Spanish Guitar") were among the most widely played on radio and music television. "Latin"-style tracks, or even longer sets, were also often played in all of the gay clubs in St. Petersburg, including one instance at *Trièl'* (a lesbian club) where, in response to the music, a conga line ensued. The fascination with warm, sunny climates is certainly related to the desire of many Russians to vacation in such locations. St. Petersburg's weather is notoriously damp and cold, and often bereft of sunshine for literally days or weeks on end; Moscow's climate is likewise less than inviting in the winter. That some of these songs appeared in the summer of 2004 and were accompanied by videos in which the band members appeared in such locations—dancing, swimming, driving, flirting, kissing—indicates that the use of the "Latin" may be related to the construction of a fantasy vacationland. A more current example of the "Latin" expressed both textually and visually (if not musically) may be seen in Sati Kazanova's 2012 song "Buenos-Aires."

31. In 2005, the group, originally fronted by singers Vlad Topolov and Sergei Lazarev, reformed, Topolov continuing on as lead singer with Lazarev pursuing a solo career. Lazarev's first solo CD, *Don't Be Fake*, was recorded entirely in English. Topolov also eventually pursued a solo career, minus the group's moniker. The group is discussed in detail in Chapter 4.

32. The English texts appear, in part (and often rife with mistakes), in the "headlines" of newspapers that are edited into the narrative of the video. One such headline—"Valerya Is New Face of Wesfalika" [*sic*]—makes explicit what is often alluded to in the video, namely the singer's having been chosen as a brand ambassador for Russian women's fashion retailer Westfalika.

33. An analysis of the formal, musical attributes of all Western, commercial popular music is obviously beyond the scope of this monograph and perhaps even impossible, insofar as the very breadth of the music might engender only the most general—and least illuminating—list of attributes possible. As such, I am assuming the reader to be familiar with at least some of these musics and will limit my discussion to those attributes of Russian popular music that are less commonly found in the West and thus serve as markers of a musical difference.

34. The spatial ramifications and manifestations of this split are discussed in Chapter 5.

35. On jazz, Yurchak notes: "Between the 1940s and 1970s, jazz was continuously praised for its roots in the creative genius of the slaves and the working people *and* condemned as bourgeois pseudo-art that lost any connection to the realism of people's culture" (2006: 165). It is important to highlight that Yurchak is not primarily concerned with a top-down reading of Soviet "control" of expressive culture; rather, his aim is to show how Soviet citizens—who viewed themselves as *good* Soviet citizens—did not see anything subversive or anti-Soviet in their connections to Western expressive culture.

36. Many, although not all, of these examinations focus on the works of Mikhail Glinka. See especially Frolova-Walker (1997, 2007); Gasparov (2005); Maes (2002); and Taruskin (1997a). All of these authors are concerned with problematizing a simplistic addition of the adjective "nationalist" to either styles or composers. Gasparov, for example, suggests that the "nationalist" quality of Glinka's *Ruslan i Liudmila* was its imperialist (rather than nativist) character, while Frolova-Walker, focusing on the same opera, contends that it is a "myth" to see anything particularly "plagal" (where plagal function marks Russianness) in the work. Both Taruskin and Maes, in their discussions of Glinka's *Kamarinskaia*—a work Tchaikovsky categorized as the acorn from which the oak of Russian music grew—find that, although it did indeed make use of "folk" material (a wedding song, "*Iz-za gor, gor vysokikh*," and a dance song, "*Kamarinskaia*"), taken in the context of his having previously written two "Spanish" pieces (*Jota aragonesa* and *Recuerdos de Castilla, or Souvenir d'une nuit d'été à Madrid*), the piece is simply "what Glinka himself called picturesque music, and in this case the national element lends no more than local color" (Maes 2002: 27).

37. "Ivan Prach," the author of the accompaniments, was, according to Taruskin, "a Bohemian from Silesia whose original name was either Jan Bogumir Práč or Johann Gottfried Pratsch" (1997b: 17).

38. See also Manuel (1989) on the connections among Ottoman, Western, and Eastern European musics. As he shows, bidirectional influences have been common for centuries in the area around the eastern Mediterranean, often as a result of peripatetic musicians (most notably the *Rom* and professional Jewish secular musicians, the *klezmorim*), as well as transnational ethnic groups. He notes, for example, that "the Ottomans chose to rule Rumania through a Greek elite transplanted from Constantinople, which appears to have exerted considerable influence on musical life until the Rumanian revolution of 1821. Meanwhile, Greek communities in Smyrna (Izmir) and Constantinople played important roles in cultural life until their expulsion in 1922" (1989: 76).

39. Zemtsovsky (1999) in his discussion of *kant*, a "subgenre of *knizhnaia pesnia*" (literally, book songs) notes that such songs included "melodies [that] were transformed from hymn tunes and Polish and Ukrainian songs, one of whose features was the use of sequences and dominant-tonic cadences" (767), thus suggesting another external (albeit Slavic) influence on Russia's popular music.

40. Professional "gypsy" musicians were a vital and visible component of Russia's musical life from at least the nineteenth century onward, and contributed to making the *romans* one of the most popular genres in Russia. On the *romans* (and *tsyganshchina*, or "gypsiness"), see MacFadyen (2002b: Chapters 1 and 2) and Von Geldern and McReynolds (1998: 173ff). On Gypsy choruses, see Fraser (1992: 200ff); Olson (2004: 19); and Scott (2008).

41. See Nelson (2004: 103–108) whose examination of the ideological basis for the post-Revolutionary abhorrence for *romansy* includes a discussion of the musical attributes found to be objectionable by the Left, due to their resemblance to those

found in *tsyganshchina*. These included "harmonies with suspensions, modulation from a major key to its parallel minor, and particular melodic conventions (*oborota*)" as well as "melodic chromaticism" (106).

42. For example, Verka Serdiuchka and *Gliuk'oza*'s "*Zhenikha khotela*" ("She Wanted a Fiancé"), Verka Serdiuchka's "*Chita drita*," Katia Lel"s "*Moi marmeladnyi*" ("My Jelly Candy"), or Fabrika's "*Rybka*" ("Little Fish").

43. Krutoi's song featured the voices of Kseniia Larina, Irina Dubtsova, and Aleksandra Chvikova (stage name Aleksa), all contestants from *Fabrika zvezd*. All three also appeared in the video for the song.

44. The band's name references the holiday celebration of the Summer Solstice in Russia and Ukraine. Literally, it is also an old Russian title for John the Baptist.

45. Not incidentally, the video for Nika's song "*Podari mne potselui*" ("Give Me a Kiss") features famous drag queens, including Zaza Napoli.

46. See also discussion in Hass (2008: 33ff).

47. For Merleau-Ponty and Lingis, perception is not made up of discrete *qualia* later assembled interiorly ("in the mind"); rather, the subject perceives complex *Gestalten*, the (theoretical, discrete) attributes of which are comprehensible only in relation to other (theoretically discrete) attributes. Alphonso Lingis—one of Merleau-Ponty's translators, and deeply influenced by his thinking—gives the example of an apple, noting that "When we see [it], this identity is not something conceived at once like a concept. . . . We see it . . . by looking at the way this shiny red and dense white involves—makes visible—a certain sense of pulpiness, a certain juiciness, even a certain clear and homogenous taste" (1994a: 5).

48. The concept of a "third space" is also invoked in the work of D. W. Winnicott. In his theorization (1971), the self in contact with the other produces a third term—that is, an intermediate area of *experiencing* first effectuated in infancy, via transitional objects. Such intermediate space—in which, according to him, the musical lies—is neither purely inside nor outside the self, and it belongs neither wholly to the realm of subjective nor the objective; rather, this space, "to which inner reality and external life both contribute" (3), and which is also termed as a "potential space" "between the individual and environment, that which initially both joins and separates the baby and the mother" (138) is the site of play and culture—exactly those things that allow a merging of fantasy and reality, internal (subjective) and external (objective).

49. The *stiliagi* (from the Russian word *stil'*, style) were youths who first appeared in the 1950s, and were later greatly influenced by Western-influenced Russian bands such as *Bravo* and *Brigada S* (Omel'chenko 2000; see also Troitsky 1987). According to Omel'chenko, although they were "always connected with the Western, bourgeois form of life" ("*vsegda sviazyvalis' s zapadnym burzhuaznym obrazom zhizni*") (89); their style came about via a "[mastery of] the elements of the past Soviet culture" (92). Certain members might be known, for example, as "Brezhnev" "because they wore many badges [*znachki*] (resembling medals)" (92). Their clothing was assembled from hand-me-downs, secondhand shops, and friends and they are characterized by Omel'chenko, because of their ability to "appropriate elements of culture of the Soviet

past" as not having been "dragged to a youth culture of capital, that is, by Western clothes" (92).

50. Pilkington's (2002) research showed the Russian youths distinguished between Russian and Western musics as being for either the "soul" or the "body," respectively. And Yurchak (2006), drawing upon an epistolary exchange between two students—Alexander and Nikolai—quotes the former as saying of rock music, "when I hear [it] I want to dance, dance improvisationally and wildly, spill out all my extra energy and forget myself as much as possible" (228). The same letter writer, however, found that such music was not solely physically involving; in another letter he "explicitly argued . . . that the best examples of Western rock music, like any music, must affect the person physiologically, aesthetically, and spiritually" (231). Although none of my informants explicitly characterized these musics in the same terms, I did note that Western musics were often listened to in the context of having a good time or "partying," either in clubs or at home with friends. Russian musics could also be used in both types of situations but were also apparently preferred in instances where intimacy (with close friends, with one's thoughts) was deemed important.

51. In 2004, Ukrainian president Viktor Yushchenko and Georgian president Mikhail Saakashvili both evinced a leaning toward the West and away from the Russian/CIS sphere of influence. Moreover, Georgia, in 2005, voted to abolish visa requirements for all citizens of the United States and the European Union, partially in an attempt to bolster tourism in the country. Such a move, of course, not only allows a greater influx of (Western) bodies, but also a symbolic invitation for intercourse with the West.

52. The statement, by Putin Aide Modest Kolerov, seemed more an opportunity to criticize the status of ethnic Russians in Estonia, in the context of the country's turn toward the West and concomitant lack of Russian influence there ("Putin Aid Hails Multicultural Russia").

53. In most cases, attacks were on students who were visibly ethnically different—that is, nonwhite. In St. Petersburg in 2004, for example, both a Syrian and a Vietnamese student were killed, the former pushed in front of an oncoming subway train, the latter stabbed thirty-seven times. In 2005, a student from Cameroon was stabbed and killed as well, "the fourth victim of murder . . . in what many see as an ongoing wave of hate crimes that has rocked the city in the past three months" (Nassor 2005). In 2006 yet another African student—from Senegal—was killed as well. Such killings are not, according to Natal'ia Rusakova, teacher of the murdered Vietnamese student, Wu An Tuan, a recent phenomenon; as she told *Novye Izvestiia*, the attacks had been "going on for years" ("*uzhe mnogo let podriad*") (Terekhov and Berseneva 2005). On the numerous attacks and murders in various cities throughout Russia, see also Corwin (2005); Kovalyev (2004); Mite (2006); Walsh (2005); "2 Killed as Skinheads Attack Gypsy Camp in Central Russia"; "Two Mongolian Students Attacked in Petersburg"; and "*V moskovskom metropolitene skinkhedami byl ubit kurd*."

54. The sentencing of the killers to relatively short prison terms—for "hooliganism," not murder—elicited an outcry from several groups in the city (Bigg 2006; see

also Walsh 2006). Indeed, the refusal of authorities to admit to the seriousness of xenophobic and nationalist extremism, to minimize such actions as no more than youthful mischief, makes them, in the eyes of Iurii Vdovin, a representative of the St. Petersburg office of the Citizens Watch human rights group, complicit in the escalating violence. Vdovin, a friend and colleague of murdered ethnologist Nikolai Girenko—an expert on hate crimes and, in this capacity, an expert witness in several court proceedings involving such dynamics—is quoted as saying that Girenko's murderers "were able to carry out this vendetta largely because city authorities have long ignored the existence of skinheads and extremists in the city by portraying their activities as hooliganism" (Yablokova 2004).

55. See, for example, "Russian Skinheads Most Numerous in World" (2004). For a detailed examination of skinhead subculture in contemporary Russia, including a discussion of its "homosocial" and anti-racist elements, see Pilkington, Omel'chenko, and Garifzianova (2010). See also Putzel's documentary, *From Russia with Hate*, produced as part of the *Vanguard* series for Current TV.

56. See note 54, supra.

57. A website set up by Kacharava's friends—including information about the victim, and pictures from the crime scene—can still be found at http://www.stop-it.narod.ru (last accessed 21 August 2013).

58. Many people from the Caucasus work in Russia selling produce, thus the connection with melons. This was certainly the case in both Moscow and St. Petersburg.

59. The commercial can currently be seen at http://truba.com/video/137313/ (last accessed 21 August 2013).

60. The group's webpage is no longer accessible as of July 2010. Perhaps not incidentally, *Nash gorod* is also the name of a Russian musical group whose main style of music is *shanson*.

61. See, for example, the logo on the group's website at http://www.demushkin.com/ (last accessed 21 August 2013).

62. The party's moniker may seem to suggest a politics in line with those of two of its constituent terms (*liberal* and *democratic*), defined in a Western sense. However, the party—headed by Vladimir Zhirinovskii, one of the most outspoken nationalist and xenophobic/homophobic politicians on the Russian scene—is better defined as ultranationalist and reactionary, often evincing an antimigrant, xenophobic mindset, as well as a staunch opposition to communism (Laruelle 2009; Pilkington, Omel'chenko, and Garifzianova 2010). In 2004, Zhirinovskii called for punishment of homosexuality by the death penalty, and has in the past expressed admiration of Hitler (among other anti-Semitic views), although he himself is Jewish (see "Criminal Responsibility"). Kur'ianovich was expelled from the party in 2006 for violating party discipline.

63. Although initially confined to its website, in the past several years the group's videos have appeared on YouTube as well. Such videos are rife with Nazi-inspired imagery (see, for example, the video at http://www.youtube.com/watch?v=t5rTAIQMYRo&skipcontrinter=1), and the group has even posted a "Partial Discography of

the S[lavianskii]S[oiuz]" ("*Nepolnaia diskografiia SS*" at http://www.youtube.com/watch?v=5jUe5dB-gzk) (both sites last accessed 15 August 2012).

64. "*My reshitel'no krome togo, chtoby pidary zarazhali nashikh detei fizicheskimi i dushevnymi boleznami! NET zapadnoi zaraze! NET paradu pidarov!*" The image was removed from the group's site some time in 2007.

65. Both Subramaniam (2001) and Zerner (2003) investigate the ways in which the threat of biological invasion often mirrors (or attempts to mask) fears of "cultural" invasion, these frequently related to discourses and dynamics of immigration.

66. As Weeks points out in the book's introduction, Kinsey's research indicated that, at the time the data was compiled, anal intercourse was the "exception" among gay men (Hocquenghem 1978: 24).

67. Weeks states: "So when homosexuals as a group publicly reject their labels, they are in fact rejecting Oedipus, rejecting the artificial entrapment of desire, rejecting sexuality focused on the Phallus. And they are rejecting the Symbolic Order" (Hocquenghem 1978: 25).

68. Grosz, among many others, highlights the fact that the creation of male phallic power is indissolubly linked to the desire to create a male body that is "sealed-up" and "impermeable" (1994: 201). See also Longhurst (2001: Chapter 5) on the role of the "business suit" in presenting the image of the masculine, impermeable body.

69. Such a classificatory system is conceptually similar to the current, most common American categorizations: "top," "bottom," and "versatile."

70. Russians use both the Russified version of the original French (*fellatsiia*), but more commonly the phrase "*delat' minet*" (literally, "to do/make a blowjob"). Anal sex is indicated by the verbs *ebat'* or *trakhat,'* both of which translate as "to fuck."

71. This is not to suggest, of course, that there are not men who are entirely either active or passive regarding oral sex, and this is often the case in terms of BDSM (Bondage-Discipline-Sadism-Masochism) relationships in which one partner is subservient to the other.

72. On the ability of music to construct identities that are concurrently both local and international, see Hawkins (2007).

73. See, for example, Mironov's "*Parizh, Parizh*" ("Paris, Paris") (2004), which serves not to familiarize the reader with the historical or cultural sites of the city but with its bar and club culture and cruising habits. The article is followed by information regarding a tour to the city sponsored by St. Petersburg tour firm "*Piter-Meil*" ("Peter-male/mail"). It is also notable that the gay meeting site, qguys.ru—aimed largely at men in Eastern Europe, especially Russia and former Soviet or current CIS states—is affiliated with the gay travel website bluway.com, whose president and founder Alexander Khodorkovsky also launched gotorussia.com, a site that offers, among other services, trips for gay (American) men to "gay Russia." (The bluway.com site, open since 2001 is, at the time of this writing—August 2013—"under construction.") Although the conflation of sex and travel may conjure up disturbing images of a modern "sex tourism," Littlewood (2001) suggests that the sexual has been an integral component of international travel since the time of the eighteenth-century "Grand Tour." I discuss *Kalendar'/Time Out* further in Chapter 5.

74. Accusations of "racism" must, however, be taken in a cultural context. For example, it was common for some men I knew to refer to black men as "*shokoladnyi*" ("chocolate"), an appellation that would certainly be considered unacceptable in the United States. In one instance, however, when Vadim had used this term in a conversation with me—and after I had balked at its use—he explained that he meant it as a compliment, saying that chocolate was "sweet and delicious." Indeed, the term was used in the title of one of the most popular songs in 2003 in Russia, "*Shokoladnyi zaiats*" ("A Chocolate Hare") sung by P'er Nartsis—himself black.

75. Many of my informants—the majority—had traveled abroad, and a few had even lived outside of Russia for extended periods of at least three months.

76. As Stanislav said, "for me, this is like a dream, a total fantasy, and I know it's never going to happen—so why waste time thinking about it?" Oleg also said that he had not given much thought to the idea of where he would most like to travel or live, possibly due, again, to his financial situation, which precluded large expenditures on such luxuries. However, it had not prevented him from developing a "fetish" (his word) for the German language (he was trying to learn German on his own), and he did offer that he had a certain desire to see, if not live in, Austria. Likewise, Volodia, although unable to entertain the idea of emigration due to both financial and bureaucratic considerations, still had learned both German and English and had developed a partiality to English language literature, including the writings of authors such as Margaret Atwood, Irish Murdoch, and (especially) Toni Morrison.

77. After numerous bureaucratic obstacles (and several years), Petia succeeded in emigrating to the West, while Artur and Vova remain in Russia as of 2013.

78. Flynn and Starkova (2002) highlight just how differentiated "the West" can be to Russians, noting that while the United States is often considered to produce the best films, it is the United Kingdom that, in the view of Russians, produces the best music. Additionally, fashion was "sited in Europe, primarily France, Britain and Italy" (55).

79. Such contrasts were not only made between Russia and foreign countries, but between Russian locations as well. For example, virtually all of my informants from St. Petersburg were highly critical of Moscow, seeing it as a vulgar, commerce-driven—even ugly—city, full of people who were unfriendly and closed. Likewise, the majority of my informants from Moscow were critical of St. Petersburg and its inhabitants, seeing it as a "backwards" city full of "snobs." And one man, Gleb, was dismissive not only of the stereotypes of the "warm," "open" Russian, but also of those whom he felt embodied these characteristics.

Chapter 3. Phantom Faggots

1. See, for example, Borenstein (2000, 2008). Additionally, an entire corpus of academic works focusing on sex and gender issues was published in the past two decades by Moscow publisher Ladomir (see, inter alia, Golod 2005; Levitt and Toporkov 1999; Toporkov 1995, 1996; Zolotonosov 1999). Kon notes, however, that this "sexophobia" was not entirely a product of the Soviet era, having, rather, deep roots in Orthodox Christianity's antipathy toward sexual pleasure in general (Kon 1993c, 2004: esp.

109–115). But in Kon's estimation, Soviet sexophobia was indeed very real, as "the majority party saw in unmanageable sexuality a threat to their ideology of total control over an individual" (2004: 115–116). Soviet citizens were, as a result, largely unable to obtain any information regarding not only homosexuality, but such subjects as birth control, abortion, STDs, and general sexual pleasure and health (Kon 1993c). Although Kon (2001c) notes that there was a type of "sexual revolution" in the 1960s and '70s, similar to that occurring simultaneously in the West, a new, post-Soviet antisex campaign (focusing often on the "evils" of sex education for young people) appeared in the 1990s.

2. See Baer (2009: 155) and Borenstein (2008: 28). Baer contends that the statement, made by an audience member of a TV talk show, was misquoted and taken out of context; according to him, the woman's statement was "widely cited as evidence of the sexophobia of Soviet culture, although most commentators were unaware that the audience's reaction—mostly guffaws—drowned out the second part of her statement: 'on television.'"

3. The title of the show is most probably a reference to Maiakovskii's poem of the same name, but here used ironically, insofar as the original was, in part, a paean to modesty. According to Baer, this is "an example of a post-Soviet (sexualized) appropriation of Soviet (sexophobic) culture" (personal communication). On the topic of such appropriations, see also Borenstein (2000). It is notable that the show's "otherness" was embodied in the person of its host, Elena Khanga—a black woman of African, Russian, and Polish (Jewish) descent, often in a blond wig. Khanga has, since the show's demise, gone on to host the talk show *Printsip domino* (*The Domino Principle*).

4. The store's opening in the winter of 2004 was announced on at least one gay website in Russia, gayly.ru ("*V Peterburge otkryli*"). Perhaps not incidentally, the establishment was located within steps of one of the city's most popular cruising spots (*pleshka*) for gay men, the *Kat'kin sadik* (Little Catherine Garden, discussed in Chapter 5), as well as cafés popular with gay men. The Moscow location of *Indigo* opened in the winter of 2005 and the St. Petersburg location in the fall of 2006.

5. I use the scare quotes here to denote the fact that I am not suggesting anything about the men's actual sexual orientations or practices; rather, I am noting men who were often assumed to be, by both my informants and by various members of the media, of *netraditsionnaia orientatsiia*.

6. Filipp Kirkorov was the husband of Alla Pugacheva until their divorce in 2005. Galkin, perhaps best known as a comedian and television host, also released musical material on occasion; he married Pugacheva—twenty-seven years his senior—on 23 December 2011.

7. As noted in Chapter 1, there are also many women who are assumed to be lesbian in Russian popular music. My focus, however, will be exclusively on men.

8. Moiseev was part of Pugacheva's backing troupe *Ekspressiia*.

9. Although only Leont'ev was born in Russia, all three artists may unquestionably be considered Russian—or, at the very least, Russian-language—stars. The texts of both Danilko/Serdiuchka's and Moiseev's releases are generally Russian (save for some English-language songs by the former), not Ukrainian or Belarusian, respectively.

Both also speak Russian in television interviews and are frequently featured in the Russian entertainment press. An analogy—aside from language—may be drawn with such singers as Avril Lavigne, Sarah MacLaughlin, k.d. lang, Justin Bieber, Bryan Adams, Celine Dion, Joni Mitchell, and Leonard Cohen, among many others, all of whom are Canadian, but who achieved high levels of success in the United States. While Danilko apparently lives in Kiev, Moiseev has lived in Barvikha (in the Moscow *oblast'*) for many years.

10. See Levin (1989: Chapter 4).

11. On abortion, see Remennick (1993) in the same volume.

12. While Karlinsky (1989) sees the omission as a serendipitous outcome of the Bolsheviks eliminating the bulk of Tsarist legislation, an oversight at best, both Healey and Engelstein read the removal of sodomy from the criminal codes as a deliberate, "principled" decision (Healey 1993; Engelstein 1995).

13. For example, psychiatrists E. K. Krasnushkin and N. G. Kholzakova postulated an etiology based on glandular dysfunction, while forensic expert N. P. Brukhanskii of Moscow's Institute of Neuropsychiatric Prophylaxis suggested that "authentic homosexuality" was the result of "constitutional factors," which might be impacted upon by social context (Healey 2001a: 136–137). Such belief in the biological basis for homosexuality could also be seen in two key Soviet encyclopedias of 1929 and 1930, both of which "conveyed a heady optimism about the imminence of discoveries about the biological mechanisms of sexual anomaly as well as a libertarian enthusiasm for the acceptance of the individual homosexual" (170).

14. See the appendix in Healey (2001a) regarding the number of men convicted under Article 121. As he notes, it is difficult, if not impossible, to ascertain the actual number of victims who were punished following the Article's adoption.

15. Livers (2004) notes that the use of corporeal metaphors was not unique to the Soviet era, having existed in the religious writings of the *khlysty* (a sect of Spiritual Christians split from the Russian Orthodox church) and the *skoptsy* (the "self-castraters" who sought deeper spiritual connection with God via the removal of sexual organs), as well as the philosophical writings of Nikolai Fedorov. On the *skoptsy*, see Engelstein (1999). On the use of corporeal metaphors, see also Borenstein (2008); Kaganovsky (2006); and Naiman (1997).

16. The subject also disappeared from academic inquiry, the psychiatric literature of the 1930s being remarkable for total absence of any research on or discussion of either male or female homosexuality.

17. See Healey (2001a: 183–186).

18. Ibid., 192.

19. *Boria* is a common diminutive of Boris.

20. Lip-synching (*fanera*, in Russian) is extremely common in both contemporary *èstrada* and *popsa*. As MacFadyen (2002a) notes, while some singers have advocated it, others, notably Filipp Kirkorov, have abjured the practice altogether, considering it "dishonest" (97). However, Kirkorov has himself been caught lip-synching. In a frequently viewed YouTube clip, the singer's stage microphone was apparently left on (with a feed to the sound booth), recording all of the panting and slightly off-key singing

during what was obviously to have been a performance making use of prerecorded music. (The clip may be found at http://www.youtube.com/watch?v=FHV9tlogMXw; last accessed 17 August 2013.)

21. In an interview, Moiseev admitted the transition from dancer to vocalist was extremely difficult, noting that vocal training was necessary. However, he also insisted that, criticisms aside, he was an "extremely musical person" who not only danced but also sang and played the piano quite well (Limpert 2003).

22. Moiseev did, however, in at least one recent instance, appear in female attire, as a female character, this in the 2004 *STS* television production of a musical version of *Ali-Baba i sorok razboinikov* (*Ali Baba and the Forty Thieves*), which featured many of Russia's most famous *popsa* and *èstrada* singers.

23. Moiseev noted in an interview that all of his dancers were "completely heterosexual"; "I specially choose dancers like that, so that among them there weren't gays or bisexuals. I have never wanted, and never want to have love near the stage, because it can destroy my career, and that person whom I would have chosen" (Limpert 2003).

24. Not incidentally, the song was a duet, performed with Ukrainian singer and actress Liudmila Gurchenko, one of the most famous gay divas in the Russian-speaking world.

25. Both articles appear to have been written from the same material, but appear in different newspapers—the first in *Argumenty i fakty*, the second in *Dni*.

26. It is probably not coincidental that the article specifically notes singer Nikolai Baskov—married, but widely assumed to be gay—as one of the first artists to answer Moiseev's call for entertainers to assist the victims of the massacre.

27. See "*Boris Moiseev zhenitsia!*" ("Boris Moiseev to Marry!") and "*Boris Moiseev ne podderzhivaet*" ("Boris Moiseev Doesn't Support"). On the denouement of the marriage announcement, see the Epilogue.

28. It was not until 2009 when Moiseev implied that the long-alluded-to son had never existed; at a press conference promoting his anniversary show "*Desert*" ("Dessert"), the singer replied "with a smile"—in response to journalists' questions as to whether or not his son would be in attendance—"yesterday my son died." The article's author states that, according to those close to Moiseev, the son was an "invention," and that the singer's report of his "death" was his way of putting and end to this "tale" (*baika*) (Zharova 2009).

29. See "*Gei ne dolzhny razdrazhat.*"

30. Moiseev's use of the trope of "the children" (and their nurturing) may be seen as a manifestation of what Edelman (2004) terms "reproductive futurism"—the basis of a heteronormative politics that sees "fighting for the children" as its fundamental task. In Edelman's account, a queer politics would be one that would abjure this imperative, and the notion of a redemptive future.

31. The performance in question is that of "*Vot i vse*" ("That's All"), and may be seen at http://www.youtube.com/watch?v=tb-UR4ppZlM (last accessed 17 August 2013).

32. In one article, Leont'ev is remembered by people in his hometown as "a very talented, vulnerable, and nonstandard [*nestandartnogo*] child. . . . He sewed his own

costumes... [and] appeared at a New Year's carnival in an ox-eyed [*volookoi*] coquettish gypsy skirt.... He went to classes in makeup, eyelashes tinted, walking in high heels, his face sometimes smeared with *Snezhinka* [Snowflake] cream." Additionally, he "tried to be like [girls]," and was not generally friendly with boys, although "he had a school friend with whom, according to the teachers, he connected the most tender feelings" ("*Valerii Leont'ev brosil*").

33. See Boikov (2004); Maistrenko (2007) and "*Liubovnik Leont'eva*." Note that the word "*liubovnik*," translated as "lover," indicates one who is male; a female lover would be indicated by the word "*liubovnitsa*."

34. Svetlana Annapol'skaia, who worked for Channel 1's musical department from the 1970s until the 1990s and was involved with the production of such shows as *Goluboi ogonek*, however, asserts that the singer's sexual orientation had nothing to do with his inability to garner screen time ("there was no persecution of gays [*golubykh*] on television at that time. The leadership simply did not know who was 'gay'"); rather, it was the singer's style and outfits—considered outrageous or simply too sexual—that kept him off the small screen. According to Annapol'skaia, "Leont'ev was guilty of having too-long hair, and costumes which, according to our officials, were not suited to television. I remember Valerii brought to me a bunch of all sorts of costumes. 'This won't work!'—I said to him. Red leather pants—that's fine. But the top, through which the naked body appears—that's too much. I finally convinced Valerii to wear a grey three-piece [suit]. And on the third try, I managed to get him into [*The Little Blue Light*]" (Boikov 2004). It seems difficult, however, to imagine that the Soviet censors did not, in fact, know (or suspect) which performers were "blue," or that Leont'ev's sartorial/sexual excesses, implicitly subversive of rigid guidelines of gendered propriety, did not in and of themselves confer the label of "*goluboi*" upon him. Especially in light of such subversion, it may have been implicitly incumbent upon Leont'ev to present the image of heterosexual normalcy, via marriage, to the public. As Karlinsky (1989) notes, many of the Soviet era's greatest artists (such as Sergei Eisenstein), although their homosexuality was an "open secret," still felt compelled to marry, to put on the public illusion of heterosexuality (see Chapter 1, note 21).

35. See "*Zhena Valeriia Leont'eva*."

36. The forum was found at http://lovehate.ru/blog/54357/27, but as of 22 August 2012, the link is dead. Svetlana Annapol'skaia (see Chapter 3, note 34) also asserted that "I think that [their] marriage was purely a formality. Liusia is a strong-willed woman. But she obviously couldn't have any sex with him. She's *rozovaia* (lesbian)." On the translation of the word *muzhik*, see note 98, infra.

37. See Bolotin (2005) and "*Leont'ev ostalsia bez boifrenda*."

38. The character was originally part of Danilko's live *SV Shou* (*SV* meaning "*spal'nyi vagon*," a sleeping car on a train), which featured several comic characters, allowing the actor to show off his talents for broad, social satire in a number of guises. Danilko had released several CDs since 2002 (as well as videos of his *SV Show*), but it was not until 2003 and the release of the song "*Khorosho*" ("It's Good") that he

became internationally known and successful, especially throughout the CIS and former Soviet states.

39. See "*Andrei Danilko: 'Serdiuchka nikogda ne budet zhlobikhoi.'*"

40. A subtitled version of the commercial may be found at http://www.youtube.com/watch?v=scUoqhbmxmg (last accessed 17 August 2013).

41. In 2004, Russia was shaken by the downing of two jets by Chechen terrorists, resulting in the deaths of all aboard, as well as the almost unimaginable massacre of hundreds (half of them children) in the Beslan school siege.

42. Although Sediuchka's references are overwhelmingly Ukrainian, it is important to note that the connections between Ukrainian and Russian cultures are extremely strong, something that was asserted to me on many occasions by numerous Russians, and something that was seen by many of them as especially disturbing in light of Ukraine's having turned away from Russia and toward the West in the wake of Viktor Yushchenko's election as president in 2004. It should furthermore be noted that the texts of Serdiuchka's songs are overwhelmingly in Russian, and thus geared toward Russian-speaking audiences, both in Russia and in Ukraine. Although Ukrainian is the official language of Ukraine, there are large numbers of people living within the country's borders—including ethnic Ukrainians and ethnic Russians whose families have resided in the country for generations—who may speak either primarily or solely Russian. According to one of my informants, an ethnic Ukrainian who had emigrated to the United States, the vast majority of his family spoke only Russian, the language which, especially during the Soviet era, was the language of the "educated classes" and official business. He himself spoke mainly Russian and English, and admitted to speaking (or understanding) very little Ukrainian.

43. In her Tide commercial, when Vladimir Tishko—host of television show of *Moskva instruktsiia* (*Moscow Instruction*), and the pitchman for this series of ads—pays an "impromptu" visit to Verka's apartment, Verka yells to her mother, "Mom, a young man has come to see us—and he's handsome, too!"

44. In the videos for both "*Chita drita*" and "*Khorosho*," Verka boisterously grabs, two-handedly, and "fluffs" the breasts of her mother and a prostitute, respectively.

45. Similar insinuations, but regarding a more serious topic, appeared in conjunction with another celebrity widely assumed to be gay, television host Andrei Malakhov. In this case, the insinuations were not only of proscriptions on his (homo)sexual activity (the title of one article read, "*Malakhovu zapreshchaiut zanimat'sia seksom*" ["Malakhov Is Forbidden to Have Sex"]) (Stepanov 2007) but of his having contacted a "dangerous virus"—the implication being AIDS. In reading the articles (Boziev and Didenko 2007; Stepanov 2007), although it is clear that the virus is, in fact, hepatitis, the illness is not named. Additionally, Malakhov's account of how he contracted the illness (according to him, on a trip to Valaam, a group of islands situated in Lake Lagoda in Northern Russia) are contradicted, according to the article, by his attending physicians, who noted that the incubation period does not tally with the time frame of his visit, thus also allowing speculation as to how he acquired the virus.

46. For example, in an article in *Komsomol'skaia pravda* (Lapteva and Remizova 2005) about the reason for Kirkorov and Pugacheva's divorce, (suggesting it might have been related to a daughter born to Kirkorov out of wedlock), one reader wrote in the accompanying forum, "Kirkorov is gay, and all of this is a well-played farce" ("*khorosho razygrannyi fars*"). Another account, appearing in a Latvian newspaper, claimed that Kirkorov paid three hundred dollars an hour to a male hustler for sadomasochistic sex, although the veracity of the account seemed dubious (Savel'ev 2003). MacFadyen (2002a: 15) also offers an account of singer Tat'iana Bulanova, in a fit of anger (over what she considered unacceptably low remuneration for a performance), casting aspersions on the singer's sexuality.

47. See "*Andrei Danilko: Serdiuchka*."

48. The word is also used to describe a short-legged clumsy person.

49. The forum was originally found at http://musik-blog.ru/article/297/; as of 22 August 2012, the link is dead.

50. See Rozanov (1913 [1911]). See also Baer (2008, 2009) and Bershtein (2012). I will return to the idea of the "spiritual homosexual" in Chapter 6. It should be noted that Rozanov was not celebrating the ascetic, but rather, in the context of his critique of Christianity, condemning it. According to Matich (2005), Rozanov's book was a "polemic against the morbid cult of Christian asceticism . . . [which celebrated] Judaism as a procreative life-affirming religion." Rozanov considered Christianity "thoroughly decadent, celebrating death, with Christ at its necrophilic helm" (243).

51. Trubach's stage name means, literally, trumpet; his given name is Khar'kovets. Although Trubach and Moiseev garnered "fame resounding throughout the entire country" for the song, in a 2009 interview Trubach characterized himself as a "terrible homophobe" ("*strashnyi gomofob*"), admitting that for the first six months of touring with Moiseev, he was afraid to ride in an elevator alone with him (about which, Moiseev reportedly replied, "it's not contagious"). Trubach's views on homosexuality are "tolerant" at best: "I'm against gay pride parades, all this garbage. I would say to them: 'Guys, no one is going to crawl into your bed. Do what you want. But to make it public is savagery.' They cancelled the article in the Penal Code—let them rejoice. They have their own clubs, their own hangouts [*tusovki*]. I think it's sinful in some way to take part in the promotion of all of this" (Liakhovich 2009).

52. On the concept of *byt* in Russian culture see, inter alia, Boym (1994) and Kaier and Naiman (2006).

53. The presentation of homosexuality as ontologically nonsituated with regard to both temporality and spatiality—an eternal "gayness"—is a criticism levied by Baer (2000) in his review of two Russian books dealing with homosexuality: K. K. Rotikov's *Drugoi Peterburg* (*The Other Petersburg*) (1998) and V. N. Dumenkov's *Liubov bez granits: Antologiia shedevrov mirovoi literatury* (*Love without Borders: An Anthology of Masterpieces of World Literature*) (1997). This same dynamic is at play in the creation of more popular texts dealing with homosexuality, such as *Lesbiianki i gei* (*Lesbians and Gays*) (Petrovets 1997), a compilation of, among other things, "gays" through history, wherein, again, gayness is not theoretically engaged, but taken as a "given."

54. Healey (2001a) discusses in detail the move from scientific/biological explanations for homosexuality, common in the early Soviet era, to those focused on the role of society—a dysfunctional society—which became the norm in the beginning of the Stalinist era. The "naturalness" of the homosexual is, according to Watton (1994) in keeping with Rozanov's (1911) argument as well. She notes, that, according to Rozanov, "moonlight people are an organic entity," noting further that "Rozanov figures the sodomite as the descendent of a primordial and prehistoric race, thereby an organically discrete entity that cannot reasonably be condemned as unnatural" (374).

55. The lyricist of the song is Karen Kavalerian. In addition to Moiseev's work, she has also has written lyrics for some of Russia's most popular artists, including singers Filipp Kirkorov and Alla Pugacheva, and the group *Prem'er-ministr* (Prime Minister).

56. MacFadyen notes several songs of Leont'ev's that may be read as referring to the status of outsider but relates these texts to problems the singer had with his career—that is, not having gleaned official approval due to his performance/sartorial style—rather than his sexual orientation. However, it is equally possible to analyze the texts of many of Leont'ev's songs as alluding to the latter as well as the former: "So many problems. I'm all mixed up! What do I do and how do I go on?" ("*Problemy*," "Problems"); "Let each person choose as he wishes" ("*Delo vkusa*," "A Matter of Taste"); "Am I to blame if I'm a black sheep? I was born that way" ("*Belaia vorona*," "White Cow") (MacFadyen 2001: 188).

57. *Kvas* is a malted, fermented mildly or nonalcoholic beverage popular in both Russia and Ukraine, made from wheat, rye, or barley and often flavored with fruits. It is also used, especially in the summer, to make a cold soup known as *okroshka*, a favorite of many Russians.

58. Interview with Igor' Kon, 3 December 2004.

59. In the song "*Klenovyi list*" ("Maple Leaf"), Leont'ev even invokes the international symbol of the gay community, in the line "My life with the colors of the rainbow/Taunts me, gladdens me" ("*A zhizn' moia tsvetami radugi/To muchaet menia, to raduet*"). A contention that the song alludes to homosexual love is supported by inclusion of the text "We are not a couple in the eyes of others" ("*Ne para my dlia glaz chuzhik*").

60. The appellation alludes to the supposed fact that the club is popular with the many sailors—closeted or not—living in St. Petersburg. Although I did on occasion see men in uniform at the club, this was not common; of course, sailors may have been in civilian dress, as it seems unlikely that a member of the military would risk being known as such, in a public space for gay men. Additionally, some of the men with whom I spoke noted that while they too, knew of the supposed popularity of *Kabare* with sailors and other military men, they were not certain whether or not it was true.

61. In the song "*Chita drita*"—the name of a fictitious dance—for example, Serdiuchka asserts her desirable, Slavic pulchritude, singing "I'm a beauty . . . a braid to my waist . . . and I like you." And in both this song and in "*Ia popala na liubov*'" ("I Fell in Love"), as well as others, the objects of her romantic attentions are unambiguously male.

62. Verka's mother, a recurring character in her videos, is played by actress Inna Belokon'.

63. See, for example, the performances of Vadim Tonkov and Boris Vladimirov as Veronika Mavrikievna and Avdot'ia Nikitichna, or Igor' Kasilov and Sergei Chvanov as the *Novye russkie babki* (The New Russian Grandmas).

64. The text of the chorus uses the imperative construction, i.e., "*devochki liubite mal'chikov*," rather than "*devochki liubiat mal'chikov*." The first would be translated as "girls, love boys," the latter as "girls love boys."

65. Another of Serdiuchka's songs "*Ia—revolutsiia*" ("I'm a Revolution") may be read as an expression of an international/Western LGBT-rights discourse. In the text, she proclaims, "Those such as I rise from the ashes. . . . That we don't fall in love, believe me, it's absurd"; the "we" possibly alludes to homosexual men and women. That the song stresses the theme of revolution ("you are a revolution, we are a revolution . . . we will all be victorious!"), however, places the text in relation to a specifically Russian history (e.g., the Bolshevik Revolution, one of the outcomes of which was a decriminalization of homosexuality).

66. Serdiuchka's music may also be stylistically related to both Ukrainian and Serbian music—indeed, to much music common in Eastern Europe—via fast tempi and foundational rhythmic patterns placing the stress on the "off" beat (that is, an "oom-*pah*"–like pattern of one *and* two *and*, and so forth), the use of brass ensembles to deliver hooks, frequent use of the "gypsy" scale, and harmonic vocabularies focusing largely (sometimes exclusively) on tonic-dominant progressions.

67. Of course, asserting that the text is based on a true story does not foreclose the possibility that such historical facts might have been based upon a homosexual (not simply homosocial) connection between the two "real" men. That Leont'ev has often chosen to use a woman for the soldier in staged performances for the songs, wherein dancers take the roles of the characters, suggests a cognizance of the fact that many listeners may indeed envision a homosexual tryst between the protagonists, the woman's appearance being a means to short-circuit just such a reading.

68. Of the song itself, Trubach says "it's just a song, just a history. This isn't t.A.T.u, who kiss on stage . . . when I sang with Boris, it does not mean I'm gay" (Liakhovich 2009).

69. On the dialogic relationships among texts, see Bakhtin (1982).

70. It was not only Verka's music that was part of gay clubs, but also her "personification" as well. For example, at the Moscow club 911, a Verka impersonator served as the mistress of ceremonies for the evening's show, one that featured not only other impersonators of Russian pop stars, but a male stripper as well.

71. Kollmann (2002), for example, notes a change in ideals of masculinity in Petrine Russia of the eighteenth century, a milieu in which there was a conscious awareness of and desire for various Western mores. Coupled with the move of marriage from a sociopolitical contract to one based on affects was a move to a masculinity—in keeping with the Western codes so favored by Peter the Great—that was "energetic, voluntaristic and self-determining" (29). Additionally, Smith (2002), focusing on nineteenth-century St. Petersburg, suggests concurrent types

of conflicting notions of masculinity. On the one hand was the worker who, feeling disempowered within the capitalist workforce and removed from the control of his home and land, enacted a masculinity dependent upon "strength, fighting prowess, a capacity to hold one's drink, womanizing and certain types of wit"; on the other hand was the class-conscious minority, emerging in the 1880s, which "modeled itself on the intelligentsia," and "valorized self-control, the assertion of reason over emotion, autonomy in personal relations, and a more respectful, but not necessarily egalitarian attitude toward women" (100–101). Finally, Friedman (2002), in the same volume, notes these same types of conflicting ideals of masculinity among Nicholaevan University students: the powerful, hard-drinking, pugnacious male versus the cultured, refined, educated ideal.

72. Conformity to narrowly defined gender roles did not, of course, begin with the Soviets, and traditional, rural Russian societies were also remarkable for the strict gender codes enacted therein. Shchepanskaia and Shangina (2005), for example, show the myriad ways in which the gendered subject is produced in Russian peasant society, starting from before his/her birth. The authors, for example, note that it was believed that if parents behaved "incorrectly" from the time of conception, and onward through pregnancy, "the female child could become amoral or masculine [*muzhepodobnaia*], and a boy could in the future fail to have man's work, or could have feminine characteristics." The inculcation of "correct" gender attributes would continue immediately following the actual birth of the child; the ritual of cutting the umbilical cord was carried out on the spinning wheel in the case of a girl's birth, and by an ax in the case of a boy's. In the first years of the child's life, adults would "for a boy, spread out on the floor symbols of masculine work: ax, plane, stirrup, bridle, sling, whip, and for a girl, trappings of a feminine future: kerchief, spindle, threads, scissors, lace frame, [tatting] shuttle. They would allow the child to choose the instrument that [she or he] liked, serving as an indication of his future calling [*prizvanie*]" (11–12). Such gendered instruction continued throughout the child's early life, and was performatively reenacted throughout adulthood. It is perhaps important to highlight that, despite the fact that many in contemporary Russian society believe in the immutability of gendered characteristics, the authors posit early on their belief in the fact that, while sex, defined in the context of reproductions, has a biological basis, "in the social environment, its expression, as with other functions of the human organism (nourishment, defecation, displays of emotion, and so forth), is regimented by culture" (5).

73. For a collection of essays on this subject, see Corrin (1992).

74. She notes: "Women comrades differed little from men: short haircuts, pants, cigarettes, a style of behavior that turned them into 'their own boys.'" There were sexless figures in boots and road workers, construction workers, vegetable farmers, etc. . . . What are labeled as sexist stereotypes in the West are accepted by Russian women as a return to individuality and the forcibly wrested feminine 'I'" (1993: 277).

75. The gendering of the workforce is still an existing dynamic in contemporary Russia, and several of the gay men I knew were in jobs that were gendered as "femi-

nine," especially teaching and medicine. Some, such as Maksim, loved working with children, and loved being in an atmosphere with largely female coworkers; others, such as Nikolai, could not stand to be in a "feminized" work space. In general, those who were employed as teachers were interested in changing their profession, as teachers' salaries were extremely low.

76. In the context of the contemporary United States, Savran (1998) examines the idea of men's fantasies of loss of power, focusing, in part, on the evolution of the "white hipster" "into several variations upon the theme of the white male as victim" (5).

77. As discussed earlier in relation to gender roles (see note 72, supra), negative reactions to gender transgressors did not begin with the Soviet system but were often encountered in folk culture as well. According to Shchepanskaia and Shangina (2005), such transgressors—including those that marked the person as somehow impeding the reproductive imperative of human life (e.g., those who were sterile, or who deliberately avoided marriage)—were often suspected of witchcraft, and the cause of misfortunes that may have befallen the village (10).

78. Levin does note that such prohibitions were not exclusively applied to homosexual activity; rather, any activity that was deemed "unnatural," that "violate[d] the proper order of the universe and society" was seen worthy of condemnation: "In sum, 'unnatural' sex inverted accepted social relationships, and for that reason constituted a serious offense" (1989: 199).

79. Morozov (2004) discusses this roiling of gendered bodies and roles in contemporary cinema, postulating the appearance of the *otesemat'* (literally, *fathermother*; his term) as a reflection of the breakdown of traditional gender roles in modern society.

80. See Borenstein (2008); on demographics, see Eberstadt (2005, 2009, 2010, 2011); Perevedentsev (2009); Rybakovskii (2010); and Shlapentokh (2005).

81. Moss (1995), engaging Eve Sedgwick's (1990) postulation of a homo/hetero divide around which Western society has been constructed, finds that the foundational binary in Soviet society, rather than revolving around sexuality, was the divide between dissident and pro-Soviet discourses. This distinction, however, does not foreclose upon the appositeness of sexuality as implicated within the Soviet sphere as well, for as Moss shows, the same (linguistic) structures (e.g., "preterition"—that is, invoking something by not mentioning it) that operate to make the unspeakable (the dissident) speakable, are in evidence within discourses of "dissident sexuality" (homosexuality) as well. A conflation of sexual and political dissidence, both of which have "come out of the closet into the public arena" (246) thus suggests the possibility of employing Sedgwick's posit as not entirely apropos only of the West.

82. Meshkov also takes issue with the genre of *shanson*, which idealizes and glorifies the criminal underworld.

83. Note that Meshkov's invocation of the term "gay propaganda" (or "propaganda of homosexuality") occurred eight years in advance of the national law banning the same.

84. The website of the National Vanguard, an American white supremacist group, carried the story of Zhirinovskii's call for the death penalty for homosexuality and

wholeheartedly supported the initiative, claiming "homosexuality is intensively promoted by Jewish and other multiracial groups, as it breaks down the fundamental unit of our race, the family, damages the psyche of uncounted victims, and causes literally millions of White children to never be born" ("Russia: Zhirinovsky Proposes"). That Zhirinovskii is Jewish seems to have been missed or overlooked by the author.

85. Although juridically validated by government actions, homophobia does not circulate only in the realm of the political, of course; for example, a graduate student in Moscow in 2005 filed a lawsuit against *MGU* (*Moskvskii gosudarstvennyi universitet*, Moscow State University), alleging discrimination based on sexual orientation ("*MGU otvetit*"). Charges of homophobia, however, are not univocal among gay men; for example, when the website gay.ru levied such charges against psychologist Irina Petrovskaiia, another gay site—gayclub.Ru (now gaynews.ru) suggested that these charges had distorted Petrovskaiia's words (and intent) ("*Gay.ru razoblachil gomofoba?*"; "*Irina Petrovskaia*").

86. The most well-known example of this is the trial and imprisonment of Mikhail Khodorkovskii, head of the Russian oil company YUKOS (*IuKOS*). Having become one of the richest men in the world through acquisition of the company in the perestroika years, Khodorkovskii's arrest and conviction were ostensibly on charges of fraud (and, in the retrial in 2009, two years before his scheduled release, charges of embezzlement and money laundering). Many, however, have suggested that Khodorkovskii was targeted for his increasing involvement in politics, something that was seen as dangerous to the continuation of Putin's power. I discuss the most recent possible target of Putin's political wrath—Aleksei Naval'nyi—in the Epilogue. On the state takeover or control of media outlets, see Arutunyan (2009) and Kara-Murza (2011).

87. In light of the 2013 national legislation against "gay propaganda," I revisit, in the Epilogue, these questions—the "regulation" or "control" of men of nontraditional orientation within the music industry and the possibility of a regime in which visibility enables discipline.

88. In full, Baev says, "This is the social reality of hatred and aggression towards all 'objectionable,' 'incorrect,' 'non-traditional.' . . . Aggression, which has reached, in the present time, open fascism. This is the reality of the supporting of a social ghetto of homosexuals, which the authorities enclose by an even denser ring of barbed wire" (2006). The irony, in the context of the current discussion, is that Baev sees this social reality as one in which Moiseev is complicit. In his estimation, as one of the "privileged few" homosexuals with access to power (and connections to powerful people) Moiseev, in his pronouncements against events such as Moscow's gay parade, naïvely fails to see that he is simply being used by the establishment to carry out their policy of intolerance and discrimination. The word "*petukh*"—literally, "rooster"—in the article's title ("*Petukhi protiv geev*," "Roosters against Gays") must be understood as having emanated from Russian prison slang. In this context, the *petukh* is the man who is forced to take the passive homosexual role. Such men were seen as occupying the lowest status in prison culture. On gay Russian slang, including this term, see Mogutin (1995).

89. Certain phenomenological readings of the body do indeed engage just such themes as the disciplining of the body. See, for example, Lingis (1994a: Chapter 4).

90. Gibson-Graham (2001) attempts such a theoretical dethronement of an assumed patriarchal power. Invoking Marcus's (1992) rereading of the "rape script," one wherein sites of possible agency and refusal are posited, they compare this to the "script" of globalization (and capitalism), seeking ultimately to explore the possibility of "rewriting the globalization script from within, denying the inevitability and 'reality' of [multinational corporations'] power over workers and communities, and exploring ways in which the hard and penetrating body of the MNC can be seen as soft, fragile, and vulnerable" (264).

91. The video of the award presentation was televised on the Russian news program *Vesti*, and can be found at http://www.vesti.ru/videos?vid=230854 (last accessed 17 August 2013).

92. Lukashenko is reported as having told openly gay German Former Minister Guido Westerwelle that he "hates fags," additionally advising Westerwelle himself to lead a "normal life" (*"Bélarus: Loukachenko 'hait les pédés'"*) Another source quotes the president as saying he had "nothing against lesbians, but would gladly send gay men to state farms" (*"imeet nichego protiv lesbiianok, no geev s udovol'stviem vyslal by v sovkhozy"*) (*"Lukashenko zaiavil Vestervelle"*).

93. Artur also suggested that the money and backing Moiseev had were contributory to this success and further suspected that some of this was from the Mafia, which meant "you couldn't touch him." Moiseev himself has spoken of sexual encounters with Communist Party and komsomol members in the Soviet era; in one interview he highlights the coercion on the part of the officials, saying, "I remember the end of the 70s. These Communists and *komosomol* members took dancers to the baths, and wanted to have sex with us. They pulled us horribly into all that! And we, young boys, played games with them. We sucked the dirty pricks [*kontsy*] of these old geezers [*mudakov*]—these aged komosomol members! They forced us to do this, they intimidated us" (Mogutin 2001). The dynamic here is obviously—at least according to Moiseev—one in which the boys are victimized by the party members; however, it is also possible that such liaisons panicked the Communist/komosomolets members after perestroika, insofar as they feared the publication of these trysts. It is not unthinkable, as such, that Moiseev could have used such liaisons to his advantage, these contributing to his "untouchability."

94. For various articles regarding picketing or boycotting of Moiseev's concerts, see *"Dikie nravy"*; *"*Gay Showman Barred from Dagestan*"*; *"Gomofobiia shagaet"*; *"V Obninske"*; *"Voinstvuiushchie khristiane"*; and Avdeev (2005).

95. The spellings *pidar* and *pidor* are both encountered in Russian, although the first is more common. Both are pronounced identically.

96. Grosz here is drawing upon the conceptualizations of both Lacan (the *object petit a*) and Kristeva (the abject).

97. The subject of masculinity in relation to gay men—often related to body image (or body fascism)—has been explored through numerous disciplinary and historical lenses. See, for example (among many others), Atkins (1998, 1999); Blotcher (1998);

Crouthamel (2011); Durgadas (1998); Echols (2010: esp. Chapters 1 and 4); Edwards (2006: Chapter 5); Loftin (2007); Mann (1998); Ridge et al. (2006); Signorile (1998); Yeung et al. (2006). As only one example, Durgadas, focusing on body weight, suggests that "fatness is equitable to feminization for a man, for heterosexual men, but even more so for gay and bisexual men" (369).

98. The forum can be found at http://www.lovehate.ru/opinions/722 (last accessed 17 August 2013). The word *"muzhik"* is not easily translated into American English, although the word "bloke" may be a close translation in British English. I discuss the term, in the context of masculinity, in Chapter 4. The word *"baba"* may be translated as "woman," but this, too, lacks nuance, as the term is often used in a slightly derogatory way; the word "broad" might be a closer translation. Although the site erektrofon.gay.ru notes Shura as being one of only two openly gay male performers in Russia, the singer himself has often equivocated when asked about his sexual orientation. In a 1999 interview, for example, he is quoted as saying "I have an absolutely normal, traditional orientation. I'm not gay. But if a person loves me, then I don't care what their sex is" (Mekhtiev 1999); in a later interview, however, in response to questions of his orientation, he replied "I love beautiful people, and it's not important to me what their sex is" (*"Ia liubliu krasivykh liudei, mne ne vazhno, kakogo oni pola"*) (Snezhinskaia 2004). In 2010, the singer introduced his "fiancée" to the public—a woman known only as "Liza"—but it is unclear whether the two actually wed (Redreeva 2010; *"Shura pokazal zhenu"*).

Chapter 4. Corporeal Intentions

1. In both St. Petersburg and Moscow, it is common for people to flag down cars, rather than relying upon taxis, as the latter are both expensive and relatively uncommon. When a driver stops to pick up a potential passenger, the fare is generally negotiated in advance.

2. A gay club, *Dusha i telo* nonetheless admitted women as well as men, although the numbers of the former were far fewer than those of the latter. Most gay (and lesbian) clubs—both in Russia, and in the West—have specific door policies instituted in order to ensure the gender demographics that they wish to maintain in the establishment.

3. The ability to view live, naked men was probably partially responsible for the St. Petersburg club *Metro*'s having been considered *miks* (mixed). Here, on Monday nights, amateur male stripteases were hosted, allowing ostensibly heterosexual or bisexual men the opportunity to view male bodies without having to enter a gay club (and risk social opprobrium).

4. Ivanov's fascination with the male body may be seen in numerous paintings, including *Apollon, Giatsint i Kiparis zanimaiushchiesia muzykoi i peniem* (*Apollo, Hyacinthus and Cyparissus Singing and Playing Music*) (1831–1834), *Iavlenie Khrista narodu* (*The Appearance of Christ to the People* (1837–1857), and his numerous studies of young male nudes, including *Sem' mal'chikov* (*Seven Boys*; sometimes titled *Sem' mal'chikov v tsvetnykh odezhdakh i drapirovkakh/Seven Boys in Colorful Clothes and Draperies*), *Nagoi mal'chik* (*Nude Boy*), and *Tri nagikh mal'chika* (*Three Nude Boys*;

sometimes entitled *Na beregu Neapol'skogo zaliva/On the Shore of the Bay of Naples*), all from the period ranging from the 1940s to 1950s. Such fascination has been cause for some to question the artist's sexual orientation (Gray 2001).

5. The journalists contend that the KK Bulla studio, the source of the photographs, "was the first to record the discreet gay culture to which tsarist Russia turned a blind eye."

6. See Bonnell (1997) and Clark (1993).

7. At a press conference following the film's premiere at the Cannes Film Festival, Sokurov inveighed against the press's ascribing of a homoerotic element, saying "for the movie you have seen, there is no such low meaning" (Peary 2004). The director's protestations notwithstanding, the film's opening images are certainly open to a reading that allows for the homoerotic: two apparently nude male bodies, both exquisitely formed, first in an almost violent struggle, then in an undeniably tender and intimate embrace, the father holding his son in his arms, the son's hand caressing or kneading the father's muscular chest, the father's hand stroking the son's hair, the son ultimately, quietly stating, "*ia liubliu tebia*" ("I love you"). The film's supposed homoeroticism was not only remarked upon within the Western press, however, but in the Russian press as well. One reviewer, noting the aforementioned scene, and recalling Sokurov's fury at the suggestion of homoeroticism, states with complete and palpable sarcasm, "Only a completely wicked person could see two naked entwined bodies on a bed, performing rhythmic movements facing each other, accompanied by moans and exhaled whispers 'well, a little more, well, well . . . thank you. I love you' as an act of physical closeness" (Barabash 2003). Referencing the budding open of the son's mouth in the same scene—from which escapes a low, almost orgasmic moan—another Russian reviewer stated that "I know for sure that in world cinema the human mouth has never reminded one so much of an anus" ("*chelovecheskii rot eshche nikogda tak ne napominal anus*") (Brashinskii 2003). Critic Armond White (2004), in an apologia for Sokurov, suggests that the director's remarks not be taken as "homophobic," but rather as an argument "against a limited sexual interpretation of the film." Kostylev (2003), however, finds that the director's indignation was disingenuous, at best, noting "Sokurov chose the most amusing way—to bring everything to a white heat, and later to publicly be indignant at the Cannes press conference by the perversity of the contemporaries who were taking spirituality and elevated love for sex." To add yet another layer of complexity, one reviewer present suggested that Sokurov's chagrin may have been due, in part, to "repeated rumors" that the director himself is gay (Peary 2004), a rumor alluded to in another reviewer's (again sarcastic) comment: "That Aleksandr Sukurov doesn't like women (meaning in movies, of course) we know from many of his previous films" (Barabah 2003).

8. Although Danilko is Ukrainian, it must be noted that the vast majority of his work is marketed toward Russian-speaking audiences, both inside and outside of Russia. See Chapter 3, note 9.

9. On the connection between the gay male listener (the opera queen) and female divas, see Koestenbaum's seminal work (1993).

10. The use of the word "boy" here—and in many instances among gay men—is not meant to indicate someone who is legally a minor but, rather, a (relatively) younger gay man. The word "relatively," however, must be understood very broadly, as it is not uncommon for gay men in their forties, or even older, to refer to one another as "boys."

11. The artwork on the wall is also indicative, purposely or not, of a "gay sensibility" through the use of a poster drawing stylistically on Hippolyte Flandrin's nineteenth century painting *Figure d'Étude*. In the 1990s, in both the United States and Western Europe, this painting became somewhat of a "gay icon," visible in numerous gay sites, both homes and businesses (Camille 1994). Kon (2004), although he suggests that there is nothing explicitly erotic about Flandrin's painting, finds that it "opened up a large space to homosexual imagination, giving rise to many imitations and variations" (285); indeed, the painting served as the cover for Fernandez's (2002) volume on art and homosexuality. Although the original features a young, muscular, nude, white male, the portrait in the video is of two muscular, nude, black males; in both portraits, however, the poses are identical: the seated body is viewed from the side, head resting on knees brought close to the chest, genitals obscured by the position of the thighs.

12. While Danilko himself was born in 1973, the character of Verka Serdiuchka is clearly middle-aged.

13. See "*Timofei Pron'kin*."

14. In the video, Oleshko, generally not opposed to showing her body, is uncharacteristically covered with a sweatshirt from the waist up. In a recorded interview, she related that she had been extremely ill the day of the shooting, and did not want to get wet and compromise her health further by catching a chill.

15. The conflation of body hair and masculinity was one made by several of my informants; as Kolia told me, "men should have hair on their bodies." Although the current version of archetypal male beauty in the United States is often one in which the male body is almost unnaturally smooth, it is worth noting that, up until the 1980s, the image of the hirsute male—at least judging from gay erotica—was far more common (and far more aligned with conceptions of masculinity) than in the present day.

16. In several interviews, Fomin notes that he left university, where he was training to become a pediatrician, to pursue his music career. He did, however, ultimately receive his degree.

17. One website (www.smash4u.ru), however, describes the band as comprising "two fantastic gays" ("*sostoit iz dvukh zamechatel'niky geev*") (site last accessed 1 June 2012).

18. See note 19, infra.

19. The original article—an interview with the singer—appeared in the Russian newspaper *Gazeta* (Romanov 2006), and portions were reproduced on several gay websites, including that of gaynews.ru ("*Sergei Lazarev: 'U nas'*"). The comments quoted in the text are from readers of the article as it appeared on the website xsgay.ru; the comments and article have since been removed (last accessed 1 July 2012), but several of the later comments are preserved at http://lazarevs.ucoz.ru/publ/1-1-0-1 (last accessed 21 August 2013).

20. In the same forum, another poster refers to Topolov as a "coward" (*trus*) and a "homophobic schmuck" (*gomofobnoe chmo*).

21. Of course, there were those who disagreed with Stanislav; Il'ia, for example, thought that being gay was, in fact, simply a matter of the biological sex of one's sexual partner, a contention with which Gleb agreed. The idea that gay men and women might be in some way superior to heterosexuals is not, according to Watton (1994), a contemporary occurrence; Russian philosopher Vasilii Rozanov, in his *Liudi lunnogo sveta* (1911), for example, considered homosexuals to have been "endowed with a cultural and intellectual superiority" (Watton 1994: 374). However, there appear to be at least some homosexual men or women in Russia who disagree with the idea of a supposed gay superiority; on the "gay" Russian website/magazine bfmg.ru, for example, the editors maintain that "sexual orientation does not make a person worse, but also does not make him better. We're against homophobia, but also against the unfounded assertion [*vypiachivanie*] of our pseudo-uniqueness" (http://www.bfmg.ru/about/; last accessed 21 August 2013). Although the site purports to be for all people regardless of sexual orientation (a "magazine for outstanding people"), the abundance of homoerotic imagery (the June 2012 issue, for example, features the almost nude male members of the group *Dik*), as well as the implications of its very title (the "BF" standing for "Best For," but most certainly referencing the international shorthand for boyfriend as well—a shorthand used in Russia, i.e., БФ) suggest that there is an active courting of a gay audience.

22. In Russia, many refer to cousins as "brothers" or "sisters." Although there is a specific term for such relatives (*dvoiurodnyi brat* or *dvoiurodnaia sestra*), most people I knew dispensed with the adjective, simply referring to cousins/brothers/sisters with the same word—*brat* or *sestra*.

23. The video can be seen at http://www.youtube.com/watch?v=6xT0q20YsHc (last accessed 21 August 2013).

24. According to Shaburova, the *muzhik* "is a significant mark of Russianness ... by definition is Russian" (2002; quoted in Kon 2003: 394), "a rigidly structured norm of masculinity, which then also serves as a concentrate of Russianness" (2005a: 90). Kon's definition of the *muzhik* draws not only upon Shaburova's work, but also Vladimir Ivanovich Dal''s *Tolkovyi slovar' zhivogo velikorusskogo iazyka* (*Explanatory Dictionary of the Living Great Russian Language*), originally published in 1880. Dal''s dictionary does not include an entry for *muzhik* but, rather, *muzh*. The entry may be seen online at http://vidahl.agava.ru/P102.HTM#15942 (last accessed 21 August 2013).

25. The common word for woman is *zhenshchina*; *baba* is a coarser word, one many consider to be somewhat derogatory and misogynistic. See Chapter 3, note 98.

26. It is clear, in the context of Kon's article, that this "sexuality" is not a *sensuality*, and is one not concerned with the pleasure of the female partner; according to one St. Petersburg woman (whom Kon quotes), a *muzhik* is "completely indifferent to his body," but "not indifferent to [his] dick [*chlen*] ... in sex, the majority of them think only about their dicks—if it's erect [*vstanet*], if it's not erect, how it's erect" (Kon 2003: 394).

27. Kay (2006) notes the appearance in post-Soviet consumer culture of *Muzhik* (which she translates as "bloke") brand cigarettes, which appear with the advertising slogan "it's just a man thing" (23).

28. As Kon notes: "In the 2001 elections, the movement 'Unity' [*Edinstvo*] successfully positioned itself merging one with the other, the images of the *muzhik* and the bear—something clearly meant to connote masculinity and power" (2003: 394).

29. The group—and Shnurov, as the singer—make use of a derogatory term for homosexuals in one of their popular songs, "*Vybory! Vybory! Kandidati—pidori!*" ("Elections! Elections! The Candidates Are Faggots!") Although the song is intended to critique Russia's political system and not homosexuality per se, it is telling that the ultimate epithet used to impugn the process is one that is homophobic.

30. Kon gives the example of the magazine *Men's Health*—one of many Western publications available in Russia—as one avenue for the production of a new type of masculinity on Russian soil. According to Erofeev (1999: 9), "a man [*muzhchina*]—this is the kind of *muzhik* who found . . . his own identity and translated the concept into Russian" (in Kon 2003: 399). It is remarkable that Erofeev, in highlighting the Westernness of this transformation, uses the phrase "his own identity" in English.

31. Kon's assertion that the female gaze doesn't "count," and that the female has "nothing" is meant to highlight the devaluation of the female in the phallocentric/patriarchal system, not to confer worthlessness upon it. Additionally, Kon notes that such dynamics are dependent upon the specific historical and cultural situation of the body: "The individual perception of the nude body, as with the methods of its representation, are dependent upon a corporeal canon peculiar to a given culture, including characteristic prohibitions for it, taboo, norms of modesty, and many other instructions which may not be in different cultures, and which are one way or another connected with gender stratification" (1999).

32. Bannister (2006) discusses the problematics of the gaze vis-à-vis 1980s indie guitar rock, a genre of music that was, according to the author, remarkable for its reliance upon strict codes of masculinity. The lead singer's appearance as a gazed-upon sex symbol, however, often troubled the construction of such binary (masculine/feminine) codes.

33. See Baer (2009) for a more detailed reading of this film, as well as additional filmic and literary examples of male visibility in post-Soviet culture.

34. Bordo's (1999) definition of "action" is more inclusive than Kon's; for example, she notes the stare of the model ("the rock") as being a site of a certain type of action, suggesting that even the engagement of the viewer, via the spectacular body, is a form of action. Also, McDonald (1997), writing on the dancing male body in music video, suggests that such bodies have not only become so commonplace in contemporary music video as to have ceased functioning as a "feminized" object, but that, additionally, the dancing in some videos (for example, the band Take That, the focus of his study) reveals an engagement with issues such as romance, via a modality that is not reliant upon phallic power.

35. Although I am specifically drawing upon Merleau-Ponty's usage here, the term is perhaps most widely associated—in its phenomenological meaning—with Husserl. For Husserl, intentionality is a central concept of consciousness, whereby our perceptions are "of" or "about" something. For a detailed discussion see, for example, Smith and McIntyre (1982).

36. Merleau-Ponty is clear that such intentionality is rooted, in part, in embodied experience. Regarding, for example, "motor intentionality," he posits that "for the normal person every movement is, indissolubly, movement and consciousness of movement. This can be expressed by saying that for the normal person every movement has a *background*.... The background to the movement is not a representation associated or linked externally with the movement itself, but is immanent in the movement inspiring and sustaining it at every moment" (2002 [1962]: 127).

37. The work of Ukrainian video director Alan Badoev, for example, is rife with images of beautiful male bodies: VIA-Gra's "*Potselui*" ("Kiss") and "*Anti-geisha*," Verka Serdiuchka's "*Kiss pliz*" ("Kiss, Please"), and Maks Barskikh's "*Student*" all feature shirtless, attractive male bodies (in the case of Barskikh, his own). While Badoev is married (to a woman) the rumors about his possible homosexual orientation are common. Additional examples of Badoev's work are noted in the Epilogue.

38. One major difference, however, is that Ridgeley did not actually sing, while Topolov does.

39. An additional, albeit more attenuated, link between the group and homosexuality may be drawn from both Topolov's and Lazarev's previous membership in the children's singing group *Neposedy*, a group that also featured Iuliia Volkova and Lena Katina, who would later form the "lesbian" group t.A.T.u.

40. Here, the connection with homosexuality is not only Michael's song but also the Emperor himself. As Hinsch (1990) notes, "Although copious evidence exists to confirm the homosexuality of Puyi, final ruler of the Qing, the creative heterosexual love scenes in the acclaimed film *The Last Emperor* have created a lasting impression in both Asia and the West that Puyi zestfully took full advantage of his female concubines" (quoted in Norton 2005).

41. Such foppish outfits were in fact in vogue in Moscow in 2004, in terms of theatrical appurtenances to gay parties or clubs. For example, several similarly attired boy dancers were present at Moscow's DecaDance—a party sponsored by the gay website qguys.ru (discussed in Chapter 5)—and in the drag show *Fabrika grez* (*Factory of Dreams*) at Moscow's *Dusha i telo* (Soul and Body). For further discussion of *Fabrika grez*, see Chapter 5.

42. Some people have questioned whether this voice actually belongs to Fomin or is, in fact, that of Esenin. One source (Rybik 2000) avers that it is Fomin, citing a live performance in Moscow in which the singer "proved" it was he who actually sang. However, the same voice is heard on several tracks of Shura's *Skazka* (*Fairy Tale*) ("*Ne ver' slezam*" ["Don't Believe the Tears"], "Are You Ready?" "*Vechnost'*" ["Eternity"], and "I Know") for which Esenin was, as with Hi-Fi, the main composer, writing the

music for sixteen of the CD's eighteen tracks. A listener to a radio interview with the group on *Èkho Moskvy*, clearly having doubts about the origin of the voice portrayed as Fomin's, submitted an online question in which he asked Fomin if the voice in the recordings was his or Esenin's ("*Argentum*"). I discuss the question of Fomin's singing in the Epilogue.

43. For example, background vocals on "*Ia liubliu*" ("I Love"), "*Sh. No. 7*" ("Sh[anson] No. 7"), and "*Beda*," as well as some lead vocals on both "*Gliupye liudi*" ("Foolish People") and "Call me Misha."

44. The vocal tracks on both "*V poslednyi raz*" ("For the Last Time") and "*Ty pogliadi*" ("[You] Look") are obviously sung by a woman with a much lower voice than any of the other tracks; as such, it is clear that numerous female singers contribute to the vocal tracks of Hi-Fi's songs and, again, it is far from certain whether any of these voices belong to any of the women appearing on stage or in videos.

45. As one contributor to a listener's forum asked, after a radio broadcast devoted to Hi-Fi on *Èkho Moskvy*, "And what does Timofei do in the group? Not a sound can be heard from him. I understand, if he were a cute boy [*smazliven'kii mal'chik*] who would be nice to look at, but that guy—he doesn't fit with the group. Mitia and the girl together would look a bit better" ("*Argentum*"). It is notable that the commentator, "Veronica," identifies both of the men by name, but not the woman.

46. Larsen (2003) examines a similar dynamic of homosocial bonding in recent Russian film. For example, in Nikita Mikhalkov's 1997 *The Barber of Siberia*, the main emotional and physical contacts appear not between the protagonist, Andrei, and his girlfriend, Jane, but between Andrei and his fellow cadets. As Larsen notes, "central to . . . the film's concept of a heroic Russian masculinity . . . is the passionate bond that unites the cadets to one another." She further highlights the fact that "unlike the talky love scenes between Jane and Andrei, the cadets' love for each other is conveyed primarily through visual imagery, not words. . . . In contrast to Andrei and Jane's single love scene, very little of which depicts them in the same frame at the same time, the cadets are repeatedly filmed in one another's arms at moments of crisis" (502). On homosocial bonding and triangulation in 1980s indie guitar rock, see Bannister (2006).

47. Ahmed's arguments also extend to dynamics of race and suggest that the concept of whiteness—as the default "here," "proximate"—acts as just such a straightening device (2006b: 121).

48. Alsou placed second in 2000 with the song "Solo." Other Russian entries who have fared well in the competition, but have not won, include t.A.T.u (third place in 2003 with the song "*Ne ver,' ne boisia*" ["Don't Believe, Don't Be Afraid"]) and *Serebro* (third place in 2007 with "Song #1"). Russia's most successful singer for decades, Alla Pugacheva, appeared at Eurovision in 1997, placing fifteenth.

49. See, for example, the video to the song "*Mulatka*" ("Mulatta"), which features numerous instances of movements graphically representing sexual activity.

50. One internet site devoted to "hunky men" carried out a poll regarding Bilan's sexuality; the results showed that 65 percent of the site's visitors thought Bilan was

homosexual, 29 percent believed he was bisexual, and only 6 percent assumed he was heterosexual. The site's author suggests, "According to our readership, it's time Dima Bilan got out of the closet!!" (http://pictures.styledanvers.com/?p=193; link currently dead; accessed through http://styledanvers.blogspot.nl/2008/06/dima-bilan-is-gaywho-are-we-to.html; last accessed 21 August 2013). Although this is a site devoted to English speakers, there are numerous Russian language forums where the same sort of sentiments are expressed; the comments on such forums will be discussed later in this chapter.

51. Bilan is reported to have responded, "You know, I don't even know how to [answer] you. How to disappoint you or make you happy—I still don't understand. But the question is rather strange for me. . . . I don't even know how, in Russian, to speak further. It's a very odd question, which doesn't even have any sense, or any basis."

52. With such connections in mind, it is notable that Andrei Danilko, as Verka Serdiuchka, released the song "*Dol'che Gabbana*" in 2011.

53. The interview can be seen at http://www.russia.ru/video/baturin2/ (last accessed 21 August 2013). It is clear from Baturin's comments that there was, at the time of the interview, an acrimonious disagreement between himself and the singer regarding ownership of copyrights and, as such, his comments may certainly be read as an attempt to "smear" Bilan with the "taint" of homosexuality. Other articles, however, have similarly called into the question the authenticity of his relationship with Kuletskaia, suggesting that the two are more like "intimate girlfriends" than lovers (Rein 2009). In one journalist's opinion (quoted in Rein), "there is not even a hint of sincerity" in their relationship; "when they kiss, they do it in the manner of [Nikolai] Baskov and [Oksana] Fedorova"—here, making reference to yet another widely-perceived-to-be-gay Russian singer and his former Miss Universe (2002) "girlfriend." Yet another journalist (also quoted in Rein) asserts that "the emergence of beauties in [Bilan's] life had to be very opportune . . . rumors appeared with a vengeance about his nontraditional orientation."

54. The statistics listed under each video do not, of course, indicate how many *unique* viewers have opened a specific video, nor how many of them have viewed it in its entirety, only how many times the specific video has been accessed. As of 21 August 2013, the video (found at http://www.youtube.com/watch?v=lZOn5DMv5A4) had been seen 1,786,358 times.

55. The diminutives used here—Kolen'ka instead of Kolia for Nikolai, for example—is probably intentional, and these particular forms might almost be considered diminutives of diminutives, most often encountered with very young children; the relation to gay men thus connotes, obviously, immaturity, weakness, and possibly even femininity (where weak = feminine). Stryalko's not-so-tacitly homophobic "humor," based on stereotypes of gay men (overly emotional, sexually voracious and indiscriminate, effeminate, cross-dressing) would seem to support this.

56. The comments appeared on the otvety@mail.ru website, a Russian site similar to answers@yahoo.com (*otvety* = answers) (http://otvet.mail.ru/question/1986119/; last accessed 21 August 2013).

57. I should note that the video to DJ Gruv's song ("*Muzhiki ne tantsuiut*"), through the use of fierce drag queens and parodic representations of "real men," indicates unambiguously that he is critiquing, rather than condoning, these sorts of gender stereotypes.

58. The forum can be found at http://otvety.google.ru/otvety/thread?tid=2427d7 ad8368c41c (last accessed 21 August 2013). Another poster, in line with many of the vicious and homophobic comments on such forums, answers simply "because faggot and gay are synonyms" ("*potomu chto pidor i gei—sinonimy*").

59. Jarman-Ivens (2006), for example, suggests an inherent queerness in rap music based, in part, on the foregrounding of the artists' muscular/unclothed bodies.

60. On gayness in Eurovision see, for example, Raykoff (2007) and Lemish (2007).

61. Miazhevich (2010) considers this partial disrobing to be an "openly gay gesture" (258).

62. Not only are the viewers assumed gay, but the performers as well; see, for example, Haugh (2006) regarding the closet in men's figure skating.

63. Of course, the need to make such "high" culture comprehensible to "the masses" often involved a watering-down of the source material, a middle-brow approach often resulting in the well-known Socialist Realist kitsch. See Chapter 1.

64. The video appears to have been shot originally in an English language version, with the Russian language version coming afterward; those scenes in which numerous people are present while Bilan sings, have been reedited to avoid synching the audio with the video—that is, "hiding" the fact that Bilan is singing in English. Although the scenes in which he sings alone have obviously been shot with Bilan singing to both English and Russian texts, it seems clear that those that would have required additional capital (the group scenes) were shot only in English versions.

65. The text appears, surprisingly, only in the Russian version, not the English. It is possible that the awkwardness of the translation ("backbone" instead of "spinal," for example) may have become known to the producer and/or distributors, and was accordingly edited out.

66. On the question of demographics, see Chapter 3, note 80.

67. That the doctor in the video and the majority of the medical staff are portrayed by men is also remarkable, as work within the medical sphere in Russia is overwhelmingly coded as feminine. Such a reality is certainly related to the fact that women often are forced to take lower-paying positions, and remuneration for medical professionals in Russia is far below that in the West. As such, the casting of a male "doctor" is in keeping not only with the video's overwhelming valuation of masculinity, but also in line with Soviet propaganda that sought to demonize the "*babka*," a female practitioner of "folk medicine," entreating the populace to make use of "modern," "scientific" (and, in the visuals of the propaganda, overwhelmingly male) doctors (Bernstein 2007; see esp. 106–128).

68. Lordi—a hard rock band in theatrical monster garb—was both praised and reviled for their performances at Eurovision. Sylvia Night (stage name of Ágústa Eva Erlensdóttir) made headlines by throwing mock diva "hissy fits" throughout the competition, including a filmed paparazzi-type "interview" (after her loss) in

which she referred to other contestants as "sluts," and spewed obscenities at the assembled journalists. (The interview can be seen at http://www.youtube.com/watch?v=vd4ZHR_fSu4; last accessed 21 August 2013.)

69. Schütz, for example, suggests that music engenders a specific sort of time, an "inner time," one that is experienced differently from objective, "outer time." The phenomenological apprehension of such "inner time," experienced by groups of listeners and/or performers is instrumental in bringing about social relationships "founded upon the partaking in common of different dimensions of time simultaneously lived through by the participants" (1951: 96) (including "outer time").

70. *Stiob*, as defined by Yurchak (2006), is a late-Soviet "form of irony that differed from sarcasm, cynicism, derision, or any of the more familiar genres of absurd humor." It stood apart from a type of Bakhtinian carnivalesque parody, however, insofar as it "cannot be understood simply as a form of resistance to authoritative symbols because it also involves a feeling of affinity or warmth towards them" (250; quoted in Miazhevich 2010: 254).

71. According to Miazhevich, performers such as Bilan "ironise the global media's obsession with gay culture using a manufactured 'western' homoeroticism in order to flatter (Western) European viewers, and at the same time knowingly disparage the West's cultural imperialism for the benefit of domestic audiences. Bilan—a Russian heterosexual performer—presents himself as a 'global gay.' . . . The fact that the fakery remains largely 'uncovered' by the Western public is part of the very point of the performance" (2010: 260).

72. According to Kon, "so far as women practically until the last third of the twentieth century did not have the right to discuss male nudity, and heterosexual men were embarrassed by it," only the homosexual gaze (*vzgliad*) could bring the male body to the foreground, a body in which "the aesthetic relationship . . . was indissolubly entwined with the erotic" (2003: 274).

73. Lazarev also appeared at the club Gay in London in the same year and at *Tsentral'naia stantsiia* (Central Station)—then a newly opened gay club in St. Petersburg—in 2011. Former bandmate Topolov had also been slated to appear at the latter club, but backed out upon learning it was a gay club (and was later sued). Topolov claimed that he had nothing "in principle" against gays, but should have been "warned" in advance about the specifics of the club's patrons. One journalist in the gay internet press archly noted that how the singer generally goes about finding out the sexual orientations of his audiences is unreported. See "*Topalov sryvaet*"; "*Vlad Topalov kinul*"; and "*Vlad Topalov otkazalsia*."

74. See Ivanov 2006; "*Sergei Lazarev*." See also fn 19, supra.

75. Fomin, for example, appeared on the cover of *Kvir* in March of 2009. See also the Epilogue.

Chapter 5. Gay-Made Space

1. Tuan makes a sharp distinction between space and place, the former defined by its abstraction, undifferentiation, and freedom, the latter by concreteness, stability,

and security, the former suggesting movement, the latter suggesting pause. Massey, however, is skeptical of such a split seeing both as co-constitutive.

2. *Kalendar'* (*Calendar*), a weekly listings magazine devoted to events in St. Petersburg, was taken over in 2004 and gradually changed its name over to the new trademark. As such, for several months, the front cover featured both names (Календарь/*TimeOut*, in a combination of Cyrillic and Latin script), while inside the cover a complete duplicate was found, absent the Cyrillic, but including the line "*skoro my smenim nazvanie*" ("soon we will change our name"). In Moscow, the publication was titled *TimeOut* from the first issue.

3. The guide appeared in the 27 March–2 April 2006 issue.

4. A small note on the bottom left corners of both covers alerts the reader that one issue is the "*muzhskoi variant oblozhki*" ("the masculine variant of the cover"), the other the "*zhenskii*" ("feminine"). While the majority of listings were geared toward gay men, rather than lesbians, the few existing establishments for the latter were also listed (for example, *Trièl',* the only lesbian bar/club in the country at the time, located in St. Petersburg).

5. In Petersburg, for example, movie theater *Dom kino* (The House of Cinema), located in the town's historic center, was listed under the "*Posmotret' kino*" (Watch Cinema) section—the only one listed. Although there was nothing manifestly "gay" about the establishment, it was the one place in Petersburg where "art" films, many of them produced outside of Russia, were shown, and it was also notable for its numerous retrospectives of films of famous directors. It should be noted that this "mapping" of gayness in the former capital was not the first instance of such; a youth organization, *Molodezhnaia assotsiatsiia HS*, in both 2002 and 2004 published a "gay map" (*gei-karta*) of St. Petersburg.

6. The magazine's name, which makes obvious reference to bisexuality (rather than specifically homosexuality) seems to have been connected to the editorial staff's desire to reach as wide an audience as possible; in Russia, judging by anecdotal evidence as well as the opinions of my informants, the number of men who term themselves "bisexual," despite the fact that the majority (if not all) of their intimate/sexual contacts are with other men, is considerable, probably due to social proscription. The magazine's contents, however, were notable for the fact that virtually all images and articles were of or devoted to men (including, in the case of the former, photographs of sexualized male bodies, the female counterparts of which were seldom seen).

7. Initially, *Kvir* was available only by mail (from the gay.ru online "store"), or at limited locations in major cities—generally, gay clubs or bathhouses, or "sex" shops. In 2005, however, the magazine became much more widely available, and its associated website offered a map of all Metro kiosks in which it might be purchased. In St. Petersburg, all but four of the city's Metro stations were noted to have been "stocked" with the magazine, although it is likely that not all of them carried it at all times. Additionally, availability became greater outside Russia's two largest cities as well, and in such places as Ekatarinburg, Vladivostok, and Omsk, *Kvir* was said to have been available for purchase—although here, again, such sites were generally limited to "sex"

shops and/or clubs. Several of my informants noted other magazines which, while not geared specifically for gay men were, due to their having been considered "stylish," "international," or "hip," read by homosexuals. Gleb, for example, described *Om*—a magazine devoted to music, style, film and so forth—as "not officially gay, but read by many gay people," and the magazine *Mir* was similarly considered to be popular with a gay readership. An online version of *Kvir* became available early in 2013.

8. Grosz (1999) uses the term *interface* to explain the dynamic between body and city, one she contrasts with both the "causal" (human consciousness, operating through the body, creates cities) and the "representational" (cities are constructed to mirror the construction of the body) theories. Additionally, Ahmed (2006b) notes how for the queer subject, "bodily direction 'toward' objects shapes the surfaces of bodily and social space" (68). Shilling (2008), drawing upon the work of Bachelard (1964), Ingold (2004), and Tilley (1994), highlights the same mutually constitutive interaction, whereby bodies assimilate geographic details into their "muscular consciousness," as well as leaving their imprint upon the surfaces of the geography, "carving out grooves, affecting where plants can grow and gradually wearing down hard material surfaces" (86).

9. For examinations of gay urban space see, inter alia, Forest (1995); Higgs (1999); Sibalis (2004); and Turner (2003).

10. On the influence of the market economy on the creation of gay communities, see Peñazola (1996).

11. As noted in Chapter 1, Gleb did have access to private space, but preferred not to use it on a regular basis. I should note that not all my informants had a desire for "communal living," however. For example, Konstantin was in the process of purchasing his own apartment, something about which he was very excited and something that would enable him to live on his own, rather than with his mother and sisters (his then-current living situation). And Petr, a violist, lived happily on his own in a small apartment in St. Petersburg, one that he had inherited from a family member. Petr's case is instructive, insofar as it indicates that the ability to procure space was not always contingent upon earning power.

12. On the "imaginary" uses of the rural/urban dichotomy in the formation of gay identity—that is, the association of urban sites as gay spaces—see Weston (1998). See also Chisholm (2005) and Herring (2010).

13. Maksim, for example, who had moved from a small city in central Russia, considered himself fortunate to have made his way to St. Petersburg, not only for social but for economic reasons. In his opinion, "if I had stayed in [my hometown], there would have been no way to earn a living; I'm very lucky to be here."

14. I note "in theory," as I was acquainted with a few people in both St. Petersburg and Moscow who were living there illegally, hoping to either navigate through the system, via bribes, and receive the necessary papers, or simply to purchase counterfeit residency permits.

15. For example, in late 2004, flocks of protesters took to the streets of St. Petersburg in response to Putin's changes in "social welfare" programs, many of which

impacted negatively on pensioners. Under the new legislation many elderly people and/or veterans lost benefits related to public transportation and medical care. The protest march, which I attended, and which progressed up *Nevskii prospekt* (one of St. Petersburg's main, central streets) featured numerous groups of senior citizens carrying banners and signs in support of communism—a system under which, in their estimation, their needs had been met.

16. Dobrenko (2004), for example, noting that everyday "realities" in the Soviet (Socialist) space were substituted by representations of "Socialism"—the signifier taking the role of the signified—states that, "The peculiarity of Soviet culture was that the object of the substitution was the here-and-now. This was a special kind of modality—not replacing the present with the future but representing the future as the present" (700).

17. Healey notes that "the first commercial baths appeared in Moscow in the mid-1600s, and laws demanded scrupulous segregation of the sexes. Authorities differ on how rigorously men and women were separated, and on the extent to which the *bania* represented a desexualized space in Russian culture. Regulations decreeing separate facilities for men and women created a homosocial environment that enabled male prostitution in a later era" (2001b: 242). It is, however, certainly possible that sexual encounters, either commercial or mutually agreed upon, could have existed far before the later eighteenth century. Healey himself notes that "urban spas staffed by beardless youths were probably sites of mutual male sexual relations long before the recorded instances of the nineteenth century" (243).

18. Healey notes that "[a]lthough few references to this trade in Moscow appear in forensic texts or the city court records . . . there are enough discussions of the phenomenon in St. Petersburg baths to suggest that what [was] encountered at the bathhouse in Moscow persisted and flourished until the 1917 revolution" (1999: 45).

19. The fact that Pavel was the "patient" of a psychiatrist should not necessarily indicate any sort of mental illness; rather, it is an illustration of the growing medicalization of homosexuality in pre- and post-Revolutionary Russia. Later, when male homosexuality was criminalized, it was lesbian women who were put under the "care" of doctors, lesbianism being deemed not a crime but a psychological/medical disorder. The type of "treatment" such women received, however, was probably not any more humane than men's experiences in prisons (on this see, for example, Essig 1999, esp. Chapter 2).

20. Healey, for example, contrasts information contained in the 1861 court case (as well as the diaries) of a man named Medved'ev with that found in Pavel's psychiatric records of the early 1900s. But Medved'ev's accounts that he would have had sex with either a man or a woman, that the sex of the partner was subordinate to the act itself, must be must be accepted with some caution, understanding that one's own internalized prohibitions may prevent a full "disclosure"—may, in fact, invite a "masking"—of one's desires, even in the putatively "private" sphere of a diary. Furthermore, Healey notes that Prince Iusupov, one of Pavel's "sponsors," was also known to have sexual relations with both men and women. If, in fact, there was a movement of sexual desire from something polymorphous to something more binarized (homosexual/

heterosexual), with a concomitant creation of a sexual-object–based identity, these accounts cannot be taken as incontrovertible proof of this; at the very least, they are simply too scant to allow any sort of certainly regarding such conjectures.

21. Healey notes that "by 1908, one jaundiced critic was able to map the daily routine for 'an entire band of suspicious young people,' the male prostitutes he considered part of the 'little homosexual world'" (2001b: 248).

22. For example, as Baer (2000) notes, it is lacking in any sort of documentary evidence, such as citations or bibliography. Baer also critiques the work for focusing almost exclusively on the elite strata of Russian society, thus engendering the author's "'rose-colored' look at Russia's gay past," one Baer finds "unjustified" (2000: 186). In his view, "for anyone who has read Konstantin Romanov's anguished diary account of his personal battle against his 'secret vice' or Petr Ilyich Tchaikovsky's tortured letter to his brother in which he declares his intention to wed, unable to bear the idea that he could be a source of shame to those who love him, Rotikov's insouciant tone seems out of keeping with the realities of gay life in Russia—both then and now. Indeed, the author's decision to publish his work under a pseudonym suggests precisely the concerns left largely untreated in his history" (186). The view of Tchaikovsky as "tortured," however, is not universally shared; see, for example, Poznansky's (1991) biography, in which the composer is portrayed as a man who is not only sanguine about and relatively at peace with his sexual orientation, but one whose sexual encounters were often the source of much pleasure and happiness. See also Poznansky (1998).

23. Healey (2002a), for example, argues against the presumption that "Moscow's policing of homosexuals was more totalitarian and therefore more relentlessly efficient than that of London, New York City, or even Nazi Berlin" (368).

24. One such site, the toilets located on the banks of the Moika river, not far from the Church of Our Savior on the Spilled Blood (*Khram Spasa na Krovi*), was pointed out to me by Gleb. They have now been converted to a restaurant.

25. Healey (2001a) notes that under Soviet rule, male homosexuals "occasionally managed to use domestic or other semiprivate venues (halls, cabarets) to gather. Parties, masquerades, and artistic performances brought scores of men together to socialize and be socialized, and make sexual contacts" (44). Additionally, parties held by a "pederasts' club"—one of which was raided in 1921, resulting in the arrest of ninety-five men—appeared to have been, according to the statements of some of those arrested, relatively common occurrences (45–46). Although it may appear surprising, some of my informants recounted their experiences as homosexual men under Soviet rule to have been generally positive, and in fact denied that there had been any real persecution of homosexuals. Both Gleb and Kirill, for example, said that it was extremely rare for men to have been convicted of homosexuality; rather, according to them, accusations of homosexuality, whether true or not, were levied against those seen as dissidents but against whom "legitimate" charges were lacking.

26. The *Kat'kin sadik/zadik* is apparently known not only by gay men, but by at least some members of the general populace as a *pleshka*. This became clear in the fall of

2004, when the monument itself was "profaned with a swastika and an inscription 'death to gays'" (Gusarenko 2004).

27. While in St. Petersburg in 2003 and 2004, one gay club—Rush—opened and closed within the span of a year. This was not uncommon, according to my informants, who noted that places appeared and disappeared regularly, although they disagreed as to the cause. Some thought that there were simply not enough people with money to support them (through attendance) on a regular basis, while others claimed it was related to harassment by the police, governmental offices, and/or organized crime. Moscow, in comparison with St. Petersburg, boasted far more bar/club-type establishments—around ten or so—but witnessed the same dynamic of regular openings and closings.

28. As with other imported parts of the gay lexicon, the term *gay-friendly* is also used, either in English or in its transliterated form (рей-френдли, *gei-frendli*), often in conjunction with clubs and parties. For example, a series of Sunday dance parties held at the club Jaba Bar in 2007 in St. Petersburg were advertised, on gay websites, using just this term. That DJs Kosinus and Slutkey, the pair who released the *Gay CD* and *Gay CD Blue Edition* (see Chapter 2), were the ones spinning at the parties no doubt added to the perception that homosexual men would be welcomed.

29. In St. Petersburg, such sites included, for example, the cafés on *Malaia Sadovaia*, a few yards from the *Kat'kin sadik*, or the restaurant *Ingbir'* (Ginger); or, in Moscow, the café located off the lobby in the hotel *Pekin* (Peking).

30. Gleb, with whom I went to the *Iamskie* on a couple of occasions, told me that many of the gay men at the *bania*—most of whom had at least a passing acquaintance with one another—would generally take up a collection of a few rubles per person, and use this as an "incentive" for the manager to open the door leading out of the steam room and onto the back stairs of the building. Here, men could have sex relatively free from the worry of intrusion by those who did not know what was occurring (and who might not take kindly to it). Although I cannot know with certainly whether men were engaging in safer sexual practices, my discussions with some informants revealed that the vast majority of them knew what such practices entailed and, additionally, most men claimed to follow them. However a few, although they claimed to know about "safe sex" (*nebesopasnyi seks*), seemed to have an incomplete understanding of the concept, and did, in fact, engage in higher-risk behaviors; Kolia, for example, said he practiced anal intercourse without a condom, if he felt his partner was a "good person." And although another informant said he both understood and practiced safe sex, he also evidenced a certain ignorance about certain aspects, telling me once that he had decided not to have sex at the *Iamskie* because the lights were out on the stairs, and he "couldn't see if the person was healthy or not."

31. Entrance fees at clubs, running anywhere from three hundred to five hundred rubles, were likewise out of reach of many of my informants.

32. This particular song was in keeping with the New Year's holiday as the film from which it came is shown every year on New Year's Day—several times, all day—all over Russia. "*S legkim parom*" may be literally translated as "with a light steam," but it implies good wishes.

33. Because of the intense heat of the *bania*, many visitors choose to cover their heads with wool or felt hats, specially made for this purpose, and immediately recognizable due to their shape: somewhat pointed at the top, with a floppy "brim" around the forehead and ears.

34. Beating the body with a *venik* while at the *bania* is said by Russians to be beneficial to one's health by promoting better circulation and opening pores (allowing impurities to escape), among other things. Additionally, it is seen as improving the skin itself, due to the release of essential oils from the plants' leaves. In St. Petersburg, *veniks* were on sale not only at the *bani* themselves, but also in stores and on the streets.

35. The duo itself was not a favorite with my informants, and their self-presentation is decidedly aggressively heterosexual. It is notable that their website's home page for a period of time indicated a gendered musical split as well—specifically, the split between *popsa/èstrada* (feminine) and *rok* (masculine)—via the highly visible words (in English), "Fuc*in Rock n'Roll." Although the duo does largely perform pop and dance music, this latter genre is not "feminized" (or "gayed") the way it often is in the United States, because dance music is widely disseminated and listened to by both gay and straight people in Russia. Suggesting an intended audience (or perhaps a differentiation from a reviled homosexual audience), many dance music compilations in Russia, as well as some in Europe and the United States, feature images of scantily clothed, sexy women as the visual accompaniments to the sounds—for example, on jewel box covers, or accompanying YouTube uploads.

36. On musical repetition, see Kivy (1993). Kivy finds that "absolute" music "does not merely contain repetition as an important feature, but as a defining feature" (359). "Musical repeats . . . perform an obvious and vital function in that they are the composer's way of allowing us, indeed compelling us to linger; to retrace our steps so that we can fix the fleeting sonic pattern" (352). Although Kivy's discussion focuses on "absolute" (classical) music, many of his observations are transportable to examinations of popular musics as well.

37. Music's ability not only to detemporalize, but, in the Deleuzian sense, to deterritorialize as well, is addressed briefly in Chapter 6.

38. The use of "Moorish" styles was evident in other "trendy" locations in Russia, including the club Jet Set (with branches in both St. Petersburg and Moscow), the restaurant/club M on St. Petersburg's *Nevskii prospekt*, and the gay sauna *Nartsis*, located in the same city.

39. The group's moniker refers to a drug-laced drink in the film *A Clockwork Orange*, and is also the Russian word for milk.

40. Although some women were present at both clubs, their attendance was discouraged, in part, by door policies that charged them prices almost or more than double those of men. Clubs such as *Greshniki* and *Kabare* were thus quite different from other *miks* establishments in St. Petersburg such as *Monro* or *Metro*, whose clienteles included both men and women. *Mono*, a tiny and ostensibly *miks* club in the city as well, also had a clientele made up largely of gay men.

41. Andrei was not the only person who assumed *Greshniki* to be a site for the "dissolute." On one of my first visits to the club, having met a man named Georgii

and having spent some time speaking with him, I was approached by another young man, Valera, who asked if Georgii was my "*boifrend*." When I said that he was not, that we had only just met that evening, he warned me to be careful, as "some of the guys here work in pairs—they'll put something in your drink, and when you're out, they'll rob you." At first I assumed this to be a warning applicable only to foreigners who might look like targets. Later, however, I learned, through other informants, that while not common, similar things could happen to Russians as well, especially if they had compromised their faculties by having drunk too much.

42. The building has since been renamed a "*dvorets bouling i bil'iard*" ("palace of bowling and billiards"), an appellation announced by large, yellow, neon letters around its dome.

43. In 2005, due to the expansion and renovation of the nearby *Mariinskii theatr*—an expansion that necessitated the demolition of the *dvorets*—*Kabare* was forced to move twice within the following months. My discussion of the club is in reference to its 2004 location.

44. On any given weekend night, for example, no more than five to ten customers appeared to be foreigners, even during the height of the summer's tourist season.

45. *Kabare* did, however, ultimately develop a website in the years following my fieldwork in Russia, a small segment of which is in English.

46. Other "texts" were visible in the logos of the companies that were displayed, such as Lacoste or Abercrombie and Fitch.

47. *Greshniki* was also seen as having more male hustlers, possibly due in part to the fact that they attracted (or were assumed to attract) more Westerners.

48. Other songs that were frequently played included Jennifer Lopez's "Jenny from the Block," Britney Spears's "Toxic" and "My Prerogative," Madonna's "Hollywood" and "Love Resurrection," The Sugarbabes's "Caught Up in the Middle," and Usher's "Yeah!"

49. Additionally, several songs from the Eurovision song contest were played, including Dana International's "Diva," Ruslana's "Wild Dances," and Iuliia Savicheva's "Believe Me." Although all songs were in English, the last two performers have a connection with Russian audiences: Ruslana, winner of the 2004 competition, was the contestant from Ukraine, and Savicheva was Russia's contestant in the same year. The playing of songs from Eurovision was something I encountered at gay clubs in other European cities—namely Helsinki and Reykjavík—although in these locations it was, unsurprisingly, the Scandinavian contestants who were favored.

50. Other songs in frequent rotation from *Fabrika zvezd* included Irina Dubtsova's "*O nem*" ("About Him"), Iuliia Savicheva's "*Vysoko*" ("High") and "Believe Me," and Iurii Titov's "*Ponaroshku*" ("For Fun"). Both "*O nem*" and "*Vysoko*" were originally recorded as ballads rather than dance tracks and, although they might be played in dance-style remixes, they were also played at their original, slower tempos at various times throughout the evening, offering an opportunity for close, intimate dancing. While the majority of Savicheva's output was sung in Russian, "Believe Me," which she performed to an international audience at Eurovision in 2004, was recorded in English.

51. Other songs by Russian (and Ukrainian) artists included *VIA-Gra* and Valerii Meladze's *"Pritiazhen'ia bol'she net"* ("No Greater Attraction"), Dima Bilan's *"Ty tol'ko ty"* ("You, Only You") and *"Ia tak liubliu tebia"* ("I So Love You"), Filipp Kirkorov's *"Zhestokaia liubov'"* ("Cruel Love"), and the group *Chai dvoem*'s ("Tea for Two") *"Den' rozhdeniia"* ("Birthday"). As with those songs from *Fabrika zvezd*, several of these were also ballads.

52. During this time period, Serdiuchka's most popular tracks included *"Khorosho"* ("Good"), *"Zhenikha khotela"* ("She Wanted a Fiancé," a duet with Natasha Inova, lead singer of the group *Gliuk'oza*), and *"Chita drita."*

53. The extent to which Serdiuchka's nationality, as a Ukrainian, marked her as "other" was not universally agreed upon by my informants. Some expressed the belief that Russians and Ukrainians were completely different, culturally, linguistically, and historically, while others, although certainly cognizant of the fact that Ukraine and the Ukrainian people were not Russian, believed they were nonetheless extremely close in terms of culture. It was this supposed deep cultural connection to Russia that led many of them to be angered at Ukraine's turn to the West during the Orange Revolution.

54. Songs frequently played included *"Grustnye skazki"* ("Sad Fairy Tales"), *"Vse resheno"* ("Everything Is Decided"), *"Begi ot menia"* ("Run from Me") and *"On chuzhoi"* ("He's Another's").

55. As noted in Chapter 2, however, the group did make occasional use of English and/or French in several of their songs of that period, such as *"Liubi menia po-frantsuzskii"* ("Love Me in French") Their more current songs such as "Mama, Good-Bye," (entirely in Russian save for the phrase that is the song's title) and *"Ia tvoia kiska"* ("I'm Your Pussycat") have also made use of the English language, while *"Ia tebia tozhe net (Je t'aime)"* ("I Also Don't [Love You]") includes lyrics in French (see Chapter 2 note 28).

56. One of the group's most famous songs, *"Begi ot menia"* was widely believed—by both my informants and, judging from articles in the press, many of the general public—to be about lesbianism, leading many to question Pol'na's sexual orientation. Pol'na, much like singers Moiseev, Leont'ev, and Danilko, has generally been equivocal when discussing her sexuality (see Amico 2009).

57. Oleg, however, was a fan of the Russian duo *Nozh dlia Frau Müller* (A Knife for Frau Müller), whose music drew upon the various aesthetics of lounge, dance, retro, and cheese, among others. The duo was probably among the more sophisticated purveyors of popular music and was not widely played on either radio or television. The name of the group, written with both Cyrillic and Latin characters (Нож для Frau Müller) graphically indicates its placement on the border of "domestic" and "foreign," something underscored by their use of music styles and samples from both "locations" as well.

58. Christy noted that one of her favorite performers is Madonna. According to her, Madonna was "everything that is modern, and absolutely one of the most creative artists. Everything that is new and exciting, she does."

59. It is notable that DJ Partyphone, although highly talented as a turntablist, and certainly a person with a high regard for music, was less interested in details such as correct attribution of styles or even names of groups. For example, during our interview, he used descriptive monikers (such as "house") to describe a myriad of different styles, and was not always sure of the names of records he was spinning—either their titles or their producers/performers.

60. Some of the artists he mentioned were dance music creators An2, Step2Sun, and SCSI-9, as well as pop group A'Studio (А-Студио); regarding the last group, he said that he listened to them "once in a while" but added that he would never play them while working as a DJ.

61. DJ Partyphone, in fact, contrasted *Propaganda* with another locale at which he was working, one that catered to just such "new Russians"—the club *Tabu*. According to him, the establishment was really more of an expensive restaurant than a club, and a place in which music occupied "third place."

62. Although *Metro* was often ostensibly a "straight" club, Monday nights at one time were widely known to be nights for gay and/or bisexual men as well, largely owing to the amateur, male striptease contests.

63. According to the group's originators, the show has traveled throughout Russia, and has generally met with a very positive response (Kirsanov 2003).

64. Both clubs, additionally, had a *temnaia komnata* (dark room) where sexual encounters could be initiated and/or consummated.

65. The term refers to New York City's Chelsea district, one of the city's "gay ghettos." There, many of the men adhere to such a hyper-"masculine" style of dress and comportment.

66. Zhenia also said, however, that *Kabare* was, at the time we spoke, in the process of hiring a new art director, and that he had heard—through friends who were in the business—that they were attempting to change their format, to become more "hip."

67. Many of St. Petersburg's more fashionable clubs were, during the period I lived there, although ostensibly for heterosexuals, at least somewhat "gay-friendly." According to informants, this continues to be the case currently.

68. The term *sponsor* (identical in Russian, *sponsor*) may be roughly translated as "sugar daddy."

69. Lingis here draws largely upon Mishima's *Sun and Steel* (2003 [1970]).

70. While illegal drugs were sometimes consumed by customers at gay clubs in Russia, my observations (as well as the opinions of my informants) seem to indicate that drugs such as ecstasy, cocaine, or crystal meth—all popular drugs among certain segments of gay communities in the West—were not terribly prevalent; it was, rather, alcohol that was sometimes consumed to excess in these clubs. The relative paucity of such party drugs was explained to me by some informants as being reliant upon several possible factors. Some suggested drugs were difficult to obtain or simply too expensive, others that the fondness for alcohol over drugs was a "cultural" dynamic in Russia, and still others that the cognizance of draconian punishments for the possession and use of illegal drugs served as a powerful disincentive.

71. See, for example, Bell (2001) and Ryan and Fitzpatrick (1996).

72. *Pleshki*, of course, are also sites where gay men might congregate to express sexual desire in the context of others with similar desires. They are, however, quite obviously different from clubs in several regards including, not at all incidentally, the absence of music, a main site of affective production.

73. Whether or not the DJs were, in fact, "the best in the capital" is certainly debatable, as much of the mixing was fairly egregious. Throughout the evening there were repeated instances of records skipping, clumsy fade-outs, and a jolting slowing of the beat of one track to segue (awkwardly) into another. The situation was not helped by the extremely poor sound system, which could handle neither the very lowest or highest frequencies of the music, often producing feedback and buzz.

74. The site was founded in 2002, and originally marketed to English speakers (as qguys.com). However, by 2003, it became geared largely toward CIS countries, a move reflected in the membership figures. For example, on the site in 2005 there were approximately 29,000 registered users from the United States, 27,000 from Russia, but only 2,500 from the United Kingdom. France, at approximately 600 members, had about the same numbers as both Latvia and Estonia (whose populations are much smaller), and nearby Finland had only about 150 members. By 2011, however, there were approximately 35,000 members from the United States, but over 157,000 from Russia, 38,000 from Ukraine, and 4,000 from Kazakhstan. It is notable that the site is allied with several other enterprises that might certainly count the "gay consumer" among their clients, including gay travel agencies (bluway.com and sistertrip.com), hotels and vacation rentals in Moscow (atlantahotel.ru, euroflats.ru), and a discount airline booking site (russiatogo.com).

75. A previous party, also hosted by the site and also in Moscow, was held at the *Sad èrmitazh* (not to be confused with the Hermitage museum in St. Petersburg), another large hall.

76. Additionally, several of my informants used other international meeting sites not specifically aimed toward CIS countries. There were (and are) also numerous Russian-language sites not primarily devoted to meeting in existence, offering everything from LGBT-themed news items (for example, gaynews.ru and gayrussia.eu) to online gay videos. The site xsgay.ru is devoted to gay life in St. Petersburg, and gayly.ru focuses largely on Moscow; several smaller cities, such as Tomsk, Murmansk, and Tiumen', however, also have (or have had) their own gay websites, as do several former Soviet republics with large Russian-speaking populations (such as Belarus and Kazakhstan).

77. There is also a sister site geared specifically toward lesbians, lesbi.ru.

78. Another online radio station, gayradio.ru, claims on its website to have been in existence from 2002. Moreover, a search on google.ru for "*gei radio*" (гей радио) will bring up several additional similar sites, including *Moskovskoe gei radio* (Moscow Gay Radio). One online station, the aptly named gaymusic.ru, appeared to be in the works as well throughout 2011; however, despite an announcement on the home page that it was to have been inaugurated in June of 2011, the station failed to materialize, and the site was down by August of that year.

79. Perhaps one of the most widely publicized instances of illegal download-

ing concerned the now-defunct website allofmp3.com (later mp3sparks.com and memphismembers.com), run by Moscow-based Mediaservices Inc. The catalog was international in scope, and members could download tracks for the relatively low price of approximately eight to ten cents per track. The site closed in 2007, partially under pressure from American trade negotiators, who warned that the site's continuing alleged infringement of copyright might jeopardize Russia's inclusion in the World Trade Organization (see Crampton 2006a, 2006b; Sandoval 2007). Currently, it is possible to download music, free of charge, from any number of Russian sites, which can be found by typing a few key (Russian) words—in Cyrillic, not transliterated—into virtually any search engine.

80. In late 2006, Anton took gaysongz.narod.ru off the Internet; the home page of miditext.ru was blank for several years, save for the announcement "site is under reconstruction" ("*sait nakhoditsia na rekonstruktsiia*"). With the plethora of websites offering free lyrics to virtually any song imaginable, it was unlikely that miditext.ru, at least in its former guise, would be resurrected. As of late 2012, the address belongs to a site named *Novosti na segodnia* (*News of the Day*).

81. The site, although it has a completely different layout and graphics, appears to be hosted by the gay.ru site (erectrofon.gay.ru; last accessed 14 August 2013). Many of the articles listed under the "*muzyka*" ("music") rubric on the latter site link to items on the former.

82. As discussed in Chapter 1, although the editor of *Kvir* claimed that the magazine was not geared solely toward a homosexual male reader, the imagery in and content of the magazine does in fact more than suggest that such an audience was courted, as does the very suggestion that the magazine might be instrumental in the formation of a "gay life."

83. I was present at a "Eurovision Party" in St. Petersburg in 2003; the majority of the guests were gay men, with several women present as well. That year, many had hoped for a strong showing for Russia, via their representation in the contest by the group t.A.T.u. (whose performance for the evening omitted their usual faux-lesbian kissing). Much to the disappointment of the majority of people present, the group finished third, behind Turkey (first place) and Belgium (second place).

84. These last two shows are musical "variety" shows featuring many of Russia's most famous singing stars from both *popsa* and *èstrada*.

85. The show and its contestants were also featured in gay Russian magazines such as *XXBi*. See, for example, Fandeev (2004).

86. For example, on one readers' forum dedicated to *Fabrika zvezd*, several visitors commented on Veselov's supposed homosexuality, both in positive and negative terms. Postings of a positive nature included "Mishan'ka, all the gays of the country are for you," and "Gays are with you! Hold on," while negative comments included "in one word: faggot," and, in reference to the singer's relatively high tenor, the tessitura was "probably like that because he doesn't have any balls [*iaits*]" (http://www.theforum/ru/reality/FabrikaZvezd/MihailVeselov.html; link currently dead). Veselov, a performer since childhood, and from a musical family (his mother was a singer in the ensemble of Lev Leshchenko, one of the most famous *èstrada* singers of the

Soviet era, and his father was a musical director and musician) is currently singing with the group *Novye samotsvety* (New Gems) headed by Inna Malikova.

87. Although transgender role reversal is uncommon in general, among the Russian songs I have surveyed for this study I have found three instances of the female taking on the role of the male: Anna German's performance of "*Vykhozhu odin na dorogu*" ("I Will Leave Alone for the Road"), in which the singer is grammatically male ("*odin*," the masculine, as opposed to "*odna*," the feminine); Klavdiia Shul'zhenko's "*Sinii platochek*," in which the singer takes on the role of the male soldier remembering his female beloved; and Alla Pugacheva's "Primadonna," the Russian entry at the Eurovision Song Contest in 1997, originally written for a man. Pugacheva stepped in to perform the song at the last minute, when the scheduled male singer (probably Valerii Meladze) became ill. I have not found any instances of men taking on the role of the female.

88. The term was used by Karl Heinrich Ulrichs in an 1864 pamphlet entitled *Vindex*.

89. Certainly many gay men, in Russia no less than in the West, may adopt hypermasculine styles, and may abjure any suggestion of the "feminine" in their self-presentation. However, this does not erase the fact that many gay men—again, both in Russia and the West—may playfully refer to themselves or their friends via feminine pronouns or slang (*tetki*, for example), and that drag artists are often a constituent part of gay clubs and/or performances.

90. Both the use of a pseudonym and the fact that "Pravdin" partially obscures his face in the photograph accompanying the article highlight the fact that even in the early part of the twenty-first century, gay Russian men were cognizant of the fact that "coming out" might engender extremely negative consequences.

Chapter 6. Conclusion

1. Several gay organizations appeared with the dissolution of the Soviet Union, but the vast majority have ceased to exist; for an overview, see Essig (1999: Chapter 3). Many were accused of having squandered the large amounts of Western money they had received on personal expenditures and, whether true or not, some in contemporary Russia feel that even the perception of misappropriated funds have made it much more difficult to find financial backing from the West today. In my interview with Kukharskii, he stated that "in the beginning in the '90s when there were much more lesbi-gay organizations in Russian than now, most of them were headed by not very socially adapted people. Alcoholics, drug addicts—and their main goal was to attract as much money from the Western interest in the Russian gay community at that time, as possible, and to misuse this funds. And our organization, [it] was keeping its good name—and vice versa, I can tell you for sure, its existence I mostly supported by my personal money—because I am sure that such type of organization should exist, if we Russians want that our civil society will be founded" (Interview with Aleksandr Kukhuarskii, St. Petersburg, 21 December 2004). Kukharskii went on to tell of a supposed embezzlement or misappropriation of funds (approximately

$85,000) donated by ILGA in 1995 for the formation of three gay community centers in St. Petersburg, Moscow, and Tallinn. Because of this, he maintained, it would be virtually impossible to get funding from the West in the future. I should note, however, that although Kukharskii implicated one ILGA member by name, another person with close connections to the organization categorically denied the claims he made.

2. See http://www.krilija.sp.ru (last accessed 7 August 2013).

3. For example, according to Kukharskii, in 2002 the group instituted a mass mailing to members of the Russian parliament in order to counteract proposed antigay legislation that was being discussed within the government at that time; the legislation, however, having to do with "pornography" (the *duma* sought to make possession of nude pictures of boys under eighteen a crime, while members of Kril'ia sought to keep the age at sixteen, in line with "heterosexual pornography") was unlikely to gather much support, financial or otherwise, from the West. Copies of the information sent to the politicians are memorialized in one of the center's publications, *Apollon (Apollo)*.

4. I should note that none had ever met Kukharskii personally and were basing their opinions on information they had heard through friends and acquaintances.

5. My own experiences in trying to register my visa and place of residence seem to bear this out. An exasperatingly labyrinthine process, it required the assistance of several Russian friends, a few thousand rubles, meetings with unknown people to receive "official" documents, and more than one box of candy offered to various civil servants. Russian friends who were living in St. Petersburg illegally recounted similar experiences in their attempts to obtain the necessary "official" documents.

6. The association's website, which was functioning during a portion of 2003 and 2004 was, as of 2005, no longer in operation; likewise, its email contact ceased to function at approximately the same time. The "HS" of the moniker, indicating the group's desire to be inclusive of all sexual orientations, stood for "Homo Sapiens, Homosexual and Heterosexual"—but also included, despite the inability to fit, acronymwise, bisexuals. The group, founded by students of the St. Petersburg State University, took part in international gay events, including Stockholm Pride in 2001, and joined both ILGA and ILGYO (the International Lesbian and Gay Youth Organization) as a provisional member.

7. I met Fialkovskii shortly before leaving from St. Petersburg and, due to our schedules, unfortunately had very little time to speak with him. Through email, however, he told me that he is no longer involved with the group.

8. In his discussion of Merleau-Ponty's placing of experience as primary to perception, Hass notes, "consciousness is in the first place not a matter of 'I think that' but 'I can'" (2008: 159).

9. See, for example, Hass (2008: 91–99) and Grosz (1994: 103–111), both of whom highlight the extent to which any discussion of gender is absent from Merleau-Ponty's work. Here, although the body is postulated as the "universal" body, it is revealed to be not "all," but male.

10. See Chapter 1, note 7.

11. Human rights abuses are not, of course, limited to homosexuals in Russia; in fact, Russia has the second-highest number of appeals pending in the European Court of Human Rights in Strasbourg ("European Court of Human Rights"). Putin's moves in 2005 to limit the activities of NGOs in Russia—in part through draconian registration procedures and strict limits on funding by foreign capital—likewise caused alarm among some human rights advocates (Buckley 2005).

12. The antipathy toward others in the context of a perceived sense of subjective instability has also been studied from a psychological standpoint. For example, in a review of several experiments, Solomon, Greenberg, and Pyszczynski (2003) found that when subjects are subconsciously made to reflect upon their own mortality, they exhibit far more negative reactions to those they perceive as being different from themselves.

13. Interview with Aleksandr Kukharskii, 21 December 2004.

14. Interview with Igor' Kon, 4 December 2004.

15. See Chapter 1, fn 36.

16. See, inter alia, Adam, Duyvendak, and Krouwel (1999); Aldrich (2003); Blasius (2001); D'Emilio (1983a, 1983b, 1992, 2002); Drucker (2000a, 2000b); Fuss (1991); Hawley (2001); Warner (1993, 2002); and Weeks (2000).

17. Baer notes that Russian academic Lev Samuilovich Klein asserted just such a "political motivation" behind his imprisonment (2005: 24). Two of my informants in St. Petersburg—both over forty—even suggested that Article 121 was not, in fact, used in order to punish homosexuals, but used explicitly for the types of purposes Klein suggests.

18. Of such groups, Kukharskii expressed the opinion that "it's very difficult to conclude is this a real activity or this is only internet activity. Because some groups, maybe it's one man only, they just expose themselves that they are very active, but the activity is only in the internet, which is a virtual activity, not a real activity" (Interview with Kukharskii, 21 December 2004). In keeping with Kukharskii's assessment, I should note that there were other gay and lesbian "organizations" in cyberspace, but that the majority of attempts to reach several of them over a period from 2003 to 2009—either via phone or email—failed. Additionally, some of them appeared on the internet, only to remove their pages in a matter of months.

19. Appeals to Luzhkov to allow the parade also emanated from the West, and also connected the event to the ECHR. In a letter from Paula Ettelbrick, the executive director of the International Gay and Lesbian Human Rights Commission (IGLHRC), the mayor was informed that "the European Court of Human Rights has held that discrimination based on sexual orientation is a violation of the ECHR. Not only is this ban a breach of both the ICCPR [International Covenant on Civil and Political Rights] and the ECHR, it additionally directly contravenes the Russian constitution." The author goes on to relate such discrimination to Russia's relationship—financial and otherwise—to the West, stating "we would also like to point out that at stake is Russia's reputation as a member of the Council of Europe and as a host of the G8 summit this summer" ("Russia: Mayor Luzhkov"). The international gay and lesbian

communities have, in fact, tied the granting of equal rights to sexual minorities to inclusion in the European Union, cautioning those governments guilty of human rights abuses that such actions might jeopardize member status. According to ILGA, for example, "Turkey has made wide-ranging reforms aimed at bolstering human rights and individual freedoms as part of its EU bid. But the EU says the reforms must also be fully implemented" ("Kaos GL Association").

20. Mishin also contributed to the highlighting of the issue of gay marriage by attempting to register a marriage between himself and human rights activist and deputy of the Bashkortostan parliament Eduard Murzin (Gessen 2005; "*Odnopolye braki*"; Petrov 2005b). That the marriage was wholly fictitious was clear, in part, from the fact that Murzin was married and heterosexual; indeed, both men stated that the goal was only to highlight the problem, and to push for legislation allowing marriage to all citizens. Although ostensibly meant to help the "gay community," some members viewed the attempt as nothing more than publicity, a stunt that would ultimately cheapen and harm the fight for legitimate, same-sex marriages (Alekseev 2005).

21. According to the man from whom I received my books, the online store received hundreds of orders weekly. Because of its situation in a residential building, and its status as a "business," however, the center faced eviction early in 2005, which some assumed to have been brought about not because of any sort of legal infraction but, rather, homophobia. The group's commercial practices were subsequently moved to a public site—the store *Indigo* in Moscow, which was originally to have been a gay "cultural center" (Terskii 2004).

22. The third "b," in Russian, is "*bliadstva*" (singular *bliadstvo*) meaning, as noted, "fucks."

23. Volodia's response was received via email, as news of the parade surfaced after I had left Russia. Italics indicate those words he had written in English. Kliment, Senia, and Nikita, all of whom lived in Moscow, and all of whom I had corresponded with via email or chat sites, were also generally against the idea of a parade, due largely to the fact that in their opinions Russia was "not ready" for such an event.

24. For a more detailed account of gay and lesbian political movements in Eastern Europe in the same volume, see Long (1999).

25. SETA's website defines the group as the "national human rights organisation in the field of legal equality and social justice for sexual and gender minorities such as lesbians, gay men, bisexuals and trans-people in Finland" (www.seta.fi; last accessed 17 August 2013).

26. Interview with Jussi Nissinen, 27 May 2004. It is interesting to note, in terms of the concept of an "international" "gay community" that Finns—according to both Nissinen and gay Finnish men with whom I spoke—have almost no contact with Russian gay men or organizations, despite their close geographic proximity. Part of this is, in the opinion of both Nissinen and other Finnish contacts, related to the conflicts between the two countries during World War II and the death of tens of thousands of Finnish soldiers and civilians. But Nissinen felt that, "these wounds we have, we have to treat them somehow; it's not treated that we get so silent about

it, it must be taken openly. I think in some years we must meet this problem, what we have, what's the problem with us—with Russians. I think it must be taken on the table some way."

27. Additionally, Adam, Duyvendak, and Krouwel (1999) contend that "processes of international diffusion play a significant role" in the formation of gay and lesbian movements, continuing that such movements "do not 'invent the wheel' again" (368). In short, they see a "transnational diffusion" in which "gay and lesbian movements all around the world influence and imitate each other" (368).

28. It is important to note that while Schluter's work was published in 2002, his research took place over a decade earlier, placing his analyses in approximately the same time frame as those of Gessen (1994).

29. The absence of social structures may, according to Schluter, be related—unsurprisingly—to the historical suppression and punishment of homosexuals in Russia, the proscription of public gatherings of homosexuals, and a still-present homophobia in contemporary Russian society.

30. See, for example, among many others Connell and Gibson (2003); DeNora (2000); Djumaev (2005); Green (2003); and Frith (1996).

31. Adam, Duyvendak, and Krouwel, for example, suggest that "[t]he very idea of a movement by homosexual people becomes imaginable only if people have sexual identities" (350).

32. Connections may be made here between worth/transcription (read: writing) in music, as well as the social sciences in general. Clough (1992), for example, notes a masculine bias in ethnographic writing, one related to (Oedipal) narrativity and one that attempts to erase desire while concurrently reifying sexual difference. That the creation of the "masculine" authority is often tied up with the taming of a putatively restive feminine is, again, an example of the alignments that are often constructed in which the "masculine" (transcribable) side is valued, and the "feminine" (untranscribable) is debased.

33. The importance of the "feel" of music—something that cannot be fully communicated via prescriptive notation—has been discussed, inter alia, by both Keil (1966, 1994) and Washburne (1990). It is notable that transcription also figured in the Soviet relationship to the various, largely non-Russian republics. As MacFadyen (2006) notes, Soviet Russians' attempts to solidify political control in Uzbekistan often included control over cultural, including musical, production, as well: "Once Asian harmonies were on paper and transcribed in recognizable forms, the first substantial intrusion of Slavic musical mores could begin" (44). In consort with the "control" afforded by notation, however, were other means of controlling musical production via the linguistic. First, the Soviets attempted to change texts of Uzbek songs, discarding "trivial" subjects such as romance, and replacing them with more civic-minded lyrics (47). And second, they sought to "explain" the development of Uzbek music in a manner keeping with their own political and cultural agendas. According to MacFadyen, "these simplified views of musical development served one purpose. They lay the theoretical foundation for explaining and substantiating cultural enlightenment in the nineteenth century, becoming a template for the way

Russians wished to remember and interpret their own contributions to local custom" (44). More recently, in the twenty-first century, Russian courts have sought to make Cyrillic the official alphabet of all regions, despite protests coming from, for example, the republic of Tatarstan (Danilova 2004).

34. Lerdahl (2003), for example, notes the congruence between the phonological attributes of both music and speech. See also Feld and Fox (1994) for an exhaustive review of the literature.

35. Blacking notes that, "music-making is not entirely a human invention created as part of an ideology of social life: it also resulted from the discovery and use of a set of interrelated capabilities as intrinsic to defining an organism's humanity as its capacity to speak a natural language. The essence of music is non-verbal and hence cannot be conceived as a product of word-based ideological construction" (1992: 310).

36. See, for example, Hisama's (2001) discussion of formal attributes of "the twist" in Ruth Crawford's *String Quartet*—that is, a transgression of the common hierarchy of instrumental voices—and of unconventional hand positions in Marion Bauer's *Toccata*. In both cases, such devices may be seen as a questioning of gender-related power; as Hisama notes, in the case of Bauer's work, "power is not wielded by only one party as a means of control of a weaker party, but flows in both directions" (106).

37. Currid (1995) notes how the use of the anterior aesthetics and artifacts of disco—reassembled in the present, in house music—serves as a way of circumventing such teleological conceptions and, concurrently, questioning authenticity. In his view, "House serves as a site where queers create historical narratives of continuity across time and space, centered around the continuous production and consumption of meaning in these musical signifiers. At the same time . . . [it] provides an alternative to unilinear white middle class understandings of queer history" (173).

38. Stokes (1997), for example, focusing on music in Istanbul, finds that the various interactions of popular, Turkish art, and national folk (*halk*) musics produced a questioning of time, place, and gender, often in the context of "nostalgia" juxtaposed against modernity. In his estimation, "musical experience builds on this kind of knowledge, since it deals so insistently with time and repetition" (687), noting the inherent "paradox" that "what is repeated can never be exactly the same" (687).

39. One of the most unabashed attempts by an artist to capitalize on past successes by adherence to stylistic attributes of the initial success may be heard in a string of hits released by singer Katia Lel' in the first decade of the century. Her exceptionally popular song, "*Moi marmaladnyi*" ("My Jelly Candy," and also known informally by the title "*Dzhaga-dzhaga*") was followed by "*Musi-pusi*," and then "*Kruchu-verchu*" ("I'm Twirling, I'm Spinning"). The songs are similar not only in their titles (hyphenated couples of two-syllable assonant words) and their lyrical content ("love" that makes the narrator "dizzy"), but their harmonic and melodic content as well. In all three, the harmony is based upon tonic-dominant relationships, and there is a pronounced use of chromatic harmony and/or nonharmonic tones—for example, the use of seventh and/or ninth chords in each, the addition of the supertonic to the tonic triad in the first song, and the use of secondary dominants in the second and third songs. This chromaticism is evident not only in the harmonies, but in the

melody lines of the first two songs as well. An additional melodic similarity is that all three songs feature a descending melody line leading to the cadence in the chorus (and, in the case of the first, also in the verse). Lel"s fourth single was "*Ruli-ruli*," which differed from the first only marginally more than the second and third. The discernment of these similarities was not dependent upon advanced musical training; remarking, for example, on "*Musi-pusi*," Gleb laughed, asking me, "have you heard it? It's just like ['*Moi marmaladnyi*']—it's *the same song!*"

40. Kon also notes the idea of nostalgia in contemporary Russia, finding that it is often used in consort with militarism and fascism; see Chapter 5, p. 141.

41. The refusal to implicate the body in the reception of popular (or any other) music is often tied to privileging such "masculine," public spheres as the political; indeed, Zuberi (2001) rightly highlights the valuing of the such spheres, noting that "for theorists of popular music, the sixties may have been the worst thing ever to have happened: because some small percentage of the music produced during those few years articulated protests against the Vietnam War or class oppression, our attention has been distracted from the issue more consistently fought over in popular music—even during the paradigmatic decade. More than that, in positioning the physicality of music in opposition to whatever the political substance of the 'real stuff' was supposed to be, such theories reinscribe the polemics against the body that have characterized attempts at policing music throughout western history" (70). Shiraev and Danilov's (1999) discussion of contemporary Russian popular music seems to typify just such a stance, valuing the socially aware music of Russian rockers, while dismissing those musics related to dancing (read: the body).

42. On identity in post-Soviet Russia, see inter alia, Clowes (2011); Fitzpatrick (2005); Olson (2004); and Tsygankov (2012).

43. This was a "live" (lip-synched) performance, included on the DVD *Alla Pugacheva: The Best Video* (2001).

44. The song did, however, feature the standard harmonic progressions examined in Chapter 2.

45. See also Tishkov and Olcott (1999), who contend that with the dissolution of the Soviet Union, and the emergence of ethnically based rights discourses, the question of a "national identity" in Russia has become fraught with difficulties. As both they and Kon (1993a) note, an unfortunate consequence of such identity-based instability may also lead to particularly virulent forms of nationalism and xenophobia.

46. As Green (2002) suggests, queer theory's valuing of subversion ignores the essentiality of social structures in the formation of identity among nonheterosexual persons. While his argument focuses on the extent to which labels such as "gay" and "lesbian"—rather than "queer"—may be integral to the definition of those structures to which individuals are allied (and in relation to which their identities are formed), and not concerned with the family, his highlighting of the extent to which "subversion" is theorized absent context is apropos.

47. See, for example, Buchanan (2004) on the Deleuzian concept of "strata." In Buchanan's view, "outside strata neither forms nor substances, organisation nor development, content nor expression, exist. It is a chaotic, disarticulated realm not even

supported by the minimal connection of rhythms. Life cannot obtain there. So while destratification is constantly courted for its liberating effects, one must nevertheless proceed with caution because moving too quickly can result in profound psychosocial disconnection, autism, catatonia, even death" (6).

48. Kon had been a visiting scholar at Cornell University, Harvard University, Wellesley College, and the University of Southern California.

49. Healey (2002b) suggests that authors such as Zhuk (1998) attempt to "[distance female homosexuality] from the Soviet-era criminality and vulgarity it is associated with in the popular imagination, and [realign it] with a 'higher' (and older) national tradition"; moreover, Rotikov (1998), in relation to male homosexuality, attempts to "persuade a metropolitan readership of the contributions that homosexuals have made to Russia's intellectual life" (367).

50. Baer, with reference to Berberova's (1997) biography of the composer suggests that Tchaikovsky remains "for many Russians the archetype of the suffering, solitary Russian (homosexual) artist" (2009: 100). Taruskin (2009) in a deliciously and appropriately savage article examines the genesis and perpetuation of Tchaikovsky's pathologization via what appears to be, by all accounts, rather unrigorous (and wholly homophobic) musicological enquiries, largely by British academics. In Taruskin's estimation, "many people, it seems, simply cannot bear the thought of a homosexual man enjoying life" (98). See also Brown (2002).

51. Shilling here is making reference to the experience of Holocaust and gulag survivors, places in which "prisoners were no longer treated as embodied *subjects*, with the right to exercise agency, but as enfleshed *objects* that were to be turned in the most efficient manner possible into units of production" (131). He offers that survivor accounts often noted the ritual of washing one's self as "most important as a symptom of remaining vitality, and necessary as an instrument of moral survival" (Levi 1987: 46; in Shilling 2008: 136). Ceasing to care for one's body was often an early sign that an inmate was to become a *Muselmänner*, one who had given up and been reduced to lifeless flesh (133; 136).

Epilogue

1. See Ivanov and Besfamil'naia (2012).

2. See "State Corporation Head" and "A Just Russia."

3. See Barry (2012); Herszenhorn (2013); and "Russian Blogger Navalny." Following his conviction on 18 July, Naval'ny was released only one day later, and is currently (as of 7 August 2013) free while preparing his appeal.

4. The word *vykhod* is probably better translated as *exit* (as a noun) or *leave* (as a verb, *vykhodit'*); however, taking into account the site's internet address, it is clear that the organizers have chosen the word to mean *coming out*. Judging from internet searches and informant contacts, it appears the term—usually encountered transliterated into Cyrillic (каминг-аут, *kaming-aut*)—is becoming more widely used by Russian speakers.

5. The home page of the group *Vykhod*, for example, notes that the organization is "fighting for equal civil rights, and the acceptance of LGBT [persons] (lesbians, gays, bisexuals, and transgenders) by society," while the Rossiiskaia LGBT"s webpage

includes as its first aim "to achieve recognition and respect by the government for the collection of rights and freedoms that are minimally essential to uphold the human dignity of LGBT people, and for the further realization of human rights activities." The former site, according to one of its informational brochures, has connections to ILGA Europe, Stockholm-based Civil Rights Defenders, and the Heinrich Böll Stiftung, among other Western organizations, and the latter notes that its activities have included the preparation of reports on the situation of LGBT people in Russia for the United Nations, the Council of Europe, and the OSCE (Organization for Security and Co-Operation in Europe).

6. The arrest, trial, and convictions of three members of the band (Mariia Alekhina, Ekaterina Samutsevich, and Nadezhda Tolokonnikova) has also garnered considerable attention from the West, including pop star Madonna (see Herszenhorn, Michaels, and Weaver, all 2012).

7. See http://queerfest.ru/queer.php (in Russian); last accessed 7 August 2013.

8. See http://queerfest.ru/queer.php (in English); last accessed 7 August 2013.

9. The definition can be found on the main page of the website.

10. Source: WorldBank (http://www.google.com/publicdata/explore?ds=d5bncppjof8f9_&met_y=it_net_user_p2&idim=country:RUS&dl=en&hl=en&q=internet+usage+russia; last accessed 7 August 2013). Citizens' increased access to information via social media in particular has troubled some in Russia's government. For example, presidential Security Advisor Nikolai Patrushev suggested that "the internet was being used by unspecified sources 'interested in aggravating the socio-political situation,'" leading some to worry about a possible crackdown on access to social media sites (de Carbonnel 2012).

11. See, for example, the website of the *Federatsiia LGBT-Sporta Rossii* (http://gay-sport.ru; last accessed 30 June 2013). The group sponsored a Winter Sport LGBT Festival (*Zimnii sportivnyi LGBT-festival'*) around Moscow in early 2012, an event advertised on *V Kontakte* (the Russian version of Facebook). HIV and AIDS information can be found at the websites of *Parni Plius* ("Guys Plus [positive]," http://parniplius.ru; last accessed 7 August 2013) and *Profilaktika VICh/SPIDa v Rossii* ("Prevention of HIV/AIDS in Russia," http://o-spide.ru). While the first site is geared toward LGBT persons, the second is addressed to a general audience, with a special section for men who have sex with men. It is notable that this section, previously freely accessible, now requires (as of September 2012) registration in order to receive a username and password, clearly a result of the passage of statutes outlawing the dissemination of "gay propaganda" to minors (noted supra).

12. I was also able, via the Google search engine, to find the names of songs simply by typing in a small portion of lyrics I might have heard (on the radio, at a restaurant, at a club), something that was simply not possible when I was conducting research in Russia.

13. The clip may be viewed at http://www.youtube.com/watch?v=QAptnsSt49Y (last accessed 7 August 2013).

14. See Grigor'ev (2010).

15. See "*Moiseev posle insul'ta.*"

16. Photographs may be found, in addition to numerous other sites, at Ukraine's *Khochu* (http://hochu.ua/cat-stars/novosti-shou-biznesa/article-28375-boris-moiseev-zhenilsya-na-molodoy-devushke-foto/#slider_top); Russia's *Lady* (at mail.ru) (http://lady.mail.ru/article/470328-boris-moiseev-zhenilsja-na-zhenshhine/); and Estonia's *Bublik* (http://bublik.delfi.ee/news/glamour/foto-boris-moiseev-zhenilsya-na-zhenschine.d?id=64652688) (all last accessed 7 August 2013).

17. See the entry at http://bmoiseev.com/news/boris-moiseev-nachal-podgotovku-k-svadbe (last accessed 7 August 2013).

18. The event may be seen at http://www.youtube.com/watch?v=gZlbDnoIaNU (last accessed 7 August 2013).

19. The filming of what was apparently meant to have been the video for the song—a video that has yet to materialize—was presented on the Ukrainian television show *ProNovosti*, and may be found at http://www.youtube.com/watch?v=Ql4Y6lSdXig (last accessed 7 August 2013). An audibly and visibly different, poststroke Moiseev appeared on *NTV Utrom* on 25 April 2012 in order to publicize the CD; the interview and performance, which garnered only 3,429 views on YouTube (as of August 2013), may be found at http://www.youtube.com/watch?v=LOSby7I6jaA.

20. The video may be found at http://www.youtube.com/watch?v=TS3CKexGvsc (last accessed 7 August 2013).

21. See, for example, "*Bienie serdtsa*" ("Beating Heart") or "*Zachem pridumali liubov'*" ("Why Was Love Invented?"). Despite the inclusion of a (supposed) female love object in both clips, however, neither features the type of unbridled, "steamy" sexuality between the actors/singer that one might expect in songs purporting to be about heterosexual passion.

22. On the implications of Lazarev's homosexuality, see Poltavskaia and Sorokin (both 2012). On the purported causes of the breakup between Kudriavtseva and Lazarev, see Krylova (2012) and "*Kudriavtseva ofitsial'no.*"

23. See Iastrebov (2011). It is probably not coincidental, in the context of the writer's comments, that he chose to pair an item on Lazarev with one on *Eurovision*.

24. See, for example, "*Tak ne byvaet*" ("It Doesn't Happen"), "*Gore zima*" ("Sorrow, Winter"), "Not That Simple," "Take Me with You," "*Po param*" ("In Pairs"), "*So mnoiu ty*" ("You with Me"), "*Zadykhaius'*" ("I Suffocate"), and "*Liubov'—suka*" ("Love Is a Bitch") (with t.A.T.u. vocalist Iulia Volkova) (Bilan as sexual object); "Safety" (with Anistacia), "*Ledi*" ("Lady"), "Not That Simple," "*So mnoiu ty*," or "*Po param*" (Bilan and female love object); "Take Me with You," or "*Zadykhaius'*" (Bilan in "masculine" roles).

25. See, for example, "*Vse budet khorosho (la-la-la)*" ("Everything Will Be Good," also released as an English-language version, "It's Gonna Be OK"); "*Ogni bol'shogo goroda (Paninaro)*" ("The Lights of the Big City"); "*Sadovnik*" ("The Gardner") and "*Perezimuem*" ("We'll [Spend] the Winter") (Fomin's body as sexual object); "*Dve zemli*" ("Two Lands"); "*Perezimuem*," with rapper StuFF and model/"dancer" Gaetcha; "*Vse budet khorosho*," with rapper StuFF and ex–Hi-Fi "band mate" Oksana Oleshko [Ksiusha]) (triangulation); and "*Perezimuem*" and "*Sadovnik*" (Fomin and female love object).

26. A censored version of the video may be seen on YouTube (http://www.youtube.com/watch?v=S6qffaGItOQ; last accessed 21 August 2013), while the uncensored version has circulated on Russian social media.

27. The group's four original members are Kirill Fedorenko, Stas Pavlov, Oleg Zhezhel' (all Ukrainian), and Artur Gasparian (born in Armenia and trained as a dancer in Russia). All four men are, in fact, trained professional dancers, with Zhezhel' responsible for having brought the group together. In 2011, Pavlov left the group for a period of months, and was temporarily replaced by Italian Francesco Borgato until his return. The group was featured in 2012 in Madonna's video for the song "Girl Gone Wild."

28. See the club's website at http://malevich-club.ru/about.html (last accessed 7 August 2013).

29. According to one press account, the owner of the building, the All-Russian Society for the Blind (*Vserossiiskogo obshchestva slepykh*), unilaterally terminated the lease due to complaints of lawlessness on the part of the club's patrons, as well as infractions of the health and fire codes (Boiko 2009).

30. The *Iamskie bani* are still in existence as well, and still caters, on certain days, to gay men.

31. St. Petersburg's *Trièl',* the country's one bar expressly for lesbian women for several years, is still in operation, and has been joined by another, *Kapriz.* Another establishment, the *Art-kafe SAFO* has also recently opened.

32. The first such law was passed in the Riazan' district on 22 April 2006.

33. See Stout (2012) and Vasil'ev (2012). The statute itself may be found online (in Russian); see "*Zakon Sankt-Peterburga no. 238.*"

34. See Berezina (2012).

35. The entire text of the statute may be found, in Russian, at http://base.consultant.ru/cons/cgi/online.cgi?req=doc;base=LAW;n=148269; an overview in English may be found at http://www.gaylawnet.com/laws/ru.htm (both sites last accessed 21 August 2013). See also Elder (2013) and Grekov (2013).

36. For example, two anti-Putin protests—one, in April, preceding the law's passage, the other, in August, following it—were held in Amsterdam, both of which drew thousands of supporters and activists. Mayor Eberhard van der Laan was on hand at the second event, in clear and vocal support of the protesters.

37. For example, in one incident, a fifteen-year-old boy was taunted and physically attacked by a group of homophobic teenagers who ultimately attempted to pour a bottle of urine over his head. The abuse was filmed and posted on Russian social media (see McCann 2013).

38. See "Gay Parades Banned," "Gay Pride Parade Banned," "*Mosgorsud priznal zakonnym,*" "*Mosgorsud zapretil,*" and Zlobin (all 2012).

39. The Court's judgment was issued on 21 October 2010, becoming final on 11 April 2011 after a rejection of the Russian government's referral request to the Court's Grand Chamber. The judgment in the case (*Alekseyev v. Russia,* Applications nos. 4916/07, 25924/08 and 14599/09) may be accessed by searching the database at the European Court of Human Rights's website (www.echr.coe.int; last accessed 7 August 2013).

40. An overview of the events of the day's planned actions may be found at Alekseev's website (http://www.gayrussia.eu/gayprides/moscow/2009.php, in Russian; http://www.gayrussia.eu/en/pride/moscowpride/2009.php, in English; last accessed 7 August 2013).

41. The press conference may be viewed at http://www.youtube.com/watch?v=X3HURTFXqYU (last accessed 7 August 2013).

Works Cited

Adorno, Theodor. 1990 (1941). "On Popular Music." *On Record: Rock, Pop and the Written Word* (ed. Simon Frith and Andrew Goodwin). New York: Pantheon Books. 301–314.
Ahmed, Sara. 2006a. "Orientations: Toward a Queer Phenomenology." *GLQ: A Journal of Lesbian and Gay Studies* 12(4): 543–574.
Ahmed, Sarah. 2006b. *Queer Phenomenology: Orientations, Objects, Others*. Durham: Duke University Press.
"A Just Russia Leader Believes Political Changes Are at Hand." *Èkho Moskvy Radio/ BBC Monitoring International Reports*, 1 June 2012.
Aldrich, Robert. 2003. *Colonialism and Homosexuality*. London: Routledge.
"Aleksandr Novikov: '. . . pederasty—trusy i nedocheloveki'" ("Aleksandr Novikov: '. . . Fags Are Cowards and Subhumans'"). gay.ru, 13 October 2004 (http://www.gay.ru/news/rainbow/2004/10/13-4223.htm). Last accessed 21 August 2013.
Alekseev, Nikolai. 2005. "*Fiktivnyi gei-brak v Moskve: fars goda*" ("A Fictitious Gay Marriage in Moscow: Farce of the Year"). gaynews.ru, 15 February 2005 (original link currently dead; accessed through http://www.sxnarod.com/index.php?showtopic=161865). Last accessed 17 August 2013.
Alekseev, Nikolai (Alekseyev, Nikolay). 2013. "Fighting the Gay Fight in Russia: How Gay Propaganda Laws Actually Only Help." *Russia Today*, rt.com, 24 August 2013 (rt.com/op-edge/russia-gay-rights-sochi-945/). Last accessed 25 August 2013.
Aleksei II. 2006. "*Pis'mo patriarkha Moskovskogo i vseia Rusi Aleksiia II meru Moskvy Iu. Luzhkov po povodu idei povedeniia v stolitse gei-parada*" ("Letter of the Patriarch of Moscow and All Russia, Aleksei II, to the Mayor of Moscow, Iurii Luzhkov, on the Idea of Carrying Out a Gay Parade in the Capital"). interfax.ru, 16 March 2006 (http://www.interfax-religion.ru/?act=documents&div=364). Last accessed 21 August 2013.
Al'perina, Susanna. 2004. "*Zhenikha khotela, vot i zaletela: Andrei Danilko zapisal s GliukoZoi novyi khit*" ("She Wanted a Fiancée, and Then Flew Off: Andrei Danilko

Has Recorded a New Hit with GliukoZa"). *Rossiiskaia Gazeta*, rg.ru, 2 April 2004 (http://www.rg.ru/2004/04/02/Serdyuchka.html). Last accessed 17 August 2013.

Altman, Dennis. 1996. "Rupture of Continuity? The Internationalization of Gay Identities." *Social Text* 14(3): 77–94.

Amico, Stephen. 2006. "Su Casa es Mi Casa: Latin House, Sexuality, Place." *Queering the Popular Pitch* (ed. Sheila Whiteley and Jennifer Rycenga). New York: Routledge. 131–151.

Amico, Stephen. 2009. "Visible Difference, Audible Difference: Female Singers and Gay Male Fans in Russian Popular Music." *Popular Music and Society* 32(3): 351–370.

"*Andrei Danilko: Kakaia liubov'? Mne prosto negde znakomit'sia!*" ("Andrei Danilko: What Love? There's Simply No Place to Meet"). newsmusic.ru, 11 June 2008 (http://www.newsmusic.ru/news_3_11363.htm). Last accessed 17 August 2013.

"*Andrei Danilko: 'Serdiuchka nikogda ne budet zhlobikhoi*'" ("Andrei Danilko: 'Serdiuchka Will Never Be Boorish'"). *Chas*, chas-daily.com, 15 January 2005 (http://www.chas-daily.com/win/2005/01/15/g_019.html?r=33&). Last accessed 17 August 2013.

Anmegichean, Maxim. 2006. *Moscow Pride March 27 May 2006: Detailed Account of the Events* (Report prepared by ILGA Europe) (http://www.ilga-europe.org/home/guide/country_by_country/russia/moscow_pride_27_may_2006/gay_pride_events_in_moscow_erupt_in_violence_moscow_militia_fails_to_ensure_order). Last accessed 17 August 2013.

Aparicio, Frances, and Cándida Frances Jásquez. 2003. *Musical Migrations: Transnationalism and Cultural Hybridity in Latin/o America*. New York: Palgrave Macmillan.

"*Argentum: Gruppa Hi-Fi*." *Èkho Moskvy*, echo.msk.ru, 3 April 2005 (http://www.echo.msk.ru/programs/argentum/35493/q.html; link currently dead). Last accessed 21 January 2009.

Artem. 2004. "Verka Serduchka [sic] Named Honorary Transsexual of Ukraine." *Ukraine Now*, ukrnow.com, 21 August 2004 (http://www.ukrnow.com/index.php?option=content&task=view&id=398; link currently dead). Last accessed 21 January 2007.

Arutunyan, Anna. 2009. *The Media in Russia*. Maidenhead, U.K.: Open University Press.

Atkins, Dawn, ed. 1998. *Looking Queer: Body Image and Identity in Lesbian, Bisexual, Gay, and Transgender Communities*. New York: Haworth Press.

Atkins, Dawn. 1999. "Body Image." *The Encyclopedia of Gay Histories and Cultures, Vol. 2* (ed. George E. Haggerty). New York: Garland.

Attali, Jacques. 1985 (1977). *Noise: the Political Economy of Music* (trans. Brian Massumi). Minneapolis: University of Minnesota Press.

Austern, Linda Phyllis. 1998. "'For, Love's a Good Musician': Performance, Audition, and Erotic Disorders in Early Modern Europe." *Musical Quarterly* 82: 3–4 (Special Issue, "Music as Heard"): 614–653.

Austern, Linda Phyllis. 2002. "Introduction." *Music, Sensation, and Sensuality* (ed. Linda Phyllis Austern). New York: Routledge.

Avdeev, Sergei. 2005. "*Ieromanakh zaslonil prokhod k Moiseevu svoim telom*" ("A Monk Has Covered the Passage to Moiseev with His Body"). *Izvestiia*, izvestia.ru, 22 November 2005 (http://izvestia.ru/news/308545). Last accessed 17 August 2013.

Bachelard, Gaston. 1994 (1964). *The Poetics of Space* (trans. Maria Jolas). Boston: Beacon Press.

Baer, Brian. 2000. "The Other Russia: Re-Presenting the Gay Experience." *Kritika: Explorations in Russian and Eurasian History* 1(1): 183–194.

Baer, Brian. 2002. "Russian Gays/Western Gaze: Mapping (Homo)Sexual Desire in Post-Soviet Russia. *GLQ* 8(4): 499–521.

Baer, Brian. 2005. "Engendering Suspicion: Homosexual Panic in the Post-Soviet Detektiv." *Slavic Review* 64(1): 24–42.

Baer, Brian. 2008. "Texts, Contexts, Subtexts: Reading Queerness in Contemporary Russian Culture." *Kultura* 2: 3–8.

Baer, Brian. 2009. *Other Russias: Homosexuality and the Crisis of Post-Soviet Identity*. New York: Palgrave Macmillan.

Baer, Brian. 2011. "Body or Soul: Representing Lesbians in Post-Soviet Russian Culture." *Journal of Lesbian Studies* 15(3): 284–298.

Baev, Nikolai. 2006. "*'Petukhi' protiv geev*" ("'Cocks' against Gays"). gayrussia.ru, 10 June 2006 (http://www.gayrussia.ru/events/detail.php?ID=5408&phrase_id =57692; link currently dead). Last accessed 1 June 2012.

Bakhtin, Mikhail. 1982. *The Dialogic Imagination: Four Essays* (ed. Michael Holquist; trans. Caryl Emerson and Michael Holquist). Austin: University of Texas Press.

Bannister, Matthew. 2006. *White Boys, White Noise: Masculinities and 1980s Indie Guitar Rock*. Aldershot, U.K.: Ashgate.

Barabash, Ekaterina. 2003. "*Propoved' v stile miakogo porno*" ("A Sermon in the Style of Soft Porn"). *Nezavisimaia Gazeta*, ng.ru, 26 May 2003 (http://www.ng.ru/culture/2003-05-26/8_kann.html). Last accessed 17 August 2013.

Barker, Adele Marie. 1999. "The Culture Factory: Theorizing the Popular in the Old and New Russia." *Consuming Russia: Popular Culture, Sex and Society since Gorbachev* (ed. Adele Marie Barker). Durham: Duke University Press. 12–45.

Barry, Ellen. 2012. "Russia Charges Anticorruption Activist in Plan to Steal Timber." *New York Times*, nytimes.com, 31 July 2012 (http://www.nytimes.com/2012/08/01/world/europe/aleksei-navalny-charged-with-embezzlement.html?_r=2). Last accessed 7 August 2013.

Beaudoin, Luc. 2006. "Raising a Pink Flag: The Reconstruction of Russian Gay Identity in the Shadow of Russian Nationalism." *Gender and National Identity in Twentieth-Century Russian Culture* (ed. Helena Goscilo and Andrea Lanoux). DeKalb: Northern Illinois University Press. 225–240.

"*Bélarus: Loukachenko 'hait les pédés*'" ("Belarus: Lukashenko 'Hates Fags'"). *Le Figaro*, lefigaro.fr, 19 February 2011 (http://www.lefigaro.fr/flash-actu/2011/02/19/97001 -20110219FILWWW00452-belarus-loukachenko-hait-les-pedes.php). Last accessed 17 August 2013.

Bell, David. 2001. "Fragments for a Queer City." *Pleasure Zones: Bodies, Cities, Spaces* (ed. David Bell et al.). Syracuse: Syracuse University Press. 84–102.

Berberova, Nina. 1997. *Chaikovskii*. St. Petersburg: Limbus Press.

Berezina, Alena. 2012. "*Rossiiskaia èlita prosit Putina lishit' deputata Milonova mandata 'za gomofobiiu i markobesne'*" ("Russian Elite Asks Putin to Deprive Deputy

Milonov of the Mandate 'For Homophobia and Bigotry'"). *Neva 24*, neva24.ru, 20 December 2012 (http://www.neva24.ru/a/2012/12/20/Artisti_i_sportsmeni_pros/). Last accessed 21 August 2013.

Berger, Harris M. 2008. "Phenomenology and the Ethnography of Popular Music: Ethnomusicology at the Juncture of Cultural Studies and Folklore." *Shadows in the Field: New Perspectives for Fieldwork in Ethnomusicology (Second Edition)* (ed. Gregory F. Barz and Timothy J. Cooley). New York: Oxford University Press. 62–75.

Bernstein, Frances. 2001. "Visions of Sexual Health and Illness in Revolutionary Russia." *Sex, Sin, and Suffering: Venereal Disease and European Society Since 1870* (ed. Roger Davidson and Lesley A. Hall). London: Routledge. 93–119.

Bernstein, Frances. 2007. *The Dictatorship of Sex: Lifestyle Advice for the Soviet Masses*. DeKalb: Northern Illinois University Press.

Bershtein, Evgenii. 2012. "The Notion of Universal Bisexuality in Russian Religious Philosophy." *Understanding Russianness* (ed. Risto Alapuro, Arto Mustajoki, and Pekka Pesonen). London: Routledge. 210–231.

Beumers, Birgit. 2001. "The 'Blue' Stage: Homosexuality in Russian Theatre and Drama of the 1990s." *Gender and Sexuality in Russian Civilisation* (ed. Peter I. Barta). London: Routledge. 295–310.

Beumers, Birgit. 2005. *Pop Culture Russia!* (Popular Culture in the Contemporary World Series). Santa Barbara: ABC-CLIO.

"*Bez Striptiza*" ("Without striptease"). *XXBi* 1 (October 2004): 4.

Biamonte, Nicole. 2008. "Augmented-Sixth Chords vs. Tritone Substitutes." *Music Theory Online* 14(2).

Bigg, Claire. 2006. "Russia: Sentences in Tajik Girl's Slaying Spark Public Outcry." *Radio Free Europe/Radio Liberty*, rferl.org, 31 March 2006 (http://www.rferl.org/content/article/1067292.html). Last accessed 21 August 2013.

Blacking, John. 1983. "Movement and Meaning: Dance in Social Anthropological Perspective." *Dance Research* 1(1): 89–99.

Blacking, John. 1992. "The Biology of Music-Making." *Ethnomusicology: An Introduction* (ed. Helen Myers) (Norton/Grove Handbooks in Music). New York: W. W. Norton. 301–314.

Blasius, Mark, ed. 2001. *Sexual Identities, Queer Politics*. Princeton: Princeton University Press.

Blotcher, Jay. 1998. "Justify My Love Handles: How the Queer Community Trims the Fat." *Looking Queer: Body Image and Identity in Lesbian, Bisexual, Gay, and Transgender Communities* (ed. Dawn Atkins). New York: Haworth Press. 359–366.

Bogdanova, Tat'iana. 2005. "*Boris Moiseev i ego ledi: Mama. Alla. Gurchenko*" ("Boris Moiseev and His Ladies: Mama. Alla. Gurchenko"). *Argumenty i fakty*, aif.ru, 28 June 2005 (http://www.aif.ru/online/superstar/66/26_01; link currently dead; accessed through http://gazeta.aif.ru/_/online/superstar/66/26_01). Last accessed 17 August 2013.

Boiko, Aleksandr. 2009. "*V Moskve zakryli gei-klub 'Dusha i telo'*" ("In Moscow, Gay Club 'Soul and Body' Is Closed"). *Komsomol'skaia pravda Moskva*, msk.kp.ru, 17 November 2009 (http://msk.kp.ru/online/news/571795/). Last accessed 7 August 2013.

Boikov, Aleksandr. "*Zhena Leont'eva sbezhala v SShA s liubovnitsei*" ("Leont'ev's Wife Ran Away to the USA with Her [Female] Lover." *Ekspress Gazeta Online*, eg.ru, 19 March 2004 (http://eg.ru/daily/adv/5420/). Last accessed 17 August 2013.

Bolotin, Valerii. 2005. "*SMI: Leont'ev zastavil svoego byvshego molit' o proshchenii*" ("Mass Media: Leont'ev Forces His Former [Boyfriend] to Beg for Forgiveness"). *Utro*, utro.ru, 22 November 2005 (http://www.utro.ru/articles/2005/11/22/497399.shtml). Last accessed 17 August 2013.

Bonnell, Victoria E. 1997. *Iconography of Power: Soviet Political Posters under Lenin and Stalin*. Berkeley: University of California Press.

Bordo, Susan. 1999. "Beauty (Re)Discovers the Male Body." *The Male Body: A New Look at Men in Public and in Private*. New York: Farrar, Straus and Giroux.

Borenstein, Eliot. 2000. "'About That': Deploying and Deploring Sex in Post-Soviet Russia." *Studies in Twentieth Century Literature* (Special Issue, "Russian Culture of the 1990s") 24(1): 51–83.

Borenstein, Eliot. 2008. *Overkill: Sex and Violence in Contemporary Russian Popular Culture*. Ithaca: Cornell University Press.

"*Boris Moiseev. Biografiia*" ("Boris Moiseev. Biography"). starchat.ru, n.d. (http://www.starchat.ru/vip/95/; link currently dead; accessed through http://www.vdanchenko.narod.ru/Archive/part21.htm). Last accessed 17 August 2013.

"*Boris Moiseev ne podderzhivaet svadebnykh nastroenii Èltona Dzhona*" ("Boris Moiseev Doesn't Support Elton John's Type of Wedding"). gay.ru, 13 July 2005 (http://www.gay.ru/news/rainbow/2005/07/13–5520.htm). Last accessed 17 August 2013.

"*Boris Moiseev zhenitsia!*" ("Boris Moiseev to Marry!"). *Afisha@mail.ru*, afisha.mail.ru, 2 November 2009 (http://afisha.mail.ru/stars/news/26110/). Last accessed 17 August 2013.

Bourdieu, Pierre. 1973. "Cultural Reproduction and Social Reproduction." *Knowledge, Education, and Social Change: Papers in the Sociology of Education* (ed. Richard Brown). London: Tavistock. 71–112.

Bourdieu, Pierre. 1977. *Outline of a Theory of Practice* (trans. Richard Nice). Cambridge: Cambridge University Press.

Boym, Svetlana. 1994. *Common Places: Mythologies of Everyday Life in Russia*. Cambridge: Harvard University Press.

Boziev, Akhmed, and Inna Didenko. 2007. "*Andrei Malakhov popal v bol'nitsu*" ("Andrei Malakhov Has Landed in the Hospital"). *Tvoi den'*, tden.ru, 15 January 2007 (http://www.tden.ru/articles/stars/006701/; link currently dead; accessed through http://for-ua.com/fun/2007/01/15/105458.html). Last accessed 17 August 2013.

Brandstetter, Gabrielle. 2007. "Dance as Culture of Knowledge: Body Memory and the Challenge of Theoretical Knowledge." *Knowledge in Motion: Perspectives of Artistic and Scientific Research in Dance* (ed. Sabine Gehm, Pirkko Husemann, and Katharina von Wilcke). New Brunswick: Transaction Publishers. 37–48.

Brashinskii, Mikhail. 2003. "*Otets i syn: Èroticheskaia fantaziia na muzhskuiu temu*" ("*Father and Son*: An Erotic Fantasy on a Masculine Theme"). *Afisha*, msk.afisha.ru, 27 August 2003 (http://msk.afisha.ru/cinema/movie/?id=328341; link currently dead, last accessed 21 January 2007; abbreviated review accessed through http://www.afisha.ru/movie/167975/review/147963/). Last accessed 17 August 2013.

Brett, Philip, and Elizabeth Wood. 2002. "Lesbian and Gay Music." *Electronic Musicological Review* 7 (http://www.rem.ufpr.br/_REM/REMv7/Brett_Wood/Brett_and_Wood.html). Last accessed 21 August 2013.

Brown, Malcolm Hamrick. 2002. "Tchaikovsky and His Music in Anglo-American Criticism, 1890s-1950s." *Queer Episodes in Music and Modern Identity* (ed. Sophie Fuller and Lloyd Whitesell). Urbana: University of Illinois Press. 134–149.

Buchanan, Ian. 2004. "Introduction: Deleuze and Music." *Deleuze and Music* (ed. Ian Buchanan and Marcel Swiboda). Edinburgh: Edinburgh University Press. 1–19.

Buckley, Neil. 2005. "NGOs Fear Russian Rule Change Would Limit Their Scope." *Financial Times*, ft.com, 9 November 2005 (http://www.ft.com/cms/s/530bf734-50c6-11da-bbd7-0000779e2340.html). Last accessed 7 August 2013.

Bull, Michael. 2000. *Sounding Out the City: Personal Stereos and the Management of Everyday Life*. Oxford: Berg.

Burkhart, Geoffrey. 1996. "Not Given to Personal Disclosure." *Out in the Field: Reflections of Lesbian and Gay Anthropologists* (ed. Ellen Lewin and William Leap). Urbana: University of Illinois Press. 31–48.

Burrows, David L. 1990. *Sound, Speech, and Music*. Amherst: University of Massachusetts Press.

"Butch: 'Moi rasskazy ob odnopolnoi liubvi—obychnyi piar'" ("Butch: 'My Stories about Same-Sex Love Are the Usual PR'"). newsmuz.com, 13 May 2005 (http://newsmusic.ru/news_2_476.htm). Last accessed 21 August 2013.

Butler, Judith. 1993. *Bodies That Matter: On the Discursive Limits of "Sex."* New York: Routledge.

Bystrov, Anton. 2005. "*Moskva: XXBi ushel . . . ne po-angliskii*" ("Moscow: XXBi Has Left . . . Not in English"). xsgay.ru, 11 March 2005 (http://xs.gay.ru/content/show_news.php?subaction=showfull&id=1110488400&archive=&start_from=&ucat=&template=archive; link currently dead). Last accessed 10 July 2012.

Camille, Michael. 1994. "The Abject Gaze and the Homosexual Body: Flandrin's Figure d'Étude." *Gay and Lesbian Studies in Art History* (ed. Whitney Davis). Binghamton, N.Y.: Harrington Park Press. 161–188.

Chantsev, Aleksandr. 2009. "'Our Attitude Toward This Passion': Lesbian Literature, from Subculture to Culture." *Russian Studies in Literature* 45(3): 53–94.

Chasin, Alexandra. 2000. "Interpenetrations: A Cultural Study of the Relationship between the Gay/Lesbian Niche Market and the Gay/Lesbian Political Movement." *Cultural Critique* 44: 145–168.

Chernov, Sergey. 2001. "The Music Business, Where Pirates Reign." *St. Petersburg Times*, sptimesrussia.com, 16 March 2001 (http://www.sptimesrussia.com/index.php?action_id=2&story_id=14780). Last accessed 21 August 2013.

Chisholm, Dianne. 2005. *Queer Constellations: Subcultural Space in the Wake of the City*. Minneapolis: University of Minnesota Press.

Clark, Toby. 1993. "The 'New Man's' Body: A Motif in Early Soviet Culture." *Art of the Soviets: Painting, Sculpture, and Architecture in a One-Party State, 1917–1992* (ed. Matthew Cullerne Brown and Brandon Taylor). Manchester: Manchester University Press. 33–50.

Clarke, Eric. 2005. *Ways of Listening: An Ecological Approach to the Perception of Musical Meaning*. Oxford: Oxford University Press.

Clough, Patricia Ticineto. 1992. *The End(s) of Ethnography*. Newbury Park, Calif.: Sage Publications.

Clowes, Edith. 2011. *Russia on the Edge: Imagined Geographies and Post-Soviet Identity*. Ithaca: Cornell University Press.

Connell, John, and Chris Gibson. 2003. *Sound Tracks: Popular Music, Identity and Place* (Critical Geographies, ed. Tracey Skelton). London: Routledge.

Corrin, Chris, ed. 1992. *Superwomen and the Double Burden: Women's Experience of Change in Central and Eastern Europe and the Former Soviet Union*. Toronto: Second Story Press.

Corwin, Julie. 2005. "Russia: Racist Attacks Plague St. Petersburg." *Radio Free Europe/Radio Liberty*, rferl.org, 30 September 2005 (http://www.rferl.org/content/article/1061791.html). Last accessed 21 August 2013.

Costlow, Jane, Stephanie Sander, and Judith Vowles. 1993. Introduction. *Sexuality and the Body in Russian Culture* (ed. Jane Costlow, Stephanie Sandler, and Judith Vowles). Stanford: Stanford University Press. 1–38.

"Counterfeit Goods Overwhelm Russia's Entertainment Market." mosnews.com, 23 March 2005 (http://www.mosnews.com/news/2005/03/23/piratecds.shtml; link currently dead). Last accessed 21 January 2007.

Coyne, Richard. 2010. *The Tuning of Place: Sociable Spaces and Pervasive Digital Media*. Cambridge: MIT Press.

Crampton, Thomas. 2006a. "On a Russian Site, Cheap Songs with a Backbeat of Illegality." *New York Times*, nytimes.com, 5 June 2006 (http://www.nytimes.com/2006/06/05/technology/05music.html?ex=1307160000&en=9cd7cbe638a3d615&ei=5088&partner=rssnyt&emc=rss). Last accessed 21 August 2013.

Crampton, Thomas. 2006b. "Russian Download Site Is Popular and Possibly Illegal." *New York Times*, nytimes.com, 1 June 2006 (http://www.nytimes.com/2006/06/01/world/europe/01cnd-mp3.html). Last accessed 21 August 2013.

"Criminal Responsibility for Homosexual Activities Likely to Be Introduced in Russia." pravda.ru, 10 October 2004 (http://english.pravda.ru/society/stories/05-10-2004/7158-homosexual-0/). Last accessed 21 August 2013.

Crouthamel, Jason. 2011. "'Comeradeship' and 'Friendship': Masculinity in Germany's Homosexual Emancipation Movement after the First World War." *Gender and History* 23(1): 111–129.

Currid, Brian. 1995. "'We Are Family': House Music and Queer Performativity." *Cruising the Performative: Interventions into the Representation of Ethnicity, Nationality, and Sexuality* (ed. Sue-Ellen Case, Philip Brett, and Susan Leigh). Bloomington: Indiana University Press. 165–196.

Dal', Vladimir Ivanovich. 1955 (1880). *Tolkovyi slovar' zhivogo velikorusskogo iazyka* (*Explanatory Dictionary of the Living Great Russian Language*). Moscow: Gosudarstvennoe Izdatel'stvo Inostrannykh i Natsional'nikh Slovarei.

Danilova, Maria. 2004. "Russian Court Weighs Regions' Alphabet." *The Guardian*, guardian.co.uk, 6 October 2004 (www.guardian.co.uk/worldlatest/story/0,1280,-3970619,00.html; link currently dead; accessed through http://tech.groups.yahoo.com/group/bcn_2004/message/599). Last accessed 17 August 2013.

Dashkova, Tat'iana. 2008. "*Uvidet' èrotiku: prestrastnyi vzgliad na sovetskie fil'my 1930-kh godov*" ("To See Erotica: A Sensual Look at Soviet Films of the 1930s"). *Teoriia mody* 9: 193–208.

Daughtry, J. Martin. 2003. "Russia's New Anthem and the Negotiation of National Identity." *Ethnomusicology* 47(1): 42–67.

Davies, Stephen. 2001. "Philosophical Perspectives on Music's Expressiveness." *Music and Emotion: Theory and Research* (ed. Patrik N. Juslin and John A. Sloboda) (Series in Affective Science, ed. Richard J. Davidson, Paul Ekman, and Klaus R. Scherer). Oxford: Oxford University Press. 23–44.

DeAngelis, Michael. 2001. *Gay Fandom and Crossover Stardom: James Dean, Mel Gibson, and Keanu Reeves*. Durham: Duke University Press.

de Carbonnel, Alissa. 2012. "Russia Security Chief Says Foreign Sites Foment Protests." *Reuters*, reuters.com, 1 June 2012 (http://www.reuters.com/article/2012/06/01/us-russia-internet-freedom-idUSBRE8500UA20120601). Last accessed 7 August 2013.

DeChaine, D. Robert. 2002. "Affect and Embodied Understanding in Musical Experience." *Text and Performance Quarterly* 22(2): 79–98.

"*Deklaratsiia prav seksual'nikh men'shinstv v Rossii*" ("Declaration of the Rights of Sexual Minorities in Russia"). lgbtnet.ru, 2 June 2006 (http://lgbtnet.ru/news/detail.php?ID=2405; link currently dead; accessed through http://piter.lgbtnet.ru/right/article.php?ID=2303). Last accessed 7 August 2013.

D'Emilio, John. 1983a. "Capitalism and Gay Identity." *Powers of Desire: The Politics of Sexuality* (ed. Ann Snitow, Christine Stansell, and Sharon Thompson). New York: Monthly Review Press. 100–113.

D'Emilio, John. 1983b. *Sexual Politics, Sexual Communities: The Making of a Homosexual Minority in the United States 1940–1970*. Chicago: University of Chicago Press.

D'Emilio, John. 1992. *Making Trouble: Essays on Gay History, Politics, and the University*. New York: Routledge.

D'Emilio, John. 2002. *The World Turned: Essays on Gay History, Politics, and Culture*. Durham: Duke University Press.

DeNora, Tia. 2000. *Music in Everyday Life*. Cambridge: Cambridge University Press.

"*Dikie nravy goroda Obninska: Boris Moiseev otmeniaet svoi kontsert*" ("The Wild Customs of the City of Obninsk: Boris Moiseev Cancels His Concert"). gay.ru, 11 February 2005 (http://www.gay.ru/news/rainbow/2005/02/11-4805.htm). Last accessed 21 August 2013.

Djumaev, Alexander. 2005. "Musical Heritage and National Identity in Uzbekistan." *Ethnomusicology Forum* 14(2): 165–184.

Dobrenko, Evgeney. 1997. *The Making of the State Reader: Social and Aesthetic Contexts of the Reception of Soviet Literature* (trans. Jesse M. Savage). Stanford: Stanford University Press.

Dobrenko, Evgeney. 2004. "Socialism as Will and Representation, or What Legacy Are We Rejecting?" *Kritika: Explorations in Russian and Eurasian History* (trans. Jesse Savage and Gust Olson) 5(4): 675–708.

Dolar, Mladen. 1996. "The Object Voice." *Gaze and Voice as Love Objects* (ed. Renata Salecl and Slavoj Žižek). Durham: Duke University Press. 7–31.

"*Domashnii mal'chik*" ("Domestic Boy"). *Kalendar'/TimeOut Peterburg* 21(50) (11–24 October 2004): 11.

Drucker, Peter, ed. 2000a. *Different Rainbows*. London: Gay Men's Press.

Drucker, Peter. 2000b. "Introduction: Remapping Sexual Identities." *Different Rainbows*. London: Gay Men's Press. 9–41.

Dumenkov, V. N. (pseud.). 1997. *Liubov' bez granits: Antologiia shedevrov mirovoi literatury* (*Love without Borders: An Anthology of Masterpieces of World Literature*). St. Petersburg: KET.

Durgadas, Ganapati S. 1998. "Fatness and the Feminized Man." *Looking Queer: Body Image and Identity in Lesbian, Bisexual, Gay, and Transgender Communities* (ed. Dawn Atkins). New York: Haworth Press. 367–372.

Eberstadt, Nicholas. 2005. "Russia, The Sick Man of Europe." *Public Interest* 3–20.

Eberstadt, Nicholas. 2009. "Drunken Nation: Russia's Depopulation Bomb." *World Affairs* 171(4): 51–62.

Eberstadt, Nicholas. 2010. *Russia's Peacetime Demographic Crisis: Dimensions, Causes, Implications*. National Bureau of Asian Research Project Report.

Eberstadt, Nicholas. 2011. "The Dying Bear: Russia's Demographic Disaster." *Foreign Affairs* 90(6): 95–108.

Echols, Alice. 2010. *Hot Stuff: Disco and the Remaking of American Culture*. New York: W. W. Norton.

Edelman, Lee. 2004. *No Future: Queer Theory and the Death Drive*. Durham: Duke University Press.

Edwards, Tim. 2006. *Cultures of Masculinity*. London: Routledge.

Elder, Miriam. 2013. "Russia Passes Law Banning Gay 'Propaganda.'" *The Guardian*, theguardian.com, 11 June 2013 (http://www.theguardian.com/world/2013/jun/11/russia-law-banning-gay-propaganda). Last accessed 7 August 2013.

Engelstein, Laura. 1995. "Soviet Policy toward Male Homosexuality: Its Origins and Historical Roots." *Gay Men and the Sexual History of the Political Left* (ed. Gert Hekma, Harry Oosterhuis, and James D. Steakley). New York: Harrington Park Press. 155–178.

Engelstein, Laura. 1999. *Castration and the Heavenly Kingdom: A Russian Folktale*. Ithaca: Cornell University Press.

Epstein, Mikhail. 1995. *After the Future: The Paradoxes of Postmodernism and Contemporary Russian Culture* (Critical Perspectives on Modern Culture, ed. David Gross and William M. Johnston; trans. Anesa Miller-Pogacar). Amherst: University of Massachusetts Press.

Erofeev, Viktor. 1999. *Muzhchiny* (*Men*). Moscow: Podkova.

Essig, Laurie. 1999. *Queer in Russia: A Story of Sex, Self, and Other*. Durham: Duke University Press.

"European Court of Human Rights Inundated with Russian Cases." mosnews.com, 21 April 2005 (http://www.mosnews.com/news/2005/04/21/hrcourtrussia.shtml; link currently dead). Last accessed 21 January 2007.

"'Fabrika zvezd-5' ne budet, budet 'Fabrika Ally Pugachevoi'" ("There Won't Be a 'Factory of Stars 5,' There Will Be the 'Factory of Alla Pugacheva'"). *Rosbalt-sever.com*, 21 September 2004 (http://www.rosbaltnord.ru/6895; link currently dead). Last accessed 1 July 2006.

Fandeev, Nikolai. 2004. "'Fabrika zvezd': krizis pereproizvodstva" ("Factory of Stars: A Crisis of Overproduction"). *XXBi* (June): 1021–104.

"*Fashisty po-prezhnemu sloniaiutsia po Moskve tolpami*" ("Mobs of fascists Are Still Hanging around Moscow"). gaynews.ru, 3 May 2006 (http://gaynews.ru/news/article.php?PAGEN_3=5&ID=2295&sphrase_id=3929). Last accessed 10 July 2012.

Feld, Steven, and Aaron A. Fox. 1994. "Music and Language." *Annual Reviews in Anthropology* 23: 25–33.

Fernandez, Dominique. 2002. *A Hidden Love: Art and Homosexuality*. Munich: Prestel.

Filippova, Sasha. 2004. "*Nochnye snaipery: SMS*" ("Night Snipers: SMS"). *Kalendar'/Time Out Peterburg*, kalendar.spb.ru, December 2004 (http://www.kalendar.spb.ru/site/prizes/20041180_42513.shtml; link currently dead). Last accessed 4 October 2005.

Fitzpatrick, Sheila. 2005. *Tear Off the Masks! Identity and Imposture in Twentieth-Century Russia*. Princeton: Princeton University Press.

Flynn, Moya, and Elena Starkova. 2002. "Talking Global? Images of the West in the Youth Media." *Looking West? Cultural Globalization and Russian Youth Cultures* (ed. Hilary Pilkington, Elena Omel'chenko, Moya Flynn, Ul'iana Bliudina, and Elena Starkova). University Park: Pennsylvania State University Press. 50–76.

Forest, Benjamin. 1995. "West Hollywood as Symbol: The Significance of Place in the Construction of a Gay Identity." *Environment and Planning D: Society and Space* 13: 133–157.

Foucault, Michel. 1990 (1978). *The History of Sexuality: An Introduction* (trans. Robert Hurley). New York: Vintage.

Fraser, Angus M. 1992. *The Gypsies*. Oxford: Blackwell.

Friedman, Rebecca. 2002. "From Boys to Men: Manhood in the Nicholaevan University." *Russian Masculinities in History and Culture* (ed. Barbara Evans Clements, Rebecca Friedman, and Dan Healey). New York: Palgrave. 33–50.

Frith, Simon. 1996. "Music and Identity." *Questions of Cultural Identity* (ed. Stuart Hall and Paul du Gay). London and Thousand Oaks, Calif.: Sage. 108–127.

Frith, Simon. 2000. "The Discourse of World Music." *Western Music and Its Others: Difference, Representation, and Appropriation* (ed. Georgina Borne and David Hesmondhalgh). Berkeley: University of California Press. 305–322.

Frolova-Walker, Marina. 1997. "On *Ruslan* and Russianness." *Cambridge Opera Journal* 9(1): 21–45.

Frolova-Walker, Marina. 2007. *Russian Music and Nationalism: From Glinka to Stalin*. New Haven: Yale University Press.

Funk, Nanette. 1993. "Introduction: Women and Post-Communism." *Gender Politics and Post-Communism: Reflections from Eastern Europe and the Former Soviet Union* (ed. Nanette Funk and Magda Mueller). New York: Routledge. 1–14.

Fuss, Diana, ed. 1991. *Inside/Out: Lesbian Theories, Gay Theories.* New York: Routledge.

Garcia, Luis-Manuel. 2005. "On and On: Repetition as Process and Pleasure in Electronic Dance Music." *Music Theory Online* 11(4).

Gaspacho (pseud.). 2006. "*Kosinus & Slutkey: reputatsiia geev pribavliaet nam populiarnosti!*" ("Kosinus & Slutkey: Gay Reputation Increases Our Popularity"). geometria.ru, 31 January 2006 (http://geometria.ru/blogs/culture/26626). Last accessed 21 August 2013.

Gasparov, Boris. 2005. *Five Operas and a Symphony: Word and Music in Russian Culture.* New Haven: Yale University Press.

"*Gay CD v Peterburge*" ("A Gay CD in Petersburg"). gayly.ru, 1 July 2004 (http://www.gayly.ru/gp/life/news/news1652.html). Last accessed 21 August 2013.

"Gay Parades Banned in Moscow for 100 Years." bbc.co.uk, 17 August 2012 (http://www.bbc.co.uk/news/world-europe-19293465). Last accessed 7 August 2013.

"Gay Pride Parade Banned for 100 Years in Russia." *Human Rights First*, humanrightsfirst.org, 7 June 2012 (http://www.humanrightsfirst.org/2012/06/07/gay-pride-parade-banned-for-100-years-in-russia/). Last accessed 7 August 2013.

"*Gay.ru razoblachil gomofoba?*" ("Has Gay.ru Exposed a Homophobe?") gaynews.ru, 11 February 2004 (link currently dead).

"Gay Showman Barred from Dagestan." mosnews.com, 16 April 2004 (http://www.mosnews.com/news/2004/04/16/moiseyev.shtml; link currently dead; accessed through http://archive.globalgayz.com/europe/russia/gay-russia-news-and-reports-20-3/#article4). Last accessed 21 August 2013.

"*Gei ne dolzhny razdrazhat*" ("Gays Must Not Irritate"). *Segodnia*, segodnya.ua, 6 February 2006 (http://www.segodnya.ua/oldarchive/c2256713004f33f5c225710c005e175d.html). Last accessed 17 August 2013.

"*Gei-pogromy v Moskve*" ("Gay Pogroms in Moscow"). queermir.ru, 3 May 2006 (http://www.queerumir.ru/articles/192/1/Gej-pogromy-v-Moskve/Page1.html). Last accessed 17 August 2013.

Gessen, Masha. 1994. The Rights of Lesbians and Gay Men in the Russian Federation: An International Gay and Lesbian Human Rights Commission Report (*Prava gomoseksualov i lesbiianok v Rossiiskoi Federatsii: otchet mezhdunarodnoi komissii po pravam cheloveka dlia gomoseksualov i lesbianok podgotovlen*). San Francisco: IGLHRC.

Gessen, Masha. 2005. "Gay Marriage for Fun and Profit." *Moscow Times*, themoscowtimes.com, 31 January 2005 (http://www.themoscowtimes.com/stories/2005/01/31/007; link currently dead). Last accessed 22 December 2006.

Gibson-Graham, J. K. 2001. "Querying Globalization." *Postcolonial, Queer* (ed. John C. Hawley) (Explorations in Postcolonial Studies, ed. Emmanuel C. Eze). Albany: State University of New York Press. 239–276.

Gil-Robles, Alvaro. 2005. *Report by Mr. Alvaro Gil-Robles, Commissioner for Human Rights, On His Visits to the Russian Federation, 15 to 30 July 2004, 19 to 29 September*

2004 (20 April 2005). Strasbourg: Office of the Commissioner for Human Rights, Council of Europe.

Golod, S. I. 2005. *Chto bylo porokami, stalo nravami: lektsii po sotsiologii seksual'nosti (What Were Sins Became Traditions: Lectures on the Sociology of Sexuality).* Moscow: Ladomir.

"*Gomofobiia shagaet po Rossii: Tol'iatti osuzhdaet pevtsov-'izvrashchentsev*'" ("Homophobia Walks across Russia: Tol'iatti Condemns Singer-'perverts'"). gay.ru, 29 September 2004 (http://www.gay.ru/news/rainbow/2004/09/29–4143.htm). Last accessed 17 August 2013.

Gorin, D. G. 2003. "*Globalizatsiia i dialog tsivalizatsii vostoka i zapada*" (Globalization and the Dialog of Civilization of the West and the East). *Sankt-Peterburg v dialoge tsivilizatsii i kul'tur vostoka i zapada* (St. Petersburg in the Dialog of Civilization and Culture of the East and West) (ed. U. V. Iakovtsa and T. G. Bogatyreva). Moscow: Mezhdunarodnyi in-t P. Sorokina-N. Kondrateva. 135–139.

Gover, Dominic. 2013. "First Image of Russia Gay Hate Murder Victim Vladislav Tornovoi." *International Business Times*, ibtimes.co.uk, 13 May 2013 (http://www.ibtimes.co.uk/articles/467252/20130513/vladislav-tornovoi-lgbt-murder-homophobia.htm). Last accessed 21 August 2013.

Granishevskaia, Elena. 2005. "*Serdiuchka vyshla iz dekreta*" ("Serdiuchka Has Left by Decree"). *Komsomol'skaia pravda*, kp.ru, 17 November 2005 (http://www.kp.ru/daily/23613.3/46830/). Last accessed 17 August 2013.

Gray, Rosiland Polly. 2001. "The Homo-Erotic Paintings of Aleksandr Ivanov." *Gender and Sexuality in Russian Civilization* (ed. Peter I. Barta). New York: Routledge. 163–180.

Green, Adam Isaiah. 2002. "Gay but Not Queer: Toward a Post-Queer Study of Sexuality." *Theory and Society* 31(4): 521–545.

Green, Lucy. 2003. "Music Education, Cultural Capital, and Social Group Identity." *The Cultural Study of Music: A Critical Introduction* (ed. Martin Clayton, Trevor Herbert, and Richard Middleton). New York: Routledge. 263–274.

Grekov, Innokenty. 2013. "Russia's Anti-Gay Law, Spelled Out in Plain English." policymic.com, August 2013 (http://www.policymic.com/articles/58649/russia-s-anti-gay-law-spelled-out-in-plain-english). Last accessed 21 August 2013.

Grigor'ev, Aleksandr. 2010. "*Boris Moiseev paralizovalo posle insul'ta*" ("Boris Moiseev Paralyzed after Stroke"). lifenews.ru, 21 December 2010 (http://lifenews.ru/news/47284). Last accessed 17 August 2013.

Grindal, Bruce T., and Frank A. Salamone. 1995. *Bridges to Humanity: Narratives on Anthropology and Friendship.* Prospect Heights, Ill.: Waveland Press.

Grosz, Elizabeth A. 1994. *Volatile Bodies: Toward a Corporeal Feminism.* Bloomington: Indiana University Press.

Grosz, Elizabeth. 1999. "Bodies-Cities." *Feminist Theory and the Body: A Reader* (ed. Janet Price and Margrit Shildrick). New York: Routledge. 381–387.

Guru Ken (pseud. Vadim Aleksandrovich Ponomarev). 2005. "*Gei-vliublennosti Valeriia Leont'eva prikhodiat i ukhodiat*" ("Gay Loves of Valerii Leont'ev Come and Go").

guruken.ru, 14 January 2005 (http://www.guruken.ru/love/vlyublennosti_Valeri). Last accessed 17 August 2013.

Guru Ken (pseud. Vadim Aleksandrovich Ponomarev). 2007. "*Gei-skandal na press-konferentsii Dimy Bilana*" ("A Gay Scandal at the Press-Conference of Dima Bilan"). newsmuz.ru, 6 March 2007 (http://newsmuz.com/news_3_4636.htm). Last accessed 21 August 2013.

Gusarenko, Elena. 2004. "*Pamiatnik Ekaterine II oskvernili svastikoi i nadpis'iu 'smert' geiam.*'" ("Monument to Catherine II Profaned with Swastika and Inscription 'Death to Gays"). lesbi.ru, 27 September 2004 (http://www.lesbi.ru/news/rainbow/2004/09/27-4133.htm). Last accessed 21 August 2013.

Haavio-Mannila, Elina, and Anna Rotkirch. 2012. "Sexuality and Family Formation." *Handbook of European Societies: Social Transformations in the 21st Century* (ed. Stefan Immerfall and Göran Therborn). New York: Springer. 465–495.

Hainge, Greg. "Is Pop Music?" *Deleuze and Music* (ed. Ian Buchanan and Marcel Swiboda). Edinburgh: Edinburgh University Press. 36–53.

Halberstam, Judith, and Ira Livingston, eds. 1995a. *Posthuman Bodies*. Bloomington: Indiana University Press.

Halberstam, Judith, and Ira Livingston. 1995b. "Introduction: Posthuman Bodies." *Posthuman Bodies* (ed. Judith Halberstam and Ira Livingston). Bloomington: Indiana University Press. 1–20.

Hass, Lawrence. 2008. *Merleau-Ponty's Philosophy*. Bloomington: Indiana University Press.

Haugh, David. 2006. "Heeere's Johnny: Whispers of Gay Lifestyle Creep to Forefront, but Few Skaters or Officials Want to Discuss It." *Chicago Tribune*, chicagotribune.com, 16 February 2006 (http://articles.chicagotribune.com/2006-02-16/sports/0602160319_1_johnny-weir-rudy-galindo-champions-on-ice-tour). Last accessed 21 August 2013.

Hawkins, Stan. 2007. "Those Norwegians: Deconstructing the Nation-State in Europe through Fixity and Indifference in Norwegian Club Music." *Music, National Identity, and the Politics of Location: Between the Global and the Local* (ed. Ian Biddle and Vanessa Knights). Aldershot, U.K.: Ashgate. 179–189.

Hawley, John C., ed. 2001. *Postcolonial, Queer* (SUNY Series: Explorations in Postcolonial Studies, ed. Emmanuel C. Eze). Albany: State University of New York Press.

Healey, Dan. 1999. "Moscow." *Queer Sites: Gay Urban Histories since 1600* (ed. David Higgs). London: Routledge. 38–60.

Healey, Dan. 2001a. *Homosexual Desire in Revolutionary Russia: The Regulation of Sexual and Gender Dissent*. Chicago: University of Chicago Press.

Healey, Dan. 2001b. "Masculine Purity and 'Gentlemen's Mischief': Sexual Exchange and Prostitution between Russian Men, 1861–1941." *Slavic Review* 60(2): 233–265.

Healey, Dan. 2002a. "Homosexual Existence and Existing Socialism: New Light on the Repression of Male Homosexuality in Stalin's Russia." *GLQ* 8(3): 349–378.

Healey, Dan. 2002b. "Review of Ol'ga Zhuk, *Russkie Amazonki: Istoriia lesbiiskoi subkul'tury v Rossii XX vek*." *Kritika* 3(2): 362–368.

Healey, Dan. "A History of Russian Homophobia." *St. Petersburg Times*, sptimes.ru, 1701(12), 28 March 2012 (http://www.sptimes.ru/index.php?action_id=100&story_id=35384). Last accessed 21 August 2013.

Healey, Daniel. 1993. "The Russian Revolutions and the Decriminalisation of Homosexuality." *Revolutionary Russia* 6(1): 26–54.

Herring, Scott. 2010. *Another Country: Queer Anti-Urbanism*. New York: New York University Press.

Herszenhorn, David. 2012. "Anti-Putin Stunt Earns Punk Band Two Years in Jail." *New York Times*, nytimes.com, 17 August 2012 (http://www.nytimes.com/2012/08/18/world/europe/suspense-ahead-of-verdict-for-jailed-russian-punk-band.html?pagewanted=all&_r=1&). Last accessed 21 August 2013.

Herszenhorn, David. 2013. "Leading Putin Critic Is Freed Pending Appeal after Putin Protests." *New York Times*, nytimes.com, 19 July 2013 (http://www.nytimes.com/2013/07/20/world/europe/judge-frees-navalny-russian-opposition-leader-during-appeal.html?pagewanted=all). Last accessed 7 August 2013.

Higgs, David. 1999. *Queer Sites: Gay Urban Histories since 1600*. London: Routledge.

Hinsch, Bret. 1990. *Passions of the Cut Sleeve: The Male Homosexual Tradition in China*. Berkeley: University of California Press.

Hirschkind, Charles. 2006. *The Ethical Soundscape: Cassette Sermons and Islamic Counterpublics*. New York: Columbia University Press.

Hisama, Ellie. 2001. *Gendering Musical Modernism: The Music of Ruth Crawford, Marion Bauer, and Miriam Gideon*. Cambridge: Cambridge University Press.

Hocquenghem, Guy. 1978. *Homosexual Desire* (trans. Daniella Dangoor). London: Allison and Busby.

Human Rights Watch. 2006. *Pride and Violence: A Chronicle of the Events of May 27, 2006 in Moscow—Human Rights Watch Briefing Paper*. Human Rights Watch, hrw.org (http://hrw.org/backgrounder/eca/russia0606/russia0606.pdf). Last accessed 21 August 2013.

Hutnyk, John. 2000. *Critique of Exotica: Music, Politics and the Culture Industry*. London: Pluto Press.

Iastrebov, Aleksandr. 2011. "*Kontsert Sergeia Lazareva i 'Evrovidenie'*" ("Sergei Lazarev Concert and *Eurovision*"). *TimeOut Moskva*, timeout.ru, 6 May 2011 (http://www.timeout.ru/journal/feature/21414/). Last accessed 7 August 2013.

Il'chenko, Sergei. 2004. "*A dusha poet: 'Musi-pusi'*" ("And the Soul Sings: 'Musi-Pusi'"). *Nevskoe vremia*, nvspb.ru, 23 April 2004 (http://www.nvspb.ru/stories/a_dusha_poet_musipusi). Last accessed 21 August 2013.

Inglehart, Ronald, and Wayne E. Baker. 2000. "Modernization, Cultural Change, and the Persistence of Traditional Values." *American Sociological Review* 65(1): 19–51.

Ingold, Tim. "Culture on the Ground: The World Perceived through the Feet." *Journal of Material Culture* 9(3): 315–340.

"*Irina Petrovskaia: Lesbiianki . . . oni uzhe psikhicheski nezdorovye*" ("Irina Petrovskaia: Lesbians . . . - they Are Already Psychically Unhealthy"). gay.ru, 31 October 2004 (http://www.gay.ru/news/rainbow/2004/10/31-4341.htm). Last accessed 21 August 2013.

"*I. S. Kon: 'Segodniashniaia rossiiskaia gomofobiia—dymovaia zavesa totalitarizma'*" ("I. S. Kon: 'Today's Russian Homophobia Is a Smokescreen of Totalitarianism'"). gaynews.ru, 15 May 2006 (http://gaynews.ru/society/article.php?ID=2308). Last accessed 7 August 2013.

Ivanov, Dmitrii. 2006. "Fake Disco Party." *TimeOut Moskva*, timeout.ru, 15 July 2006 (http://www.timeout.ru/text/display/32071/). Last accessed 21 August 2013.

Ivanov, Maksim, and Anna Besfamil'naia. 2012. "*Grazhdane poshli na chetvertyi srok*" ("To the Citizens for the Fourth Term"). *Komersant*, komersant.ru, 27 April 2012 (http://kommersant.ru/doc/1924836). Last accessed 7 August 2013.

Jarman-Ivens, Freya. 2006. "Queer(ing) Masculinities in Heterosexist Rap Music." *Queering the Popular Pitch* (ed. Sheila Whiteley and Jennifer Rycenga). New York: Routledge. 199–220.

Joas, Hans. 1996. *The Creativity of Action*. Chicago: University of Chicago Press.

Kaganovsky, Lilya. 2006. "Visual Pleasure in Stalinist Cinema: Ivan Pyr'ev's *The Party Card*." *Everyday Life in Early Soviet Russia: Taking the Revolution Inside* (ed. Christina Kiaer and Eric Naiman). Bloomington: Indiana University Press. 35–60.

Kaier, Christina, and Eric Naiman. 2006. "Introduction." *Everyday Life in Early Soviet Russia: Taking the Revolution Inside* (ed. Christina Kiaer and Eric Naiman). Bloomington: Indiana University Press. 1–22.

"*Kak Moiseev poterial nevestu*" ("How Moiseev Lost [His] Fiancée"). dni.ru, 11 October 2005 (http://www.dni.ru/news/showbiz/2005/10/11/71131.html). Last accessed 17 August 2013.

"Kaos GL Association Will Not Be Closed: Turkish Gays Win First Legal Victory on Road to EU." *International Lesbian and Gay Association*, ILGA.org, 3 January 2006 (http://ilga.org/ilga/en/article/732). Last accessed 17 August 2013.

Kara-Murza, Vladimir. 2011. "Russia, Ten Years without Freedom." *World Affairs*, worldaffairsjournal.org, 13 April 2011 (http://www.worldaffairsjournal.org/blog/vladimir-kara-murza/russia-ten-years-without-freedom). Last accessed 20 August 2013.

Karlinsky, Simon. 1989. "Russia's Gay Literature and Culture: The Impact of the October Revolution." *Hidden from History: Reclaiming the Gay and Lesbian Past* (ed. Martin Bauml Duberman, Martha Vicinus, and George Chauncey Jr.). Markham, Ontario: NAL Books (New American Library). 348–364.

Kaufmann, Dimitrina. 2000. "The Pitch as Body-Movement and Spatial Expression." *European Meetings in Ethnomusicology* 7: 10–19.

Kay, Rebecca. 2006. *Men in Contemporary Russia: The Fallen Heroes of Post-Soviet Change?* Aldershot, U.K.: Ashgate.

Keil, Charles. 1966. "Motion and Feeling through Music." *Journal of Aesthetics and Art Criticism* 24(3): 337–349.

Keil, Charles. 1994. "Participatory Discrepancies and the Power of Music." *Music Grooves: Essays and Dialogues* (ed. Charles Keil and Steven Feld). Chicago: University of Chicago Press. 96–108.

Kelly, Catriona. 1998. "Popular Culture." *The Cambridge Companion to Modern Russian Culture*. Cambridge: Cambridge University Press.

Kelly, Catriona, and David Shepherd, eds. 1998. *Russian Cultural Studies: An Introduction*. Oxford: Oxford University Press.

Kilgour, Maggie. 1990. *From Communion to Cannibalism: An Anatomy of Metaphors of Incorporation*. Princeton: Princeton University Press.

Kirsanov, Vladimir. 2003. "*Fabrika grez: russkie Prsitsilly*" ("The Factory of Dreams: The Russian Priscillas"). kvir.ru, December 2003 (http://www.kvir.ru/05-fabrika .html; link currently dead). Last accessed 22 June 2012.

Kishkovsky, Sophia. 2005. "It's Like 'Sex in the City,' Only the City Is Moscow." *New York Times*, nytimes.com, 29 December 2005 (http://www.nytimes.com/2005/12/29/ arts/television/29sex.html). Last accessed 21 August 2013.

Kishkovsky, Sophia. 2006. "Notes from a Russian Musical Underground: The Sound of Chanson." *New York Times*, nytimes.com, 16 July 2006 (http://www.nytimes.com/ 2006/07/16/arts/music/16kish.html). Last accessed 21 August 2013.

Kivy, Peter. 1993. "The Fine Art of Repetition." *The Fine Art of Repetition: Essays in the Philosophy of Music*. Cambridge: Cambridge University Press. 327–359.

Koestenbaum, Wayne. 1993. *The Queen's Throat: Opera, Homosexuality, and the Mystery of Desire*. New York: Poseidon Press.

Kolesnikov, Andrei. 2005. "*Upravliaemaia ksenofobiia*" ("Manageable Xenophobia"). gazeta.ru, 8 November 2005 (http://www.gazeta.ru/column/kolesnikov/470598 .shtml). Last accessed 21 August 2013.

Kollmann, Nancy Shields. 2002. "'What's Love Got to Do with It?' Changing Models of Masculinity in Muscovite and Petrine Russia." *Russian Masculinities in History and Culture* (ed. Barbara Evans Clements, Rebecca Friedman, and Dan Healey). New York: Palgrave. 15–32.

Kon, Igor'. 1993a. "Identity Crisis and Postcommunist Psychology." *Symbolic Interaction* 16(4): 395–410 (accessed through http://sexology.narod.ru/english/igor_kon005 .html). Last accessed 21 August 2013.

Kon, Igor'. 1993b. "Sexual Minorities." *Sex and Russian Society* (ed. Igor' Kon and James Riordan). Bloomington: Indiana University Press. 89–115.

Kon, Igor'. 1993c. "Sexuality and Culture." *Sex and Russian Society* (ed. Igor' Kon and James Riordan). Bloomington: Indiana University Press. 15–44.

Kon, Igor'. 1995. *The Sexual Revolution in Russia: From the Age of the Czars to Today* (trans. James Riordan). New York: The Free Press.

Kon, Igor'. 1999. "*Muzhskoe telo kak èroticheskii ob"ekt*" ("The Male Body as an Erotic Object"). *Gendernye issledovaniia* (*Gender Studies*) 3: 297–317 (accessed through http://sexology.narod.ru/publ016.html). Last accessed 21 August 2013.

Kon, Igor'. 2001a. *Liubov' nebesnogo tsveta* (*Sky-colored Love*). Sankt-Peterburg: Prodolzhenie Zhizni.

Kon, Igor'. 2001b. "*Muzhskie issledovaniia: meniaiushchiesia muzhchiny v izmeniaiushchemsia mire*" ("Men's Studies: Changing Men in a Changing World"). *Vvedenie v gendernye issledovaniia, chast' 1: Uchebnoe posobie* (*Introduction to Gender Studies, Part 1: A Handbook*) (ed. I. A. Zherebkina). Khar'kov: Khar'kovskii Tsentr Gendernykh Issledovanii; St. Petersburg: Aleteiia. 562–606 (accessed through http:// sexology.narod.ru/publ018.html). Last accessed 11 August 2012.

Kon, Igor.' 2001c. "Sexual Culture and Politics in Contemporary Russia." Paper Presented at the International Social Science Conference, Dubrovnik, Croatia, 12–16 June 2001 (accessed through http://sexology.narod.ru/english/igor_kon004.html). Last accessed 11 August 2013.

Kon, Igor.' 2003. *Muzhskoe telo v istorii kul'tury* (*The Male Body in the History of Culture*). Moscow: Slovo.

Kon, Igor.' 2004. *Seksologiia* (*Sexology*). Moscow: Akademiia.

Kon, Igor.' 2006. "*Gomofobiia kak forma ksenofobii*" ("Homophobia as a Form of Xenophobia") (http://www.sexology.narod.ru/info167.html). Last accessed 7 August 2013.

Kon, Igor,' and James Riordan. 1993. *Sex and Russian Society*. Bloomington: Indiana University Press.

Kostylev, Anton. 2003. "*Skandal vmesto skandala*" ("A Scandal instead of a Scandal"). gazeta.ru, 12 September 2003 (http://www.gazeta.ru/2003/09/12/sokurov.shtml). Last accessed 17 August 2013.

Kovalyev, Vladimir. 2004. "Asian Student Stabbed to Death." *Moscow Times*, moscowtimes.ru, 15 October 2004 (http://www.moscowtimes.ru/stories/2004/10/15/003.html; link currently dead; accessed through http://www.accessmylibrary.com/article-1G1-123285898/asian-student-stabbed-death.html). Last accessed 21 August 2013.

Kozinets, Robert. 2010. *Netnography: Doing Ethnographic Research Online*. Los Angeles: Sage.

Kramer, Andrew E. "Ikea Plans to Halt Investment in Russia." *New York Times*, nytimes.com, 23 June 2009 (http://www.nytimes.com/2009/06/24/business/global/24ruble.html). Last accessed 21 August 2013.

Kramer, Andrew E. "Ikea Fires 2 Officials in Russia Bribe Case." *New York Times*, nytimes.com, 16 February 2010 (http://www.nytimes.com/2010/02/16/business/global/16ikea.html). Last accessed 21 August 2013.

Krylova, Marta. 2012. "*Lera Kudriavtseva priznalas,' pochemu ushla ot Sergeia Lazareva*" ("Lera Kudriavtseva Reveals Why She Left Sergei Lazarev"). woman.ru, 5 September 2012 (http://www.woman.ru/relations/medley4/article/84075/). Last accessed 7 August 2013.

"*Kudriavtseva ofitsial'no rasstalas' s Lazarevym*" ("Kudriavtseva Has Split with Lazarev"). *Segodnia*, segodnya.ua, 27 August 2012 (http://www.segodnya.ua/culture/stars/Kudryavceva-oficialno-rasstalas-s-Lazarevym.html). Last accessed 7 August 2013.

Kudymov, Dmitrii. 2004a. "*Na vykhod!*" ("Come out!"). *Kalendar'/TimeOut Peterburg* 20(49) (September 27–October 10): 103.

Kudymov, Dmitrii. 2004b. "*V pautine*" ("In the Web") (n.b.: the title is a play on words—"web" as "worldwide web," and as "spider's web/intrigue"). *Kalendar'/TimeOut Peterburg* 21(50) (11–24 October): 107.

Kumar, Nita. 1992. *Friends, Brothers, and Informants: Fieldwork Memoirs of Banaras*. Berkeley: University of California Press.

Kuntsman, Adi. 2004. "Cyberethnography as Home-Work." *Anthropology Matters* 6(2) (accessed through http://www.anthropologymatters.com/index.php?journal=anth_matters&page=article&op=view&path%5B%5D=97). Last accessed 21 August 2013.

Kuortti, Joel, and Jopi Nyman, eds. 2007. *Reconstructing Hybridity: Post-Colonial Studies in Transition*. Amsterdam: Rodopi.

Kuzmin, Mikhail. 1980 (1923). *Kryl'ia* (*Wings*). Letchworth, U.K.: Prideaux Press.

Lapovsky Kennedy, Elizabeth, and Madeline Davis. 1996. "Constructing an Ethnohistory of the Buffalo Lesbian Community: Reflexivity, Dialogue, and Politics." *Out in the Field: Reflections of Lesbian and Gay Anthropologists* (ed. Ellen Lewin and William Leap). Urbana: University of Illinois Press. 171–199.

Lapteva, Elena, and Mariia Remizova. 2005. "*Prichina razvoda Ally i Filippa: Kirkorov skryval vnebrachnuiu doch'?*" ("The Reason for the Divorce of Alla and Filipp: Did Kirkorov Hide an Illegitimate Daughter?"). *Komsomol'skaia pravda*, kp.ru, 24 November 2005 (http://www.kp.ru/daily/23617/47134/). Last accessed 21 August 2013.

Larsen, Susan. 2003. "National Identity, Cultural Authority and the Post-Soviet Blockbuster: Nikita Mikhalkov and Aleksei Balabanov." *Slavic Review* 62(3): 491–511.

Laruelle, Marlène. 2009. "Rethinking Russian Nationalism: Historical Continuity, Political Diversity, and Doctrinal Fragmentation." *Russian Nationalism and the National Reassertion of Russia* (ed. Marlène Laruelle). London: Routledge. 13–48.

Lemish, Dafna. 2007. "Gay Brotherhood: Israeli Gay Men and the Eurovision Song Contest." *A Song for Europe: Popular Music and Politics in the Eurovision Song Contest* (ed. Ivan Raykoff and Robert Deam Tobin). Aldershot, U.K.: Ashgate. 123–134.

"*Leont'ev ostalsia bez boifrenda*" ("Leont'ev Is Left without a Boyfriend"). from-ua.com, 17 November 2005 (http://www.from-ua.com/news/437bb3875c773/). Last accessed 17 August 2013.

Lerdahl, Fred. 2003. "Two Ways in Which Music Relates to the World." *Music Theory Spectrum* 25(2): 367–373.

Levi, Primo. 1987. *If This Is a Man; The Truce*. London: Abacus.

Levin, Eve. 1989. *Sex and Society in the World of the Orthodox Slavs, 900–1700*. Ithaca: Cornell University Press.

Levitt, Marcus, and Andrei Toporkov, eds. 1999. *Èros i poronografia v russkoi kul'ture* (*Eros and Pornography in Russian Culture*). Ladomir: Moscow.

Levkovich, Evgenii, and Pavel Grinshpun. "*Boris Moiseev: 'Ia s geiami voobshche ne tusuius'*" ("Boris Moiseev: 'I Generally Don't Hang Out with Gays'"). *Rolling Stone*, rollingstone.ru, 11 January 2007 (http://www.rollingstone.ru/articles/music/article/158.html). Last accessed 17 August 2013.

Levy, Adrian, and Cathy Scott-Clark. 2006. "Muscle Maryas." *The Guardian*, theguardian.com, 28 January 2006 (http://www.theguardian.com/artanddesign/2006/jan/28/photography.russia). Last accessed 19 June 2013.

Liakhovich, Tat'iana. "*Nikolai Trubach: 'S Borei Moiseevym pervye polgoda ia boialsia v odnom lifte ezdit,' a potom on skazal mne': 'Slushai, Kolia, èto ne zarazno'*" ("Nikolai Trubach: 'For the First Half Year with Boris Moiseev, I Was Afraid to Ride in the Same Elevator, but Then He Said to Me': 'Listen, Kolia, It's Not Contagious.'" *Bulvar gordona*, bulvar.com.ua, 14 January 2009 (http://www.bulvar.com.ua/arch/2009/2/496e56bfe0e70/). Last accessed 17 August 2013.

Limpert, Polina. 2003. "*Boris Moiseev: liubov' prikhoditsia pokupat'*" ("Boris Moiseev: Love Should Be Bought"). pravda.ru, 30 October 2003 (http://culture.pravda.ru/culture/2003/4/68/195/14514_moiseev.html). Last accessed 17 August 2013.
Lingis, Alphonso. 1994a. *Foreign Bodies*. New York: Routledge.
Lingis, Alphonso. 1994b. *The Community of Those Who Have Nothing in Common*. Bloomington: Indiana University Press.
Lingis, Alphonso. 1998. *The Imperative*. Bloomington: Indiana University Press.
Lipsitz, George. 1994. *Dangerous Crossroads: Popular Music, Postmodernism and the Poetics of Place*. London: Verso.
Lissyutkina, Larissa. 1993. "Soviet Women at the Crossroads of Perestroika." *Gender Politics and Post-Communism: Reflections from Eastern Europe and the Former Soviet Union* (ed. Nanette Funk and Magda Mueller). New York: Routledge. 274–286.
Littlewood, Ian. 2001. *Sultry Climates: Travel and Sex*. Cambridge, Mass.: Da Capo Press.
"*Liubimye zhenshchiny Borisa Moiseeva*" ("Boris Moiseev's Beloved Ladies"). dni.ru, 29 June 2005 (http://www.dni.ru/news/showbiz/2005/6/29/65718.html). Last accessed 17 August 2013.
"*Liubovnik Leont'eva besprobudno p'et*" ("Leont'ev's [Male] Lover Drinks Hard"). news.rin.ru, 27 December 2008 (http://news.rin.ru/news/34860/). Last accessed 17 August 2013.
Livers, Keith A. 2004. *Constructing the Stalinist Body: Fictional Representations of Corporeality in the Stalinist 1930s*. Lanham, Md.: Lexington Books.
Loftin, Craig M. 2007. "Unacceptable Mannerisms: Gender Anxieties, Homosexual Activism, and Swish in the United States, 1945–1965." *Journal of Social History* 40(3): 577–596.
Long, Scott. 1999. "Gay and Lesbian Movements in Eastern Europe." *The Global Emergence of Gay and Lesbian Politics: National Imprints of a Worldwide Movement* (ed. Barry D. Adam, Jan Willem Duyvendak, and André Krouwel). Philadelphia: Temple University Press. 243–265.
Longhurst, Robyn. 2001. *Bodies: Exploring Fluid Boundaries*. London: Routledge.
Löw, Martina. 2008. "The Constitution of Space: The Structuration of Spaces through Simultaneity of Effect and Perception." *European Journal of Social Theory* (trans. Rhodes Barrett) 11(1): 25–49.
"*Lukashenko zaiavil Vesterwelle, chto gomoseksualistov nado vysylat' v sovkhozy*" ("Lukashenko Declares to Westerwelle that Homosexuals Should Be Sent to State Farms"). *Regnum*, regnum.ru, 14 February 2011 (http://www.regnum.ru/news/polit/1374465.html#ixzz1Rv2wzNBD). Last accessed 17 August 2013.
"*Luzhkov zapretit gei-parad v Moskve*" ("Luzhkov Will Not Allow a Gay Parade in Moscow"). lenta.ru, 29 July 2005 (http://lenta.ru/news/2005/07/29/gay/). Last accessed 17 August 2013.
Lyon, M. L., and J. M. Barbalet. 1994. "Society's Body: Emotion and the 'Somatization' of Social Theory." *Embodiment and Experience: The Existential Ground of Culture and Self* (ed. Thomas J. Csordas) (Cambridge Studies in Medical Anthropology 2, ed. Ronald Frankenberg, Byron Good, Alan Harwood, Gilbert Lewis, Roland

Littlewood, Margaret Lock, and Nancy Scheper-Hughes). Cambridge: Cambridge University Press. 48–66.

MacFadyen, David. 2001. *Red Stars: Personality and the Soviet Popular Song, 1955–1991*. Montreal: McGill-Queen's University Press.

MacFadyen, David. 2002a. *Estrada?! Grand Narratives and the Philosophy of the Russian Popular Song since Perestroika*. Montreal: McGill-Queen's University Press.

MacFadyen, David. 2002b. *Songs for Fat People: Affect, Emotion, and Celebrity in the Russian Popular Song, 1900–1955*. Montreal: McGill-Queen's University Press.

MacFadyen, David. 2006. *Russian Culture in Uzbekistan: One Language in the Middle of Nowhere*. London: Routledge.

Maes, Frances. 2002. *A History of Russian Music: From Kamarinskaya to Babi Yar*. Berkeley: University of California Press.

Maistrenko, Victoria. "*Zhena Valeriia Leont'eva zhivet v Amerike*" ("Valerii Leont'ev's Wife Lives in America"). *gazeta.ua*, 13 October 2007 (http://gazeta.ua/ru/post/186398). Last accessed 17 August 2013.

Mann, William J. 1998. "Laws of Desire: Has Our Imagery Become Overidealized?" *Looking Queer: Body Image and Identity in Lesbian, Bisexual, Gay, and Transgender Communities* (ed. Dawn Atkins). New York: Haworth Press. 345–354.

Manuel, Peter. 1989. "Modal Harmony in Adalusian, Eastern European, and Turkish Syncretic Musics." *Yearbook for Traditional Music* 21: 70–94.

Manuel, Peter. 1995. "Music as Symbol, Music as Simulacrum: Postmodern, Pre-Modern, and Modern Aesthetics in Subcultural Popular Musics." *Popular Music* 14(2): 227–239.

Marcus, Sharon. 1992. "Fighting Bodies, Fighting Words: A Theory and Politics of Rape Prevention." *Feminists Theorize the Political* (ed. Judith Butler and Joan W. Scott). London: Routledge. 385–403.

Margolis, Mikhail. 2006. "*Pevets Boris Moiseev: 'Po povodu geev u nas s Luzhkovym odinakovoe mnenie*" ("Singer Boris Moiseev: 'Regarding Gays, I Have the Same Opinion as Luzhkov'"). *Izvestiia*, izvestia.ru, 6 June 2006 (http://www.izvestia.ru/news/314384). Last accessed 21 August 2013.

Mascia-Lees, Frances E., Patricia Sharpe, and Colleen Ballerino Cohen. 1989. "The Post-modernist Turn in Anthropology: Cautions from a Feminist Perspective." *Signs* 15(1): 7–33.

Massey, Doreen. 2005. *For Space*. London: Sage.

Matich, Olga. 2005. *Erotic Utopia: The Decadent Imagination in Russia's Fin-de-Siècle*. Madison: University of Wisconsin Press.

Mauss, Marcel. 1973 (1934). "Techniques of the Body." *Economy and Society* 2: 70–88.

May, Michael. 2000. "Swingin' under Stalin: Russian Jazz during the Cold War and Beyond." *Here, There, and Everywhere: The Foreign Politics of American Popular Culture* (ed. Reinhold Wagnleitner and Elaine Tyler May). Hanover, N.H.: University Press of New England. 179–191.

McCann, Jaymi. 2013. "Russian Neo-Nazis Torture Gay Teenager They Tricked into Meeting Them as Part of Online Scam." *Daily Mail*, dailymail.co.uk, 27 July 2013 (http://www.dailymail.co.uk/news/article-2379967/Russian-neo-Nazis-torture-gay-teenager-tricked-meeting-online-scam.html). Last accessed 17 August 2013.

McDonald, Paul. 1997. "Feeling and Fun: Romance, Dance and the Performing Male Body in the Take That Videos." *Sexing the Groove: Popular Music and Gender* (ed. Sheila Whiteley). London: Routledge. 277–294.

Mead, George Herbert. 1962 (1934) (orig. essay, 1904). "The Function of Imagery in Conduct." *Mind, Self, and Society from the Standpoint of a Social Behaviorist* (ed. Charles W. Morris). Chicago: University of Chicago Press.

Mekhtiev, Artur. 1999. "*Shura: 'orientatsiia u menia normanl'naia*'" ("Shura: 'My Orientation Is Normal/Straight'"). *Vechernyi Minsk*, vminsk.by, 6 September 1999 (http://www.vminsk.by/news/30/14486/). Last accessed 21 August 2013.

Merleau-Ponty, Maurice. 2002 (1962). *Phenomenology of Perception* (trans. Colin Smith). London: Routledge.

Merleau-Ponty, Maurice. 1964. "The Child's Relation with Others." *The Primacy of Perception and Other Essays on Phenomenological Psychology, the Philosophy of Art, History, and Politics* (ed. James M. Edie; trans. William Cobb). Evanston, Ill.: Northwestern University Press. 96–155.

Meshkov, Aleksandr. 2005. "*Pochemu gei i lesbiianki zapolonili nashu stsenu?*" ("Why Have Gays and Lesbians Filled Our Stage?"). *Komsomol'skaia pravda*, kp.ru, 24 October 2005 (http://www.kp.ru/daily/23599.4/45825/). Last accessed 17 August 2013.

"*Metropolit Kirill: Russkaia pravoslavnaia tserkov' za prava cheloveka bez gomoseksualizma*" ("Metropolitan Kirill: The Russian Orthodox Church Is for Human Rights without Homosexuality"). gay.ru, 11 October 2005 (http://www.gay.ru/news/rainbow/2005/10/11-6027.htm). Last accessed 7 August 2013.

Meyer, Leonard. 1956. *Emotion and Meaning in Music*. Chicago: University of Chicago Press.

"*MGU otvetit za diskriminatsiiu geev*" ("Moscow State University Answers to Discrimination of Gays"). gaynews.ru, 1 March 2005 (original link currently dead; accessed through http://www.gayly.ru/news/news2149.html). Last accessed 21 August 2013.

Miazhevich, Galina. 2010. "Sexual Excess in Russia's Eurovision Performances as a Nation Branding Tool." *Russian Journal of Communication* 3(3/4): 248–264.

Michaels, Sean. 2012. "Madonna: Pussy Riot Verdict Is 'Inhumane.'" *The Guardian*, theguardian.com, 20 August 2012 (http://www.theguardian.com/music/2012/aug/20/madonna-pussy-riot-verdict). Last accessed 21 August 2013.

Middleton, Richard. 1983. "'Play It Again Sam': Some Notes on the Productivity of Repetition in Popular Music." *Popular Music* 3: 235–270.

Middleton, Richard. 1990. *Studying Popular Music*. Milton Keynes, U.K.: Open University Press.

"*Mikhail Veselov: iz gei-kluba na 'Fabriku zvezd*'" ("Mikhail Veselov: From Gay Club to 'The Factory of Stars.'") gay.ru, 22 September 2004 (http://www.gay.ru/news/rainbow/2004/09/22c.htm; link currently dead; accessed through http://www.gayru.org/t198.html). Last accessed 17 August 2013.

Miller, Neil. 1989. *In Search of Gay America: Women and Men in a Time of Change.* New York: Atlantic Monthly Press.

Mironov, Nikita. 2004. "*Parizh, Parizh*" ("Paris, Paris"). *Kalendar'/Time Out Peterburg,* kalendar.spb.ru, December 2004 (http://www.kalendar.spb.ru/site/prizes/20041180_48091.shtml; link currently dead; accessed through http://www.gorodovoy.spb.ru/rus/news/culture/382253.shtml). Last accessed 21 August 2013.

Mishima, Yukio. 2003 (1970). *Sun and Steel* (trans. John Bester). Tokyo: Kodansha International.

Mishin, Èd (pseud. Mikhail Edemskii). 2004a. "*MSM*." *Kvir* 14 (September 2004): 1.

Mishin, Èd (pseud. Mikhail Edemskii). 2004b. "*Ironiia syd'by*" ("The Irony of Fate"). *Kvir* 17 (December 2004): 1.

Mite, Valentinas. 2006. "Russia: African Student Killed in St. Petersburg in Possible Hate Crime." *Radio Free Europe/Radio Liberty,* rferl.org, 7 April 2006 (http://www.rferl.org/content/article/1067491.html). Last accessed 21 August 2013.

Mogutin, Iaroslav. 1995. "Gay in the Gulag." *Index on Censorship* 24(1) (accessed through http://slavamogutin.squarespace.com/gay-in-the-gulag/). Last accessed 21 August 2013.

Mogutin, Iaroslav. 2001. *30 interv'iu (30 Interviews).* St. Petersburg: Limbus Press (accessed through http://www.gay.ru/art/music/singer/russian/moiseev/mois_mog.html). Last accessed 17 August 2013.

"*Moiseev i Baskov pomogli zhertvam terrora v Beslane*" ("Moiseev and Baskov Helped the Victims of the Terror in Beslan"). *Zheltaia pressa,* yellowpress.ws, 10 September 2004 (http://yellowpress.ws/?public=1474). Last accessed 17 August 2013.

"*Moiseev posle insul'ta pereosmyslil zhizn'*" ("After Stroke, Moiseev Rethought Life"). dni.ru, 23 June 2011 (http://www.dni.ru/showbiz/2011/6/23/214351.html). Last accessed 7 August 2013.

Morozov, Andrei. 2005. "*Boris Moiseev: 'Ia sygraiu Lenina'*" ("Boris Moiseev: 'I'm Going to Play Lenin'"). *Novye Izvesntiia,* newizv.ru, 14 April 2005 (http://www.newizv.ru/news/2005-04-14/22965/). Last accessed 17 August 2013.

Morozov, I. A. 2004. "'*Muzhskoi èlement' ili v poiskakh 'muzhskogo': neskol'ko slov ot sostavitelia*" ("The 'Masculine Element,' or in Search of the 'Masculine': A Few Words from the Compiler"). *Muzhskoi sbornik, vyp. 2: "Muzhskoe" v traditsionnom i sovremennom obshchestve (Masculine Collection, Volume 2: The "Masculine" in Traditional and Modern Society)* (comp. I. A. Morozov; ed. D. V. Gromov and N. L. Pushkareva). Moscow: Labarint. 5–12.

"Moscow Prosecutors Will Not Charge MP3 Web Site." monsews.com, 9 March 2005 (http://www.mosnews.com/money/2005/03/09/mp3crim.shtml; link currently dead). Last accessed 29 January 2007.

"Moscow Says Banned Gays Because 'Cleaner' than West." *Reuters,* reuters.com, 30 May 2006 (original link currently dead; accessed through http://www.redorbit.com/news/international/520455/moscow_says_banned_gays_because_cleaner_than_west/). Last accessed 17 August 2013.

"*Mosgorsud priznal zakonnym zapret na gei-parady do 2112 goda*" ("Moscow City Court Upheld Ban on Gay Parades until 2112"). gazeta.ru, 7 June 2012 (http://www

.gazeta.ru/social/news/2012/06/07/n_2378221.shtml). Last accessed 7 August 2013.

"*Mosgorsud zapretil gei-parady na sto let vpered*" ("Moscow City Court Bans Gay Parades for the Next Hundred Years"). gomoscope.ru, n.d. (http://gomoscope.ru/?p=485; link currently dead). Last accessed 20 October 2012.

Moskowitz, Marc L. 2010. *Cries of Joy, Songs of Sorrow: Chinese Pop Music and Its Cultural Connotations*. Honolulu: University of Hawai'i Press.

Moss, Kevin. 1995. "The Underground Closet: Political and Sexual Dissidence in Eastern Europe." *Postcommunism and the Body Politic* (ed. Ellen E. Berry, *Genders* 22). New York: New York University Press. 229–251.

Myers, Steven Lee. 2006. "Russia: Moscow Court Bars Gay Parade." *New York Times*, nytimes.com, 27 May 2006 (http://www.nytimes.com/2006/05/27/world/europe/27briefs-brief-004.html). Last accessed 17 August 2013.

Naiman, Eric. 1997. *Sex in Public: The Incarnation of Early Soviet Ideology*. Princeton: Princeton University Press.

"*Napadenie fashistov na klub 'tri obez'iany*'" ("Attack of Fascists at the Club 'Three Monkeys'"). gaynews.ru, 1 May 2006 (http://gaynews.ru/news/article.php?PAGEN_3=2&PAGEN_4=3&ID=2268). Last accessed 17 August 2013.

Nartova, Nadya. 2007. "'Russian Love,' or What of Lesbian Studies in Russia?" *Journal of Lesbian Studies* 11(3/4): 313–320.

Nassor, Ali. 2005. "African Student Killed Near Metro Station." *St. Petersburg Times*, sptimes.ru, 29 December 2004 (http://www.sptimes.ru/story/16476). Last accessed 21 August 2013.

Neederveen Pieterse, Jan. 2004. *Globalization and Culture: Global Mélange*. Lanham, Md.: Rowman and Littlefield.

Nelson, Amy. 2004. *Music for the Revolution: Musicians and Power in Early Soviet Russia*. University Park: Pennsylvania State University Press.

Newton, Esther. 2000 (1992). "My Best Informant's Dress: The Erotic Equation in Fieldwork." *Margaret Mead Made Me Gay: Personal Essays, Public Ideas* (Q Series, ed. Michèle Aina Barale, Jonathan Goldberg, Michael Moon, and Eve Kosofsky Sedgwick). Durham: Duke University Press. 243–257.

"*Nizhnyi Novgorod: Boriu Moiseeva vstretili . . . matom*" ("Nizhnyi Novgorod: Boris Moiseev Was Met with . . . Foul Language"). bluesystem.ru, 2 June 2005 (http://bluesystem.ru/news_topic/?aid=208). Last accessed 17 August 2013.

"*Nochnaia vylazka mrakobesov*" ("Night Sortie of the Obscurantists"). gaynews.ru, 1 May 2006 (http://www.gaynews.ru/gaylife/article.php?PAGEN_3=33&PAGEN_7=9&PAGEN_4=16&ID=2249). Last accessed 17 August 2013.

Norton, Rictor. 2005. "The Suppression of Lesbian and Gay History" (http://rictornorton.co.uk/suppress.htm). Last accessed 1 June 2012.

"*Odnopolye braki v Rossii: shansov net*" ("Same-sex Marriages in Russia: Not a Chance"). *Izvestiia*, izvestia.ru, 19 January 2005 (http://izvestia.ru/news/298624). Last accessed 17 August 2013.

Olson, Laura J. 2004. *Performing Russia: Folk Revival and Russian Identity*. New York: RoutledgeCurzon.

O'Mahony, Mike. 2006. *Sport in the USSR: Physical Culture—Visual Culture*. London: Reaktion.
Omel'chenko, Elena. 2000. *Molodezhnye kul'tury i subkul'tury* (*Youth Cultures and Subcultures*). Moscow: Institut sotsiologii.
"*Oprosy 'Levada-tsentra': Rossiiane protiv diskriminatsii i nenavisti v otnoshenii seksual'nykh men'shinstv*" ("Survey of the 'Levada Center': Russians Are against Discrimination and Hatred in Relation to Sexual Minorities"). gayrussia.ru, 16 May 2006 (http://www.gayrussia.ru/society/detail.php?ID=5016&phrase_id=101934; link currently dead; accessed through http://www.liveinternet.ru/users/1060453/post15413747/). Last accessed 17 August 2013.
Pacini Hernandez, Deborah. 2009. *Oye Como Va! Hybridity and Identity in Latino Popular Music*. Philadelphia: Temple University Press.
Peary, Gerald. 2004. "Sokurov Speaks." bostonphoenix.com, 9–15 July 2004 (http://www.bostonphoenix.com/boston/movies/film/documents/03959028.asp). Last accessed 17 August 2013.
Peñazola, Lisa. 1996. "We're Here, We're Queer and We're Going Shopping! A Critical Perspective on the Accommodation of Gays and Lesbians in the U.S. Marketplace." *Gays, Lesbians and Consumer Behavior: Theory, Practice and Research Issues in Marketing* (ed. Daniel L. Wardlow). New York: Hawthorn Press. 9–41.
Perevedentsev, V. I. 2009. "The Demographic Prospects of Russia." *Sociological Research* 41(3): 61–80.
Pesman, Dale. 2000. *Russia and Soul: An Exploration*. Ithaca: Cornell University Press.
Petrov, Igor'. 2005a. "*Evropa-Putinu: v Rossii est' seksual'nye men'shinstva*" ("Europe to Putin: In Russia There Are Sexual Minorities"). gaynews.ru, 20 July 2005 (http://piter.lgbtnet.ru/society/article.php?ID=1455). Last accessed 17 August 2013.
Petrov, Igor'. 2005b. "'*Russkii put' legalizatsii gei-brakov*" ("The Russian Way of Legalization of Gay Marriages"). gaynews.ru, 10 April 2005 (http://piter.lgbtnet.ru/right/article.php?ID=1763). Last accessed 17 August 2013.
Petrov, Igor'. 2005c. "*V Rossii poiavilos' 'pravitel'stvo' gomofobov*" ("In Russia There Has Appeared a 'Government' of Homophobes"). gaynews.ru, 13 March 2005 (link currently dead; accessed through http://gay-talk.sexnarod.ru/topic70419_35.html). Last accessed 17 August 2013.
Petrov, Igor'. 2006. "*Sobor neseksual'nogo men'shinstva*" ("Cathedral of the Asexual Minority"). gaynews.ru, 5 April 2006 (http://piter.lgbtnet.ru/society/article.php?ID=2225). Last accessed 11 July 2012.
Petrovets, T., ed. 1997. *Lesbiianki i gei* (*Lesbians and Gays*). Moscow: Ripol Klassik.
Philips, Roel. 2005. "Esctoday.com Interview with Natalia Podolskaya." esctoday.com, 11 March 2005 (http://www.esctoday.com/4021/esctoday-com_interview_with_natalia_podolskaya-2/). Last accessed 21 August 2013.
Pilkington, Hilary. 1996. "Farewell to the *tusovka*: Masculinities and Femininities on the Moscow Youth Scene." *Gender, Generation and Identity in Contemporary Russia* (ed. Hilary Pilkington). London: Routledge. 237–263.
Pilkington, Hilary. 2002. "Reconfiguring 'the West': Style and Music in Russian Youth Cultural Practice." *Looking West? Cultural Globalization and Russian Youth Cultures*

(ed. Hilary Pilkington, Elena Omel'chenko, Moya Flynn, Ul'iana Bliudina, and Elena Starkova). University Park: Pennsylvania State University Press. 165–200.

Pilkington, Hilary, and Elena Starkova. 2002. "'Progressives' and 'Normals': Strategies for Glocal Living." *Looking West? Cultural Globalization and Russian Youth Cultures* (ed. Hilary Pilkington, Elena Omel'chenko, Moya Flynn, Ul'iana Bliudina, and Elena Starkova). University Park: Pennsylvania State University Press. 101–132.

Pilkington, Hilary, Elena Omel'chenko, and Albina Garifzianova. 2010. *Russia's Skinheads: Exploring and Rethinking Subcultural Lives*. London: Routledge.

Piper, Elizabeth. 2005. "Moscow's Prosecutor Probes 'Racist' Campaign TV Ad." *Reuters*, reuters.com, 9 November 2005 (original link currently dead). Last accessed 23 February 2007.

"*Pis'ma*" ("Letters"). *Kalendar'/TimeOut Petruburg* 22(51) (25 October–7 November): 128.

Poltavskaia, Veronika. 2012. "*Sergei Lazarev snova okazalsia v tsentre gei-skandala*" ("Sergei Lazarev Once Again at the Center of Gay Scandal"). woman.ru, 11 March 2012 (http://www.woman.ru/stars/events/article/74741/). Last accessed 7 August 2013.

Polupanov, Vladimir. 2000. "*Kuda toropitsia Valerii Leont'ev?*" ("Where Is Valerii Leont'ev Rushing To?"). *Argumenty i fakty*, aif.ru, 27 December 2000 (http://gazeta.aif.ru/_/online/aif/1053/13_01). Last accessed 17 August 2013.

Polupanov, Vladimir. 2004. "*A. Novikov: 'Na èkrane—negodiai i grekhovodniki'*" ("A. Novikov: 'On the Screen Are Scoundrels and Sinners'"). *Argumenty i fakty*, aif.ru, 24 March 2004 (http://gazeta.aif.ru/_/online/aif/1221/25_01). Last accessed 21 August 2013.

Poznansky, Alexander. 1991. *Tchaikovsky: The Quest for the Inner Man*. New York: Schirmer Books.

Poznansky, Alexander. 1998. "Tchaikovsky: A Life Reconsidered." *Tchaikovsky and His World* (ed. Leslie Kearney). Princeton: Princeton University Press. 3–54.

Pravdin, Igor' (pseud.). 2003. "*Ot pervogo litsa: 'K. P. Olovo'*" ("From the First Person: 'K. P. Olovo'"). xsgay.ru, 13 November 2003 (http://xs.gay.ru/pressa/interview/11.html; link currently dead; moved to http://xs.gay.ru/interview/item_interview/17). Last accessed 7 August 2013.

"Protesters Disrupt Lecture by Oscar Wilde's Grandson Ahead of Moscow Gay Parade." mosnews.com, 26 May 2006 (http://mosnews.com/news/2006/05/26/protestgay.shtml; link currently dead; accessed through http://groups.yahoo.com/group/SovietBelarus/message/1041). Last accessed 17 August 2013.

"Putin Aide Hails Multicultural Russia, Criticizes Baltic States." itar-tass.com, 15 October 2005 (original link currently dead; accessed through http://www.russia-channel.com/forums/showthread.php?t=23963&page=10). Last accessed 21 August 2013.

Rabinow, Paul. 2012. "Fieldwork and Friendship in Morocco." *Ethnographic Fieldwork: An Anthropological Reader (Second Edition)* (ed. Antonius C. G. M. Robben and Jeffrey A. Sluka). Mladen, Mass.: Blackwell. 520–527.

Raykoff, Ivan. 2007. "Camping on the Borders of Europe." *A Song for Europe: Popular Music and Politics in the Eurovision Song Contest* (ed. Ivan Raykoff and Robert Deam Tobin). Aldershot, U.K.: Ashgate. 1–12.

Redreeva, Elena. 2011. "*Shura: 'Ia slishkom mnogoe perezhil, chtoby i dal'she stradat'*" ("Shura: I've Been through Too Much to Suffer any Longer"). *Moskovskii komsomolets*, mk.ru, 13 August 2011 (http://www.mk.ru/social/interview/2011/08/12/614097-ispoved-poslednego-shuta.html). Last accessed 17 August 2013.

Reid, Susan. 1998. "All Stalin's Women: Gender and Power in Soviet Art of the 1930s." *Slavic Review* 57(1): 133–173.

Rein, Ol'ga. 2009. "*Nastoiashchaia liubov' Dimy Bilana*" ("Dima Bilan's True Love"). *Ekspress Gazeta Online*, eg.ru, 15 October 2009 (http://eg.ru/daily/stars/14985/). Last accessed 21 August 2013.

Remennick, Larissa I. 1993. "Patterns of Birth Control." *Sex and Russian Society* (ed. Igor' Kon and James Riordan). Bloomington: Indiana University Press. 45–63.

Rice, Timothy. 2008. "Toward a Mediation of Field Methods and Field Experience in Ethnomusicology." *Shadows in the Field: New Perspectives for Fieldwork in Ethnomusicology (Second Edition)* (ed. Gregory F. Barz and Timothy J. Cooley). New York: Oxford University Press. 42–61.

Ridge, Damien, David Plummer, and David Peasley. 2006. "Remaking the Masculine Self and Coping in the Liminal World of the Gay 'Scene.'" *Culture, Health, and Sexuality* 8(6): 501–514.

Riordan, James. 1977. *Sport in Soviet Society: Development of Sport and Physical Education in Russia and the USSR*. Cambridge: Cambridge University Press.

Riordan, James. 1993. "Introduction." *Sex and Russian Society* (ed. Igor' Kon and James Riordan). Bloomington: Indiana University Press. 1–14.

Riordan, James. 1999. "The Impact of Communism on Sport." *The International Politics of Sport in the 20th Century* (ed. James Riordan and Arnd Krüger). New York: Routledge. 48–66.

Romanov, Nikolai. 2006. "*Sergei: 'Odezhda skryvaet samye krasivye chasti tela'*" ("Sergei: 'Clothing Hides the Most Beautiful Parts of the Body'"). gazeta.ru, 20 December 2006 (http://www.gazeta.ru/style/2006/12/a_1172797.shtml). Last accessed 21 August 2013.

"*Rossiiu gubiat evrei i pederasty*" ("Russia Is Being Ruined by Jews and Fags"). gay.ru, 30 June 2004 (http://www.gay.ru/news/rainbow/2004/06/30-3618.htm). Last accessed 21 August 2013.

Rotikov, Konstantin Konstantinovich (pseud.). 1998. *Drugoi Peterburg (The Other St. Petersburg)*. St. Petersburg: Liga Plius.

Rozanov, Vasilii. 1913 (1911). *Liudi lunnogo sveta: Metafizika khristianstva (People of the Moonlight: Metaphysics of Christianity)* (Second Edition). St. Petersburg: pub. unknown.

"Russia Buries 3 Million Pirated CDs in Moscow Pit." mosnews.com, 31 May 2005 (http://www.mosnews.com/news/2005/05/31/piratedcds.shtml; link currently dead). Last accessed 22 February 2007.

"Russia: Mayor Luzhkov of Moscow Violates European Convention on Human Rights by Banning First Gay Pride Parade on May 27." *International Gay and Lesbian Human Rights Commission*, iglhrc.org, 23 May 2006 (http://www.iglhrc.org/cgi-bin/iowa/article/takeaction/partners/269.html). Last accessed 17 August 2013.

"Russian Blogger Navalny Charged with Embezzlement." bbc.co.uk, 31 July 2012 (http://www.bbc.co.uk/news/world-europe-19060444). Last accessed 7 August 2013.

"Russian Gays Take Homophobic Moscow Mayor Luzhkov to Strasbourg Court." gayrussia.ru, 19 September 2006 (http://archive.gayrussia.eu/en/news/detail.php?ID=7178). Last accessed 20 June 2012.

"Russian Skinheads Most Numerous in World." mosnews.com, 18 April 2004 (http://www.mosnews.com/news/2005/04/18/russianskinheads.shtml; link currently dead; accessed through http://dokmz01.blogspot.nl/2005/04/russian-skinheads-most-numerous-in.html). Last accessed 21 August 2013.

"Russia: Zhirinovsky Proposes Death Penalty for Homosexual Activity." *National Vanguard*, nationalvanguard.org, 5 October 2004 (http://222.nationalvanguard.org/story.php?id=3964). Last accessed 23 February 2007.

Rybakova, Nadezhda. 2006. "*Dima Bilan stanet geem?*" ("Will Dima Bilan Become Gay?"). kleo.ru, 9 October 2006 (http://www.kleo.ru/items/news/2006/10/09/bilan.shtml). Last accessed 21 August 2013.

Rybakovskii, L. L. 2010. "A Comparative Assessment of Demographic Distress in the Regions of Russia." *Sociological Research* 49(2): 37–49.

Ryan, Jenny, and Hilary Fitzpatrick. 1996. "The Space That Difference Makes: Negotiation and Urban Identities through Consumption Practices." *From the Margins to the Centre: Cultural Production and Consumption in the Post-industrial City* (ed. Justin O'Connor and Derek Wynne). Aldershot, U.K.: Arena. 169–201.

Rybik, Sergei. 2000. "*Hi-Fi: 'My ne znaem, chego ozhidat' ot zavtra'*" ("Hi-Fi: 'We Don't Know What to Expect from Tomorrow'"). *Segodnia*, segodnya.ua, 1 February 2000 (http://www.segodnya.ua/oldarchive/c2256713004f33f5c22568770049e995.html). Last accessed 21 August 2013.

Sanderson, Terry. 2004. *The Gay Man's Kama Sutra*. New York: St. Martin's Press/Thomas Dunne Books.

Sandoval, Greg. 2007. "U.S. to Russia: Allofmp3.com Closes Door on Your WTO Chances." cnet.com, 29 August 2007 (http://news.cnet.com/8301-10784_3-9768658-7.html). Last accessed 21 August 2013.

Savel'ev, Anton. 2003. "*Kirkorovu naviazali sadista-prostituta*" ("Kirkorov Linked to Sadist-Prostitute"). *Ekspress Gazeta Online*, eg.ru, 4 June 2003 (http://www.eg.ru/daily/stars/4520/). Last accessed 21 August 2013.

Savran, David. 1998. *Taking It like a Man: White Masculinity, Masochism, and Contemporary American Culture*. Princeton: Princeton University Press.

Scheffler, Israel. 1974. *Four Pragmatists: A Critical Introduction to Peirce, James, Mead, and Dewey*. New York: Humanities Press.

Schilder, Paul. 1978. *The Image and Appearance of the Human Body: Studies in the Constructive Energies of the Psyche*. New York: International Universities Press.

Schluter, Daniel. 2002. *Gay Life in the Former USSR: Fraternity without Community* (Issues in Globalization, ed. Stuart Bruchey). New York: Routledge.

Schrand, Thomas. 2002. "Socialism in One Gender: Masculine Values in the Stalin Revolution." *Russian Masculinities in History and Culture* (ed. Barbara Evans Clements, Rebecca Friedman, and Dan Healey). New York: Palgrave. 194–209.

Schütz, Alfred. 1951. "Making Music Together: A Study in Social Relationship." *Social Research: An International Quarterly* 18(1): 76–97.
Schwirtz, Michael. 2011. "Russia's Best-Known Gay Activist Has an Uphill Fight." *New York Times*, nytimes.com, 17 June 2011 (http://www.nytimes.com/2011/06/18/world/europe/18russia.html). Last accessed 7 August 2013.
Scott, Erik R. 2008. *The Nineteenth-Century Russian Gypsy Choir and the Performance of Otherness*. PhD dissertation, University of California, Berkeley.
Sedgwick, Eve Kosofsky. 1985. *Between Men: English Literature and Male Homosocial Desire*. New York: Columbia University Press.
Sedgwick, Eve Kosofsky. 1990. *Epistemology of the Closet*. Berkeley: University of California Press.
"*Serdiuchka poteriala orientatsiiu*" ("Serdiuchka Lost [Her] Orientation"). dni.ru, 11 October 2005 (http://www.dni.ru/news/showbiz/2005/10/qq/71117.html; link currently dead; accessed through http://www.km.ru/music/2cf658c4f9ab4d58b17f2cbda1438eca). Last accessed 17 August 2013.
"*Sergei Lazarev: 'U nas ochen' gomofobnaia strana'*" ("Sergei Lazarev: 'Our Country Is Very Homophobic'"). gaynews.ru, 20 December 2006 (http://www.gaynews.ru/news/article.php?ID=2778). Last accessed 21 August 2013.
Severianin, Mark. 2006. "*Tolerantnost' po-peterburgski*" ("Tolerance the Petersburg Way"). gaynews.ru, 28 September 2006 (http://gaynews.ru/gaylife/article.php?ID=2625). Last accessed 17 August 2013.
Shaburova, Ol'ga. 2002. "*Muzhik ne suetitsia, ili pivo s kharakterom*" ("A *Muzhik* Doesn't Fuss, or a Beer with Character"). *O muzhe(n)stvennosti* (*On Masculinity*) (ed. Sergei Oushakine). Moscow: Novoe Literaturnoe Obozrenie. 532–556.
Shaburova, Ol'ga. 2005a. "*Voina, soldat, i pesnia: natsional'no-patrioticheskii diskurs v konstruirovanii rossiiskoi maskulinnosti*" ("War, Soldier, and Song: National-Political Discourse in the Construction of Russian Masculinity"). *Gendernye issledovaniia* 13: 85–100.
Shaburova, Ol'ga. 2005b. "'*Muzhik*' *kak konstrukt russkoi muzhestvennosti i ego reprezentatsiia v rossiiskoi massovoi kul'ture*" ("The '*Muzhik*' as a Construct of Russian Masculinity, and His Representation in Russian Mass Culture"). *Vater Rhein und Mutter Wolga: Diskurse um Nation und Gender in Deutschland und Russland* (ed. Elisabeth Cheauré, Regine Nohejl, and Antonia Napp). Würzburg: Ergon. 485–497.
Shchepanskaia, T., and I. Shangina. 2005. "*Pol i narodnaia kul'tura*" ("Sex and Folk Culture"). *Muzhiki i baby: Muzhskoe i zhenskoe v russkoi traditsionnoi kul'ture* (*Men and Women: The Masculine and the Feminine in Russian Traditional Culture*). St. Petersburg, Russia: Iskusstvo-SPB.
Shilling, Chris. 2008. *Changing Bodies: Habit, Crisis, and Creativity*. Los Angeles: Sage.
Shiraev, Eric, and Sergei Danilov. 1999. "Pop Music as Mirror of the Russian Transformation." *The Russian Transformation: Political, Sociological, and Psychological Aspects* (ed. Betty Glad and Eric Shiraev). New York: St. Martin's Press. 213–225.
Shlapentokh, Vladimir. 2005. "Russia's Demographic Decline and the Public Reaction." *Europe-Asia Studies* 57(7): 951–968.

"*Shura pokazal zhenu*" ("Shura Shows His Wife"). *Ekspress Gazeta Online*, eg.ru, 21 May 2010 (http://www.eg.ru/daily/stars/19440/). Last accessed 17 August 2013.

Sibalis, Michael. 2004. "Urban Space and Homosexuality: The Example of the Marais, Paris' 'Gay Ghetto.'" *Urban Studies* 41(9): 1739–1758.

Signorile, Michelangelo. 1997. *Life Outside: The Signorile Report on Gay Men, Drugs, Muscles, and the Passages of Life*. New York: HarperCollins Publishers.

Silant'ev, Valerii. 2006. "*Ot moskovskikh pogromov k peterburgskim vesel'iam*" ("From the Moscow Pogroms to the Petersburg Merriments"). gaynews.ru, 6 June 2006 (www.gaynews.ru/gaylife/article.php?ID=2416). Last accessed 17 August 2013.

Sluka, Jeffery A. 2012. "Fieldwork Relations and Rapport: Introduction." *Ethnographic Fieldwork: An Anthropological Reader (Second Edition)* (ed. Antonius C. G. M. Robben and Jeffrey A. Sluka). Mladen, Mass.: Blackwell. 137–142.

Smith, David Woodruff, and Ronald McIntyre. 1982. *Husserl and Intentionality: A Study of Mind, Meaning, and Language*. Dordrecht and Boston: D. Reidel.

Smith, S. A. 2002. "Masculinity in Transition: Peasant Migrants to Late-Imperial St. Petersburg." *Russian Masculinities in History and Culture* (ed. Barbara Evans Clements, Rebecca Friedman, and Dan Healey). New York: Palgrave. 94–112.

Snezhinskaia, Alena. 2004. "*Zhenshchiny Shury: Sekrety lichnoi zhizni*" ("Shura's Women: Secrets of a Private Life"). pravda.ru, 14 December 2004 (http://www.pravda.ru/culture/2004/4/70/199/18656_shura.html). Last accessed 21 August 2013.

"Sodomy Not a Crime—Duma." mosnews.com, 28 May 2004 (http://www.mosnews.com/news/2004/05/28/gays.shtml; link currently dead). Last accessed 22 February 2007.

Solomon, Sheldon, Jeff Greenberg, and Tom Pyszczynski. 2003. "Fear of Death and Human Destructiveness." *Psychoanalytic Review* 90(4): 457–474.

Sorokin, Denis. 2012. "*Sergei Lazarev snova okazalsia v tsentre gei-skandala*" ("Sergei Lazarev Once Again at the Center of Gay Scandal"). *Sobesednik*, sobesednik.ru, 6 March 2012 (http://sobesednik.ru/scandals/20120306-sergei-lazarev-snova-okazalsya-v-tsentre-gei-skandala). Last accessed 7 August 2013.

Starks, Tricia. 2008. *The Body Soviet: Propaganda, Hygiene, and the Revolutionary State*. Madison: University of Wisconsin Press.

Starr, S. Frederick. 1983. *Red and Hot: The Fate of Jazz in the Soviet Union, 1917–1980*. New York: Oxford University Press.

"State Corporation Head Predicts End of Stability in Russia." *Èkho Moskvy Radio/BBB Monitoring International Reports*, 1 June 2012.

Steinholt, Yngvar. 2003. "You Can't Rid a Song of Its Words: Notes on the Hegemony of Lyrics in Russian Rock Songs." *Popular Music* 22(1): 89–108.

Stella, Francesca. 2008. "Homophobia Begins at Home: Lesbian and Bisexual Womens' Experiences of the Parental Household in Urban Russia." *Kul'tura* 2: 12–17.

Stepanov, Anton. 2007. "*Malakhovu zapreshchaiut zanimat'sia seksom*" ("Malakhov Is Forbidden to Have Sex"). *Tvoi den'*, tden.ru, 16 January 2007 (http://www.tden.ru/articles/stars/006816/; link currently dead; accessed through http://www.galya.ru/cat_page.php?id=18838). Last accessed 17 August 2013.

Stites, Richard. 1992. *Russian Popular Culture: Entertainment and Society since 1900*. Cambridge: Cambridge University Press.

Stokes, Martin. 1997. "Voices and Places: History, Repetition and the Musical Imagination." *Journal of the Royal Anthropological Institute* 3(4): 673–691.

Stone, Ruth M. 1982. *Let the Inside Be Sweet: The Interpretation of Music Event among the Kpelle of Liberia*. Bloomington: Indiana University Press.

Stout, Brett Edward. 2012. "Russia's Closet: The Politics behind a Ban on Gay 'Propaganda.'" *Advocate*, advocate.com, 30 March 2012 (http://www.advocate.com/politics/commentary/2012/03/30/russias-closet-politics-behind-russias-ban-gay-propaganda). Last accessed 7 August 2013.

Stratton, John. 1996. *The Desirable Body: Cultural Fetishism and the Erotics of Consumption*. Manchester: Manchester University Press.

Subramaniam, Banu. 2001. "The Aliens Have Landed! Reflections on the Rhetoric of Biological Invasions." *Meridians: Feminism, Race, Transnationalism* 2(1): 26–40.

Suprycheva, Evgeniia. 2010. "*V Moskve proshel samyi masshtabnyi gei-parad za poslednie 5 let*" ("In Moscow Was the Biggest Large-Scale Gay Parade of the Last 5 Years"). *Komsomol'skaia pravda*, kp.ru, 29 May 2010 (http://www.kp.ru/daily/24498/651843). Last accessed 17 August 2013.

Taruskin, Richard. 1997a. "How the Acorn Took Root." *Defining Russia Musically: Historical and Hermeneutical Essays*. Princeton: Princeton University Press. 113–151.

Taruskin, Richard. 1997b. "N. A. Lvov and the Folk." *Defining Russia Musically: Historical and Hermeneutical Essays*. Princeton: Princeton University Press. 3–24.

Taruskin, Richard. 2009. "Pathetic Symphonist: Chaikovsky, Russia, Sexuality, and the Study of Music." *On Russian Music*. Berkeley: University of California Press. 76–104.

Tatchell, Peter. 2009. "Thank You Mayor Luzhkov." *The Guardian*, theguardian.com, 19 May 2009 (http://www.theguardian.com/commentisfree/2009/may/19/russia-gay-pride-luzhkov). Last accessed 7 August 2013.

Tchaikovsky, Peter Ilich. 1900. *Rukovodstvo k prakticheskomu izucheniiu garmoniia* (*Guide to the Practical Study of Harmony*) (trans. Emil Krall and James Liebling). Leipzig: P. Jurgenson.

Terekhov, Aleksei, and Anastasiia Berseneva. 2005. "*Obyknovennyi rossizm—2*" ("Ordinary Russism—2") (n.b.: the title is a play on words, "Russian" and "racism"). *Novye izvestiia*, newizv.ru, 5 July 2005 (http://www.newizv.ru/news/2005-07-05/27538/). Last accessed 21 August 2013.

"*Terra Muzcognito: Tri voprosa nashim chitateliam*" ("Terra Muzcognito: Three Questions to Our Readers"). 2004. *Kvir* 15 (October 2004): 58.

Terskii, Nikita. 2004. "*Moskva, tsentr, 300 kv. metrov*" ("Moscow, a Center, 300 Square Meters"). *TimeOut Moskva* 1(001) (18–25 November): 93.

Thornton, Sarah. 1996. *Club Cultures: Music, Media and Subcultural Capital*. Hanover, N.H.: University Press of New England.

"*Timofei Pron'kin: glavnyi sol'nyi proekt*" ("Timofei Pron'kin: Main Solo Project"). *Schastlivye roditeli*, parents-online.ru, 6 September 2011 (http://www.parents

-online.ru/zvezdi/znamenitie-roditeli/_article/timofej-pronkin-glavnyj-solnyj-proekt/). Last accessed 21 August 2013.

Tilley, Christopher. 1994. *A Phenomenology of Landscape: Places, Paths, and Monuments.* Oxford, U.K.: Berg.

Tishkov, Valery, and Marsha Brill Olcott. 1999. "From Ethnos to Demos: The Quest for Russia's Identity." *Russia after Communism* (ed. Anders Åslund and Martha Brill Olcott). Washington, D.C.: Carnegie Endowment for International Peace. 61–90.

Titon, Jeff Todd. 2008. "Knowing Fieldwork." *Shadows in the Field: New Perspectives for Fieldwork in Ethnomusicology (Second Edition)* (ed. Gregory F. Barz and Timothy J. Cooley). New York: Oxford University Press. 25–41.

"*'Tolerantnost' v Sankt-Peterburge: gei ne pri chem*" ("'Tolerance' in St. Petersburg: Nothing to Do with Gays"). gaynews.ru, 15 July 2006 (http://gaynews.ru/news/article.php?ID=2456). Last accessed 17 August 2013.

"*Topalov sryvaet svoi kontserty i ne vozvrashchaet dengi*" ("Topalov Backs Out of His Concerts, and Doesn't Return the Money"). *Shou-biznes*, shoowbiz.ru, 7 September 2007 (http://www.shoowbiz.ru/news/13628.html). Last accessed 21 August 2013.

Toporkov, Andrei, ed. 1995. *Ruskii èroticheskii fol'klor, pesni, obriady, i obriakovyi fol'klor (Russian Erotic Folklore: Songs, Ceremonies, and Ritual Folklore).* Moscow: Ladomir.

Toporkov, Andrei, ed. 1996. *Seks i èrotica v russkoi traditsionnoi kul'ture (Sex and Erotica in Russian Traditional Culture).* Ladomir: Moscow.

Troitsky, Artemy. 1987. *Back in the USSR: The True Story of Rock in Russia.* London: Omnibus.

Tsygankov, Andrei. 2012. *Russia's Foreign Policy: Change and Continuity in National Identity.* Lanham, Md.: Rowman and Littlefield.

Tuan, Yi-Fu. 1977. *Space and Place: The Perspective of Experience.* Minneapolis: University of Minnesota Press.

Tuller, David. 1996. *Cracks in the Iron Closet: Travels in Gay and Lesbian Russia.* Boston: Faber and Faber.

Turner, Mark. 2003. *Backward Glances: Cruising the Queer Streets of New York.* London: Reaktion.

"2 Killed as Skinheads Attack Gypsy Camp in Central Russia." mosnews.com, 14 April 2006 (http://222.mosnews.com/news/2006/04/14/gypsyattack.shtml; link currently dead). Last accessed 22 February 2007.

"Two Mongolian Students Attacked in Petersburg." *RIA Novosti*, rian.ru, 16 April 2006 (http://en.rian.ru/russia/20060416/46459419-print.html). Last accessed 21 August 2013.

Urban, Michael E. (assisted by Andrei Evdokimov). 2004. *Russia Gets the Blues: Music, Culture, and Community in Unsettled Times.* Ithaca: Cornell University Press.

"U.S. Companies Lose Billions of Dollars Annually to Russian Piracy." mosnews.com, 23 February 2004 (http://www.mosnews.com/news/2005/02/23/piracy.shtml; link currently dead). Last accessed 22 February 2007.

"*Valerii Leont'ev brosil grazhdanskuiu zhenu i doch'*" ("Valerii Leont'ev Cast Aside His Legal Wife and Daughter"). newsmuz.com, 17 February 2009 (http://newsmuz.com/news_3_14445.htm). Last accessed 17 August 2013.

Vanina, Elena. 2004. "*Drugie golosa, drugie komnaty*" ("Different Voices, Different Rooms"). *Afisha* (25 November 2004) 22(42): 36–37.

Vasil'ev, Aleksei. 2012. "*Glava Peterburga podpisal zakon protiv propagandy gomoseksualizma*" ("Head of St. Petersburg Signed Law against Homosexual Propaganda"). *Rossiiskaia gazeta*, rg.ru, 11 March 2012 (http://www.rg.ru/2012/03/11/reg-szfo/zakon-anons.html). Last accessed 7 August 2013.

"Vike-Freiberga Lashes Out at Riga City Council on Gay Pride Parade Decision." *Baltic Times*, baltictimes.com, 21 July 2006 (http://www.baltictimes.com/news/articles/15939/). Last accessed 17 August 2013.

"Vladimir Zhirinovsky Believes that Death Penalty Would Be the Most Appropriate Punishment." pravda.ru, 5 October 2004 (http://english.pravda.ru/society/stories/05-10-2004/7158-homosexual-0). Last accessed 1 February 2007.

"*Vlad Topalov kinul gei-klub*" ("Vlad Topalov Abandoned Gay Club"). e-news.com.ua, 7 September 2007 (http://e-news.com/ua/show/156335.html; link currently dead; accessed through http://vtemu.info/index.php?t=558). Last accessed 21 August 2013.

"*Vlad Topalov otkazalsia vystupat' v gei-klube*" ("Vlad Topalov Refused to Perform at Gay Club"). gay.ru, 17 August 2006 (http://www.gay.ru/news/rainbow/2006/08/17-8096.htm). Last accessed 21 August 2013.

"*V moskovskom metropolitene skinkhedami byl ubit kurd*" ("In the Moscow Metro, a Kurd Is Killed by Skinheads"). *All-Russian Civic Congress*, civitas.ru, 20 March 2006 (http://www.civitas.ru/news.php?code=76). Last accessed 21 August 2013.

"*V moskovskom metro skinkhedy izbili korrespondenta NTV*" ("Skinheads Beat NTV Correspondent in Moscow Metro"). *RosBiznesKonsalting*, top.rbc.ru, 3 April 2006 (http://top.rbc.ru/incidents/03/04/2006/79307.shtml). Last accessed 21 August 2013.

"*V moskovskom metro ubit moskvich-armianin*" ("Muscovite-Armenian Killed in Moscow Metro"). *RosBiznesKonsalting*, top.rbc.ru, 22 April 2006 (http://top.rbc.ru/incidents/22/04/2006/79583.shtml). Last accessed 21 August 2013.

"*V Obninske v vtoroi raz otmenili kontsert Moiseeva*" ("In Obninsk for the Second Time Moiseev's Concert Has Been Canceled"). gayly.ru, 12 April 2006 (http://www.gayly.ru/news/news3033.html). Last accessed 21 August 2013.

"*Voinstvuiushchie khristiane ob"iavili 'krestovyi pokhod' protiv Borisa Moiseeva*" ("Militant Christians Have Declared a 'Crusade' against Boris Moiseev"). gay.ru, 21 April 2004 (http://www.gay.ru/news/rainbow/2004/04/21-3240.htm). Last accessed 17 August 2013.

Von Geldern, James, and Louise McReynolds. 1998. *Entertaining Tsarist Russia: Songs, Plays, Movies, Jokes, Ads, and Images from Russian Urban Life, 1779–1917*. Bloomington: Indiana University Press.

"*Vpervye v Rossii! Gay CD*" ("For the First Time in Russia! A Gay CD"). xsgay.ru, 2004 (http://xs.gay.ru/gaylife/2004/gaycd.html; link currently dead). Last accessed 22 February 2007.

"*V Peterburge otkryli butik dlia geev*" ("In St. Petersburg a Boutique for Gays Opened"). gayly.ru, 2 December 2004 (http://www.gayly.ru/gp/life/news/news1944.html). Last accessed August 13, 2013.

"*V svoem osuzhdenii gei-parada v Moskve 'aktivist' Èd Mishin gotov ob"ediniat'sia s kubanskimi kazakami*" ("In the Condemnation of the Gay Parade in Moscow, 'Activist' Ed Mishin Is Ready to Be United with the Kuban Cossacks"). gayrussia.ru, 27 September 2005 (http://archive.gayrussia.eu/events/detail.php?PAGEN_2=2&ID=2262). Last accessed 17 August 2013.

Walker, Brian. 1996. "Social Movements as Nationalisms or, On the Very Idea of a Queer Nation." *Rethinking Nationalism* (ed. Jocelyne Couture, Kai Nielsen, and Michel Seymour). *Canadian Journal of Philosophy* (Supplementary Issue 22): 505–547.

Walsh, Nick Paton. 2005. "Students Bear Brunt of Racist Fury." *The Guardian*, theguardian.com, 22 December 2005 (http://www.guardian.co.uk/russia/article/0,2763,1672357,00.html). Last accessed 21 August 2013.

Walsh, Nick Paton. 2006. "Girl Aged Nine Stabbed in Face as Russian Race Tension Spreads." *The Guardian*, theguardian.com, 26 March 2006 (http://www.theguardian.com/world/2006/mar/27/russia.nickpatonwalsh). Last accessed 21 August 2013.

Warner, Michael, ed. 1993. *Fear of a Queer Planet: Queer Politics and Social Theory* (Social Text Collective Series: Cultural Politics, Volume 6). Minneapolis: University of Minnesota Press.

Warner, Michael. 2002. *Publics and Counterpublics*. New York: Zone Books.

Washburne, Chris. 1990. "'Play It con filin!'": The Swing and Expression of Salsa." *Latin American Music Review/Revista de Música Latinoamericana* 19(2): 160–185.

Watton, Lindsay F. 1994. "Constructs of Sin and Sodom in Russian Modernism, 1906–1909." *Journal of the History of Sexuality* (Special Issue, "Part 2: Lesbian and Gay Histories") 4(3): 369–394.

Weaver, Courtney. 2012. "Opposition in Two Minds over Pussy Riot." *Financial Times*, ft.com, 16 August 2012 (http://www.ft.com/intl/cms/s/0/f89aa772-e6ec-11e1-8a74-00144feab49a.html#axzz2CUx0EtOt). Last accessed 21 August 2013.

Weeks, Jeffrey. 2000. *Making Sexual History*. Cambridge, U.K.: Polity Press.

Weston, Kath. 1998. "Get Thee to a Big City: Sexual Imaginary and the Great Gay Migration." *Long Slow Burn: Sexuality and Social Science*. New York: Routledge. 29–56.

White, Armond. 2004. "Sokurov's Vision of Intimacy." Liner notes to DVD, *Father and Son* (*Otets y syn*). Wellspring: FLV5435.

Williams, Walter L. 1996. "Being Gay and Doing Fieldwork." *Out in the Field: Reflections of Lesbian and Gay Anthropologists* (ed. Ellen Lewin and William Leap). Urbana: University of Illinois Press. 70–85.

Winnicott, D. W. 1971. *Playing and Reality*. London: Routledge.

Winning, Alexander. 2013. "Homophobic Killing Sparks Outrage." *Moscow Times*, themoscowtimes.com, 13 May 2013 (http://www.themoscowtimes.com/news/article/homophobic-killing-sparks-outrage/479794.html). Last accessed 25 August 2013.

Woods, Gregory. 1995. "We're Here, We're Queer, and We're Not Going Catalog Shopping." *A Queer Romance: Lesbians, Gay Men, and Popular Culture* (ed. Paul Burston and Colin Richardson). London: Routledge. 147–163.

Yablokova, Oksana. 2004. "Skinhead Expert Shot Dead in St. Pete." *Moscow Times*, themoscowtimes.com, 22 June 2004 (original link currently dead; accessed through http://www.eng.yabloko.ru/Publ/2004/PAPERS/06/040622_mt.html). Last accessed 21 August 2013.

Yeung, King-To, Mindy Stombler, and Reneé Wharton. 2006. "Making Men in Gay Fraternities: Resisting and Reproducing Multiple Dimensions of Hegemonic Masculinity." *Gender and Society* 20(1): 5–31.

Yurchak, Alexei. 2006. *Everything Was Forever, Until It Was No More: The Last Soviet Generation*. Princeton: Princeton University Press.

"Zachem nuzhna èto èntsiklopediia?" ("For Whom Is This Encyclopedia Necessary?"). erectrofon.gay.ru (http://erectrofon.gay.ru/intro.htm). Last accessed 17 August 2013.

"Zakon Sankt-Peterburga No. 238" ("Statute No. 238 of St. Petersburg). *Rossiiskaia gazeta*, rg.ru, 29 February 2012 (http://www.rg.ru/2012/02/29/zak-piter-admin-pravonarush-reg-dok.html). Last accessed 7 August 2013.

Zaretskaia, Ol'ga. 2004. "*Odno prostoe dvizhenie*" ("One Simple Motion"). *Elle Girl Rossiia*, September 2004. 36–42.

Zemtsovsky, Izaly. 1999. "Russia." *The Garland Encyclopedia of World Music, Volume 8: Europe* (ed. Tim Rice, James Porter, and Chris Goertzen). New York: Garland. 755–788.

Zemtsovsky, Izaly. 2001. "Russian Federation: Traditional Music: Russia." *The New Grove Dictionary of Music and Musicians (Second Edition)* (ed. Stanley Sadie; executive ed. John Tyrrell). New York: Grove's Dictionaries. 1–10.

Zerner, Charles. 2003. "The Viral Forest in Motion: Ebola, African Forests, and the New Cartographies of Environmental Danger." *In Search of the Rain Forest* (ed. Candace Slater). Durham: Duke University Press. 249–284.

Zharova, Milena. 2009. "*U Borisa Moiseeva umer syn*" ("Boris Moiseev's Son Is Dead"). dni.ru, 26 January 2009 (http://www.dni.ru/showbiz/2009/1/26/157964.html). Last accessed 17 August 2013.

"Zhena Valeriia Leont'eva: 'Esli Leont'ev khochet imet' detei, pust' imeet!'" ("Valerii Leont'ev's Wife: 'If Leont'ev Wants to Have Children, Let Him!'"). newsmuz.ru, 30 August 2005 (http://newsmuz.com/news_3_1177.htm). Last accessed 17 August 2013.

Zhuk, Ol'ga. 1998. *Russkie Amazonki: Istoriia lesbiiskoi subkul'tury v Rossii XX vek* (*Russian Amazons: The History of Lesbian Subculture in Twentieth-century Russia*). Moscow: Glagol.

Zlobin, Vadim. 2012. "*Gei-parady zapretili na 100 let*" ("Gay Parades Banned for 100 Years"). *Utro*, utro.ru, 7 June 2012 (http://www.utro.ru/articles/2012/06/07/1051454.shtml). Last accessed 7 August 2013.

Zolotonosov, Mikhail. 1999. *Slovo i telo: seksual'nye aspekty, universalii, interpretatsii russkogo kul'turnogo teksta XIX-XX vekov* (*Word and Body: Sexual Aspects, Universals, Interpretations of the Russian Cultural Text of the 19th and 20th Centuries*). Ladomir: Moscow.

Zuberi, Nabeel. 2001. *Sounds English: Transnational Popular Music*. Urbana: University of Illinois Press.

Index

ABBA, 160
Abercrombie and Fitch, 254n46
ACT-UP, 173
Adams, Bryan, 227n9
Afisha (magazine), 136, 137
Aguilera, Christina, 61
Aguzarova, Zhanna, 49
Air Supply, 37, 75
Alekhina, Mariia, 267n6
Aleksa (Aleksandra Chikova), 150, 221n43
Aleksandrinskii teatr, 143
Aleksandrov, Aleksandr, 89–90
Alekseev, Nikolai, 2, 174, 175, 191–192, 200–201, 203, 207n5, 269n39, 270n40
Aleksei, DJ, 146
Ali-Baba I sorok razboinikov, 228n22
Alibi (musical group), 198
Allofmp3.com, 257n79
Aloud (musical group), 32
Alsou (Alsu Ralifovna Abramova), 34, 37, 123, 244n48
American Idol, 217n20
Amsterdam, 136, 269n36
An2, 256n60
Anastacia, 149
Anastezia, 37
Andreia i Galena, 26–27
Annapol'skaia, Svetlana, 229n34, 229n36
anus, and permeability, 55–56. See also penetration
Arbenina, Diana, 27, 214n66
Article 121, 64, 68, 187, 227n14, 261n17
Article 995, 67

Art-Kafe SAFO, 269n31
A-Sortie, 37
Astashenok, Aleksandr, 162
A'Studio, 37, 38–39, 256n60
atlantahotel.ru, 257n74
Atwood, Margaret, 225n76
"*A ty budi menia*," 163–164
Aventura (musical group), 219n30
Azis (musical artist), 65

Bachi, 68
Badoev, Alan, 197–198, 243n37
baian, 49, 51
Baltic States, 53
Bal'zakovskii vozrast, ili vse muzhiki svo . . ., 30
Bananarama, 149
bania: as gay space, 10, 11, 17, 19, 142, 144–145, 250n17n18, 252n30 (see also *Iamskie bani*); hygiene and, 12, 13, 16, 19; as social space, 19
Barber of Siberia, The, 244n46
Barcelona, 136
bardovskaia pesnia, 22
Barskikh, Max, 198, 243n37
Baskov, Nikolai, 66, 103, 199, 228n26, 245n53
Baturin, Viktor, 103, 124–125, 245n53
Beatles, The, 96
Bellinger, Trudy, 123
Belokon', Inna, 233n62
Belyi roial', 44
Benassi Brothers, The, 152
Benetton, 52, 146, 215n1
Berlin, 150, 251n23

Bertolucci, Bernardo, 118
Beslan massacre, 73, 169, 230n41
Beyoncé, 152
bfmg.ru, 241n21
Bieber, Justin, 227n9
Big Brother, 215n2
Bilan, Dima (Viktor Belan), 3, 29, 66, 103, 105, 117, 122–132, 133, 134, 164, 199, 203, 217n12, 255n51; "Believe"/"*Vse v tvoikh rukakh*" and, 123, 126–130; display of body and, 126–127, 130–132, 196; Eurovision and, 122–123, 126–128, 130, 203; physical appearance and, 123–124, 127; relation to West and, 132, 247n71; sexual orientation and, 124–126, 131–132, 196, 244–245n50
BiS, 38, 198
bisexuality, Russia, 10, 248n6
Björk, 31, 33
Black Eyed Peas, The, 59, 149
Blaze (musical group), 159
Blestiashchie, 49
bluesystem.ru, 11, 159
Blur, 159
bluway.com, 224n73, 257n74
Bobina, DJ (Dmitrii Almazov), 197
body, male, Russia: display of and, 111–112, 242n33; homoeroticization of in film and, 104, 239n7; homoeroticization of in gay magazines and, 8; homoeroticization of in Soviet propaganda and, 17, 212n49, 50; popular music and, 3, 105–111, 114, 117–118, 119, 132–134, 195–198, 204
body, Soviet Union: *fizkul'tura* and, 14, 16, 17, 19, 113–114, 130; gender and, 112–114, 211n40; hygiene and, 12–13, 14; post-Soviet reactions and, 14–15; relation to state and, 12–15, 68–69, 70; sexuality and, 13–14; sexuality and biological etiology and, 14, 227n13
Bogdanovich, Aleksandr, 77
"Bogoroditsa, Putina progoni," 192
Bol'shoi brat, 215n2
Bombdogs, 159
Bondarchuk, Vasilii, 198
Boney M, 152
Boogie Corporation, 152
Boogie Pimps, 59
Borgato, Francesco, 269n27
Bourdieu, Pierre, 212n53
Boy George, 3, 153
Bravo (musical group), 199, 221n49

Braxton, Toni, 219n30
Brigada S, 221n49
Brighton Beach, Brooklyn, 28
Brukhanskii, N. P., 227n13
Budapest, 168
Bulla, Karl (K.K.), 17, 104, 239n5
Bunker (club), 199
Bush, Kate, 90
Butch (musical group), 27

CafeMax, 11, 210n35
Callas, Maria, 105–106
Cannes Film Festival, 239n7
Carey, Mariah, 37
Carnival Celebration, St. Petersburg, 2
Castro District, San Francisco, 139
Chai dvoem, 255n51
Channel 8 (Russia), 194
Chelsea, New York City, 65, 256n65
Cher, 70
Christy, DJ, 34, 38, 151, 214n65
Chubais, Anatolii, 191
Chvanov, Sergei, 233n63
Circuit Party, 153
Citizens Watch (St. Petersburg), 223n54
Civil Rights Defenders (Stockholm), 267n5
Clockwork Orange, A, 253n39
Cocteau Twins, 61
Cohen, Leonard, 227n9
community, gay, 6, 19, 74, 85, 86, 144, 172, 173, 175, 177–178, 192
Council of Europe, 65, 171, 207n2, 261n19, 267n5
Cranberries, The, 33

Daineko, Viktoriia, 37
Dal', Vladimir, 241n24
Dana International, 160, 254n49
Danilko, Andrei, 3, 28, 59, 66, 70, 77–80, 87, 88, 92, 94, 99, 105–106, 111, 114, 116, 117, 134, 150, 226–227n9, 245n52, 255n56; "Kukla" and, 106; "*Posle tebia*" and, 105, 106; sexual identity and, 79–80, 94–95; *SV Shou* and, 229n37. *See also* Serdiuchka, Verka
DecaDANCE, 158–159, 243n41
Deepest Blue, 32
Deetron, 152
Defense of Marriage Act, 173
Deineka, Aleksandr, 17
Del'fin (musical artist), 16

Demushkin, Dmitrii, 54
Deutschland sucht den Superstar, 217n20
Diesel (brand), 52, 146, 148, 215n1
Dik (musical group), 197, 198, 241n21
Diskoteka Avariia, 38
Dmitrievich, Alesha, 43
Dolce and Gabbana, 124
"Dol'che Gabbana" (song), 245n52
Dolgorukii, Iurii, 2
Dom kino, 248n5
Dom 2, 215n2
Don't Be Fake, 219n31
Don't Be Fake (CD), 133, 219n31
Dubtsova, Irina, 221n43, 254n50
Duran Duran, 159
Dusha i telo (club), 103–104, 152, 159, 198, 238n2, 243n41

Edinaia Rossiia, 191
Edinstvo, 242n28
Edwards, Joel, 32
Eisenstein, Sergei, 209n21, 229n34
Ekspressiia, 226n8
El'tsin, Boris, 71, 89–90, 191
Elka (musical artist), 38
embodiment: experience of music and, 23–24, 39, 50–51, 131, 154–158, 265n41; intentionality and, 114–116; musical text and, 90; phenomenology and, 23–24, 58–59; pleasures of musical repetition and, 181–183; queerness and, 185; space/place and, 136, 249n8; Western theory and, 185. *See also* embodiment, Russia; homosexuality; penetration; popular music, Russia
embodiment, Russia: homosexuality and, 6, 9, 11–12, 16–19, 66, 86, 99–100, 105, 116–117, 162–163, 186–187, 204; relation to Western popular culture and, 52–53, 222n50; relation to Western popular music and, 52; social relationships and, 19–20. *See also* embodiment; homosexuality, penetration; popular music, Russia
Erektrofon, 161–162
Erkenov, Hussein, 104
Èrmitazh (museum), 135, 168
Esenin, Pavel, 107, 197, 243–244n42
"Esli u vas netu teti," 145
ethnography, 23–28; online ethnography and, 27–28; relationship of researcher to informants and, 25–26, 214n66

euroflats.ru, 257n74
European Court of Human Rights, 97, 174, 203, 261n11, 261n19
Eurovision Song Contest, 29, 105, 130–131, 163, 203–204, 217n12, 244n48, 246–247n68, 254n49, 254n50, 258n83, 259n87, 268n23. *See also* Bilan, Dima
Evraziiskogo soiuza molodezhi, 175
Evzerov, Vladimir, 90

Fabrika (musical group), 48, 221n42
Fabrika grez, 152, 243n41
Fabrika zvezd, 3, 36–37, 70, 150, 163–164, 221n43, 254n50, 255n51
FaceOff, VJ, 146
Faktor strakha, 215n2
fanera, 227–228n20
Fantasy (musical group), 37
Farmer, Mylèye, 33
Fear Factor, 215n2
Federatsiia LGBT-Sporta Rossii, 267n11
Fedorenko, Kirill, 269n27
Fedorov, Nikolai, 227n15
Fedorova, Oksana, 245n53
Fialkovskii, Ignat, 169, 260n7
Figure d'Étude (Flandrin), 240n11
Fitnes-Sauna, 199
Flandrin, Hippolyte, 240n11
Fomin, Dmitrii (Mitia), 3, 66, 107–110, 111, 114, 119–121, 134, 164, 189, 196; display of body and, 109–110, 196–197; sexual identity and, 109, 196–197. *See also* Hi-Fi
Foster, Jodie, 194
Freestyler, 153
Freeway (CD), 110
Friche, Vladimir, 209n18
From Russia with Hate, 223n55
Furnish, David, 74

G8, 203, 261n19
Gadjo, 159
Galkin, Maksim, 66, 226n6
Garland, Judy, 160
garmon,' 45, 49
Gasparian, Artur, 269n27
Gay (club), 247n73
Gayborhood, Philadelphia, 65
Gay CD, 31–33, 59, 252n28
Gay CD Blue Edition, 31–33, 252n28
gayclub.ru/gaynews.ru, 12, 210n36, 236n85, 240n19, 257n76

gay clubs, Russia, 3, 92, 138, 144, 146–158, 161, 163–164, 166, 198–199; clienteles and, 148–149, 152, 153–154, 253n40, 254n47; DJs and, 151–152, 154, 161; drug use and, 256n70; foreign patrons and, 148, 152, 253–254n41, 254n44, 254n47; gay men's assessments of and, 147; internationalism and, 148–150, 152; longevity and, 166, 198–199, 252n27; modernity and, 149–150; music and, 149–153; musical spatiotemporal negotiation and, 146–147, 149–151, 152–153, 158; relation to West and, 149–150; Russian popular music and, 150–152; sex/sexuality and, 63–64, 104, 157–158; stage shows and, 63–64, 147, 152–153, 158; strippers and, 63, 104, 107, 153, 154, 157; *temnye komnaty* and, 104, 157, 256n64; use of English and, 146, 148, 199; Western popular music and, 149–150, 151–152. *See also* individual clubs
gaydar.net, 11
gayly.ru, 11, 33, 159, 160, 226n4, 257n76
Gay magazines, Russia, 7–8. *See also* individual publications
Gay Man's Kama Sutra, 64
gay men, Russia; apolitical stance and, 18, 19, 168–169, 170, 176, 191–192; audiences and, 163–164; body style and, 153–154; housing and, 139–141, 249n11; internet and (*see also saity znakomstv*), 25, 64, 134, 159–161, 192, 193, 200, 213n63, 215n68, 257n76; musical space and, 138–139, 145–158, 165; musical spatiotemporal negotiation and, 23, 91; online musical media and, 160–161; opinions of West and, 20, 37, 60–61, 176–177, 225n76; politics and, 169, 171, 174–176, 192, 199–202, 260n3; popular music preferences and, 21, 33–37, 49, 61–62, 101,133, 154, 161, 162; relationship to Westerners and, 24–25, 57, 62, 161; safer sex and, 252n30, 267n11; social space (pre-Revolutionary) and, 17, 141–143; social space (Soviet/Post-Soviet) and (*see also bania*; gay clubs, Russia; *pleshka*), 136–141, 143–145, 251n25; virtual/mediated spaces and, 158–166, 193. *See also* homosexuality, Russia; popular music, Russia
gaymusic.ru, 257n78
Gaynor, Gloria, 160
Gay Pride Parade, 1, 176, 202, 203, 204; Riga, 208n10; Russia, 1–2, 54–55, 101, 170–171, 174–176, 202–204, 207–208n7, 236n88, 262n23; violence and, 2, 175, 208n10; Warsaw, 208n10
gayradio.ru, 257n78
gay.ru, 8, 11, 64, 74, 159, 160, 170, 175, 236n85, 248n7, 258n81
gayrussia.eu/gayrussia.ru, 192, 257n76
Gay Village (Montréal), 65
gender, Russia, 92–93, 95–96, 100, 234n72, 234–235n75, 235n77, 246n67; masculinity and, 92–96, 101, 130, 233–234n71; *muzhik* and, 103, 111, 116, 126, 238n98, 241n24, 241n26, 242n27, 242n28, 242n30, 246n57
gender, Soviet Union, 92–95
Georgia, 53, 222n51
Gere, Richard, 194
German, Anna, 259n87
Gil-Robles, Alvaro, 65, 171
Girenko, Nikolai, 53, 223n54
GLAAD, 173
Glinka, Mikhail, 90, 220n36
Gliuk'oza, 38, 221n42, 255n52
Golubaia ustritsa, 199
Golubye pesni (Gay Songs, gaysongz.narod.ru), 160–161
Gor'kii, Maksim, 68
Gosmedizdat, 12
Gosti iz budushchego, 27, 38, 39, 59, 151, 160, 218n28
Gosudarstvennyi muzykal'nyi kolledzh imeni Gnesinikh (Gnesin State Music College), 123
gotorussia.com, 224n73
Great Soviet Encyclopedia (1936), 14
Grebenshchikov, Boris, 213n56
Greshniki (club), 34, 63–64, 86, 147–151, 152–154, 159, 167–168, 198, 214n65, 253n40, 253–254n41, 254n47
Gruv, DJ (DJ Groove) (Evgenii Rudin), 16, 37–38, 49, 103, 151, 212n48, 246n57
Gubin, Andrei, 66
gulag, 1, 69, 157, 209n21, 266n51
Gurchenko, Liudmila, 31, 73, 228n24

habitus, 18, 212n53
Hayes, Darren, 34
Heidegger, Martin, 165
Heinrich Böll Stiftung, 267n5
Helms, Jesse, 173
Helsinki, 24, 144, 150, 254n49
Hendrix, Jimi, 96
hexis, 18, 22, 212n53

Hi-Fi (musical group), 3, 15–16, 29, 35, 37, 39, 66, 105, 106–109, 114, 117, 118, 119–121, 133, 189, 196–197, 243n42, 244n44, 244n45, 268n25; lip-synching and, 121, 196–197; "Ne dano" and, 109, 114; "Pro leto" and, 108. *See also* individual members

Hitler, Adolph, 223n62

Holland, Merlin, 207n7

Homophile movement, 173

homophobia, Russia, 2, 4, 5, 35, 60, 65, 96, 98, 100, 117, 133, 141, 167, 171, 174, 187, 190, 199, 202, 203, 210n36, 223n62, 231n51, 236n85, 262n21, 263n29, 269n37; Perm' legislation and, 4; relation to demographic statistics and, 95–96; relation to economic factors and, 171–172; violence and, 170–171 (*see also* Gay Pride Parade)

homophobia, Soviet Union, 4, 202

homosexuality: attitudes toward, international, 5; "gay culture" and, 177–178; international connections and, 9, 176, 177, 263n27; musical dynamics and, 131; musical transcription and, 178, 179–180; orientation (phenomenology) and, 122, 131, 138, 163; relation to the linguistic and, 178–181; sociopolitical movements and, 139; theorization of through embodiment and music, 178–184

homosexuality, Russia: attitudes toward, 4–5; "blue notes" and, 179–180; embodied intersubjectivity and, 162–163, 165–166; embodiment and, 162–163, 169–170, 204; embodiment and Soviet models and, 15; exogenous theorizations/constructions of and, 6–7, 177, 239n7; identity and musical repetition and, 183–184; idiomatic expressions (for) and, 3, 9, 81, 236n88, 259n89; indigenous/contextualized theorizations/constructions of and, 7–8, 9–12, 142–143, 178, 186, 209n18, 241n21, 250–251n20, 266n49; lesbianism and, 207n1, 210n30, 215n68, 215n69, 250n19, 257n77; LGBT organizations and, 192–193, 201, 259–260n1, 261n18, 266–267n5; modernity and, 32; Orthodox Slavs and, 67, 95; pre-revolutionary criminalization of and, 67; re-criminalization of and, 96–97 (*see also* Legislation against Gay Propaganda); relation to English and, 192–193, 252n28, 266n4; relation to legal-juridical complex and, 171, 178–179, 192, 199–202, 261–262n19, 266–267n5; relation to queerness and, 6, 8, 10–11, 185, 192–193; relation to West and, 19, 86, 95, 175, 177, 184, 185, 187, 192, 199–203; spiritual homosexuality and, 80–81 (*see also* Moiseev, Boris), 133, 186, 194; theorization of biological etiology and, 16–17; visibility and, 63–66, 97, 142–143, 178, 200, 203, 204. *See also* embodiment; popular music, Russia

homosexuality, Soviet Union: attitudes toward, 5, 67–70; attitudes toward, ex-Soviet republics, 5, 98; criminalization of and, 67–70, 207n1, 209n21; decriminalization of and, 67, 207n2, 227n12; discursive erasure of and, 69–70; relation to anthropomorphized state and, 68–70; relation to fascism and, 68, 173–174; spatiality and, 69; theorization of biological etiology and, 14, 67

homosexuality, Western: relation to capital and, 8, 139, 172–173, 210n27; relation to juridical-political complex and, 85, 173, 177, 178–179

Husserl, Edmund, 243n35

Ia+Ia, 175

Iamskie bani, 19, 144, 145, 252n30, 269n30

identity, gay, 6, 9, 19, 172–173, 178, 179, 184, 192, 201

identity, Post-Soviet, 183–184

Idols, 217n20

IKEA, 30, 215n1

Indigo, 64, 175, 226n4, 262n21

Infiniti (musical group), 45

Ingbir' (restaurant), 252n29

In-Grid, 149, 152

Inova, Natasha, 255n52. See also *Gliuk'oza*

Institute of Ethnology and Anthropology, Moscow, 184

Institute of Neuropsychiatric Prophylaxis, Moscow, 227n13

International Covenant on Civil and Political Rights (ICCPR), 261n19

International Gay and Lesbian Human Rights Commissions (IGLHRC), 261n19

International Lesbian and Gay Association (ILGA), 168, 208n9, 260n1, 260n6, 262n19, 267n5

International Lesbian and Gay Youth Association (ILGYA), 260n6

Irakle (musical artist), 150

Irèn (musical artist), 38
Ironiia sud'by, ili s legkim parom, 145, 252n32
Isakovich, Liudmila, 76–77. *See also* Leont'ev, Valerii
IuKOS, 236n86
Iusupov, Feliks (Prince), 250n20
Ivan kupala (musical group), 49
Ivanov, Aleksandr, 104, 238n4
Ivanushki International, 37
Izvestiia, 68
"Iz-za gor, gor vysokykh," 220n36

Jaba Bar, 252n28
Jagger, Mick, 162
Jakata, 146–147, 148
Jet Set (club), 253n38
Joala, Jaak, 43, 44
Johannesburg, 1
John, Elton, 74, 143, 162
Jonsi (musical artist), 131
Jota aragonesa, 220n36
Junior Jack, 149

Kabare (Matrosskaia tishina) (club), 84, 86, 147–151, 152–154, 159, 170, 198, 199, 232n60, 253n40, 254n43, 254n45, 256n66
Kacharava, Timur, 53, 223n57
Kadysheva, Nadezhda, 45, 48
Kalendar'/TimeOut Peterburg, 59, 136–138, 166, 214n67, 248n2
Kamarinskaia (Glinka), 220n36
Kamon!!!, 197
Kapriz, 269n31
Kasheparov, Anatolii, 45
Kasilov, Igor', 233n63
Katina, Lena, 214n66, 243n39
"Katiusha" (song), 35–36, 217n18
Katiusha (weapon), 217n18
Kat'kin sadik/Kat'kin zadik, 143–144, 226n4, 251–252n26, 252n29
Katsuba, Valerii, 104
Kavalerian, Karen, 232n55
Kavkazkaia plennitsa, 49
Kazaky (musical group), 198
Kazanova, Sati, 219n30
Khanga, Elena, 226n3
Khlysty, 227n15
Khodorkovskii, Mikhail, 191, 236n86
Khodorkovsky, Alex, 224n73
Kholzakova, N. G., 227n13
Khram Spasa na Krovi, 251n24
Khvorostovskii, Dmitrii, 198
Kings of Tomorrow, 32

Kinsey, Alfred, 224n66
Kirkorov, Filipp, 45, 46, 66, 79, 198, 199, 226n6, 227–228n20, 231n46, 232n55, 255n51
Klein, Lev, 261n17
Kofe Khauz, 216n11
Kolerov, Modest, 222n52
kommunalka, 140
komsomol, 15, 93, 237n93
Kon, Igor', 12, 85, 171–172, 174, 184–185, 189–191, 192, 214n65
Konstantin, DJ, 146
Korni (musical group), 87, 162, 214n67
Korroziia metalla (musical group), 217n16
Kosinus and Slutkey (DJs), 31–33, 38, 216n9, 252n28
Krall, Diana, 33
Krasnushkin, E. K, 227n13
Krasnaia ploshad', 135
Kremlin, 53
Krot, DJ, 49
Krutoi, Igor', 49, 198, 221n43
Krylenko, Nikolai, 68
Kryl'ia (novel), 208n12
Kryl'ia (organization), 2, 168, 174, 214n65. *See also* homosexuality, Russia, LGBT organizations and
Kuban Cossacks, 175
Kudriavtseva, Lera, 195, 268n22
Kukharskii, Aleksandr, 2, 167–168, 171–172, 208n12, 214n65, 259–260n1, 260n3. *See also Kryl'ia* (organization)
Kuletskaia, Lena, 125, 245n53
Kul'turnyi proekt (K. P.) Olovo, 147, 149, 169
Kul'turnyi proekt Why Not?!, 146–147, 149
Kur'ianovich, Nikolai, 54, 223n62
Kuzmin, Mikhail, 208n12
Kvir (magazine), 7–8, 124, 137, 162, 175, 196, 247n75, 248–249n7, 258n82
Kvir-fest, 192, 193
Kvirkul'tura v Rossii, 192, 193

Laan, Eberhard van der, 269n36
Lacoste, 254n46
Lama (musical group), 198
lang, k.d., 227n9
Larina, Kseniia, 221n43
Last Emperor, The (film), 118, 243n40
Latter Days (film), 111
Lavigne, Avril, 227n9
Law, Jude, 126
Lazarev, Sergei, 66, 109–111, 114, 118–119, 124, 164, 219n31, 247n73; sexual identity and,

103, 109–110, 133–134, 195–196, 243n39, 268n22, 268n23
Legislation against Gay Propaganda, Russia (Article 6.21), 28, 191, 199–202, 235n83, 236n87
Lel', Katia, 35, 221n42, 264–265n39
Lemeshev, Sergei, 209n21
Lenin, Vladimir, 20, 89
Leningrad (musical group), 111
Lennox, Annie, 33
Leont'ev, Valerii, 3, 28, 66, 70, 75–77, 79, 80, 84–87, 88, 89, 90, 91, 98, 100, 101, 162, 202, 226n9, 255n56; children and, 77; gender and, 75, 94–95, 228–229n32, 229n34; "Greshniki" (song) and, 85–86; "*Kazhdyi khochet liubit*'" and, 84–85, 86, 90, 160; marriage and, 76–77; musical style and, 87; performance style and, 75; relationship to West and, 95; sexual identity and, 76–77, 103; textual allusions to homosexuality and, 84–87, 232n56, 232n59, 232n67
lesbian clubs, Russia, 144, 215n68, 219n30, 238n2, 248n4, 269n31. *See also* gay clubs, Russia; *Triel'*
lesbi.ru, 257n77
Leshchenko, Lev, 75, 258n86
Levada-Tsentr, 5, 191, 209n19
Li, Ekaterina (Katia), 107, 119, 121
Liberace, 65
Liberal'no-demokraticheskaiia partiia Rossii (LDPR), 54
Lipchanskaia, Olesia, 107, 119, 121
Liube, 35
Liudi lunnogo sveta, 186, 241n21
Loboda, Svetlana, 198
Lominskii, Aleksandr, 198
London, 61, 65, 123, 139, 150, 251n23
Lopez, Jennifer, 37, 254n48
Lorak, Ani, 195
Lordi, 131, 246n68
Luchshie pesni o glavnom, 22, 237n92
Lukashenko, Aleksandr, 98
Lukoil, 34
Luzhkov, Iurii, 1–2, 101, 172, 174, 203, 261n19
Lvov, Nikolai Alexandrovich, 41

MacLaughlin, Sarah, 227n9
Madonna (musical artist), 33, 61, 152, 162, 254n48, 255n58, 267n6, 269n27
Magreb (restaurant), 253n38
Maiakovka Sport, 144, 198
Maiakovskii, Vladimir, 12–13, 212n49, 226n3
Malafeev, Viacheslav, 199

Malakhov, Andrei, 230n45
Malevich (club), 198, 199
Malikova, Inna, 259n86
Malinin, Aleksandr, 34
Malinin, Nikita, 33–34, 38
Manana, DJ, 38
Manson, Marilyn, 96
Mapplethorpe, Robert, 168
Marais, Paris, 139
Mariinskii teatr, 254n43
Martakis, Kostas, 131
Martin, Ricky, 3
Martinez (musical artist), 152
Martos, Edvin, 128, 129, 130
masculinity, Russia. *See* gender, Russia, masculinity and
Mashina vremeni (musical group), 31
Mathieu, Mireille, 152
Mavrikievna, Veronika, 233n63
Mechta (café), 4
Meck, Nadezhda von, 7, 186
mediaservices Inc., 257n79
Medvedev, Dmitrii, 191, 199
Meladze, Valerii, 49, 255n51, 259n87
memphismembers.com, 258n79
Men's Health (magazine), 242n30
Mercury, Freddy, 162
Metro (club), 10, 152, 198–199, 210n32, 238n3, 253n40, 256n62
Metropolitan Kirill (Kirill Gundiaev), 172
Mezhinskaia, Kristina, 198
Michael, George, 118, 243n40
Middle Passage, The, 176
Mikhalkov, Nikita, 244n46
miks clubs, Russia, 3, 10, 151, 198–199, 210n32, 215n68, 238n3, 253n40. *See also* individual clubs
Military Articles of 1716, 67
Miliukova, Antonina, 186
Milk, David, 198
Milonov, Vitalii, 199
Mir (magazine), 249n7
Mironov, Sergei, 191
Mishima, Yukio, 157, 256n69
Mishin, Èd (Mikhail Edemskii), 7–8, 162, 174–175, 209n26, 262n20
Mission Impossible, 120
Mitchell, Joni, 227n9
Mobil'nye blondinki, 198
Moia prekrasnaia niania, 30
Moiseev, Boris, 3, 28, 66, 70–75, 76, 79, 80–84, 86, 87, 88, 89, 90, 91, 98–99, 101–102, 117, 133, 160, 198, 202, 217n15, 226n8, 226–227n9,

Moiseev, Boris (*continued*): 228n21, 228n22, 228n23, 228n26, 228n28, 228n30, 231n51, 232n55, 237n93, 255n56, 268n19; attitudes toward homosexuality and, 74–75, 236n88; audience and, 71, 73, 102, 195; children and, 74; coming out and, 71, 73; concert performance and, 70–73; gender and, 71–73, 94–95; "*Golubaia luna*" and, 80–82, 90, 160; "*Golubaia zvezda*" and, 81, 82–83, 91; homophobic protests and, 99; "*Ia ne mogu tebia teriat*'" and, 195; internet presence and, 193–195, 198; "*Luchshii iz muzhchin*" and, 195; marriage and 74, 193–194; musical style and, 83–84; *Pastor* and, 194–195; popularity and, 98–99; relationship to West, and, 95; sexual identity and, 73–75; spiritual homosexuality and, 80, 83, 101, 194; textual allusions to homosexuality and, 80–83
Molko, Brian, 90
Molodezhnaia assotsiatsiia HS, 169, 248n5
Moloko (musical group), 146
Mono (club), 10, 151, 198, 210n31, 210n32, 253n40
Monro (club), 10, 198–199, 210n32, 253n40
Montréal, 1, 65, 150
Morrison, Toni, 225n76
Moscow Ministry of Health, 212n49
Moskovskii dvorets molodezhi, 158
Moskovskii gosudarstvennyi universitet (MGU), 236n85
Moskovskii prospekt, 135
Moskovskii vokzal, 70
Moskovskoe gei radio, 257n78
Moskva instruktsiia, 230n43
mp3sparks.com, 257n79
Mr. Slan, 38
MTV Russia, 22, 118, 150, 213n59
Mudèka, 4
Murdoch, Iris, 225n76
Muren, Zeki, 65
Murzin, Edward, 262n20
muzhelozhstvo, 66, 67, 141, 173, 187
muzhik. See gender, Russia
"*Muzhiki ne tantsuiut*" (song), 103, 246n57
MuzTV, 22, 78, 118, 150, 194, 195, 213n59
Mylo, 32

Na beregu neba, 122
Naipaul, V.S., 176
Nanny, The (television program), 30
Napier-Bell, Simon, 118
Napoli, Zaza, 120, 197, 221n45
Narodnyi artist, 36, 163

Nartsis, P'er, 225n74
Nartsis (sauna), 144, 198, 253n38
Nash (musical group), 131
Nash gorod (musical group), 223n60
Nash gorod (political group), 54, 202
Nashi pesni, 22
National Vanguard, 235–236n84
NATO, 53
Naval'nyi, Aleksei, 191, 236n86, 266n3
Neposedy, 243n39
Nereal'nye, 198
Nesmelov, Aresenii, 90
Nevskii prospekt, 53, 135, 142, 143, 215n1, 250n15, 253n38
New York City, 1, 27, 61, 65, 136, 139, 144, 146, 153, 176, 251n23, 256n65
Night, Sylvia, 131, 246–247n68
Nika, 49, 221n45
Nikita (musical artist), 39, 66
Nikitichna, Avdot'ia, 233n63
Nikitiny, Sergei and Tat'iana, 48
911 (club), 198, 215n68, 233n70
Nissenen, Jussi, 176, 214n65, 262–263n26
Nizhinskii, Vatslav, 17
Nochnoi kuligan, 122
Nochnye snaipery, 27, 70, 218n30
Noch' v stile disko, 35–36, 145
Normal'nyi/progressivnyi, 5
Novaia volna (musical program), 22
Novikov, Aleksandr, 35, 217n15
Novogodnyi goluboi ogonek, 51, 163, 229n34
Novye russkie babki, 233n63
Novye samotsvety (musical group), 259n86
Nozh dlia Frau Müller, 255n57
NTV, 202, 215n3
NTV Utrom, 268n19

Obama, Barack, 200
Okna (television program), 215n2
Oktiabr'skii concert hall, 70, 77, 92, 98
Oleshko, Oksana (Ksiusha), 107–110, 119, 121, 240n14, 268n25
Om (magazine), 249n7
Onegin (club), 154
100 dnei do prikaza, 104, 112
158B, 144, 198
Orbakaite, Kristina, 35–36, 163–164
Organization for Security and Co-Operation in Europe (OSCE), 267n5
Orlova, Liubov', 213n56
Orthodox Church/Orthodox Christians, 2, 74, 85–86, 171, 172, 190–191, 202, 209n18, 210n36, 225–226n1, 227n15

Otets i syn (film), 104, 239n7
O-Zone, 149

"*Paninaro*" (song), 196
Par' (club), 154
Paris, 136, 139, 144, 150, 224n73
Parni Plius, 267n11
Partyphone, DJ, 151–152, 214n65, 256n59
Passazh, 142
Patriarch Alekseii II (Alekseii Ridiger), 172
"Patriotic Union." *See* Russia, national anthem and
Patrushev, Nikolai, 267n10
Pavlov, Stas, 269n27
P'ekha, Èdita, 34
P'ekha, Stas, 34
Pekin (hotel), 252n29
penetration, 52–59; embodiment and, 57; homophobia and, 54–55, 59; homosexual body and, 55–56; homosexuality, Russia and, 54–60; pleasure and, 56–57; relation to music and, 52–53, 56–57, 59; Russian-Western relations and, 54–56
Penkin, Sergei, 66
Peskov, Aleksandr, 79
Petergof, 135
Peter the Great (Peter I), 66, 233n71
Petrovskaia, Irina, 236n85
Petrov-Vodkin, Kuz'ma, 17
Pet Shop Boys, 3, 196
petukh, 236n88. *See also* homosexuality, Russia, idiomatic expressions (for) and
phallus, 55–56, 224n67, 224n68
phenomenology: difference between scientific and experiential, 26; *Gestalten* and, 23, 90–91, 221n47; intentionality and, 23; intersubjectivity and, 165; mind/body dualism and, 23–24; orientation and, 23; phantom limb and, 99–100; study of musical experience and, 23–24, 213n61; synergy and, 23. *See also* embodiment; homosexuality
Philadelphia, 65
Philippine Idol, 217n20
Pink (musical artist), 31, 61–62, 70
Pionery (group), 15–16, 93, 211–212n47, 212n49; songs and, 44, 50
piter.lgbtnet.ru, 210n36
Piter-Meil, 224n73
Placebo (musical group), 90
Plant, Robert, 75
Platonov, Andrei, 211n40
pleshka, 10, 142–144, 226n4, 251n26, 257n72
Pliazh "kurort," 11, 144

Pliushchenko, Evgenii, 128, 129, 130, 199
Ploshad' muzhestva, 143
Podol'skaia, Natal'ia, 217n12
Pogrebizhskaia, Elena (Butch), 27, 214n66
Pol'na, Eva, 27, 39, 151, 160, 218n28, 255n56
Polovoe prosveshchenie, 13
Polovoi vopros, 13, 14
Poltavchenko, Georgii, 199
Pop Idol, 36
popular culture, Soviet Union, 20–21
popular music, Russia, bisexuality and, 87, 119–120, 228n23; embodiment and, 22–23, 50–51, 91–92, 100–101; *èstrada* and, 3, 22, 34, 35, 36, 40, 43, 44, 45, 46, 49, 65, 66, 73, 75, 106, 107, 123, 145, 152, 163, 181, 183, 213n55; formal attributes of, 22–23, 39–51; formal attributes, use of circle of fifths progressions and, 44–46, 84, 87; formal attributes, use of melodic sequences and, 46–49, 83–84, 87; formal attributes, use of secondary dominant chords and, 42–44, 87; gay icons and, 3, 27, 36–37; "gay" male performers and, 65–66, 202 (*see also* individual performers); genres, 22; *Gestalten* and, 91, 92, 117; homosexuality and triangulation and, 117–122, 196; "Latin" music and, 218–219n30; lesbian performers and, 26–27, 117, 202, 214n66, 255n56; media accounts of homosexuality and, 3–4, 202; minor keys and, 46; nostalgia and, 15–16; piracy and, 22–23, 32, 160, 216n10; relation to Western popular music and, 31, 40, 123, 221–222n49 (*see also* popular music, Western); repetition and, 181–182, 264–265n39; *roma* influence on, 41–42, 220n40; *romans* and, 22, 40, 41, 42, 43, 50, 220n40, 220–221n41; television and, 22, 31, 35–37, 50, 75, 76, 77, 81, 98, 122, 145, 163–164; textual allusions to homosexuality and, 3, 70, 80–89 (*see also* individual performers); use of English and, 37–38, 107, 123, 129, 197, 218n28, 219n32, 246n64–65, 254n50, 255n55; use of French and, 38, 218n28; use of German and, 38; Western functional harmony and, 40–46; Western functional harmony, use of leading tone and, 41–42, 46; Western functional harmony, use of tonic-dominant progressions and, 46
popular music, Soviet Union, and singer-listener relationship, 21–22
popular music, temporality and, 145–146, 247n69

popular music, Western: gay Russian space and, 59; in Russia, 21, 22, 31, 37, 40, 57–58, 96, 218n24, 219n35, 222n50. *See also* gay clubs, Russia
Pornomania, 64
Portishead, 61
Poslednye kinoremiksy (CD), 212n48
Poslednyi geroi (television program), 215n2
Posle tebia (CD), 105–106
Povich, Maury, 215n2
Pratsch, Ivan, 41, 220n37
Pravda, 68
Pravdin, Igor,' 166, 259n90
Prem'er-ministr (musical group), 232n54
Primat, DJ, 146
Printsip domino, 215n2, 226n3
Pro èto (poem), 226n3
Pro èto (television program), 63, 64, 226n3
Profilaktika VICh/SPIDa Rossii, 267n11
Pron'kin, Timofei, 107–110, 114, 119–121; display of body and, 109; sexual identity and, 109. *See also* Hi-Fi
ProNovosti, 268n19
Propaganda (club), 151–152, 198, 214n65, 256n61
Proposition 8, 173
Pugacheva, Alla, 3, 22, 35, 36–37, 49, 66, 73, 79, 98, 162, 163, 183–184, 213n56, 226n6, 226n8, 231n46, 232n55, 244n48, 259n87
PUNCH (musical group), 37
Pussy Riot, 192
Pust' govoriat (television program), 64
Putin, Vladimir, 35, 65, 77–78, 90, 96, 172, 191, 192, 199, 201, 222n52, 236n86, 249n15, 261n11, 269n36
Puyi (Aisin-Gioro Puyi), 243n40

qguys.ru, 3, 11, 159–160, 161, 224n73, 243n41, 257n74
Queer Nation, 173
Quest Pistols, 37

Radio Indigo, 160
Raduga bez granits, 171, 207–208n7
Raikov, Gennadii, 96
Ramazanova, Zemfira, 27
Rammstein, 78
Recuerdos de Castilla, or Souvenir d'une nuit d'ètè à Madrid, 220n36
Red Club, 154
Reflex (musical group), 26, 37, 117, 162
Renaissance Event Club, 207n7
Reykjavík, 1, 150, 254n49

Richter, Sviatoslav, 209n21
Ridgeley, Andrew, 118, 243n38
Rivera, Sandy, 32
Robinson, Tom, 160
Rodina (political party), 53–54
Rogozin, Dmitrii, 53
Romanov, Konstantin, 251n22
Rossiiskaia LGBT-set,' 192
Rotaru, Sofiia, 3, 22, 43, 44, 152, 162
Royal Gigolos, The, 149
Rozanov, Vasilii, 80, 186, 209n18, 231n50, 232n54, 241n21
Rudenko, DJ, 38
Rudkovskaia, Iana, 129, 130
Ruki vverkh, 145, 253n35
Rusakova, Natal'ia, 222n53
Rush (club), 252n27
Ruslana, 254n49
Ruslan i Liudmila (opera), 220n36
Russia: "imaginary West" and, 34, 51–52; internet usage and, 193, 267n10; mortality rates and, 15; national anthem and, 89–90; national music style and, 40–41, 220n36; political movement/stasis and, 190; relationship to West and, 1–2, 34, 53, 54, 55, 69, 95, 96, 203, 261–262n19; relation to Ukraine and, 53, 222n51, 230n42, 255n53; Russia, and Western popular culture in and, 30–31, 51–52, [129], 218n21, 221–222n49; skinheads and, 2, 53, 54, 94, 202, 223n54, 223n55; spatiotemporal interaction, Soviet and Post-Soviet and, 141; use of English and, 24, 30, [34]; Western culture and, 2, 172, 233n71, 242n30; xenophobia and, 3, 5, 35, 53–54, 174, 190, 217n16, 222n53, 222–223n54, 223n62, 265n45
"Russia, Our Holy Power." *See* Russia, national anthem and
Russian Nanotechnologies Corporation (*Rosnano*), 191
Russia Today, 200
russiatogo.com, 257n74
Russkii obshchenatsional'nyi soiuz, 207–208n7
Rybak, Alexander, 203–204

Saakashvili, Mikhail, 222n51
Safin, Ralif Rafilovich, 34
saity znakomstv, 11, 159–160, 193, 210n29. *See also* gay men, Russia, internet and; individual sites
Samovolka (club), 144
Samutsevich, Ekaterina, 267n6

Sanderson, Terry, 64
Sankt-Peterburgskaia LGBT-organizatsiia Vykhod, 192
São Paolo, 1
Sash (musical artist), 153
saunas, gay, Russia, 11, 144, 199, 253n38
Savicheva, Iuliia, 39, 254n49, 254n50
Scandinavian Hunks, 131
Schwartz, Matt, 32
SCSI-9, 256n60
Seksuaalinen Tasavertaisuus (SETA), 176, 214n65
Semenduev, Viacheslav, 34
semistrunnaia gitara, 45, 49
Serdiuchka, Verka, 3, 28, 29, 39, 49, 59, 66, 77–80, 87–89, 90, 91, 92, 99, 101, 105, 117–118, 119, 134, 150, 197, 202, 217n12, 221n42, 226n9, 230n42, 240n12, 243n37, 245n52, 255n52, 255n53; audience and, 59, 230n42, 239n8; "Chita drita" and, 88, 92, 232n61; "Devochki" and, 88–89; image/performance style and, 59, 78, 88; "Khorosho" and, 78, 92; musical style and, 59, 89, 233n66; relationship to West and, 95, 233n65; relation to Danilko and, 78–79, 87–88; sexual identity and, 79, 87–88, 232n61; textual allusions to homosexuality and, 88–89; Ukrainian culture and, 59, 78, 88, 150, 230n42, 233n66, 255n53. *See also* Danilko, Andrei
Serebro (musical group), 244n48
Sex in the City, 30, 215n3
Sex Shops, Russia, 64. *See also Indigo; Pornomania*
shanson, 35, 49, 223n60, 235n82
Sheepshead Bay, Brooklyn, 28
Shevchenko, Zhenia, 42
Shkola remonta, 215n2
Shnurov, Sergei, 111, 242n29
"Shokoladnyi zaiats," 225n74
Shul'zhenko, Klavdiia, 43, 47, 49, 259n87
Shura, 4, 37, 39, 66, 101, 238n98, 243–244n42
sistertrip.com, 257n74
Siutkin, Valerii, 199
Skazka (CD), 243–244n42
Skoptsy, 227n15
Sky (musical group), 37, 38
Slavianskii bazaar, 98
Slavianskii soiuz, 54, 223–224n63
Sluzhebnyi roman (film), 16, 49, 151
"Sluzhebnyi roman" (song), 16, 49, 151
Smash!!, 29, 37, 39, 66, 105, 107, 109–111, 117, 121–122, 133, 219n31; display of male body and, 110–111; homoeroticism and, 118–119

SMS (CD), 214n67
Sobko, Masha, 198
Sobraniye narodnïkh pesen s ikh golosami, 41
Sochi Olympics 2014, 201
Soft Cell, 160
Soho, London, 65
Sokurov, Aleksandr, 104, 239n7
Solomon Guggenheim Foundation, 168
Somerhalder, Ian, 196
Sommersby, 194
Soviet Union: housing policies and, 139; sexophobia and, 4, 63–64, 209n18, 225–226n1, 226n2, 226n3
Spears, Britney, 61, 254n48
Spokoinoi nochi, mal'ishi, 152
Spravedlivaia Rossiia, 191
Springer, Jerry, 215n2, 216n4
Stalin, Iosif, 14, 20–21, 67, 89–90
Stalinskoe plemia, 212n50
Star Académie, 218n21
Star Academy, 218n21
Starikov, Valerii, 4
Starye pesni o glavnom, 163
Steinach, Eugen, 211n42
Step2Sun, 256n60
Stereo (club), 198
stiliagi, 52, 221–222n49
Stinatra, Frank, 90
stiob, 132, 247n70
Stolichnaya vodka, 201
Stonewall, 173, 176
Stotskaia, Anastasiia, 217n12
St. Petersburg Times, The, 148, 168
Strykalo, Valentin (Iurii Kaplan), 125–126
STS, 145, 228n22
Studio 54, 146
Sugarbabes, The, 254n48
Sultanova, Khursheda, 53
Sun and Steel, 256n69
Sunglasses Party, 146–147
Superlazer, DJ (Sergei Lazarev), 133. *See also* Lazarev, Sergei
Surganova, Svetlana, 27
Surganova i orkestr, 27
Survivor (television program), 215n2

t.A.T.u, 21–22, 26, 117, 160, 196, 214n67, 233n68, 243n39, 244n48, 258n83, 268n24
Tabu (club), 256n61
Talankin, Igor', 7
Tallahassee, 27
Tarasov, Sergei, 3

Tchaikovsky, Pyotr Ilyich (Petr Il'ich Chaikovskii), 7, 184, 186–187, 220n36, 251n22, 266n50
Tea Party, The, 173
Tereshina, Tat'iana (Tania), 107, 119–121
"Third space," 221n48
Timbaland, 123
TimeOut London, 136
TimeOut Moskva, 137, 195, 198, 210n35, 248n2
Tishko, Vladimir, 230n43
Titov, Iurii, 254n50
Tkachenko, I. M., 211n40
Todd, Adel,' 193–194
Tolerance Program, St. Petersburg, 2–3
Tolkovyi slovar' zhivogo velikorusskogo iazyka, 241n24
Tolokonnikova, Nadezhda, 267n6
2Nite (CD), 110–111, 118
Tonkov, Vadim, 233n63
Topolov, Vlad, 109–111, 114, 118–119, 219n31, 241n20, 243n38, 247n73; sexual identity and, 109–110
Tornovoi, Vladislav, 200
Trakan, 149
Triėl', 144, 215n68, 219n30, 248n4, 269n31
Tri obez'iany, 133, 164, 198, 207n7
Trubach, Nikolai (Nikolai Khar'kovets), 81, 90, 231n51, 233n68
Tsentral'naia stantsiia (club), 2, 199, 247n73
tsyganshchina, 220n40, 220–221n41. See also popular music Russia, *roma* influence on; popular music, Russia, *romans* and
Tuan, Wu An, 222n53
Turku, 150
Turner, Tina, 152
Tutsi, 219n30
Tverskaia ulitsa, 135
Tweet (musical artist), 153
12-Volt (club), 198

Ulrichs, Karl Heinrich, 259n88
"Unbreakable Union." See Russia, national anthem and
United Nations, 267n5
Usher (musical artist), 254n48

Vaikule, Laima, 152
Valeriia, 39, 45, 150, 197, 199
Vasilevskii, L. M., 211–212n47
Vdovin, Iurii, 223n54
Vedishcheva, Aida, 44
Vengerov and Federoff, 49

venik, 145, 253n34
Veselov, Mikhail, 37, 163–164, 258–259n86
VIA (*vokal'no instrumental'nyi ansambl'*), 22, 44
VIA-Gra, 49, 198, 243n37, 255n51
VIA-Pesniary, 44–45
Vicious, Sid, 90
Vīķe-Freiberga, Vaira, 208n10
Village People, The, 160
Vindex, 259n88
Vintazh (musical group), 38, 197
Vinylshakerz, 32
Vitas, 66
Vladimirov, Boris, 233n63
Voda (sauna), 144, 198
Volkova, Iulia, 196, 214n67, 243n39, 268n24
Vremia-reka (CD), 123
Vserossiiskogo obshchestvo slepykh, 269n29
Vspyshkin, MC, 38
VTsIOM, 4
Vysotskii, Vladimir, 49, 213n56

Westerwelle, Guido, 200, 237n92
Westfalika, 219n32
West Village, New York City, 65, 139
Wham!, 118
Wilde, Oscar, 207n7
Will and Grace, 194
Winnicott, D. W., 221n48

xsgay.ru, 11, 32, 110, 159, 166, 169, 210n32, 210n35, 240n19, 257n76
XXBi, 7, 8, 137, 258n85

Young, Karen, 146
YouTube, 22, 111, 125, 193–195, 198, 202, 223n63, 227n20, 268n19
Yushchenko, Viktor, 222n51, 230n42

Zdravstvuite, ia vasha tetia, 49
Zemfira, 27
Zenit (sports team), 199
Zhasmin/Jasmin, 34, 37, 38, 217n13
Zhdi menia, 215n2
Zhezhel,' Oleg, 269n27
Zhirinovskii, Vladimir, 55, 59, 96, 223n62, 235–236n84
Zimnii sportivnyi LGBT-festival', 267n11
Zolotoe koltso, 45, 48
Zolotoi grammofon, 22, 77
Zveri, 218n30
Zykina, Liudmila, 43, 44

STEPHEN AMICO is assistant professor in the departments of music and media studies at the University of Amsterdam.